SAN DIEGO PUBLIC LIBRARY

S0-CCA-624

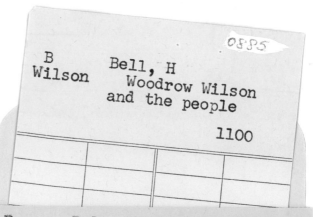

B
Wilson

Bell, H
Woodrow Wilson
and the people

0885

1100

B
Wilson

Bell, H
Woodrow Wilson
and the people

0885

11x00 5/04

1100

SAN DIEGO PUBLIC LIBRARY

LIBRARY RULES

TIME: — Books may be kept 14 days, unless dated otherwise.

RENEWALS: — Books may be renewed once at the agency where borrowed, unless on reserve. Bring book with you.

FINES: — Five cents a day will be charged for each book kept overtime.

DAMAGES: — Injury to the book from tearing, penciling, unusual soiling or other ill-usage, will be charged to the card owner. Please report to us when a mutilated book is issued to you.

CARDS—ALWAYS BRING YOUR CARD WITH YOU.

B
WILSON

Woodrow Wilson

AND THE PEOPLE

By H. C. F. BELL

SAN DIEGO PUBLIC LIBRARY
COP. A

ARCHON BOOKS
1968

0885

Copyright, 1945, by H. C. F. Bell

Reprinted 1968 by permission
Doubleday & Company, Inc.
in an unaltered and unabridged edition

Library of Congress Catalog Card Number: 68-15342
Printed in the United States of America

AUG 2 0 1968

Acknowledgments

THE AUTHOR gratefully acknowledges the kindness of authors, agents, and publishers in granting him permission to include the material listed below:

D. Appleton-Century Company, Inc.—for some extracts from the *American Year Book*.

The *Atlantic Monthly*—for extracts from Volume 126.

Ray Stannard Baker—for extracts from his *Woodrow Wilson Life and Letters*. Copyright, 1922, 1927, 1931, 1935, by Doubleday, Doran & Company, Inc.

Carnegie Endowment for International Peace—for extracts from *Italy at the Peace Conference*, by René Albrecht-Carrié, published by Columbia University Press.

Doubleday, Doran & Company, Inc.—for extracts from *Unfinished Business*, by Stephen Bonsal; *Cordell Hull*, by Harold B. Hinton; *Eight Years with Wilson's Cabinet*, by David F. Houston; and from *Woodrow Wilson as I Knew Him*, by Joseph P. Tumulty.

Farrar & Rinehart, Inc.—for extracts from *The Life and Times of William Howard Taft*. Copyright, 1939, by Henry F. Pringle.

Houghton Mifflin Company—for extracts from *Beveridge and the Progressive Era*, by Claude G. Bowers; *The Life and Letters of Walter Hines Page*, by Burton J. Hendrick; *Forty-Two Years in the White House*, by Irwin Hood Hoover; *The Intimate Papers of Colonel House*, Arranged as a Narrative by Charles Seymour; *Charles W. Eliot*, by Henry James; *Letters Personal and Political*, by Franklin K. Lane, with special permission from Mrs. Anne W. Lane; *Henry Cabot Lodge*, by William Lawrence; and from *And Gladly Teach*, by Bliss Perry.

ACKNOWLEDGMENTS

Little, Brown & Company—for extracts from *The Gentleman from Massachusetts,* by Karl Schriftgiesser, with special permission from his agents, Curtis Brown, Ltd.

Longmans, Green & Co., Inc.—for extracts from *Carter Glass,* by Rixey Smith and Norman Beasley.

The Macmillan Company—for extracts from *The Woodrow Wilsons,* by Eleanor Randolph McAdoo; and from *Great American Universities,* by E. S. Slosson.

G. P. Putnam's Sons—for extracts from *British Agent,* by Bruce Lockhart, with special permission from Putnam & Company, Ltd., London.

Charles Scribner's Sons—for extracts from *Selections from the Correspondence of Theodore Roosevelt and Henry Cabot Lodge 1884–1918;* and from *Theodore Roosevelt,* by J. B. Bishop.

Peter Smith, Publisher—for extracts from *Woodrow Wilson and His Work,* by William E. Dodd, with special permission from William E. Dodd, Jr.

The University of North Carolina Press—for extracts from *The Wilson Era,* by Josephus Daniels.

Mrs. Woodrow Wilson—for extracts from *The Public Papers of Woodrow Wilson,* Harper & Brothers, publishers.

Yale University Press—for extracts from *Memoirs of the Peace Conference,* by David Lloyd George.

Foreword

W<small>ILSON</small> once told an audience that just as Hercules (!) drew
strength from contacts with the earth, so he himself had constantly
to go among the people in order to renew his powers. Even a President
of Princeton could slip up on his mythology. Nor does the comparison
seem too exact, even if one makes the proper substitution of Antaeus
for Hercules. What Wilson wanted was interchange, communion in
thought and sentiment, with the rank and file of his fellow countrymen. If this book brings him closer to some of them, it will have
answered its purpose. It has not been written for possible use by any
special group or groups.

What I have tried to do is to show that sustained effort to establish
and maintain contact with the people was one of the strongest factors
in Wilson's public life. Since, like the rest of us, he was much shaped
by some of those who stood closest to him, much of his private life has
come in, too. I have tried to show how he was handicapped (self-
handicapped in large degree); how he still managed to win remarkable
successes for a time; and why at the end he went down to apparent
defeat that seemed the ultimate in tragedy. Since the tragedy was
perhaps national and international, as well as personal, its causes are
still worth pondering.

The story begins in Alexander Hall at Princeton, and ends in the
house on S Street, Washington. In parts it is far from a pleasant
tale; but without those parts it would not be comprehensible. If the
intention had been to cover our twenty-eighth President's public
career it would be sadly incomplete; since many things, important in
themselves but not especially relevant to the main theme, have been

passed over briefly or left out. For most of it I have drawn heavily on the work of investigators, led by Mr. Baker and his adjutant, Miss Brand, who have spent perhaps a hundred years of work on the mountain of material that the "Wilson Era" offers. But I have made my own use of some of the materials, and told the story as it appears to me. For the last part I have had to do a little more exploring on my own account, making use of Mrs. Wilson's kind permission to use the Wilson manuscripts in the Library of Congress.

In other ways I have been the recipient of much kindness. Busy people have taken time to talk to me about Wilson: in New York, Messrs. Herbert Hoover and Hugh Gibson, Sir William Wiseman and Professor Westermann; in Washington, Mr. Joseph Grew and Colonel Bonsal; in New Haven, President Seymour; in Baltimore, Mrs. Harry F. Reid and Dr. William Buckler; in Princeton, Mr. W. A. C. Imbrie and Professors Beam, Corwin, Magie, and Priest; in Haverford, Professor Lunt. At Wesleyan University, the President and Trustees have allowed me to take some leave at a none too convenient time; while the librarian and his staff have given the utmost in helpfulness.

I have lately had to keep in mind that "if it were done . . . then 'twere well it were done quickly." In consequence, the need for making a rather breathless finish (the fault of no one but myself) has prevented me from imposing on my friends for criticism that would undoubtedly have been useful. Miss Brand and my colleague Professor Schattschneider read some of the chapters and made excellent suggestions; but the time soon came when I had to quote Macbeth again: "Bring me no more reports."

H. C. F. BELL

Middletown, Connecticut
April 1945

Contents

To

RAY STANNARD BAKER

and

KATHARINE EDITH BRAND

*Benefactors to all people
interested in Woodrow Wilson
and his work*

CHAPTER I

The Academic Shades

———————◆———————

The account given in leading American newspapers on October 26, 1902, of the inauguration of Woodrow Wilson as President of Princeton was of no more interest to most of the American people than it would have been to Mr. Lloyd George and M. Clemenceau and his Imperial Majesty, William II, had any of them seen it. Only the small number of Americans who watched developments in higher education, or who had some acquaintance with Princeton's new head through his writings and lectures, had reason to feel that anything significant had happened—only they and a very few farsighted politicians who were Democrats. Senator Henry Cabot Lodge probably took time to read about the affair, especially since his friend, President Roosevelt, had intended to be present; and he probably felt that Mr. Wilson would do very well—for Princeton—in spite of what the Senator regarded as his deficiencies in exact scholarship.

The lack of interest was not entirely mutual. Wilson had thought and written and lectured a good deal about the people. Like the sound nineteenth-century liberal that he was, he had been concerned that they should have their rights. But, more than many men of his profession, he had lived in the academic shades, in a world of abstractions, constitutions, and principles. He had given the people his head but not his heart. Their hopes and fears, their joys and griefs, were outside his range. So even were practical politics. Quite often he had not bothered to vote. And even in principle he was a cautious liberal. He was all for improvement by evolution, for grafting the new upon the old. He was to spend eight years more in an academic environment, but not all of them as the detached and conservative liberal he had been. For he was to come to grips with conservatism, even with privilege. It was one thing to write and lecture; it was a very different thing to have power and responsibility, and battle for your beliefs. The bitterness of conflict (for he was a doughty warrior) and the greater bitterness of defeat were to persuade him that liberal conservatism was not always enough; that privilege had to be rooted up; that politicians had to be routed. He was not joking when he said later that academic politicians made party politicians seem mere amateurs. And, though neither he nor they could realize it for some time, the hatred of privilege and sheer politics which he developed before he left the university had commenced to place him on common ground with many of the people.

There were no outward signs of coming conflict on that perfect October day when Wilson marched at the head of an academic procession, blazing with the hoods of a hundred universities and colleges, to Alexander Hall, where he was to make his vows to serve as Princeton's President, and inform an expectant gathering of the manner in which he intended to live up to them. While the preliminary speeches were being given, and the "Veni Creator Spiritus" (so seldom heard at inaugurals in these days) was being sung, he was able to gaze around at his proud family, at the group of friendly trustees who had appointed him, at the enthusiastic alumni and undergraduates, at the distinguished guests from other universities and colleges, and at the faculty colleagues whom he was now to lead.

He was a very happy man. It was so pleasant to remember that, in June, twenty-six trustees had elected him to the presidency unanimously, and on the first ballot; pleasant to recall how surprised and proud his wife had been; pleasant to think of the way in which alumni and undergraduates had cheered and cheered, as he stood on the steps of Old Nassau. But there was something that gave him a deeper joy: the realization that he would no longer be merely one of those who suggested, discussed, and voted on plans for improving the university, but *the* one whose delightful function it would be to formulate or pass on policies, to steer them through trustees and faculty, and to see that they were carried out. For a long time he had been chafing at his powerlessness to do anything except by speaking and writing, except through argument and influence. And now the power had come to him. In the emotional reaction that he must have felt (for one side of him was strikingly emotional), the satisfaction of pride and ambition had no small place; but probably a much larger place was occupied by his happiness in thinking how much he would be able to give, to serve. A longing to serve unselfishly in some good cause, and persuade others to serve with him, was as deeply imbedded in him as anything in his whole character. The word "service" had been on his lips since the time he reached maturity, and would linger there until he died. He had long shown eagerness to do things for various groups: the family, the university, the community, the nation. He had been willing to give himself without relaxation or reserve. And now, in his forty-sixth year, an opportunity for great service had come. So his heart swelled, as he remembered all the admiration and confidence and affection that his family and the Princeton group had given him; and thought of what he might do for all of them. Of course such opportunity would have to be paid for by some sacrifice. His manner of living and working would have to be fundamentally altered; and the *magnum opus* on the philosophy of politics that he had planned and prepared to write for years would have to wait. But why feel much regret about such things when he was going into action for Princeton, for higher education in America, and so for America herself?

The regret was not so easily disposed of by the person in the audience on whom his attention most centered, and who had his welfare most at heart. Mrs. Wilson's pride and happiness in the honors her husband was receiving were all that he could have wished; but she felt pangs which she did not let him realize. To her their life at Princeton had been ideal; and it was largely she who had made it so. A woman with marked gifts of intellect, character, and taste, gracious, fine-looking, and dignified, she had made the happiness and well-being of her family, and of her husband in particular, the paramount interest of her life. She knew that he, more than most men, needed affection, comfort, and seclusion for his working hours, freedom from money troubles, a steady intellectual companionship, and the frequent company of cheerful friends. By skillful planning, and by denying herself, she had succeeded in giving him all of them. And, after many years of marriage, they were very much in love. When middle age was approaching; when his three daughters were commencing to grow up; when he was writing with cold brilliance or slashing irony; when some men had learned to treat him with caution, and many with respect, Wilson sent his wife letters that suggest the authorship of a poetic and rather lovelorn youth:

If I were looking for a poem to express what I felt when I first saw you and what all our subsequent life has shown me of yourself and of the sweet things of love, I should adopt Wordsworth's "She was a phantom of delight" line for line, word for word, dropping not a syllable, except to fit the color of your hair!

And Mrs. Wilson gave him just the sort of answers for which he must have hoped:

How do you expect me to keep my head, you dear thing, when you send me such letters . . . Surely there never was such a lover before, and even after all these years it seems almost too good to be true that you are *my* lover.

Letters even as intimate as these must find their way into print when one of the authors has been persistently described as "cold." One reason why their mutual affection held lay in Mrs. Wilson's ability to blend it with intellectual companionship. She was her husband's constant and, as he claimed, severe critic; and, when they had some leisure in the evenings, she read aloud to Wilson, or painted, as she loved to do, when it came his turn to read. They and their daughters were not afraid of being thought old-fashioned because they liked Scott and Dickens, Spenser and Tennyson, and Wilson's favorite of all poets, Wordsworth. It was not only a happy household, but a generous one. Wilson's father was part of it; and a couple of Princeton undergraduates, poor relatives by choice, were usually there. They lived in a charming, half-timbered house, to which Wilson had contributed the money cost by almost killing work in producing articles and outside lectures. Even the design was partly his. Its particular feature was a study, where Wilson was guarded against intrusion in his working hours; where his books and manuscripts and proofs piled up; and where he forced himself to sit before his typewriter for hours on end. The books had been an expensive item for people of their means; but Scotch thrift was second nature to them both; and Mrs. Wilson, an adept in sewing and in all kinds of household management, was able to make their income meet all their needs, including the entertainment of their friends.

To Mrs. Wilson, friendships were among the best of all good gifts; to her husband, they seemed a matter of necessity. His spirits, and with them his always rather doubtful health, seemed to rise as friends drew closer, and fall when separations came. In his hours of leisure he wanted outside companionship, and even gay companionship. His interest in games, though keen enough, was that of a spectator, not a participant. He played golf conscientiously; but sometimes did not bother to keep his score! But he wanted men to walk and cycle with; and he wanted intelligent and lighthearted women to talk to. Mrs. Wilson had helped in providing even these. Being both sensible and sensitive, and having (unlike her husband) the gift of much humility, she realized that humor was not one of her strong points. If men and other women could contribute to her husband's happiness in ways that she could not, she was willing to let them have their little share of him. She had given him all she could; and had been very happily rewarded by his happiness and his rapid rise to eminence. But would being President make for his happiness, their happiness? How would his health stand the added strain? He had always over-worked; and, being none too robust, had suffered what even doctors in those days called breakdowns.

His education had been interrupted in this way twice at least; and so had his years of teaching at Princeton. He often had attacks of in-digestion and neuritis; and once at least neuritis had disabled his right hand for months. It was no wonder, then, that Mrs. Wilson's pride and happiness were mixed with some misgiving and regret. The life she had built for both of them would be shaken, if not destroyed. The gaunt presidential mansion would not be home in the old sense; en-tertaining would be largely official and formal; the hours of quiet study and quiet leisure would be more difficult to secure; and even their friendships with colleagues and colleagues' wives could hardly be the same. A president could not afford to be too intimate with a few members of his faculty; and, knowing her husband through and through, Mrs. Wilson must have feared that some of his friendships might not stand the test of his new power. He expected his friends to live up to attributes and views with which he had invested them; and when they acted simply as themselves, he was inclined to feel that he had been deceived. Since June he had been pondering great plans for the remaking of Princeton, and doubtless relying on his friends for full support. How much of the glowing happiness which he was show-ing now would last?

The trustees were assailed by no such doubts. Instead, they must have been reflecting complacently that, with no effort at all, they had given Princeton a president who would rival, and might outshine, the head of any other American university. In the field of government he had long been acknowledged as one of the country's real authorities: he was well regarded by historians, and might be ranked more highly still when his *History of the American People,* now just through the printer's hands, was submitted for judgment. But what counted more perhaps with the trustees was his growing fame as an essayist and publicist. His articles were in great demand by the editors of America's leading periodicals; his lectures were sought after by the greatest universities, and by organizations of intelligent men and women in far off states. In the best sense of the word he would be an advertisement and a drawing card for Princeton.

And then he so thoroughly looked the part of the ideal president. He still seemed almost young. Of medium height and build, not athletic-looking but well set up, bronzed and rested by his summer, and alive with energy, he appeared the perfect candidate for any academic post. His face was pleasantly rugged, all intellect above and dogged strength below. Providence had given him a quick brain and a good singing and speaking voice. In his childhood days his father had trained him to argue; and, as a youth, he had practiced declaiming to audiences of trees and plants. In college he had become an expert in debating which was more of the spontaneous House of Commons type than of the set and rehearsed variety so strangely favored in most American universities and colleges. At Wesleyan and Princeton he had delighted in acting as a debating coach. But to speak of him as a good orator and debater is not enough. All through his life (for his able father's training had come in here, too) he had been greatly interested in words. Exactness in the use of words, stimulated by a close and loving acquaintance with some of the masters of English prose and verse, and married to a natural aptitude for thinking and speaking with rare clarity, had given him a literary style which would be world famous in its lean and forceful quality. The Princeton trustees knew this style well. At the inaugural they were to know it even better, and rejoice.

The trustees had further reason for self-congratulation in realizing that Wilson was heart and soul a Princeton man, and yet one who had considerable acquaintance with other universities and colleges. In some small degree he was a Princetonian by inheritance, since his father had been a student at the theological seminary for a year; and, though he spent a freshman year at Davidson College, he became by election a Princetonian of Princetonians. In the distinguished and close-knit class of 1879 (for the "College of New Jersey" in those times had much smaller classes than most of the present-day small colleges) he had been a loyal and leading though somewhat unusual figure. He had never troubled much about following the paths that custom and policy laid out. With the best brains in the class, he had been graduated with lower marks than a third of his classmates, because he preferred to give most of his time to subjects which he really cared about. His connection with athletics had been only managerial. Glad even then to form a few intimate friendships, he had appeared to most of his fellow undergraduates rather aloof. But he had thoroughly enjoyed himself; and his devotion to Princeton had remained unimpaired when his plans for his career took him to other universities and colleges. His discovery in the Princeton library of some dramatized accounts of the debates in Britain's parliament, at a time when Gladstone and Disraeli were at the height of their great duel, and Bright's oratory, even in print, still stirred men's blood, apparently fanned his natural liking for politics into flame, and caused him to decide that his career lay there.

Since the most-traveled path to politics and public life lay through the practice of law, he had studied two years at Charlottesville, incidentally observing the working of the honor system at Mr. Jefferson's university. Again two years, and he had shifted all his plans. For there had been weary months spent in waiting vainly for legal clients in Atlanta, Georgia, and bemoaning the lack of any immediate prospect of being able to support Miss Ellen Axson, to whom he was engaged.

So law, and with law a career in politics, had been put aside, for some time at any rate; and the study of politics in the abstract had been taken up instead. That had carried him to Johns Hopkins, which then, alone among American universities, offered first-rate facilities for graduate study. In consequence, it had gathered the most brilliant group of teachers and students in America. In two years of grinding work Wilson had fortified his reputation for independence; had written a thesis still regarded by many as a classic; and had seen a first-rate graduate school at work. He had also qualified for an appointment to the faculty of the brand-new college at Bryn Mawr where, now happily married, he had taught under the "group system" of studies. After three years he had moved again to Wesleyan, where he had been close to that past master in the art of teaching, Caleb Winchester. Two years at Middletown—years full of teaching, writing, lecturing, and babies—had prepared him for the final move to Princeton. That final move had been made twelve years ago; and now Princeton was an open book to him. What new president, the trustees may well have asked themselves, could be better fitted to reorganize and vitalize the university? Everyone was agreed that vital changes were long overdue.

But, since whatever novelties were in prospect would have to be grafted onto the old tree, the trustees had further reason for satisfaction in realizing that Wilson seemed perfectly qualified to head an institution which owed much, and had given much, to American Presbyterianism and its ministry; and which had a record for patriotism that could scarcely have been bettered. One could hardly have been more Presbyterian and ministerial in origin than he. Born in a a manse at Stanton, Virginia, his boyhood had been passed in other manses in South Carolina and Georgia. His mother's first recollections were of a manse in Carlisle, just within England's Scottish border. His wife had come from the same sort of family as his own. Generations of Scotch and Scotch-Irish preachers and teachers, intelligent, industrious, thrifty, rigid in religion and in standards of conduct, had supplied a fitting background for the first lay President of Princeton. It might have seemed too one-sided a background for the head of a university which drew its students from East and West and South; but the blending of a dozen different races and religions could hardly have produced a more all-round American. He was the offspring of pioneering forebears: of his father's father, who had frankly come out from Ulster to make his way, and, beginning as an apprentice in journalism in Philadelphia, had ended as a newspaper proprietor of note in Ohio and in Pittsburgh; of his father, who had taught and preached in Ohio and Pennsylvania before going South; of his mother's parents, who had ranged more widely still.

By inheritance a Middle Westerner, by birth and upbringing a Southerner, and by education and adult life an Easterner, nothing in him was really sectional. He had no colonial ancestors to boast of; but the blood of a dozen sons and daughters of the Revolution could not have made him a greater patriot. Eight years before the inaugural he had published in the *Forum* "A Calendar of Great Americans," which revealed at least as much about its author as about any of his subjects. To qualify for admission to his "calendar" it was not enough to have been a great man in a section of America, or even in all America. So the door was closed to "great Englishmen bred in America, like Hamilton and Madison; the great provincials, like John Adams and Calhoun; the authors of such thought as might have been native to any clime, such as Asa Grey and Emerson; and the men of mixed breed, like Jefferson and Benton." The exclusion of Jefferson, of all men, shows in how puckish a spirit Wilson was writing. And Jefferson was one of his own heroes, even in those days, when conservatism still clung to him. But he was able to make out an argument that was at least partly serious. The "mixed breed" in Jefferson was shown by "the strain of French philosophy that permeated and weakened all his thought," by his preoccupation with the Roman Senate, and his parade of "classical figures" in his speeches.

The "Great Americans" were men who had "created or exemplified a distinctively American standard and type of greatness." Who were they? Franklin, Clay, Jackson, and Lee all qualified; but there was no man who answered every possible requirement as did Lincoln:

> He never ceased to be a common man: that was his source of strength. But he was a common man with . . . a genius for things American, for insight into the common thought . . . The whole country is summed up in him: the rude Western strength, tempered with shrewdness and a broad and human wit; the Eastern conservatism, regardful of law and devoted to fixed standards of duty. He even understood the South, as no other Northern man of his generation did.

Wilson never regarded himself as a second Lincoln; but Lincoln's Americanism glowed before him as a pattern for his own. Just because his own Americanism was very genuine, it was too independent, too individual, too eclectic, merely to reproduce that of another man. But in his analysis of Lincoln there was not a little unconscious self-portraiture.

Wilson was typically American, not only in being enterprising, ambitious, egalitarian, and possessed of a crusading spirit, but also in his attitude toward other nations. He was too fastidious to talk of "God's own country"; but he was certain God had not made its equal. During World War I he was to prove beyond cavil that all other countries were alike to him in so far as their interests or their dignity came into conflict with America's. And, unfortunately, he knew little about them up to and even past the time when, as President of the United States, he needed to know much. He never had half the knowledge of continental Europe that Theodore Roosevelt had, nor half the knowledge possessed by some of his own Princeton faculty. He had seldom gone abroad; and when he had gone, it had been always for health, and, with one exception, always to Britain. Even the Britain that he knew was the cultural, not the economic and political Britain: it was the Britain of the past, though up to the very recent past. He would have felt more at home with Gladstone and with Bright, even with Burke and Fox, than with Asquith, Lloyd George, Haldane, and Grey. And, as with so many men who know Britain, his deep interest in its history, his admiration for its Burkes and its Bagehots, his affection for its poets and its scenery, all fed and blended into his consuming love for America. When, in the earlier part of his life as a leader in reform, the conservative side of his Americanism was uppermost, he drew upon Burke in working out his political philosophy. When he wished to show people, as he had been doing ever since his Johns Hopkins days, that the human element in American Government, the spirit and the customs of rulers and ruled, were more important than the machinery which constitutions forged, he found inspiration in Bagehot.

As for British history back of Burke, it was, of course, not only British but American. He was emotionally in love with the English Lake Country, finding exquisite pleasure in reading or reciting Wordsworth stretched out on the bank of a stream. He was captivated by Cambridge, and quite overwhelmed by Oxford with its "quadrangle" system. He delighted in a straightforward courtesy that he found among the Scots. But he never felt at home on either side of the Scottish border. America was his only home, his spiritual abiding place, the hope of all the world. Even Britain was far too swathed in traditions, in social stratification, in conservatism, for this eager planner of new things. The Princeton trustees could hardly have thought of all these things at the inaugural; but they knew their new President well enough to be certain that a lack of patriotism would never be among his faults.

Of course the thing that must have lain uppermost in the minds of most of them was Wilson's attitude toward higher education, especially at Princeton; but on that point they were already well informed. In 1896 the "College of New Jersey" had celebrated its sesquicentennial by becoming Princeton University. Wilson, just forty at the time, had been chosen to make the principal oration; and, in a gathering much like the one he faced at his inaugural, had scored a great success. In explaining his views on education, he laid bare much of the outlook on life that was to lie back of many of his struggles at Princeton, Trenton, Washington, and Paris. His very choice of a title, "Princeton in the Nation's Service," was characteristic. Even as a university president, he was to feel responsibility to the nation. As he saw it, Princeton's task would be to train a certain number of scholars, but a vastly greater number of men who would be "citizens and the world's servants." For these men learning would be important, not so much for itself as in conveying to them things of the spirit. Science, invaluable as it was, could never do that. It could not purge them of passion or "dispose" them to virtue. It could not make them less self-indulgent, ambitious, or covetous.

What was more, the imitation of the methods of the natural scientists by men in other branches of learning had caused "a certain great degeneracy," leading to "agnosticism in religion, scientific anarchism in the field of politics." Training for public service should have a moral basis; and only in religion could that basis be found. The "mild promptings" of philosophy were not enough:

If [a college] give [its students] no vision of the true God, it has given them no certain motive to practice the wise lessons they have learned.

What should be these "wise lessons"? Princeton undergraduates should be taught to believe in "progress"; but not (here Burke came in strongly) in progress dangerously rapid and radical. In the body politic, as in the human body, healthy growth was gentle, and built on "old tissue." For progress, then, a knowledge of the past was indispensable. Young Americans should, for example, realize that "the men whom Madison led in the making of the Constitution . . . had flung off from the mother country . . . not to break a Constitution but to keep it." He went on to make that appeal for "the catholic study of the world's literature" which has been heard periodically from the time of the Renaissance at least, and was popularized at the turn of the century by President Eliot's famous bookshelf.

All of his policies were, in fact, familiar. But Wilson made them as clear cut as a set of ivory chessmen, and showed that they were derived from a defined philosophy. And he left no one in doubt that he would translate them into action if he could. The trustees must have realized that when they had elected him by unanimous ballot. Some of them may also have been struck by what seemed a personal note in the sesquicentennial address:

It has always seemed to me an odd thing . . . that . . . the man whose citizenship and freedom are of the world of thought should ever have been deemed an unsafe man in affairs.

There had been some suggestion there of repressed desires. But in the six years which had elapsed the trustees had not noticed any particular desire on Wilson's part to enter public life. What they had noticed was the fact that he had come to be in great demand at other universities, especially when new presidents were needed. They had raised his salary above that of any other member of the faculty; and, lest this should not bind him, a group of trustees and alumni had supplemented it unofficially, on condition that he should not leave Princeton for any other university within five years. Now that he was their own President, they could breathe easily.

The outward evidences of enthusiasm at the inaugural were furnished by the undergraduates and alumni, especially the young alumni who had known Wilson as a teacher. The men of the early nineties had especially happy memories; for he had been especially approachable in those years. His lectures had been tremendously successful from the first. His custom had been to speak slowly and solemnly for ten minutes perhaps, while wise undergraduates tried to write down every word; but the rest of the period had been one of sheer delight for the intelligent. For then Wilson had illustrated his text with examples, quotations, and commentaries that often flashed with wit. His hearers had often broken into applause; and even if, as some of his colleagues believed, his examinations had not been so exacting as they might have been, he had achieved his main purpose in putting undergraduate minds to work. He had never had much use for facts, merely as facts. He was contemptuous of his own second book, *The State*, a dull textbook on comparative government, written while he was at Wesleyan. More even than most distinguished teachers, his great aims were to interpret and inspire.

Nor had he been content to confine his contacts to his classrooms. In his earlier years at Princeton he had somehow found time to let undergraduates invade his home, and to show interest in most of the things which interested them. The great story about him was that of his helping daily, for ten weeks, to coach a football team which had become discouraged even under the captaincy of the great Poe. The story, while exaggerated, had apparently some basis of truth. He had certainly helped to work out plays at Wesleyan. And, again continuing what he had done for Wesleyan undergraduates, he had set up a "House of Commons," and proved invaluable as a debating coach. But what the undergraduates and young alumni had probably liked best of all had been his way of trusting them, of treating them as men, as gentlemen. Since few if any secrets remain in the bosoms of faculty circles, it must have been known that he had put up a stiff and successful fight for the establishment of the honor system, as he had seen it at the University of Virginia. Here, obviously, was the right sort of President. If there was any questioning of his entire fitness, it probably came from a few men of the upperclass eating clubs, just then expanding in number, and lining Prospect Avenue with their imposing houses. For Wilson was already wondering whether the expulsion of Greek-letter fraternities from Princeton, which had been carried out before his day on the ground of their encouragement of exclusiveness, had not opened the way for a system still less desirable. Princeton was becoming steadily more fashionable; and distinctions based on wealth and "background" were becoming more deeply marked. The new President had already expressed concern.

The members of the Princeton faculty, who of course knew him much better and had much more interest in his personality and his policies than any group at the inaugural outside his family, were in general well pleased at his elevation, but could not rejoice over it so unreservedly. Every faculty in greater or in less degree represents a rather delicate balancing and co-ordination of certain divisions and interests, based, for the most part, on convictions that certain parts of a university, even certain branches of knowledge, are of paramount importance, and entitled to corresponding treatment. These convictions are not only honest, but may be so deep as to reach men's very philosophies of life. And these deep convictions are bound sometimes to tangle, unconsciously perhaps, with personal considerations—with pride and ambition, with likes and dislikes, with friendships and enmities, even with jealousy. So faculty politics often come into play; and faculty politics can be very intense indeed, both because the politicians and their families are relatively few and in continuous contact, and because motivating convictions and interests are so personal. News spreads fast, and, as among all men and women, tends to take on deeper colors as it goes.

Pity, then, the President, who must try to understand all divisions and many individuals; to make all of them feel that they are receiving full justice and something more; to hold them together, or at least to see that politics do not hurt the institution as a whole. Wilson was to be tested immediately in one of the most difficult of posts. It was impossible for the Princeton faculty to feel joy unconfined until he had been tested. He was certain to be a reformer, not only because of his views and temperament, but because it was a time of renovation on many an American campus; and Princeton men felt that Princeton was lagging. Undergraduate teaching seemed deficient in distinction and standards; the graduate school was small and showed no signs of growth; and, no doubt largely for these reasons, it was proving difficult to fill professorships with men of the highest caliber. To make all the needed changes—and one of them was a vigorous elimination of faculty "dead wood"—the new President would need not only firmness and courage, but also tact, restraint, and common sense. Wilson stepped forward prayerfully, but with little or no apparent doubt of his success.

He had some solid reasons for his confidence. His relations with his colleagues had been pleasant, and in some cases intimate. The younger members of the faculty had drawn together against their elders, and had looked to him as their leader. If he had any enemies, they were in the elder group. Not many years ago Professor Bliss Perry told of his impressions of Wilson in the nineties:

My seat . . . was next to the chair of a long-jawed, homely, fascinatingly alert man. . . . He was only thirty-six, but there was little that was youthful in him except high spirits, energy, and self-confidence. . . . Sometimes I found it hard to excuse his impatient contempt for the dullness and slowness of some of his elderly colleagues. . . . His Scotch-Irish temper was quick and not always under perfect control. But his "arrogance" and "autocracy," like his "timidity" and "vacillation" were the invention of a later epoch. I sat on committees with him very frequently, and though he knew his own mind and never hesitated to express it, he betrayed no arrogance of opinion.

Yet even in those days he was deeply aroused by what he regarded as an attack upon his loyalties or his principles:

[President Patton] took the floor himself to oppose Wilson, who was defending a verbal phrase used in the administration of the Honor System: "I pledge my honor as a gentleman that during this examination I have neither given nor received assistance." . . . Dr. Patton . . . proceeded . . . to attack caustically that romantic conception of "a gentleman's honor," which, as he declared, had once allowed a "gentleman" to seduce a woman or kill a friend in a duel, but would not allow him to cheat at cards! Now Wilson . . . was fond of phrases and knew their power over the student mind, and he resented Patton's ridicule of "chivalry" as if it were directed against Virginia and himself. He grew white and very quiet, and it was then that he was most dangerous. In his reply, he was scrupulously courteous to the President, who had for personal reasons retained his British citizenship, but Wilson understood the sentimental side of American undergraduates far better than a foreigner, and he managed to convey that impression with unmistakable clearness and with a passion that swept the faculty off their feet.

So much of the man lies in that early incident; idealism, Americanism, a love of phrases, personal pride, even some lack of delicacy in choosing his weapons.

The members of the Princeton faculty had no reason to be much disturbed by his possession of these mostly admirable, and not unusual, qualities; but some of them, realizing that idealists, when opposed, quite naturally tend to become authoritarian, may have wondered whether the new President's plans for reform might not be too hotly, too impatiently pursued. This seemed all the more possible when they remembered that with his pride went extraordinary self-confidence. Even his admiring friend, Bliss Perry, remarked on this:

In my opinion, his "tragic fault" lay in the excess of that self-confidence which was one of the most fascinating of his virtues. I have heard him quote with delight the saying that while a Yankee always thinks he is right, a Scotch-Irishman *knows* that he is right.

There was a question, then, whether Wilson would prove as liberal in action as he was in theory, once power was in his hands. Would he remember that the essence of early nineteenth-century liberalism had lain in the belief that all types of opinion should be considered sympathetically and given the widest possible liberty of action? Of course the theory had never prevailed against cupidity and selfishness in economic matters; but would the incoming President adhere to it in matters of education and religion and the arts? On the face of it, there may have seemed no room for doubt. But there had been indications that his belligerent idealism was apt to outrun his liberal belief. It was remembered that, as an undergraduate, he had almost certainly tossed away Princeton's greatest debating prize, rather than demean himself by presenting arguments for protective tariffs, even to an audience quite cognizant of the fact that he had had no choice of sides. And then there was a story about the "House of Commons" he had set up at Wesleyan. Report had it that he had been unable to forgive a group of undergraduates who had joyfully upset the "ministry," and so defeated a platform which he, the father of the whole project, had approved.

Even at Princeton there were undergraduates who, on whatever (if any) grounds, believed that disagreement with the deeper convictions of the Professor of Jurisprudence and Politics was imprudent and impolitic. Trifling and perhaps unfounded stories these, of course, but straws that bent in what might be a prevailing wind. It was certain that Wilson was ready for advice and argument on most matters, that he was open to conviction on many things, but there was room for doubt as to his understanding of others' viewpoints when his deepest principles were involved. Great liberals had often been like that, especially when they were men of strong religious bent, such as Mazzini and Gladstone. They had struggled and suffered, and made others suffer. In their enthusiasm for liberalism they had sometimes become dogmatic and deplorably illiberal. They had achieved great things; but sometimes they had failed disastrously. Sometimes more moderate men had had to carry on their work. But never did those around them live in tranquillity for long. No member of the Princeton faculty could then have dreamed that the incoming President would rank with the great liberals of history; but those who sensed the quality of his reforming spirit may have doubted whether Princeton's future was to be one of unruffled calm. They knew that trustees and alumni and they themselves had convictions, responsibilities, and powers.

It seems to be a matter of general opinion that Wilson's inaugural address was less noteworthy than the one he had delivered at the sesquicentennial. That was inevitable, although the new speech had been prepared laboriously, and would have been worthy of the president of any university. Since his views had remained unaltered, Wilson of necessity had repeated himself a good deal, even in the title "Princeton *for* the Nation's Service." There was nothing but reaffirmation in his insistence that the university's primary function was to train men for participation in affairs, and that its teachings should be "informed with the spirit of . . . the religion of Christ, and with the energy of a positive faith." When he declared that higher education in America had "gained immensely in knowledge but . . . lost system"; that knowledge had become so specialized and diversified as to lack "coherence," he was still in the spirit of his sesquicentennial talk. Where he departed from the earlier address was in coming out flatly against the "elective system" which President Eliot had instituted at Harvard, and in talking more specifically than he had done six years before about the kind of curriculum he favored, and the manner in which the various departments of the faculty could best contribute to the more "coherent" scheme of undergraduate training he had in mind. And now he offered much more definite suggestions concerning the graduate school than he had done before. Speaking hopefully of the prospect of securing money to build a "college of residence" for graduate students, he spoke very decidedly about its relations to the university as a whole:

We shall build it, not apart, but as nearly as may be at the heart, the geographical heart, of the university; and its comradeship shall be for young men and old, for the novice as well as for the graduate. It will constitute but a single term in the scheme of co-ordination which is our ideal.

The Dean of the graduate school was at the time abroad, planning the sort of building he wanted, under the inspiration of Oxford's rich spires and cloisters, its stately dining halls and spacious lawns. He may even have been impressed by the scholarly and social aloofness of All Souls. His school was becoming the consuming passion of his life; and the trustees, finding Wilson's predecessor lukewarm to it, had given the Dean a degree of autonomy unheard of at other universities. Mr. West was a talented classicist; but his taste for planning and administration had for some time outrun his interest in scholarship and teaching. He was not a man to let the most distinguished of new presidents dictate to him. He had devoted and influential friends among the trustees, the alumni, and the faculty; and he possessed the politician's art of knowing when and how to make use of them.

When the speeches and singing and cheering came to an end, and the guests were strolling across the campus to the inevitable reception at the President's mansion, professional and amateur photographers enjoyed a rare opportunity. It was disappointing that President Roosevelt had not come; but Mr. J. P. Morgan, the high priest of finance, was there. What was more, olympians of the academic world were outclassed in interest by a group of literary lights, including William Dean Howells and Mark Twain. But the photographers could not realize that among the strollers were two men then of far less note, whose photographs would one day appear frequently in books about a great President of the United States: Walter Hines Page, editor of *World's Work,* former editor of the *Atlantic,* and partner in the publishing firm of Doubleday, Page, & Company; and George Harvey, editor of the *North American Review,* and, under the aegis of Mr. Morgan, president of Harper and Brothers. Mr. Page had been a friend of the new President from Wilson's briefless Atlanta days; Mr. Harvey knew him little if at all except through his writings. But as they walked away from Alexander Hall they were alike in their admiration of Wilson's force, sincerity, and daring; the nice precision of his style; his ability to appeal to sentiment without crossing the border line into sentimentality, and to blend idealism with practicality. Both saw in him the possibilities of leadership in national affairs. But certain differences in their reactions marked, not only their differences in outlook, but the blend of liberalism and conservatism that was in the Wilson of 1902.

Mr. Page was pleased to find in the inaugural speech indications of a spirit akin to what was beginning to be termed "progressivism" even then; Mr. Harvey apparently appreciated more the underlying conservatism in Wilson's credo that "growth that is a manifestation of life . . . builds upon old tissue." Mr. Page was wondering whether he had not been listening to a man who might be useful to American liberals; Mr. Harvey was speculating on the same man's probable usefulness to the Democratic party.

Wilson no doubt greeted them both cordially; and no doubt cast a wistful glance at the line of people still waiting to be greeted. He had more than an ordinary dislike of large, formal functions. Besides, he wanted as much time as possible to think out plans for the future of Princeton.

CHAPTER II

The First Fight for Democracy

———————◆———————

THERE are certain curious resemblances between Wilson's experiences
in his two presidencies. Each of them covered a period of eight years,
divided into two well-defined sections. In each case there first came
four or five years of remarkable success. By strong, wise leadership,
and by his great capacity for planning and pushing through reforms,
Wilson achieved practical results of much permanent value. Then in
each presidency a period of stress and storm set in. The President's
ideals mounted higher. He struck for things less immediately practical,
but of far greater import when viewed at longer range. He demanded
sacrifices from others, never hesitating to sacrifice himself. In each case
a strong opposition took form, compounded both of men sincerely convinced that idealism was going too fast and far, and of other men who,
not altogether consciously, were animated by personal interests, by
rancor, and by partisan spirit. In each case the opposition found a
leader of great resolution, acting largely from the less worthy set of
motives. Each of these opposition leaders was a master of political
strategy and tactics. Bliss Perry doubted whether even Henry Cabot
Lodge was as formidable an antagonist of Wilson's as Andrew Flem-
ing West, the Dean of Princeton's graduate school. Senator Lodge
was no more successful at any rate.

The two presidencies naturally offered great contrasts. The difference in Wilson's attitude toward the American people was the most
fundamental of them all. The detached and academic viewpoint from
which he had regarded them in 1902 had been utterly transformed by
1912. By the time he was inaugurated as President of the United States
the good of the people had become his constant preoccupation, his

overmastering passion. He and they had been getting acquainted during the two years' interval between his presidencies when he was New Jersey's governor; but his passion did not spring merely from contacts. Its earliest roots were in his family heritage, his disposition, and his studies. His last years at Princeton, the years of struggle and defeat, had nourished it and brought it into light. He had been fighting for democracy at Princeton, democracy both social and intellectual. He had been defeated, as he believed at least, at the hands of forces armed by wealth and privilege, and manipulated by sheer politics. He left academic for political life with the determination to continue the fight he had made at Princeton on wider grounds. At the time he had come to think more about the people, but still in the abstract. Two years at Trenton were to teach him to see them in flesh and blood, and so to give them love and confidence, instead of mere interest and sympathy.

In 1910, the year in which Wilson retired from the presidency of Princeton, and before his retirement was announced, Professor Edwin E. Slosson wrote in his *Great American Universities:*

> Princeton is the most interesting of American universities to study just now, because it is in . . . a "mutation period." [The others] cannot be compared with it for novelty and rapidity of transformation. . . . [Princeton] is going forward by leaps and bounds.

Mr. Slosson was not forgetting that "mutations" were also occurring at other places. Nor could he give unreserved praise to Princeton by any means. He found it strikingly deficient in educating men for the professions; and in consequence "still a college in spirit." But, he insisted, Princeton was changing so rapidly as to make any judgment tentative. He found a great deal to admire and everything to hope, since Woodrow Wilson was the President. What had struck him most of all was that Princeton had "an ideal of education," and was working steadily to transform it into a reality. In those early days of the Carnegie Foundation and the General Education Board, planned and sustained effort to reach certain ends in higher education was still rare.

The ideal had been in Wilson's mind long before he had given his sesquicentennial address in 1896, and its concrete application at least as early as the time when the trustees elected him as President. Throughout his presidency he had worked for it unremittingly and courageously. He had evidenced no more hesitation in rejecting Harvard's free elective system (already undergoing some modification at its place of origin) than he had done in attacking, at the age of thirty-five, the whole conception of the proper study of government advanced by the most influential student of the subject in America, Professor Burgess of Columbia. At first he had not been domineering or precipitate. During the first five years of his presidency, before problems of fundamental reconstruction stirred Princeton to the depths, he had worked easily and pleasantly with all his faculty, retaining their liking, and commanding a safe majority of willing votes. Dissenters from his philosophy and his ideals had found that no conformity in opinion would be required of them. He had successfully faced a real test of his ability to carry his faculty with him in performing the painful preliminary task of relieving it of its "dead wood." Inevitable protests had come from the victims and from their friends. Wilson had shown real sympathy, but had made it clear that no personal feelings could be allowed to count against the general interest. Some of the undergraduates had also felt aggrieved.

Standards of scholarship had been raised; and youths who had been careless about the observance of the honor system, or about their capacity to imbibe alcohol; yes, even moral but nonchalant young men unwilling to "allow their studies to interfere with their education," had found that Princeton was no place for them. Here again the President had inflicted and endured pain. A decade later, in telling Colonel House of an important conversation at Paris with the Italian Premier, he remarked that he had found no interview so distressing since the mother of a Princeton undergraduate had insisted that she could not survive a coming operation if her son's expulsion was not canceled. Wilson had remained immovable on the first occasion, as he was to do on the second. But he had not found it easy. People who thought of him as "cold" and "hard" little knew how much he stood in fear of the emotional side of his nature. At any rate, he had gone ahead with his purges at Princeton, supported by his trustees and by his faculty, even when undergraduate registration had dropped off.

As he passed from purging the Princeton community to putting into practice the plans he had made for it, some of the qualities which were to give him unexampled success in his first years at Washington came into view. Clear perception of fundamental needs and of ways by which they could be satisfied; capacity to exert leadership by convincing argument and appeals to common sense and loyalty; courage that sometimes reached audacity—all these appeared. Some of them were evident even in the steps he took to improve the instruction of undergraduates. His attack on the "free elective system," under which an undergraduate was allowed to believe that he was getting an education by choosing a hodgepodge of courses—say in astronomy, abnormal psychology, German history, the Russian novel, and the government of dependencies—was followed up by the institution of a system by which courses were elected in groups. Wilson had explained the idea in his inaugural address:

Since [the undergraduate] cannot in the time at his disposal go on the grand tour of accepted modern knowledge, we who have studied the geography of learning and who have observed several generations of men attempt the journey, must instruct him how in a brief space he may see most of the world, and he must choose only which of several tours that we may map out he will take.

Eleven groups of courses were laid out with much regard for coherence and co-ordination, and none at all for undergraduate convenience, companionship, or caprice. Mapping these intellectual "tours" was a long and delicate job. Wilson showed wisdom and restraint by entrusting the task to a committee of the faculty and waiting patiently for its report. But this reform did not touch the real depths of Wilson's educational ideals. The university, as he saw it, must be given over wholeheartedly to the cultivation of its students' intellects. Almost all university and college presidents said that; but most of them wished rather than hoped to accomplish it. Wilson set his prominent jaw on it, and went to work on the basis of certain elementary principles. For example, since there was no use in leading a horse to water if it would not drink, undergraduates must be made intellectually thirsty. The President, by diligent search and persuasion, was soon bringing to the campus teachers who functioned as fountains, not cisterns. Again, since knowledge, to be useful, must be digested as well as absorbed, new emphasis was placed on discussion, on the easy meeting of minds at different levels of information and maturity. Here was the best method of stimulating thirst. Any young man worth educating would wish to have an active part in his own intellectual development. The fact was realized in many universities and colleges; but Wilson, by establishing the famous "preceptorial" system, won for Princeton the admiring attention of them all. The system, as he pointed out, was no mere imitation of British tutoring. Oxford and Cambridge tutors, be-

ing appointed for life, were apt to tire of doing such work for youngsters and go to seed. No, he wanted young men who would not stay
in the work for more than five years; and he wanted no less than fifty
of them. In those days, university endowments and incomes were relatively small, and Princeton could not compare with some of her
competitors in either; but Wilson, instead of worshiping the golden
calf, treated it as a bull, and grasped it firmly by the horns in the ballroom of the Waldorf:

Now I am coming to business. To start that particular thing fairly and
properly would need two millions and a quarter. [Whistles from the
audience.] I hope you will get your whistling over, because you will have
to get used to this, and you may thank your stars I did not say four millions and a quarter, because we are going to get it. [Applause.] I suspect
there are gentlemen in the audience who are going to give me two millions
and a quarter to get rid of me.

This was the language of a daring man accustomed to success; and the
Princetonians liked it. They did not, in fact, give him the sum that he
asked for. Neither did Mr. Andrew Carnegie, who answered an appeal
by pointing out that he had just contributed a lake. He could scarcely
have been pleased by Wilson's comment that he had given cake to a
university that needed bread. But certain wealthy individual alumni
and a few classes agreed to make sufficient annual gifts for a limited
period to give the preceptorial system a fair trial. Hence, when the
fall term of 1905 opened, nearly fifty young "companions and coaches,"
some destined for scholarly eminence, and all selected with great care,
trooped into the first faculty meeting, and trooped out at its close, to
"consort" with Princeton undergraduates. Wilson had scored heavily
in putting his purely educational principles into practice.

For more than four years, then, he was a successful, popular, and
happy President. The removal to Prospect, the presidential mansion,
and the assumption of the dignity that went with the presidential
office, had made him no less domestic and no less able to throw off care
and give rein to his moods of gaiety. Almost everyone who knows English history has read of the famous occasion on which the younger Pitt,
romping with some youngsters, had been floored, and was having his
face rubbed with black, when the Prime Minister and another important member of the Cabinet arrived; and of the way in which Pitt,
having hastily put himself to rights, walked with such dignity into the

room where the distinguished visitors were waiting that the temperature seemed to drop toward freezing point. Wilson seldom if ever chilled his visitors; but some features of the Pitt incident might have been paralleled at Prospect. Mrs. McAdoo has given a picture of her father, playing the part of an overmannered dowager, in a charade, dressed in one of Mrs. Wilson's hats, a velvet curtain, and a feather boa.

He was as gentle and domestic as he had ever been, singing hymns to his dying father; dressing daily the post-operational wound of one of his daughters; looking after two of them when they were ill and their mother was in Europe with the third. At Prospect there were great Christmas and New Year celebrations (toasts with one foot on the table and the singing of "Auld Lang Syne"); much coming and going of relatives; reading aloud in the evenings (Shelley and Keats, often followed by nonsense verse); family billiards and family whist. No presidential family could have rooted more vigorously at football and baseball games. Up to 1906 the only serious drawbacks to the happiness of the family came from Wilson's illnesses. Neuritis plagued him frequently, and sometimes seriously. In December 1905 he underwent an operation for hernia, and developed phlebitis as a consequence. Refusing, as usual, to give himself a real chance to recuperate, instead, adding the labor of giving public addresses to the burden of his normal work, he awoke one day in May 1906 to find one eye sightless. The first medical verdict was a shattering one: there had been the rupture of a blood vessel in his head; he had arteriosclerosis, and was permanently incapacitated for hard work. He heard this sentence with remarkable courage (probably without really accepting it); and was soon rewarded with better news. The great Dr. Stengel assured him that with a few months' rest and more caution in the future he would be able to work normally again. So he set out with his family for Rydal, in his beloved English Lake Country. The summer proved to be one of his happiest. It brought what seemed, at any rate, to be complete recovery, save for some impairment of vision. And yet life at Prospect was never quite the same after that summer. During the months of rest in England he had been considering how to put others of his educational principles into practice. He was unconsciously preparing for the period of stress, storm, and defeat.

His new objective showed some of that sheer idealism which was to bring him such fame, such enmity, and such reverses; but at first sight his aim was a simple one enough. He merely wanted to make the university one great intellectual community, in which each member, from the President down to the least promising freshman, should be a partner and participant. There would naturally be great differences in levels of information and maturity, in ranks and in degrees; but, in so far as he could help it, there should be no barriers to prevent underclassmen from mingling with upperclassmen, or to fence off undergraduates from graduates. The principle was simple; but men spend much time and energy and even loyalty in creating and maintaining barriers between groups. At Princeton very tangible barriers between the upperclassmen and lowerclassmen were created by the upperclass eating clubs. So important were they in Princeton life, so delicate the etiquette which ruled admission to their membership, that underclassmen were not supposed even to walk past the clubhouses, much less to consort with the members.

Wilson decided quite simply that the clubs would have to go. He came to this decision all the more easily, because he regarded them as conflicting with two other convictions he had greatly at heart. One was that nothing could be allowed to interfere in any serious degree with the intellectual life that is the *raison d'être* of every university or college. He had no wish to make life at Princeton all work and no play. He was merely demanding a priority. At every university the priority, while conceded in theory, was more or less denied in practice by undergraduate organizations of all kinds. It seemed to Wilson that at Princeton the clubs were primarily guilty. The minds of sophomores and even freshmen were too much occupied by hopes and fears concerning the "making" this club or that, or even any club at all. Some aspirants discreetly campaigned for election through lowerclass clubs, or by finding ways to emphasize their social, financial, or athletic desirability. Sometimes even their families arrived at Princeton to take a hand. To a lad of nineteen or twenty failure might be little short of tragedy. He might be cut off from his friends, and condemned to loneliness or association with "muckers." What would his friends at home and at other colleges think of him? At Princeton, in 1906, two thirds of all the sophomores were taken into clubs.

Wilson had long known how distracting were these sophomore and freshman hopes and fears; and the coming into force of the preceptorial system accentuated, in his mind at any rate, the evil that they did. For these reasons the clubs would have to go. And Wilson had a third reason for his decision—a reason which went deeper far. It seemed to him that the clubs were extinguishing democracy. Social position, preparation for college at certain schools, even mere wealth, increased a sophomore's chances. Lack of these qualifications relegated some good lads to the same outward status as that of the inevitable misfits and undesirables. True, such conditions existed in nearly all leading colleges; but it should be Princeton's privilege to lead in abolishing injustice and the infliction of unnecessary pain. He felt then as he did later when he talked of "America First," not in the sense of the isolationists, but in that of a man who coveted for his country the glory of being first in service to mankind. So, he decided, the clubs would have to be replaced by "quadrangles" (he seemed to love the word), to one of which each undergraduate would be assigned. Barriers and distractions and privilege would all be swept away.

Had Wilson been able to carry through his plan, Princeton would have led Harvard and Yale in undergraduate social organization, perhaps by a good margin of years. Possibly he might have carried it through had he gone more slowly and taken full account of the obstacles in his path. Almost all responsible Princetonians recognized that the club system had its evils; but there was no such unanimity in believing that its extinction offered the only cure. It was not only indigenous, but peculiar to the university. To some, its condemnation was the condemnation of a Princeton institution, and so, in a manner, of Princeton. Many of the younger alumni, especially of the sort whom money-hunting presidents and trustees of universities and colleges kept lovingly in mind, were not only attached to the clubs, but proud of them. Belonging to certain of them "placed" a man, and assured him of pleasant quarters when visiting the campus. Proud members had subscribed generously in a competition of armaments on Prospect Avenue.

Were pride, loyalty, and financial contributions all to be offered up as a sacrifice to the President's ideals? Was it necessary to deal so drastically with a system under which Princeton was thriving, merely because it gave rise to evils which existed almost everywhere? Were undergraduates to be deprived of the right of selecting their associates? Did not Wilson's plan involve an interference with free selection, free enterprise? Did it not even involve virtual confiscation of private property? Should Princeton be committed to the quadrangle system when no one knew how it would work? All these were the natural arguments of men whose occupations had taught them caution and given them little contact with idealism and idealists. But to a deeply convinced and impatient reformer they seemed no better than adhesion to the dusty maxim of "Let well enough alone." Or, rather, they seemed worse. Were they not evidence of the blindness of fortunately circumstanced materialists to idealism or common generosity, even to fair play? It was always to be difficult for Wilson to understand why other men were often so reluctant to follow him along new and rocky paths. But there was one aspect of the question which he was no more able to overlook than were the alumni. Where, oh where, was the money for the quadrangles to come from? It is the opinion today of some of those best qualified to judge that had Wilson's approaches to Mrs. Russell Sage and Andrew Carnegie produced results, he might have scored another great success. The point is not lacking in interest. The inauguration and development of his favorite scheme might have kept him in Princeton, and out of politics. But no outside donor could be found; and certain alumni who probably could and would have supplied the money otherwise were unwilling that the weight of their millions should tip the balance in a bitter quarrel between loyal Princeton men.

For a bitter quarrel it soon became, and one which brought out all the virtues and all the faults of the crusader in Wilson. In its acute stage it covered only a few months; but it helped to set the stage for a longer and perhaps even more unfortunate conflict about the graduate school. Moreover, it made up for its brevity by its bitterness and its complexity. While some of what transpired is difficult to follow, Wilson's rashness and highhandedness are unmistakable. In December 1906, without consulting his faculty, he persuaded the trustees to appoint a committee, under his chairmanship, to consider and report on the "social co-ordination" of the university. Since the matter was not much publicized, and since the committee did not report until six months later at commencement time, an apparent lull ensued. But beneath the surface opposition developed rapidly. Dean West, who had no sympathy with Wilson's idealism, and had some real grounds for demanding that the building of a graduate school should have had priority over any other large and expensive developments at Princeton, took the lead and maneuvered shrewdly. He enlisted the sympathies of his greatest friend among the trustees, ex-President Cleveland, and began to use his powers of persuasion on Professor Hibben, the closest and most trusted of Wilson's friends.

As the spring of 1907 advanced, a serious cleavage appeared in Wilson's formerly united and devoted faculty. His failure to consult it about the "quadrangle" question had been more constitutional than wise. For alumni opposition was certain to be strengthened by opposition in the faculty; and both were to the detriment of the university. Aware that serious opposition was piling up, he acted more rashly than before. The report on "social co-ordination" which, as chairman of the committee, he presented to the trustees in June was his own, even to the typing. The most that he could claim was the "general approval" of the committee as a whole. What was more, he had to be persuaded by his great friend, Cleveland Dodge, to ask the trustees for authority merely to "mature" his plans, not for authority to "mature and execute" them, as he had planned to do. On the face of it, he wanted authorization to go ahead, no matter what the alumni or faculty might feel or say or do. But such highhandedness was not really in line with Wilson's beliefs or with most of his career. Nearly all people, he believed, were fundamentally wise and good. If they were appealed to on rational and idealistic grounds, their conversion sooner or later was certain. Sooner or later he would convert Princeton's alumni and Princeton's faculty. The difficulty was that he wanted their conversion sooner, not later; and, in his impatience to get things done, saw no reason for not acting while conversion was going on. His boldness carried some of the trustees off their feet; but obscurity still surrounds the action the whole body took on his report. He was certain that his "quadrangle" plan had been adopted in principle as the policy of the university. Some of the trustees agreed with him, while others disagreed or were doubtful. So matters stood when all Princeton was suddenly informed of what was going on.

Wilson gave Princeton men one of their most exciting commencements and summers within memory. He had previously discussed his objections to the clubs with some of the members, and explained in general terms the remedy he proposed. But only on the evening before commencement day, when the clubs were filled with alumni and a resulting club spirit, was the full nature of his project realized. At the time, the clubmen apparently were stunned—so much so that Wilson, after talking with some of them, felt encouraged by their attitude. But when, in the *Alumni Weekly,* they read and digested the President's report, his statement to club representatives, and some of the horrified letters which poured in from defenders of the *status quo,* they gave plenty of evidence of life. Wilson had hoped for a summer of quiet planning in the cool, green serenity of St. Hubert's in the Adirondacks. But there was no serenity. Reports of mounting opposition came to him; and his fighting instinct, of which he was all too proud, stiffened him in his attitude.

His friends all did their best. Mr. Dodge tried to persuade him that his former preference for evolution over revolution should moderate his hot insistence upon the immediate adoption of a plan which he himself had described as "radical." Mr. Hibben and Dr. Henry van Dyke, alarmed for Princeton, as well as for their friend, its President, tried to re-enforce St. Hubert's cooling properties. Unfortunately, a suggestion that they were concerned on his account made their visit worse than useless. Meanwhile the increasing resentment of influential alumni, doubtless fed by Dean West's lament that Wilson was destroying the famous Princeton spirit, was becoming a real threat to the university's future. Most of the best and worst of Wilson was now in evidence. His reasoned idealism was perfectly shown in his indictment of the clubs. Even some of his antagonists must have admired his courage and his indifference to personal distress or loss. But his impatience, his intolerance of opposition, and his refusal to balance evil against evil, were seriously impairing his future usefulness. Never again would a united Princeton delight in giving support to a President who had showered it with great benefits.

When Wilson returned to Princeton at the end of the summer, he was already beaten. There was neither money in sight for his project nor strong enough trustee support for its adoption as a policy. Former supporters among the trustees and in the faculty had come to think that the plan should be buried, temporarily if not for good. Some classes were said to be withdrawing their contributions to the support of the preceptorial system; and the faculty had become divided into Guelfs and Ghibellines, the factions meeting separately under their leaders. It was in the faculty that Wilson received his deepest wound; yet the faculty, even apart from the block of preceptors who followed him eagerly, never failed to give him support. A resolution offered by Dr. Henry van Dyke that the trustees be asked to shelve the scheme and appoint a new committee to consider the question *de novo,* was defeated by a great majority. Wilson was cut to the heart by the fact that the motion for adoption was seconded by Mr. Hibben, the greatest friend he had outside his family. Then and there, to his own infinite hurt, he ceased to consider Mr. Hibben as a friend at all. He was going through bitter days. The trustees let him down as easily as possible. It was suggested that one quadrangle should be built as an experiment; but Wilson would have all or nothing. In view of the differences of opinion as to whether the trustees had or had not accepted his report, the most sensible solution seemed to lie in its withdrawal by its author.

But irritation lingered on. In the faculty, lines that had started as pro- and anti-quadrangles, and become pro- and anti-Wilson, were deeply furrowed. Alumni support was shaken; and even the undergraduates were partially estranged. Nor could Wilson give Princeton an example in returning to serenity. It was never easy for him to forgive, much less forget, when he had been defeated in what he regarded as a stand for righteousness. And he had discovered what he was to consider a lifelong enemy. Though he had no feeling against possessors of great wealth who made good use of it; though he numbered such men among his closest Princeton friends, it seemed to him that the forces of financial and social privilege had broken his plans for serving democracy through Princeton, and Princeton through democracy. He was gravitating toward the position that was to attract the politicians of his party. His fight had been greatly publicized, and some of the people as well as the politicians were beginning to take note of him. But his ambitions were not yet political. He would withdraw his report on social co-ordination, but only to bide his time. While he was biding it, he again encountered the power of money in a struggle with Dean West about the graduate school.

When Wilson, during the first years of his presidency, had been occupied in seeing that better instruction was offered to the undergraduates, he and the Dean had seemed to get on well enough. The Dean had a genuine interest in such matters; and his *Short Papers on American Liberal Education* show that his views touched those of Wilson at many points. He was an enthusiastic supporter of the preceptorial system, and insistent that education was "the one business of a university." Rather curiously, in view of what was to transpire, he declared for "high powers and; in grave emergencies, irresistible powers for every university president, in quick control of everything at short range." Moreover, the two men had been one in desiring the development of graduate instruction at Princeton. One of the President's first requests to the trustees, a vain one as it proved, had been that they should appropriate three million dollars for this purpose.

But when Wilson had started out to make the university a closely knit intellectual community, without barriers either horizontal or perpendicular, Dean West had soon become the moving spirit of the opposition forces. Being as practical as the President was idealistic, he had sympathized with most or all of the arguments brought against Wilson's "quadrangle" scheme. And he had been offended by the President's highhanded methods. He had scored neatly by pointing out that while the scheme had been presented as part of Wilson's educational program, its author had placed it before the trustees without troubling to consult the faculty. Moreover, his devotion to his graduate school had given him a particular grievance, and at the same time greatly strengthened his hand. During the two months just preceding Wilson's first move to get his quadrangles, the Massachusetts Institute of Technology had asked Dean West to become its President at a much greater salary than Princeton could offer him. He had declined, after receiving a highly eulogistic resolution voted by the trustees and drafted by the President. It had contained assurances that a determined effort would now be made to build a graduate students' residence. Some of Wilson's friends had even then expressed uneasiness. When, a few weeks later, the Dean and Mr. Cleveland had claimed that their project for a graduate school building was entitled to priority over the President's for quadrangles, Wilson had been able to answer that a bequest sufficient for an adequate dormitory, primarily for graduate students, had just come in. But the Dean, wanting a building far more than adequate, and rightly pointing out that endowment would also be required, had been anything but satisfied.

By the winter of 1907–08 much of the smoke of the quadrangle battle had died away, and the real issues involved in the differences between President and Dean about the graduate school were commencing to be discernible. Ostensibly the great question was as to whether the proposed building should be placed in the center of the campus, as Wilson had announced in his inaugural address, or at some little distance, as Mr. West, desiring seclusion and spaciousness, became increasingly resolved. The dispute, outwardly trivial, had implications that went deep enough to touch some of the President's ideals. A detached and cloistered graduate school, he thought, would create barriers between graduates and undergraduates, preventing the undergraduates from being stimulated to greater concentration and higher thinking by having constantly before their eyes young men who had withdrawn themselves from youthful interests and activities in order to immerse themselves in thought. He could not or would not realize that undergraduates on any campus, observing the graduate students come and go, for the most part shrug them off as rather a sad group, unfitted by a deficiency in red corpuscles for pursuits more remunerative and pleasing. If he had confined himself to insisting, like President Eliot, that graduates and undergraduates should have the same teachers and share certain courses, he would have been on firm ground.

But a more practical question was involved—the question of unity of control within the university. The President would have nothing less. Unfortunately, this question was becoming personal. The Dean's zeal for his house had eaten him up, and he was ready to satisfy it by using all the influence he could command. Wilson, who disdained mere personal conflicts and loathed academic politics, was slower than were some of his friends to realize that Princeton was not large enough for Dean West and himself. And, finally, the two great protagonists were divided on the question of plain living and high thinking. While universities far outstripping Princeton in wealth and graduate enrollment were content to house graduate students in the plainest buildings, if they were housed separately at all, Dean West was planning to give his school the magnificence of Oxford, supplemented by the luxuries of very-well-to-do America. While at other places keen students cared everything for distinguished teaching, and little or nothing for luxury or "atmosphere," Dean West was determined that his young men should dine "in hall," surrounded by oak paneling, stained windows, and fan vaulting, and retire to rooms equipped with wood-burning fireplaces and private baths. Wilson and some of his faculty wondered whether students of high intellectual and low financial endowment would not actually be repelled. Moreover, the solicitation of funds for the Dean's school was being carried on, against all precedent, independently of the university's other appeals for funds.

After commencement, in 1908, Wilson sailed all by himself for Scotland to rest up and recuperate. He was overworked, bothered by neuritis, and depressed by the failure of his "quadrangle" plans. But new horizons were opening. His fight for the quadrangles had been much publicized, and had won him so much sympathy that some of his friends even thought it possible that the Democrats would nominate him for the presidency of the United States, should a dark horse be needed. He might be selected to run for the vice-presidency at any rate. Wilson gave them no encouragement. He understood Bryan's control of the party much too well to entertain the larger hope; and he refused to have his name put forward as Bryan's possible running mate. He had a low opinion of Bryan, and he was not nearly through with Princeton yet. The trustees were clearly on his side with regard to the graduate school. But being tired and shy with strangers, he was in a somber mood. Even on the solemn Anchor liner which was taking him to Scotland other passengers must have thought him almost too academic to be true. He took his exercise every morning and afternoon by running resolutely up and down a "clear, secluded course" on one side of the boat, wearing, no doubt, his "cycling shorts." Deck games were not for him. Fellow passengers might have been more diverted had they known how "delightful" he found his running, how "much less monotonous and much more invigorating than walking." He had brought only one book along ("to keep Princeton discouragements out"), *The Oxford Book of English Verse*. His self-doctoring worked. He was recuperating fast.

The recuperation became more and more complete as he cycled about Scotland, reached his dear English Lake Country, found old friends there, communed with Lord Morley during a visit to Mr. Carnegie's Skibo Castle, and wrote entertaining letters to his wife. When he returned to Princeton in September, he was ready to match himself against anybody or anything. If he could not make righteousness prevail at Princeton, he might find broader fields on which to fight for it. Far more of the people were interested in him now than at the time of the inaugural—enough of them, in fact, to make a good many Democratic strategists believe that he could be "built up" into a valuable party asset. Before the graduate school battle had reached its close, he had made considerable contributions to the build-up himself.

Perhaps no one but Miss Dorothy Sayers (and not even she in restricted space) could do full justice to the conflict which commenced in earnest after Wilson's return in the autumn of 1908, and lasted until the summer of 1910, when, defeated, he gave up Princeton. "The plot thickened" as the struggle went on. There were interviews and conferences and meetings and legal opinions without end. Wilson, realizing, and even at last admitting, that Princeton would have to choose between Dean West and himself, not only put up a valiant fight, but showed more wisdom and moderation than he had done in the battle of the quadrangles. This probably strengthened his position with the trustees. Mr. Cleveland's death, while deeply regretted by all Princetonians, may have helped him, too, by depriving Dean West of one of his most influential allies.

Certainly things seemed at first to go Wilson's way. In February 1909 the trustees, apparently acting on the advice of some of the most distinguished members of the faculty, deprived the Dean of his position as autocrat of the graduate school, transferring control to a committee of which he was to be chairman. The committee was soon criticizing the Dean's plans. At this juncture the "money power" was interjected. A gift, large enough to be very impressive in those days, was offered by a Mr. Procter, on tactfully phrased conditions that the Dean should continue to head the school and have his way about the location of its buildings. The trustees were in an unholy fix. In the autumn of 1909, hoping both to get the money and to keep the President, they voted to accept the gift. Wilson, strongly backed by the majority of the graduate school committee, refused to accept the decision. He also made it clear that if donors were to be permitted to dictate policies, Princeton would have to find another President. The trustees partially reversed their vote of acceptance, and Mr. Procter withdrew the gift. But by this time Princeton was once more in turmoil. Thanks partly to Wilson himself, the dispute about the quadrangles was renewed, and party lines reformed.

With the situation tense and the ultimate outcome doubtful, Wilson decided to appeal to his "constituents," the alumni. With his lifelong faith that people would follow the paths of righteousness if only the true issues could be made clear to them, it was the most natural thing for him to do. He had made some such appeal before in the quadrangle fight. Soon he would be appealing in the same manner to the people of New Jersey, then to the people of the United States, once even, and very disastrously, to the people of Italy. He started on a tour. The alumni showed everything from enthusiasm at St. Louis to cold hostility at New York. But a wider audience, in which politicians were the closest listeners, was attentive at all times. For Wilson's speeches carried him beyond academic problems, and into a nationwide controversy related to "progressivism" in politics. In April 1910, when there were indications that the trustees, with the concurrence of the clergymen who sat among them, would decide against him after all, he apparently let his feelings run away with him before a Pittsburgh audience.

> . . . the churches . . . at least the Protestant churches—are serving the classes and not the masses of the people. They have more regard for pew rents than for men's souls. . . . It is the same with the universities. . . . The colleges of this country must be reconstructed from the top to the bottom . . . political parties are going to pieces. They are busy with their moral regeneration and they want leaders who can help them accomplish it.

The very exaggerations of the speech won it great publicity. And it sounded like good campaign material for a candidate appealing to left-wing Democrats. It is impossible to tell how much Wilson had politics in mind when he spoke in this way; but about this time he acknowledged privately that it was "getting a little difficult to keep out." At Princeton the balance still wavered.

In a sense, Wilson laughed himself out of Princeton; but his laugh was a very bitter one. His wife heard it, and inquired the cause. "We have beaten the living," he said, "but we cannot fight the dead. The game is up." He had just learned about the death of an old Mr. Wyman in Salem, Massachusetts, who had had two nephews at Princeton. The estate, supposedly amounting to two millions or more, had been left to the graduate school; and Dean West was to share the duties of executor with the deceased's solicitor. Even at that, Wilson could have fought on; for the money, once paid in, would be at the disposal of the trustees. He thought of doing so, but seems to have decided that the game was really up when he heard that the Procter offer would be at once renewed. The Dean would be clearly irremovable; and the best that he himself could hope for, if he stayed on, would be continuous dissension and hostility from sections of the trustees, the alumni, and the faculty. Meanwhile the politicians, convinced now that they needed him, were holding out definite prospects of his becoming the nation's chief executive in the elections of 1912. At commencement time he moved the acceptance of the Procter and Wyman gifts. He had not much opportunity to brood over his defeats, as the politicians joyfully claimed him for their own; but his resentment never died. He was never to cease contending against what seemed to him privilege or politics devoid of principle.

CHAPTER III

Wilson and the People in New Jersey

On SEPTEMBER 15, 1910, a young Irish-American, Joseph Tumulty by name, sat in the opera house of Trenton, New Jersey, watching the state Democratic convention do its accustomed work. The hall was hot and crowded, as the party platform was voted and the delegates proceeded to pick the man who was to run for governor. The gathering was noisy, at times excitingly disorderly; for the Democratic machine, commanded by ex-United States Senator James Smith, Jr., was using "steam-roller" methods to force Woodrow Wilson on the convention as its candidate. Loud protests came from many delegates, including all those from Wilson's own county and some of those from Smith's. Some delegates based their protests on the obvious unfitness of any man of Wilson's type for so high a post in politics; but far more of them were outraged that the machine was crushing the chances of three independent candidates, all estimable men, and all pledged to reform. These delegates had come to Trenton full of hope that they could rescue the party from the bosses, and perhaps the State from the domination of public-utilities corporations and other "interests." As usual, the machine was proving too strong for them. It was true that the platform called for reform; but, as a distinguished commentator was to write in 1944, "platforms are for parties to stand on and successful candidates to escape from." It was true again that the theorist from Princeton talked reform; but he would owe everything to Smith. And Smith, tied up with the public utilities, was no more willing to permit reform than was his Republican counterpart, whose connections with the Pennsylvania Railroad were so pleasant. The reformers protested, shouted unkind remarks, and even tried to stampede the gathering to revolt. It was all in vain. The Big Boss could count upon the pledges or obedience of more delegates than he needed; and his friend, Colonel Harvey, observing all things from a box, was adept in political stage management. The heart of young Mr. Tumulty was sore within him. He loved his country, his State, his party; and he also loved reform.

Many Americans in both Democratic and Republican circles felt as Tumulty did. Since the nineties discontent and the spirit of reform had been growing. People had been complaining that tariffs and business monopolies had been forcing the many to contribute to the bank accounts and incomes of the few.

They had been asking why it was so difficult to get laws that provided satisfactory conditions for labor in hours, in wages, in employers' liability; and why some men could so easily get "accommodation" from the banks, while others equally solvent could not. They had become increasingly convinced that too close a connection between high finance and politics, between such great businessmen as August Belmont and such organizations as Tammany, was largely responsible for their grievances. In most places election to office depended upon bosses, rather than on the votes of people who needed lower tariffs or better labor laws. The bosses, handing out jobs and other immediate benefits, could outbid candidates with nothing better than promises of legislation to offer. A bird in the hand of a boss seemed worth at least two in the bushes of a state legislature or Congress. And citizens not open to inducements could be fooled by editorials and doctored news (especially in papers with lots of pictures and sex) or by orators, who could make thinking seem superfluous. New citizens brought in to provide cheap labor were especially susceptible to the influence of tangible benefits, and of propaganda, too. It was wonderful what one could do with detached and selected quotations (or as often misquotations) from O'Connell and Parnell, from Mazzini and Garibaldi, from Patrick Henry and Washington. Wonderful, too, and admirable in its way was the effect of appeals for loyalty to either great party. But bribes, printed propaganda, oratory, and the party organization's own expenses cost money; and that was where the financiers came in. Contributions to a party organization and business assistance to bosses might be cheap insurance against legislators of the reforming type. In the middle Atlantic States, in parts of New England, and in Illinois, the system flourished like some luxuriant, rank growth. The bosses of the two great

parties carried it on with suavity, and with a pleasant mutual understanding that it was a great American game. Many of them played it
largely or entirely for the fun of it. Big and little bosses, with educational backgrounds supplied by institutions ranging from primary
schools up to the oldest universities, with homes palatial or proletarian,
enjoyed it as their somewhat more sophisticated successors enjoy it still.

But from 1896, when Bryan, as skilled in social and political diagnosis
as he was inept in remedies, thundered out that John Jones had been
deprived of his right to elect the men and get the laws he needed, a
swelling band of reformers decided to wake John Jones to a realization
of what was being done to him. Roosevelt and La Follette were equally
vociferous, although in different ways; and Woodrow Wilson, all
unknown to Mr. Tumulty, passed from dislike of this "invisible" and
unconstitutional type of government to a burning determination to
strike at it. It seemed to him that the men of wealth whose contributions helped to frustrate the needs of consumers and of labor for better
laws were substantially the same kind as those who had frustrated
his own plans for improving higher education in America through
Princeton. He had been stopped in one crusade; now he would embark upon a greater, and against much the same antagonists. As for
personal considerations, politics promised to fill several needs: his taste
for activity, his enjoyment of power, his delight in combat, and his
ability to look after his family. He was a poor man and a proud one.

When the time came, he plunged into politics as eagerly and as confidently as he had accepted the presidency of Princeton; but it had
been only by slow degrees, and after agonies of indecision, that he had
made up his mind. For years he had felt an obligation, a "mission"
really, to inform and guide his countrymen on the public issues of the
day; but he had never been quite sure whether he should work from
outside public life, by lecturing and writing and training up undergraduates to be good citizens, or from inside, by seeking office of some
kind. Introvert that he was, and (for all his emotionalism) a worshiper
of reason, he was tortured by seeing arguments on both sides. Homage
to reason, and especially to his own reasoning powers, had kept him in
painful doubt. Would not his clear and impartial view of public issues,
he had asked himself, be clouded once he went into politics? And
would not the nation lose by this? In his first years as President of
Princeton, when he had watched some of his dreams come true, his
political aspirations had grown dim; now, in the last years, just as he

felt himself hemmed in by forces and persons too strong for him, the door to politics, and to a "mission" with possibilities almost unlimited, had been swinging open month by month.

Colonel Harvey, who had never ceased to think of Wilson's possible usefulness to the Democrats since the time of the inaugural, had played a large part in the opening of the political door; but no one had played so great a part, how consciously or unconsciously can never be known, as had Wilson himself. In the quadrangle and graduate school conflicts, as seen through newspaper headlines and "rewrites," he had appeared even more the antagonist of wealth and privilege, more the champion of the less fortunate, than a man in his position could have been in reality. The Pittsburgh speech which, to Wilson himself, as President of Princeton, had seemed an indiscretion almost beyond pardon, had been for Wilson, the potential leader of the reforming element in national politics, a master stroke. Wilson emerged as a Democratic phoenix from the Princeton ashes.

But this phoenix was, from his entrance into politics, to keep passing through new fires; for he stood, of course, at opposite poles from the bosses who disgusted Mr. Tumulty by forcing him on the convention at Trenton. Some of his standards, his virtues, and even his experiences in the past and the future, were strikingly suggested by Kipling's *If*. Mr. Baker has pointed out how eagerly he seized on it as a personal credo, how he carried it in his pocket, and later had it framed, to hang beside him till he died. He could not live up to all of it. He was too sensitive not to be hurt at times by friends and enemies, too pugnacious to keep his poise when misrepresentation or sheer falsehood was used to mislead the people about the things he was trying to do for them. Perhaps his dreams and thoughts did occasionally run away with him. Nor was he immune to the temptations of success. But consorting with the world's great ones was to leave untouched his passionate devotion to the masses of humanity; and not even Kipling could have had in mind a figure more dauntless in what seemed irreparable defeat. No doubt there were bosses in New Jersey and elsewhere who could claim some attributes of "a Man" in Kipling's sense; but emphasis on idealism did not fit in with their methods or their aims. Neither did Wilson's speeches or writings or record; neither did the personality of the man himself. Yet Colonel Harvey could not have swung the political door in New Jersey open to Wilson if some of the biggest bosses had not claimed him for their own.

He well knew why they had. The national Democratic party, after some fifteen impotent and jobless years, was torn by dissensions between conservatives and Bryanites, and generally discredited. What it needed was a candidate who was already news, who could be "built up" into a favorite with progressive and independent voters, especially in the West and South, but who would not be too alarming to conservatives. It was essential that he should be able to hold and sway an audience; and it was desirable that he should be without a political past, since the political pasts of men of any force always included the making of some enemies. It was also desirable that he should be a man of high educational and cultural standards. Mr. Roosevelt of Harvard and Mr. Taft of Yale had set such standards at the White House for the Republicans. How useful, then, for the Democrats to have Mr. Wilson of Princeton, who could equal or surpass them.

As Colonel Harvey, practiced politician, friend of financiers, and prominent citizen of the world of print, held up Wilson for inspection to the organization, and turned him around so that all his qualifications might be exhibited, many of the organization men in New Jersey and in other States were more and more impressed. They felt that, in talking, the President of Princeton sometimes went too far toward the left. But such talk would be useful in sweeping in progressive or independent votes; and why take it very seriously? Harvey could point out a distinctly conservative tone in almost everything he said, until the time when he had grown angry and excited over campus quarrels. And besides, he knew nothing whatever of practical politics. He was not even an amateur as yet, but a man who would have to lean on experienced supporters with power and influence. Self-interest, gratitude, a little pressure if need be, would surely steady him. So gentlemen who sometimes really did have poker faces, in combination with silk hats and fat cigars, came more and more to think that he would do, even began to beckon him. That he might one day successfully use their very efforts to restrain him as a means of undermining their machine would probably have seemed to them fantastic, had anyone suggested it.

The Democrats who first beckoned Wilson were not, however, bosses or organization regulars at all, but reformers from the West and South, newspaper editors in particular. Some of them, longing for a leader as liberal and inspiring as Bryan, but at the same time sound and well-informed, had sensed something of Wilson's quality from his speeches and writings as early as had Colonel Harvey and Walter

Page. As time went on, they found that interest was being shown in the President of Princeton by conservative Democrats and organization men, eager to repudiate Bryan and all his works, and on the lookout for someone who was relatively safe but could talk the party's language with a progressive accent. The organization men knew that only by enticing independent and progressive voters in large numbers could they avoid more impotent and jobless years. The conservatives were anxious to draw such voters away from Bryan, Roosevelt, and La Follette, all very dangerous to established ways in business and in politics. Colonel Harvey, neither a progressive nor a standpatter, was an ideal person to effect a junction between the reformers and organization men; and Wilson, loyal to his party as he was to any organization or group which could lay legitimate claim to him, made speeches and wrote articles in which both reformers and conservatives could find things to approve.

Take, for example, a speech he made at the Waldorf, in November 1904, when a stinging realization of his party's latest humiliation at the polls gave him the emotional stimulus he needed for the best of his performances. He called for the rejuvenation of the party; but what he demanded was revolt. "Unsafe" leaders (one could supply the name of Bryan instantly) were to be driven out:

It is now high time that the South which has endured most by way of humiliation at the hands of this [Bryanite] faction should demand that it be utterly and once for all thrust out of Democratic counsels . . . the historic party has always stood for moderation in affairs and a careful use of the powers of the federal government in the interest of the whole people. . . .

That was exactly the sort of language that the conservative and much-organized Democrats of New York liked best; and they naturally drowned Wilson with applause. Moreover, they were not entirely mistaken in their man; for the Wilson of 1904, when things were going smoothly at Princeton, still believed that reform should be conservative. It was not the sort of language to be expected from a potential leader of progressives and liberals; but the left-wing Democrats must have realized that he was not so much denouncing Bryan's extreme liberalism as his quackery. Many of them were intelligent people who may, for instance, have remembered passages from an article called "Democracy and Efficiency" which he had published in the *Atlantic* three years before. He had struck at privilege, boasting of the way in which America had taught the world that every government should look after the welfare of all its people, not that of any special class. Then he had gone on to a scathing denunciation of the type of man who made a profession of politics:

> The boss—a man elected by no votes, preferred by no open process of choice, occupying no office of responsibility—makes himself a veritable tyrant among us, and seems to cheat us of self-government.

There would have been few cheers for that article in the Waldorf ballroom. But Colonel Harvey, as sincere in his admiration for Wilson as in his devotion to his party, observed the whole picture and rejoiced.

Harvey's joy brought him into action, and his action strained Wilson's irresolution in 1906, the year he commenced crusading against the Princeton clubs.

Wilson, attending a dinner given in his honor at the Lotus Club in February, was startled and naturally gratified at hearing Harvey declare to the diners that he possessed all the qualifications of an ideal President of the United States. Wilson's reaction will bear analysis, though the analysis leaves one in some doubt. He had heard suggestions of his qualifications as a candidate for the presidency from other quarters, and he must have realized that Harvey, most astute of observers and politicians, had sent up a trial balloon. He was much too cautious and informed to build up hopes on a foundation so insubstantial as all that; but he may have felt that it would be as well to see whether the balloon did show any winds aloft, before he himself pulled it down again.

This is at least a possible interpretation of a letter he wrote to the conservative editor of the Brooklyn *Eagle,* in answer to one suggesting that the *Eagle* might give him its support. The beginning of the letter was apparently a strong tug at the balloon. "Nothing," he wrote, "could be further from [his] thoughts than the possibility or the desirability of holding high political office." But he went on to give an attractive portrait of himself, as one who "would hold liberal and reforming programmes to conservative and strictly constitutional lines of action"; and then to express fears that, should Colonel Harvey's suggestion be taken up "immediately," a speech which he was planning to give in New York at the Jefferson Day banquet, on April 16, "would sound like a personal platform and a self-nomination." After all, if nothing was really further from his thoughts than going into politics, he could have informed both the *Eagle* and the Jefferson Day gathering of the fact, and let it go at that.

Mr. Baker, out of his unparalleled knowledge of the Wilson manuscripts, believes that Wilson never spent more time on the preparation of a speech than he did in getting up this Jefferson Day address. Apparently the result was to place him more in the progressive camp than he had ever been, both actually and in the eyes of the public. In a gathering where, as a potential candidate for the presidency, suggested by Colonel Harvey, he was bound to be sized up, he avowed himself a follower of the third President in the importance he placed on "an individual sense of responsibility in the aggregate action of the nation," on "the right of the individual to opportunity," and on "the right of the people to a development not monopolized by the few." Generalities? Of course; but the speech, while doubtless given in all sincerity, was quite possibly framed with some idea of further testing air currents. Wilson's *History of the American People* had not added to his reputation among historians; but its writing must have added to his knowledge of American politics. For that matter, how could any observer have failed to recognize the excellent strategy of allowing one's availability for office to remain in doubt as long as possible, and of talking in terms of principles, not of specific changes? If Wilson did have such strategy in mind, he was offering an effective contrast to President Roosevelt, whose enjoyment of office had been so obvious, and whose "big stick" threatened so many heads. Nor would Wilson have been out of character in keeping his options open, without having reached any decision to make use of them.

He had still four years in which he could be as quiescent as he chose, in which he could talk only of principles, and in which he could battle with himself as to whether he would be an "outside" reformer or an "inside" one. When the blood vessel broke in his head a few weeks after the Jefferson Day dinner, it seemed, of course, that all thoughts of public life would have to be given up; and when he returned from England in the fall, unfinished business at Princeton and the opening of the struggle for the quadrangles were sufficient to occupy all his thoughts. Indeed, he might well have found the affairs of the university enough to engross all his attention up to the time he left it. In point of fact, he furnished the best possible indication of an increasing interest in public life by giving more and more attention to politics during those hot and crowded years. Pulled in two directions, sometimes in an agony of indecision, he found it increasingly "difficult to keep out" of public life. For the politicians bore down on him more and more, especially after the elections of 1908. If those elections gave the Democrats no particular reason for hoping that a distinguished liberal of their party might have a chance in 1912, the sequel to the elections did. Roosevelt, deciding that he had completed his special task of exposing the iniquity of the trusts and other flaws in the existing American system, had willingly relinquished the presidency to Taft, as a cool lawyer of liberal views and unquestioned integrity, under whom reform legislation could be carried through Congress in orderly fashion. The country, "a little out of breath" in Mr. Baker's phrase, after a long period of Roosevelt's superabundant activity, had as willingly acquiesced. But it soon became all too clear that Mr. Taft was too amiable, too easygoing, to stand out against the tougher and more experienced conservatives of the party. As discontent and disillusionment increased, Democrats of all complexions became more than ever convinced that the next President would have to be a Progressive, or at least a liberal (whatever the terms are worth) of some party and some sort. It was unlikely that the conservative Republicans would permit the choice of a Progressive nominee, and even doubtful whether Republican Progressives would unite in supporting Roosevelt or La Follette. Such troubled waters promised excellent Democratic fishing if the right bait could be found.

The pressure on the seemingly attractive Wilson bait increased; but it was very live bait, with much resistant capacity. Yet the outcome of his struggles now seems to have been a foregone conclusion, or nearly so. It was not only that he felt himself increasingly hemmed in at Princeton. More and more there came to him the intoxicating realization that he could sway great masses of people. With the waning of his power at Princeton came the waxing of his influence in the country. He was more sincere than most men when he said that purely personal ambition had never moved him much; but the ambition to be a commanding figure in what he regarded as a struggle for righteousness always moved him mightily. He suffered from some irresolution to the end; but by 1910 the question was not so much as to whether he was willing to enter public life, as to whether he could enter it on his own terms. His views about the "tyranny" of the bosses and America's lack of leadership except through party managers had not changed. The bosses would have to make concessions if he was ever to be President.

Of course there was hardly anyone who seriously suggested or supposed that he could take a flying leap from Prospect to the White House. In some position less exalted than that of President he would have to prove his capacity, make connections, and acquire experience. It would naturally be best for him to start in New Jersey; and he was already a big enough figure there to be in line for a United States senatorship, or, better still, the governorship. In neither of the great parties was any other candidate of anything like his size available. But could he and the organization come to terms? That depended a good deal upon ex-United States Senator James Smith, Jr., a "Big Boss" who ranked in state Democratic organizations with such overlords as Croker of Tammany and Sullivan of Illinois. Mr. Smith was in fact a very incarnation of the system, and, as such, was an attractive parasite on American democracy. Few bosses were as handsome, none more suave or well turned out. Though of poorest Irish origin, he reached some affluence, sent his three sons to Princeton, and was on pleasant and mutually profitable terms with great financiers. Smaller New Jersey bosses and their followers looked up to him with affectionate reverence. The discovery that he had purchased a large block of sugar shares just before his vote on the sugar schedule of the tariff was given had brought him a scathing denunciation from Cleveland and his removal from Washington; but, having friends who were tolerant of such slips, he saw no reason why he should not be a senator again. Probably the Democratic voters of the State would refuse to give him a majority in the senatorial primary of 1910; but it was the two houses of the New Jersey legislature, voting jointly, which actually elected senators.

Only after hesitation did Mr. Smith make up his mind about Wilson. If only the Democrats could get a majority in the joint voting, Mr. Smith might once more find himself in the senatorial offices at Washington. A Democratic candidate for the governorship who could roll up a great vote would carry many Democratic candidates for the legislature to victory with him. Colonel Harvey, who had known the Big Boss well for many years, kept assuring him that the man to do it was Wilson. After hearing Wilson speak, Mr. Smith, who could recognize greatness, to say nothing of vote-getting ability, agreed. But there were other things to be thought of. When Wilson was talking of principles, he sometimes sounded dangerous, quite radical in fact. And suppose he (the Big Boss) and Wilson did not agree, which of them was to be the master of the New Jersey Democrats? If the organization was to back up Wilson, there would have to be negotiations and a clear agreement on that point. It would be something of a poker game; but what boss would be deterred by that? However, there was one thing more: Wilson would have to do his part in bringing the organization to his support. Mr. Smith could hardly ask his followers to buy a professor in a poke.

Meanwhile, the professor was thinking of Colonel Harvey's plan in quite a different way. New Jersey would be simply an ideal state in which to start on his new mission. Being a paradise for trusts and bosses, it would give him excellent practice in attacking the national evils against which his face was set; and, should his attacks succeed, a place of leadership among all Americans of similar ideals. So he found the governorship tempting. But with him, as with the Big Boss, there were other things to be thought of. Since he had no intention of being a tool of the bosses, or even under their restraint, he, too, felt that there would have to be negotiations ending in clear agreements on some points. It would be something of a chess game; but he could probably hold his own at that. Whether as poker or as chess, the game promised to be an amusing one.

The wants of the Big Boss and his immediate vassals were quite simple. They wanted things in the State and its legislature to go on very much as they had been going on. But this, of course, implied more specific things. Primarily, it meant that the party machine should remain in their control. They believed that so long as this control was theirs, no Democratic majority in the legislature would pass measures which could annoy their friends and patrons in big business. This was important. Mr. Smith, for example, could remember that without his friend, the great William C. Whitney, he could hardly have reached the United States Senate. His return to the Senate was another of his demands. These demands were to be made on Wilson, who had denounced boss rule so scathingly nine years before, and who, even in 1910, was publicly declaring himself the enemy of the interests. The Pittsburgh speech by no means stood alone. In January, for example,

speaking to the great New York bankers, again at the Waldorf, he
had deeply offended some of them, and Mr. Morgan in particular:

> Banking is founded on a moral basis. . . . The country doesn't trust
> you. You are not interested in the development of the country. . . . You
> take no interest in the small borrower and the small enterprise. . . . You
> . . . see nothing beyond your own interests and . . . take tolls of all
> passers-by.

If a man who made such speeches was to become a Democratic governor of New Jersey, he would have to be kept in leash. Of course
the machine could do that, so long as it remained intact. Wilson must
pledge that he would not try to break up the organization and build
one of his own.

Wilson was perfectly willing to give the pledge. When he actually
gave it over his signature, in June, as the negotiations were drawing
to a close, he even promised to co-operate with the organization on
the most friendly terms, so long as it "was willing to work . . . for
such policies as would re-establish the reputation of the State and the
credit of the Democratic Party in serving the State." The proviso,
being one which almost any candidate might have set down, did not
trouble the bosses. They had their pledge; but they did not know
Wilson. They did not realize that he was in deadly earnest about
what he wrote or said. They did not realize that his reputation at
Trenton and Washington, as at Princeton, would not rest on what he
said or wrote, but on his amazing ability to get things done, to push
things through. Apparently they had not even followed his struggles
at Princeton sufficiently to be aware that whenever or wherever he
met organized opposition that was official and representative, he
would go over the heads of its leaders and appeal to the "constituency,"
to the people whom the opposition was supposed to represent, and,
in his opinion, did not. He had satisfied the bosses with a promise that
he would make no attempt to break their organization; but he had
given no promise that he would not ask the people to cease supporting
it, if occasion should arise. Confident both of himself and of the people,
he had won the first move of the game.

What was more, he had secured assurances that, giving this one
pledge, he would be asked for no others. Ex-Senator Smith, knowing
that the organization could not have Wilson for a candidate if he were
asked otherwise to bind himself, and no doubt confident that the ma-

chine could prevent harm being done, had disclaimed desire that Wilson should "commit [himself] in any way as to principles, measures, or men." But there were questions on which Wilson had definitely to oppose the organization chiefs. They claimed that they could not swing the State without the support of the brewers—a support of which the party's opposition to local option was in part at least the price. Wilson believed in local option, and had said so. Nothing the organization men could say persuaded him to change his stand. Then there was the question of Mr. Smith's return to the Senate. This issue was very personal to Wilson, and also of vital importance to his progress as a cleanhanded, liberal leader. If he were to carry the Democrats to victory with him in the legislature, and they were to send the discredited ex-Senator back to Washington, it would look as though he and Smith had struck a thoroughly dishonorable bargain. Since Wilson would have to accept his nomination from the machine, he was already being labeled as its tool from both left and right. The Hearst press, all Bryanite, was calling him Wall Street's nominee; while the New York *Sun*, then and later inveterately hostile, stressed the connection of Harvey and other of Wilson's supporters with big business, and accused him of unfriendliness to labor. He could hardly declare his attitude toward the bosses and their patrons before the machine nominated him in the state convention, scheduled to meet in September at Trenton; but he was determined not to be under obligation to give apparent substantiation to the Hearst charges in case he were elected Governor. Harvey, quite understanding this, discussed the situation tactfully with Smith; and Smith, always pleasant, and as often as possible amenable, seemed ready to sacrifice his own hopes for the good of the party. After the convention, Harvey assured Wilson, Smith would announce that he was not a candidate for the Senate. Altogether, Wilson had made a bargain which did his Scotch ancestry real credit. And he, not even an amateur politician, not even a "professor in politics" as yet, had been trading with experienced professionals.

The negotiations, which ended about the middle of July, when the bosses insisted that Wilson would have to make up his mind, had taken a long time. Since it was understood that Wilson would go to Trenton only for a stop-over on his trip to Washington, they had attracted much attention, covered much ground, and involved many potentates. A curious example of their ramifications lies in the fact that an Illinois Republican, captivated by one of Wilson's speeches, was instrumental in bringing him to the serious attention of influential Chicago Democrats, including the state boss, Roger Sullivan. The same Republican even engineered a discussion of Wilson's possibilities as a presidential candidate between an influential Democrat from the "windy city" and Mr. Smith, across a lunch table in New York. Delmonico's and other famous New York restaurants catered richly to the negotiations as they went along; and the guests were so commonly notables in politics, in publishing, or in finance, that a list of them would have been invaluable to the Hearst papers or the *Sun*. When Wilson was present at these feasts, the notables examined him shrewdly. All or nearly all of them admitted his presidential possibilities; some doubted whether he would be safe; but very few had either hopes or doubts commensurate with his own plans for action, in case New Jersey should make him its Governor. He did not know the intricacies of state politics; but he knew the general situation well enough—the "political suzerainty . . . set up by Railroad and Public Service interests," of which Joseph Tumulty (of whom more soon) wrote bitterly.

Wilson was not the man to view such a scene with leniency, or, as Governor, to keep his hands off it. He did not expect, in any case, to be at Trenton for longer than two years, and national politics would have to take a great part of his time; but even at that, the "suzerainty" might be broken. He had leisure to think it all over during the summer months, as he divorced his thoughts from Princeton in the artistic atmosphere (which Mrs. Wilson specially loved) of Lyme, Connecticut. Having insisted that the nomination should come to him "on a platter," as Harvey said, he did not have to bother about the convention any further than to repel the charge that he was unfriendly to labor. He took his nomination for granted, on Smith's and Harvey's word. He was well refreshed, and back in Princeton, when Mr. Tumulty sat watching the steam roller in the Trenton opera house.

From the time of the Trenton convention one can view Wilson's debut in politics through the eyes of Tumulty, whose opportunities and capacity for observation were exceptional. He was a plump, fresh-faced young Democrat, a lawyer, a Roman Catholic, and Irish in sympathy to the core, delighting in the speeches of O'Connell and Emmet. Through his father, and through a natural bent, he had come easily to prominence in the ward politics of Jersey City, and then to

a seat in the legislature. He was on civil terms with some of the big
bosses, but he was not at their command. He and his particular circle
were hotly against boss rule for the benefit of the "interests." Hence
his depression and disgust when claques (including a group of Princeton undergraduates) provided by the organization smothered protests
by their cheers; and well-schooled delegates nominated the Smith
candidate on the first ballot. Tumulty was still in the opera house
when the nominee, summoned from Princeton by Harvey, the great
promoter and stage manager, was hastily brought in to make his
speech of acceptance, before the left-wing Democrats could leave in a
rebellious mood. Then Mr. Tumulty was surprised. The nominee, un-
expectedly easy and informal, even to the wearing of a golf sweater
beneath his coat, was saying unexpected things:

I shall enter upon the duties of the office of Governor, if elected, with
absolutely no pledges of any kind. . . . The future is not for parties
"playing politics," but for measures conceived in the largest spirit . . .
[for] leaders . . . who love . . . opportunity for service. . . . We are
witnessing . . . a revival of the power of the people. . . .

All the delegates seemed to like the speech, though not, perhaps, for
identical reasons. Mr. Tumulty liked it, too. He went home puzzled
but somewhat happier.

His attitude changed to one of delighted amazement as the short
but carefully organized campaign progressed. He began to be captivated when, in his own home town, he went to hear the nominee's
first campaign speech. Wilson, not at all "high-browish," made
Tumulty feel perfectly at home by referring to his good work in the
legislature and asking for a frank criticism of the campaign address.
Tumulty answered that it had dealt too much with generalities, evad-
ing such matters as employers' liability and the regulation of public
utilities, which the platform had taken up. Wilson (who, unknown
to Tumulty, had written the platform) thanked him; promised to
remedy the fault in his next speech; and did. What was more, he was
soon talking progressivism and poking fun at the regulars of both
parties. For instance, he was reminded of

the picture of a poor devil of a donkey on a treadmill. He keeps on
tramping, tramping, tramping, but he never gets anywhere. But there is
a certain elephant that's tramping, too, and how much progress is it making?

He had come quite into the open in his attack upon "invisible" machine government and the use of legislators as "errand boys" for financial magnates of the interests. He made a nice appeal to popular sentiment in stressing that some of the magnates were not even residents of the State. Hence, long before the election he had started to undermine the organization that had made him its nominee. He did not try to break it; but he was determined to weaken it. Republican Progressives, better organized and led than progressive Democrats, were naturally doubtful of his sincerity. Wilson, having offered to debate any politician in the State; then, being challenged by Mr. Record, leader of the progressive Republicans, answered questions put to him with a categorical denunciation of the Democratic machine and a promise that, if elected, he would feel free to act without consideration for its wishes or its influence. For good measure, he added that he hated the system, and would feel "forever disgraced" were he to give it his co-operation "in the slightest degree."

Since he had still to be elected, and since the Democratic bosses could "deliver the vote," this seems at first sight sheer audacity. It was; but his audacity, like the first Napoleon's, was grounded on good information and keen calculation of chances. Tumulty, by this time in close contact with men who were managing the campaign, found them rubbing their hands in enjoyment of Wilson's "great campaign play." A candidate would say anything, wouldn't he, to pick up votes? If the voters took him seriously, then the more fools they. Tumulty delightedly saw that it was the organization men, not the voters, who were being fooled. He was even happier to observe that the "Presbyterian priest," as Smith had once called him, by speaking to "the plain people" of every section of the State, by emphasizing "the fight against privilege," and by insisting that men go forward only by "the path of pain and struggle," was rousing many citizens to put reform before party organization, and even before party.

When the end came, Wilson's majority surpassed the party's fondest hopes. He had even put the legislature in the party's hands. Also, he had won his game with the bosses, although they did not see it yet. He had used the organization to come into power; but he had already weakened it. Like many another reformer in democracies, he had used corruption to drive corruption out, believing the end so great as to justify what seemed the only possible means. Few if any people were troubled about that; but the bosses were soon to be staggered by what they regarded as his ingratitude. One of them was ex-Senator Smith. Since ingratitude and lack of fidelity to friends were charges that would pursue Wilson for the balance of his career, the case of Mr. Smith has more than intrinsic interest.

Mr. Smith decided that, after all, there was no real reason why he should not go back to Washington as a senator. Very understandably, he wanted a chance to rehabilitate his reputation for his family's sake. Since there was rarely a Democratic majority in the legislature when the election of a senator occurred, now was the appointed time. Why not? It was true that the people, asked to show their preference in a primary, had declared heavily for a Mr. Martine. But Smith's name had not been presented in the primary; the legislature would make the actual choice; and Martine was one of those rather pompous and ineffective men who consent to be put up as candidates in elections which everyone thinks they cannot win. The only possible obstruction could come from the new Governor-elect, who might use his power of influencing the people to bring pressure on their representatives. And Harvey had told Wilson that Smith would refuse to be a candidate.

But now the election was over, things looked different to the Big Boss. There was a Democratic majority in the legislature; and the Governor-elect surely would not forget the faithful admirer who, in spite of the doubts and protests of other machine leaders, had made him the party's nominee. Promises and principles were all very well; but this was a question of politics, where promises and principles, while admitted, had to be kept in their proper place. The Big Boss went to see the Governor-elect. But the Governor-elect saw the question as one of promises and principles, where political factors and even gratitude, while admitted for consideration, had to be kept in their proper place. Wilson admitted sympathy with Smith's desire to rehabilitate himself, but would not hear of his election to the Senate. He would not for a moment consider the repudiation of an undertaking upon which he had relied, especially when it would apparently convict him of corruption and hypocrisy.

There was even more to it than that. The Governor-elect had constantly insisted that "the power of the people" freely to choose their representatives must be restored. Specifically, he stood for the direct election of senators. Was he to connive at the flouting of the people's will in their expressed preference for Martine? Instead, as he frankly told his visitor, he would do everything in his power to see that Martine went to Washington. Merely to stand aside would neither save his reputation nor satisfy his own standards. When the Big Boss left, the two men seemed committed to a fight that might cost each of them dear: Smith, his hold on the legislature, and so his greatest usefulness to the machine and to its friends; Wilson, the ability to get his reform program made into law, and his own State's support in the national convention of 1912. On this occasion Wilson showed no appetite for conflict. After delay and thought which filled Tumulty with anxiety, he tried to find someone who could persuade Smith to change his mind. Harvey refused to interfere (this was perhaps the genesis of the Wilson-Harvey break); and Colonel Watterson, the famous Kentuckian, found Smith inflexible. Wilson next appealed to one of Smith's most trusted lieutenants, going personally to the very modest home where the much-loved boss lay on his deathbed. The visit was deeply appreciated by the dying man and his friends; but their loyalty to Smith deprived it of any tangible results. Consultations with members of the legislature gave no prospect of success.

Peace seeming impossible, Wilson was ready for hostilities, ready to use his favorite weapon—an appeal to the people. Acting as his own ambassador, he called on Smith, and left an ultimatum that he would open fire if Smith did not surrender within two days. When the two days were up, the appeal appeared, insisting that good faith to the voters, fidelity to principle, and respect for at least the spirit of the law establishing the senatorial primary, all made it obligatory on the legislators to elect Martine.

The days that followed were more exciting than those of the campaign. Tumulty, who had urged opposition to Smith's election from the first, and whom the Governor-elect had now made his secretary, in order to have at hand someone who understood New Jersey politics, went joyously into action. There were packed mass meetings, attended by important people and representatives of leading newspapers from outside the State, all intent on seeing how the Democrats' rising star would acquit himself in battle. Smith, his suavity gone for once, talked of "foul play" and ingratitude. Wilson, now throwing moderation to the winds, called the bosses "warts upon the body politic," and promised that their "castles," mere "pasteboard" affairs, would crumble at the voters' touch. He would have been even more in character if he had talked of the walls of Jericho, as he marched around from meeting to meeting, blowing the reformers' horn. And the castles, though built of far more substantial material than "pasteboard," were taken by surprise. When the legislature came to ballot, after an all-night vigil at the Smith and Wilson headquarters, the vote for the Big Boss was almost pathetically small. Mr. Martine prepared to take his seat at Washington; and Mr. Smith, bewildered and incredulous, went into retirement, from which he was never really to emerge.

Wilson's campaign for the governorship and fight with Smith outlined immediately and for all time the place he was to hold in politics. At no time would he ever be a politician in the ordinary sense; at no time would the machine men of his party consider him a "regular." They would always regard him as a man who refused to play the game; worse, as a man too proud, too convinced of his superiority, too fond of dominance, to play the game. They would also regard him as an ingrate. Since there was much genuine gratitude and genuine friendship in the ties which bound these men of the machine, Wilson's attempts to exclude such human elements from politics appeared to them his cardinal sin. A boss himself might be forgiven some pride and self-esteem; and most bosses love power. But a man who seemed ungrateful, incapable of generous friendship (at the cost of almost anyone or anything) would always be a maverick in "regular" politics. Against the Republicans, most organization men would go on backing Wilson for the votes he could bring in; but the dislike which many of them felt for him was probably all the deeper because they backed him out of mere necessity.

As President, this was to cost him dear. In the months of his political debut it did not bother him in the least. Had he not the people, the "real sovereign"? He was sure that he understood them, and that they trusted him. He saw himself in a position above mere politics. As Governor, he would be the people's representative. During the campaign he had repeatedly told his audiences not to vote for him unless they were prepared to take him as their leader and spokesman. It was as the chosen "political spokesman and adviser of the people" that he had waged the battle against Smith. Since the people had elected him in that capacity, he had told the crowds, he claimed the position, with all its responsibility, and hoped that the citizens would follow him. Let who would lead the organization, he would lead not only the party, but all citizens whom he could serve. He would think for them, plan for them, and carry through the reforms that they had needed so urgently and for so many years. The crusader had taken his first objective, and was ready to press on. The next objectives were in New Jersey; and beyond these were greater ones in Washington.

CHAPTER IV

Trenton to Baltimore

———————◆———————

By the time the Smith affair was over, the Christmas of 1910 had come and gone, and the Governor-elect was beginning to settle into place. As regards personal surroundings, the settling was far from satisfactory, especially before the autumn of 1911. Refusing to live at Prospect, or to accept any salary from the university from the time in October 1910 when he ceased to be its President, Wilson found himself poor and without a home. During the summer he would have the official summer "mansion" at Sea Girt, a mansion which looked very much like a small hotel or superior boardinghouse, was set close to the railroad tracks, and was treated as public property, even to the rooms downstairs, by strangers of all kinds. An ancient official motor-car went with the mansion, but since it was driven by an ancient coach-man who detested all mechanical conveyances, it contributed less to convenience than to dignity. In fact, both the Governor and his lady found that dignity and officialdom were making impossible for both of them the convenient informality and privacy which academic surroundings had offered throughout their married life.

Even the circle of their friends was changing fast. At Sea Girt there were a good many political persons to be entertained; and as they took their places around the ponderous table in the gaunt "state" dining room, some of the men who were to be associated with Wilson's great-est days made their first entrance on the scene. One of them was William McAdoo, already a man of some note, thanks to his success in the construction of the Hudson Tunnels and general competence in handling large business affairs. He had come down from New York with the frank purpose of sizing up the Governor. Another was

Colonel House, neatly described by Wilson's third daughter, Eleanor, who was later to be McAdoo's second wife:

. . . a small man with clear, steady eyes—very quiet and calm, his manner in pleasant contrast to the aggressive self-assertion of most of the politicians we had seen. He listened with flattering attention to what was said, but seldom committed himself.

These two guests and others, such as Dudley Field Malone, made some political entertaining a real pleasure. But on the whole officialdom weighed heavily. The Governor chafed at times; and Mrs. Wilson, who had shrunk even from Prospect, seemed rather unhappy and worried. It was a strain for her when the governors of most of the States descended on Sea Girt; and it was an annoyance to Wilson that he had sometimes to don a frock coat and top hat, mount a horse, and review the National Guard on sacred Sunday afternoons. Even at Princeton, where he still lived throughout the remainder of the year, the old life was hopelessly shattered. It was partly a question of money. Entertaining at Sea Girt was expensive, his salary was none too large, and housing at Princeton was costly. Mrs. Wilson, as usual sparing her husband to the utmost, packed and stored nearly all their possessions; and, for economy's sake, established the family in three small bedrooms and a sitting room in the then Princeton Inn on Nassau Street. Wilson's three daughters, now grown up, pursuing their separate interests in music, painting, and social work, and sharing a growing interest in beaux, spent little time in Princeton, and escaped the full impact of the change. But when Wilson came home by train from Trenton, there was usually nothing to look forward to but dinner in a public dining room and an evening in a sitting room which Dean West's students might have disdained as lacking a fireplace. For Mrs. Wilson the change was harder than it was for him. There was no place to paint in or to garden in; there was little proofreading or even sewing to be done; there was not even housekeeping to fill her time. Not until the autumn of 1911, when two ladies from among the Southern "cousins" (far, far removed) gladly agreed to share a modest house in Princeton and its upkeep, were the Governor and his family able to live something like their normal lives again.

Mrs. Wilson's forced diversion from accustomed occupations had given Wilson an important political adjutant. Impossible as it is to estimate how great a part she played in her husband's progress from

Princeton to Washington, one can be sure it was not small. She dreaded the White House even more than she had dreaded Prospect or the "mansion" at Sea Girt; but since her husband was intent on going there, and since she felt he would do great things for the country, she urged and helped him on. Some of her assistance was merely secretarial. She clipped newspapers which Wilson had no time to read, and called his attention to anything which seemed especially significant. She also had many quiet talks with some of his political associates, and was affectionately frank in giving him her criticism and advice. Tumulty was soon her close ally on a "Wilson-for-President" basis. No mean authority when it came to politics, he called her "the better politician of the two." One might think of the remark as no more than a courteous pleasantry, had not another authority on political strategy remarked on her pronounced political instinct. She was especially useful in her ability to steady her husband, to calm him down when impatience and impetuosity took hold on him; but she pushed him into action, too. She was of great assistance to Tumulty in overcoming Wilson's reluctance to go on campaign speaking tours, despite her loneliness in his absence and her concern about his health and nerves.

Her most tangible contribution to his progress in the Princeton-Trenton period was her entertainment of Bryan. The Commoner was to speak at the Theological Seminary; and Mrs. Wilson or someone else (accounts differ) saw an excellent opportunity of relieving some of the strain which Wilson's attacks on Bryanism had created between him and the most powerful figure in the Democratic party. So Mrs. Wilson invited the Great Commoner to dine, summoned her husband back from a Southern speaking tour by an urgent telegram, and made arrangements that worked out perfectly. There was no one present at the quiet little dinner but two of Wilson's daughters and one of Bryan's friends; so the two men saw each other under conditions that made for perfect ease. They eschewed political talk; capped each other's stories; sized up each other's personalities; and parted with mutual liking. Tumulty, with characteristic enthusiasm and exaggeration, declared joyfully: "You have nominated your husband, Mrs. Wilson." Others congratulated her. Mrs. Wilson shrugged off her part. It was "nothing"; it was merely "a question of good manners."

In some respects Wilson was at his life's best while he was Governor. He was very hopeful of becoming President, and being able to devote all his energies to bettering conditions for the people. Events presaging war in Europe—the Agadir crisis, the seizure of Tripoli, the Italo-Turkish war, the failure of the Haldane Mission—seemed almost as remote from his plans as were the stars. The immediate task of serving the people of New Jersey gave him no real worry. New Jersey's Democratic machine seemed too stunned by the novelty and success of his methods in fighting Smith to put up much resistance to his plans. He was riding the crest of success and mastery again. He was also happier in other ways. In Colonel House he was finding a friend who would do much to fill the place of Mr. Hibben, and in addition could provide him with expert advice on politics.

He seemed better physically, too. A speaking tour in the spring of 1911, during which he covered eight thousand miles, left him stronger than when he had set out. Realization of his ability to sway great gatherings was a powerful tonic; and so was the delightful task of planning what he would do, should he arrive in the White House.

In his happy frame of mind he was nearly always an agreeable and amusing person. The "harsh and unlovely" side of him, so disastrously evident in earlier and later years, was very much submerged. He was able even to be humorous about people who bothered him. Once, badgered by an earnest and unrealistic young progressive, he suggested that the desk of every reformer should bear a sign: "DON'T BE A DAMNED FOOL."

When one of his interviewers asked him whether he would not find it more difficult to be nominated for the presidency than to be elected, he assented immediately. This was imprudent, especially at a time when Roosevelt had not yet bolted the Republicans; but the forecast proved quite accurate. His party, as a cartoonist showed graphically, was trying to ride two Democratic mules, not one. Once the party nomination was made, loyalty and interest might cause the right- and left-hand mules to run together for victory in the November elections of 1912; but it would take great skill to manage them simultaneously, before and during the choice of the party's candidate. The right-hand mule, though fed in large part by Tammany and kindred machines in other States, and by such financial "angels" as August Belmont in New York and Thomas Fortune Ryan in Virginia, possessed a certain sedate respectability. Plenty of Democrats of the highest type could shrug off its undesirable backers in view of the safe continuance of established ways that it offered. Moreover, the men who would presumably be its favorite candidates for the presidential nomination were certainly respectable or more. There was nothing objectionable about Governor Harmon of Ohio except some tendency toward pomposity. Oscar Underwood of Alabama, a veteran congressman deservedly respected and admired, was another right-wing candidate.

The left-hand mule, the younger, faster, and progressive mule, was backed by men in general more intellectual, more interested in principles, and in consequence less bound by party ties. On that side Bryan's flamboyant eloquence, his picturesque benignity of countenance, his long struggle (disfigured though it had been by quackery) to bring the party back to power with its progressive element in ascendancy, and also his genuine goodness and kindliness, had made his influence well-nigh supreme. He said repeatedly that he did not wish the nomination. He was believed to be planning to put his influence behind Champ Clark of Missouri, another much-respected veteran in Congress, who became Speaker in 1910, when the Democrats regained control of the House of Representatives. There was some uncertainty about this. Frankness was not always reckoned to be among the Great Commoner's virtues. There were rumors that his long friendship with Clark was a shade less cordial than it had been, and that Bryan's disclaimer of desire for the nomination was far from being heartfelt. Whether Clark or Bryan should stand in his way, Wilson would have powerful competition for the favor of the left-hand mule.

Of course Wilson was committed, and sincerely committed, to a decided preference for the party's left wing. Those who have written that it required some legerdemain to present him as a progressive Democrat seem to have forgotten that he had always been a liberal, and that his speeches during the last years of his presidency at Princeton (including those of his gubernatorial campaign) had given evidence of his rapid shift to the left. They seem, in fact, to have forgotten that he was too intelligent a man to be a prey to the fixity of political viewpoints which afflicts many of us as Americans—too intelligent a man, in other words, to be unable to change his mind. He who had always been so frank in his admiration of the long-established processes of Anglo-Saxon types of government now favored the use of the initiative and referendum as weapons which might be useful, for the time being at any rate, in breaking down the bosses' control of politics. To one of his interviewers he admitted frankly how greatly he had changed his mind:

For fifteen years I taught my classes that the initiative and referendum wouldn't work. I can prove it now—but the trouble is *they do!*

Yes, in so far as "progressivism" had a defined meaning, he was clearly on the progressive side. After all, the change that had taken place in him was only natural. Faith in the essential goodness and wisdom of the people as a mass had always underlain, and would never cease to underlie, his whole conception of government and politics.

With such a faith, and at a time when the political and economic shackling of the people through abuse of the power of wealth had become a commonplace to the open-minded and intelligent, how could he have failed to consider and represent himself as the candidate of men and women of progressive views? There was question only as to where among them he would take his stand. For Americans of progressive views were not joined in the acceptance of any definite articles of faith. La Follette and Roosevelt were both intent on leading the Republican party into progressivism; but while La Follette was eager to see the structure of big business in the industrial East reduced to ruins, Roosevelt had shown, and was soon to show again, that, while fulminating against the trusts, he would handle them considerately. Senator Borah was another Republican of strongly progressive views; but, like Roosevelt, he stood for a high tariff, despite the privilege it gave to big business.

Wilson was much less extreme than La Follette, and much more logical than Borah. He was no enemy of big business so long as big business did not enslave or rob consumers or wage earners, and so long as it kept its hands off politics. He was an enemy of high protective tariffs because he believed them potent instruments in the mulcting of the people. Since there was moderation in his progressivism, he might outrun Harmon and Underwood and Clark and Bryan for the nomination, if he could show a notable record at Trenton, give an effective display of his political wares throughout the country in a series of speeches, and avoid too greatly antagonizing the conservative elements in the party.

At Trenton he went to work at once. Even before his inauguration he had made an impressive start, as James Kerney, editor and publisher of the *Trenton Evening Times,* was later to point out:

There was nothing in the career of Wilson that so vastly expanded his reputation as his fight on Smith. . . . Like his conflict at Princeton, it . . . won him outside of his own State hundreds of supporters for every one he lost at home . . . it was easy to set him before the public as a sort of tribune of the people. . . . The country was filled with reformers, but Wilson . . . was a successful reformer . . . not . . . cut from any standardized pattern.

On the other hand, his fight with Smith had also won him powerful antagonists "outside of his own State"—men of Smith's own kind and their backers. He asked no favor from any boss, but when he delivered his inaugural speech as Governor, on January 17, against a background of flags and bunting, "a brass band with three bass drums," a State Guard in "magnificent" uniforms, and carriage horses that "actually pranced," he seemed distinctly conscious of the danger that would lie in alarming Democratic businessmen too much. His tone was firm, but conciliatory, too. Corporations, he said, were no longer to be regarded as "hobgoblins," but "organizations of a perfectly intelligible sort," which had proved decidedly useful. The trouble was that, "for the time being," they had "slipped out of the control of the very law that gave them leave to be." Hence "wise regulation," especially in the granting of charters, was called for.

In the same way, laws governing the relations between capital and labor would have to be revised, since they had been "framed for another age." Was it proper that a wage earner, an individual, and a poor one at that, should be forced to go to law against a corporation, a well-financed group of men, in order to get compensation for injuries received in line of duty? Or were the whole body of citizens, the consumers, of New Jersey properly provided for? Should they not be assured of service by public utilities on decent terms, through the creation of a commission with "complete regulative powers"? And did not the citizens lack something more fundamental still—the right to select, through primaries, the candidates for every elective office in the State, yes, even the officials and committees of the parties? Wilson's tone grew harsher as he spoke of a system that offered the people "nothing more than a choice between one set of machine nominees and another." Was there not need, in fact, for new election laws, for bállot reform, for the abolition of corrupt practices? Was there not need, again, for better taxation, for the conservation of natural resources, and for economy? The speech was an elaboration of the platform he had written for the party, a restatement of the promises which he had made in his campaign.

He was speaking from the heart. The party must live up to its promises; and he, the Governor, was specially bound. The bosses had nominated him, for their own reasons. But it was the people who had elected him. They had given him a majority for which the bosses could not have been responsible, an almost unprecedented majority, to which many Republicans must have contributed. His promises must be kept. But how could they be, with a Republican majority in the Senate and with so many members of both parties in the lower house who were amenable to boss control? Wilson's answer was in full keeping with the lifelong views of government on which he was prepared to act as Governor and, God willing, as President. He would be in the fullest sense a party man, leading the party, and, if need be, using legitimate means of coercion to keep it united in fidelity to its platform. But he would be more than that. He would be the servant and representative of all New Jersey citizens, not only in making sure, as "chief executive," that the laws were put in force, but in seeing to it that the people got such laws as they required. If machines and lobbyists, and legislators who feared machines and lobbyists, refused to pass needed laws, he would appeal to the sovereign people who had the vote. Used in a small State where contact with the electorate was easy, and at a time when sentiment for reform was thoroughly aroused, this was a formidable weapon. Wilson had no intention of using it unnecessarily or immediately. As a good party man, solicitous for the party's reputation and its unity, he would try persuasion first, carrying the power of appeal to the people like a pistol in its holster, visible but not to be leveled, much less fired, until persuasion failed.

Persuasion, as it proved, was possible; but only through certain innovations in the legislative process which must have made many New Jerseyites rub their eyes. When Smith was the effective party leader, and he and his staff could enforce effective discipline, the legislative process had been an odd perversion of what the makers of the State constitution had had in mind. Bills were apt to emerge from obscure places (if, for example, the offices of corporation lawyers could in this connection be called obscure) and to go through their stages under the very eyes of the Big Boss and his staff. Such legislators (and apparently they formed a good proportion) as believed that their political futures would be in the hands of the machines obeyed orders to cast their votes in certain ways at certain times, without feeling much concern about the content of the bills.

Wilson decided that all that sort of thing should end. From now on he would be the party's leader, responsible for the fulfillment of the promises in the platform. Looking over the legislature, he singled out in both houses a few men who had the point of view, the knowledge, and the ability to produce the sort of bills which the electors had apparently given the party a mandate to pass. He called them together (at first in a New York hotel room for convenience' sake); he placed the case before them; he explained what other States had done; and he parceled out among them the task of preparing the needed bills. As the drafts came in, he spent many evenings in studying and revising them, and discussing them with their drafters, seeking information and advice wherever they could be found. He got the authors of the bills to introduce them as rapidly as possible, so as to give the legislators time for study and debate. This was all highly unconventional. He was acting much like a British prime minister in ignoring the separation of the executive and legislative powers. In still another way he shattered precedent. He did not hesitate to admit Mr. Record to his confidence and to his consultations. In fact, he seemed open to suggestions from any quarter. One day he received a call from William U'Ren, a former blacksmith, who had been largely responsible for some very progressive reforms in Oregon. It was U'Ren who convinced him that the initiative and referendum (just taken up by Bryan to the horror of all conservatives) could really work in America.

It was easier, of course, to get good bills framed and introduced than to get them passed. The bosses were angry and active. The only hope was to use persuasion, allowing the pistol in its holster to be seen now and again. To use persuasion, he had to meet the legislators face to face. He did meet them, individually and in small groups, inviting them to conferences, and, in literal fashion, keeping the doors of his offices invitingly open. But that was not enough. Bosses and lobbyists could have more conferences and open doors than he. And it was in party caucuses of legislators that action regarding legislation was decided on, and that concerted pressure was applied on behalf of machines and lobbyists. To meet that situation was possible, if he was willing to break another precedent.

He was. Word reached him of the calling of a caucus of Democratic legislators for March 6, to discuss one of his favorite measures, an election bill to which the name of a Mr. Geran was attached. Quite casually he sent word that he would like to be present. No one venturing to exclude him, he walked in, brisk, persuasive (even the holster of the pistol was invisible), and with everything mapped out. His position, to say nothing of his air of assurance and his certainty as to what he wanted, gave him the leadership at once. One rebellious member asked what business lawmaking was of his. And then, just as a professor of government *would* do, he pulled out a copy of the Constitution and began to read:

The governor shall . . . at such . . . times as he may deem necessary . . . recommend [to the legislature] such measures as he may deem expedient.

If this did not precisely explain his presence at the caucus, it answered the rebellious member's question; and vocal opposition was for the moment stilled. For three hours the Governor discussed the Geran bill, clause by clause, drawing upon all his knowledge of American history and government, including that of existent laws in other States. It seemed hardly fair, this unloosing of a flood of knowledge with which no antagonist was prepared to cope. He ended with a stirring appeal for loyalty to the State and the party. One legislator, describing the whole affair, was emphatic as to its effect:

We all came out of that room with one conviction: that we had heard the most wonderful speech of our lives. Even the most hardened of the old-time legislative hacks said that. . . . That caucus settled the fate of the Geran bill, as well as the whole Democratic program.

Apparently it did. The Geran bill made it impossible for repeaters, for dead men, and for other phantoms to cast votes; for corporations to contribute to campaign funds; for bribes, even in such elegant forms as liquor and tickets, to be used. Another law snatched still more power from the bosses, by establishing primaries for all elective offices in the State. Still another allowed municipalities to adopt the commission plan of government, including the initiative and referendum, if they wished. The regulation of public utilities was provided for; and industrial employees became entitled automatically to compensation on a fixed scale for injuries received in course of work. The country looked on admiringly; and Wilson's stock as a probable nominee went up.

With as much of his legislative program as could be completed in one session safely on the statute books, the Governor could start out to appeal to the Democrats of the nation. Though he was usually reluctant to go on speaking tours, and almost invariably nervous when he got up to speak, he had no sooner launched out on an address than he went on confidently, eagerly, and happily. He always enjoyed public speaking because he knew that he did it well; and for his enjoyment of the speaking he was doing at this time there were other good reasons. He was meeting a challenge; he was face to face with the masses of people he trusted and wished so much to serve; better yet, he was giving them the aspirations and ideas they needed. For his political wares were honest ones. Not merely did he believe in them with all his heart, but they were custom built, not taken from some general stock. They were not, and hardly could have been, original. In ultimate origin they might stem from ancient Greece, or seventeenth-century England, or from the writings of some contemporary American; but Wilson had selected, combined, adopted, and adapted them, through long study, meditation, and experience.

For him, they were not so much ideas and aspirations as programs for action. He was "briefing" the people for attacks on what he regarded as the strongholds of corruption and of privilege. For the people were the sovereign, and hence ultimately the government. "The whole spirit of government," he told a Jefferson Day gathering in 1912, was "the spirit of men of every kind banded together for the common good." At the end of the campaign a cartoonist portrayed Wilson as a schoolmaster pointing to a blackboard which bore the sentence: "Politics is the business of *all* the people, not *some* of the people." The class, consisting of one top-hatted boss, looked surly, contemptuous, and on the point of going to sleep.

From his basic conception of the true nature of democratic government Wilson was able to use analogies that made some of his political offerings easier for his audiences to understand. He pictured the whole people as a living body having certain organs, upon the normal functioning of which the health of the body would depend. But normal functioning might be obstructed and destroyed by abnormal growths, such as the worst type of political machines, and the organized lobby-ing by which "pressure politics" (this was not his phrase) were carried on at Washington and at State capitals. Once he described in very con-crete terms just how these abnormal growths functioned:

Almost all [of our legislation] is framed in lawyers' offices, discussed in committee rooms, passed without debate. Bills that the machine and its backers do not desire are smothered in committee; measures which they do desire are brought out and . . . rushed through in the hours that mark the close of the legislative sessions, when everyone is withheld from vigilance by fatigue and when it is possible to do secret things . . . we no longer have representative government.

He would do all in his power, he promised, to see that the people themselves directly selected men to make and execute laws that were really for their interest.

Something would have to be done about the existing economic and financial structure, too. Changes in the economic setup of the country—for instance, the recent enormous expansion of big business— were apt to produce new needs, to stimulate new desires, and so to be responsible for new growths. There was nothing to be said against big business in itself. There were great businesses which deserved the thanks of the country, as did the wealthy and public-spirited men who headed them. There were other businesses which cut production down in order to keep prices up; which entered politics through party machines and lobbyists, in order to secure privileges at the cost of the consumers and of labor. Big corporations derived their powers from all the people who held their stocks and bonds, and could use these powers to the detriment of the whole nation. Government must there-fore have the power to regulate them in the general interest.

Other steps would be required in the handling of big business. Tariff revision would be the most fundamental, with reconstruction of the nation's system of banking and currency a close second. Other re-formers, oratorically more or less gifted, were talking on similar lines; but few if any of them issued to the people so clear a call to arms. Where in history, Wilson asked, was there record of a government or a party that had reformed itself? He could even on occasion touch the heartstrings of an audience, as when, on one occasion, he issued his familiar plea for service:

Did you ever see anybody who had lost a son hang up his yardstick over the mantelpiece? Have you not seen many families who have lost their sons hang up their muskets? . . . the yardstick was used for the man's own interest . . . the musket was used to serve no possible purpose of his own.

But it was wit, far more than sentiment, which relieved the rationality of his speeches. Introducing him at Harrisburg, A. Mitchell Palmer referred to the hopes of the Democrats in a man who had "lighted up the whole horizon." Wilson was quick. "Mr. Palmer has given me a lighting contract, and, knowing the men who undertake lighting contracts in New Jersey as I do, I don't know that I want to be associated in the work." And conservative Virginians laughed when, admitting that progressivism had run away with him, he told the story of a Scotsman whose dog ran down the street with a lobster clawed to its tail; and who, being enjoined by the fishmonger to "whustle" for his dog, suggested that the merchant "whustle" for his lobster.

Even on his speaking tours Wilson realized the difficulty of his third task—of being progressive without hopelessly antagonizing the right wing. He was too independent and too honest to make a proper job of it. From time to time he tried to administer soothing syrup to the conservatives. There was, he said, some "strain and peril" in every "process of change"; but these would be much less serious if people would accept the process in a proper mood. He was not proposing revolution, but "restoration," in which there would be "as much healing as hurt." Just where the machine men and the businessmen whom he seemed to threaten were to get the "healing" he did not explain; although he did promise that no "stable foundations," no rights of property or contract—in fact, not "any rights at all"—would be infringed.

On other occasions he seemed to throw discretion to the winds. There was, for example, an evening on which he talked to the New York Democratic Club. He must have known that some of the most politically influential figures among the men he faced were hostile to almost all of his ideas and his principles. But whether he was thinking of a larger audience to which his words might penetrate, or whether (as his whole record suggests) he was merely speaking the truth as he saw it, he showed little concern for the susceptibilities of his listeners. He opened tactfully, by declaring himself honored to be associated with an organization of Democrats pledged to tariff reform. He pleased everyone, of course, when he talked of "standpat

Republican leaders . . . unenlightened, uninformed, absolutely blind and stubborn"; and he ran no risk of giving offense when he praised "the fundamental principle of the Democratic party . . . tariff for revenue." But he was not on such safe ground in arguing that highly paid labor, like expensive machinery, was apt to be cheaper in the end, or in contending that "the high cost of production [was], in almost every instance," based "upon patronage and privilege," and thus a "cancer" eating at the hearts of all Americans. Then, with Tammany men all about him, as they must have been, he paid some of his usual compliments to the bosses. He did not care for any party organization which was "privately owned," since, as he added rather airily, he did not propose to be privately owned himself.

The New York bosses had seen enough of the tribulations of their brothers in New Jersey to realize that Wilson meant exactly what he said. They kept on realizing it up to and through the national convention at Baltimore. But it was during his great speaking tour in the spring of 1911 that he came closest to stampeding the right-hand mule beyond recall. At Kansas City he publicly praised the initiative, the referendum, and the recall of administrative officers (not of judges) as methods of combating government by partisan machines. There was consternation among his backers. Not only pronounced conservatives among the Democrats, but good, middle-of-the-road members of the party, had been shocked when Roosevelt had come out for these new heresies. The South, in particular, would never stand for them. Wilson was sharply curbed. He made only a partial recantation; but the initiative, referendum, and recall never appeared again in his speeches, and not at all in the campaign literature which his helpers sent out.

The men who managed his campaign for the nomination were more enthusiastic and devoted than experienced. Colonel House was not yet established as his adviser in chief; and Wilson, whose belief in the people and in his own powers of persuasion made him a little impatient at having to organize the campaign at all, used assistants who were as much amateurs in politics as himself. None of them was more active and enthusiastic than Walter Page. Long a champion of "the forgotten man" (whom he described as such) in his own South, he was eager to place Wilson in the White House in the interests of innumerable "forgotten men." He enlisted William Bayard Hale, who had presented Roosevelt to the reading public with great success, to give Wilson a similar "build-up" in the then popular *World's Work*. He joined Mrs. Wilson and Tumulty in urging the Governor to set out on his first great speaking tour; was one of the first to solicit campaign funds; urged (unsuccessfully) full publication of receipts and of expenditures; and generally made himself as useful as he could. In view of his later relations with Wilson, his contribution is worth remembering. Oswald Garrison Villard was another man of letters who threw himself into the campaign, making the New York *Evening Post* a Wilson organ, and playing some part in planning campaign strategy. And then there was McAdoo, most practical of the group; and finally William McCombs.

McCombs was, and remains, a tragic figure. Arkansas—a family of means—Princeton—deep affection and admiration for Wilson—a New York law office—affiliation with Tammany in apparent ignorance of some of the things that Tammany stood for—Wilson's appearance as a candidate—McCombs' dash to help him with time and brains and money: this brings McCombs to 1911. Wilson, gladly accepting the services and the homage, gave him the management of the campaign. The appointment affords clear evidence of Wilson's inexperience, or perhaps indifference, where organization was concerned. It was unfortunate for McCombs and for himself. A campaign manager needs to be rugged, tough-skinned, indifferent to personal considerations, and stout of heart when things go wrong. McCombs was frail, thin-skinned, given to suspicion and jealousy, and easily alarmed. Where propaganda was concerned, he gave excellent service; but his dislike and jealousy of the practical and hard-fighting McAdoo, and the nervous irritability he showed in contacts with other men, helped to make the Wilson headquarters a place of dissension and divided counsels.

One says "helped to make," because divisions within the party, taken in conjunction with Wilson's personality, would have made harmony difficult in any case. "Public life," as Mr. Kerney wrote, "is necessarily full of inconsistencies. . . . Politicians of all grades are wont to temper their acts and words to meet the prevailing winds." This was hard for such an idealist and amateur as Wilson. In some respects, he played the conventional game quite well. He tried (unsuccessfully) to start a German-American movement in his favor; he sought and obtained membership in the American-Irish Historical Society; he appointed the first Hebrew to a judgeship in the State's higher courts, and made an admirable speech, "The Rights of the Jews"—being rewarded, so it was said, by a much-needed subscription of four thousand dollars a month to campaign funds from Mr. Henry Morgenthau. He successfully refuted the charge of his unfriendliness to labor; he dodged woman suffrage, by becoming a strong exponent of States' rights in that respect; and he held off importunate advocates of prohibition by insisting that the liquor question had no legitimate place in politics.

But the probability of his nomination had little or nothing to do with such issues. Could he or could he not become the favorite of the party's progressive wing, without becoming anathema to the more conservative section? At the outset he did not stand too well with either side. Colonel Harvey had never been able to set the minds of his friends at rest; while Bryan's followers had found it difficult to forget the New Jersey Governor's earlier slurs on their leader and his doctrines, and the fact that he had almost contemptuously refused to run for the vice-presidency on the Bryan ticket of 1908. But from the time of Mrs. Wilson's little dinner for Bryan in the spring of 1911 the courtship of the Bryanites made steady progress. Before the year was out Colonel House and Josephus Daniels, a friend of Bryan's, and a North Carolinian of influence, were working to persuade the Commoner that Wilson, not Champ Clark, should be the candidate. Bryan was noncommittal, but apparently not unimpressed. He nodded approvingly over the Wilson reforms at Trenton, and was highly pleased when Wilson told an audience that the Democrats would merely reap, in 1912, reward for Bryan's having "borne the heat and burden of a long day."

A rude interruption of the *rapprochement* was threatened when one of the Governor's old antagonists at Princeton published a confidential letter of five years before, expressing Wilson's ardent desire to knock Bryan and all he stood for "into a cocked hat"; but Wilson's backers were equal to the test. As candidate and Commoner were about to meet at a 1912 Jackson Day dinner, swift action was required. Daniels, called by telephone, met the Commoner as he traveled North, and worked hard to plug the breach. At the dinner Wilson produced a tribute to the aging chief more touching than the first, and felt the chief's arm magnanimously placed around his back. But as the left wing warmed to Wilson, the right wing cooled, until the situation between Harvey and Wilson became impossible. Harvey's support of the Governor in *Harper's Weekly* was angering his wealthy and influential friends, and at the same time laying Wilson open to the suspicion of Western progressive Democrats that "Wall Street" was backing him. In December 1911 the two men, together with Harvey's great friend, "Marse Henry" Watterson, dined quietly together in New York. In parting, Harvey asked Wilson whether his support was keeping alive rumors of Wall Street backing. Wilson answered, a shade bluntly, that apparently it was; and went home seemingly in ignorance that anything important had happened.

He was soon undeceived. Though, on the alert Tumulty's suggestion, he twice wrote Harvey to express regret for his bluntness and his hope of keeping Harvey's support, *Harper's Weekly* announced that it had ceased to back him at his own request. It is generally believed that the affair had been engineered to relieve Harvey from his embarrassment; but on the surface it had an ugly look. The term of "ingrate" had already been fastened upon Wilson by the friends of Smith, even so far away as Washington. It was now taken up by a wider and more respectable circle. Colonel Watterson's paper did its best to defame Wilson in this way:

> He who would show himself so disloyal to a private friendship cannot be trusted to be loyal to anything. Within a single year Governor Wilson's radical change of base, his realignments and readjustments, have been exactly concurrent with his selfish aims. There seems no abasement into which he is unwilling to descend with equal facility and grace. May God preserve Democracy from such a leader and such leadership!

The dispute between Wilson's friends and those of Harvey and Watterson widened to cover the sources of Wilson's campaign funds, to cover everything which might afford some ground for accusing him of what to politicians are the cardinal sins—ingratitude and "unreliability." Wilson, consoled, perhaps, by the reflection that he had been cleared of all charges of being a favorite with "Wall Street," was admirably calm. Referring sarcastically to Colonel Watterson as "a fine old gentleman," he disposed of him in the most effective manner possible. He took a courageous attitude toward the press in general. Importuned by agents of Mr. Hearst to send a letter welcoming the great man and his papers back into the Democratic fold, as other leading candidates had done, he finally gave an unlooked-for answer.

He could not write such a letter, since he believed that Mr. Hearst's return would weaken the party.

As the national convention, scheduled to meet at Baltimore at the end of June, drew near, his chances of getting the nomination seemed anything but promising. Though he could count on delegations from a few States such as Texas, where yeoman work had been done by Colonel House and other friends of his, it was clear that, in pledged delegates, Clark was ahead of him by something like two to one. The great delegations from New York, Illinois, Massachusetts, California, and Ohio were either pledged to the Speaker, or would switch to him if the nomination of a conservative, Harmon or Underwood, proved impossible. Clark, through his long service in Washington, was some-one whom Democratic politicians knew and could count upon. And in 1910 Bryan had endorsed him to the hilt:

> I have known Mr. Clark eighteen years. He is absolutely incorruptible. . . . Never have I known him to be on any side of a question that was not the side of the people.

Bryan's own Nebraska delegation was pledged to Clark. Of course the Wilson men had some hope. Bryan could do wonders if he would; and some of his recent speeches seemed to place him behind the New Jersey Governor. The Wilson people had established some claims to gratitude by declining to set up organizations in the States whose "favorite sons" would appear as candidates. Then there was the widely diffused pro-Wilson sentiment among the voters. If the convention should be protracted, that might be called into play.

People who enjoy the game of speculating on the "ifs" of history should find the Baltimore convention a godsend. For the convention was full of "ifs"—of situations so delicate that had this man or that (on some occasions Wilson himself) moved differently, Champ Clark or Roosevelt, or even possibly Bryan, would have been in control of our foreign relations until early in 1917 at any rate. Unfortunately, the story of the convention presents not only many "ifs," but some undetermined questions that are vital. Was it really Bryan who made Wilson the chosen candidate? And, if so, did he or did he not perform this service accidentally, in trying to get the nomination for himself? We are soon to have new light on this. At any rate the general pattern of the convention is perfectly familiar: a struggle between right and left. But few convention struggles have been as dramatic or as bitter.

Bryan was a super showman; and feeling ran high, not only because social issues cut deep, but because the progressive element, having just watched the Republican conservatives reject Roosevelt for Taft in the "steam-roller" convention at Chicago, was in a bitter and suspicious mood. The New York delegation especially affronted it. The delegation contained some distinguished men, including the Governor, the Lieutenant Governor, and Judge Alton Parker, the defeated Democratic candidate of 1904. But the left wing fixed their eyes disgustedly on Mr. Murphy, the overlord of Tammany, and on August Belmont, who seemed to them the incarnation of "Wall Street." Figuratively and literally, the convention promised to be one of sweat and tears, if not of blood.

One would have looked in vain for sweat or tears at Sea Girt. Wilson, running through business, golfing, chatting, discussing the situation over the telephone, now with McCombs and now with McAdoo, showed the outward imperturbability where his personal fortunes were concerned which impressed even his antagonists, then and later. He played Mrs. Wilson's wifely and rather obvious game of pretending that what they really wanted was his defeat and an opportunity to rest again in the English Lake Country. But it does not seem possible that even Wilson remained inwardly cool, as news of the great moments of the convention came in, and personal decisions which might prove decisive were called for. The conservatives first showed their hand by deciding to nominate Mr. Parker as temporary chairman. Bryan, "specialist in conventions," called upon the leading candidates to declare how the suggested nomination impressed them. Clark, unwilling to alienate either progressives or conservatives, straddled the issue; but Wilson, to the horror of McCombs, answered flatly that the convention, being primarily one of progressives, should be organized as such. Bryan seemed to look more benignly toward the Wilson headquarters than he had done before; and progressive Democrats throughout the country became more convinced than ever that Wilson was their man.

With the actual nomination of Parker, came Bryan's first great counterthrust at the right wing. "The Democratic party," he declaimed, "is true to the people. You cannot frighten it with your Ryans nor buy it with your Belmonts." At Sea Girt, Wilson heard that Parker had been elected to the temporary chairmanship all the same. News soon followed that Democratic voters throughout the country, aroused by

Bryan's dramatization of the issue, were swamping the delegates with telegrams; and that in the vote for permanent chairman Parker had been defeated by Kentucky's progressive Congressman, Ollie James. News of a second progressive victory, breaking down the "unit rule" in voting, was equally encouraging; but then came the tense moment which always precedes the balloting. Bryan, whatever his ultimate objective may have been, chose this moment for his most daring assault on the conservatives. Undeterred by the hisses and catcalls which his former reference to the Ryan and Belmont millions had provoked, he repeated his offense in presenting, for passage by the convention, a resolution as shrewd as his eyes and as ruthless as his lips.

> . . . the party . . . is still the champion of popular government and equality before the law. As proof . . . we hereby declare ourselves opposed to the nomination of any candidate for President who is . . . under obligation to J. Pierpont Morgan, Thomas F. Ryan, August Belmont, or any other member of the privilege-hunting and favor-seeking class.

In the uproar that ensued, Bryan drove home his point by fulminating against a "most brazen" attempt to "make the nominee the bond slave of the men who exploit the people of this country." Considering that Bryan had earnestly solicited Tammany support for himself in former years, this was disingenuous, to say the least. But, determined to make the nomination of a conservative impossible, he seemed to feel that the end justified the means. His move worked perfectly. Not many delegates would lay themselves open to the charge of supporting "the privilege-hunting and favor-seeking class." News soon reached Wilson that the Bryan resolution had passed by a majority of more than four to one; and that, after the customary speeches of nomination and attempts of the backers of each candidate to outcheer and "outparade" the backers of all the rest (here the Wilson backers won with seventy-five minutes!), the balloting would begin. It was then that real strain came to the watchers at Sea Girt.

On the fifth day of the convention Wilson had to make one of the most important decisions of his life. Incidentally, it was to prove of considerable importance to the world. The question was whether he would or would not surrender his delegates to Clark, who had a clear majority but lacked the two-thirds vote which Democratic rules required. This was after the tenth ballot. On nine ballots Wilson's support had been impressive; and the Speaker, while having enough pledged delegates to keep ahead of him by more than a hundred votes, had still been lacking a majority. Then, on the next ballot a break had come. New York's delegation of ninety, surrendering whatever hope it may have had of nominating a conservative, had gone over to the Speaker. Both at Baltimore and at Sea Girt there was a general impression that the end had come; for there had been no case since 1844 in which a candidate securing a majority had not become the party's nominee.

Wilson's position was embarrassing. He had been outspoken in his denunciation of the "undemocratic" character of the two-thirds rule; and Clark's friends reminded him of the fact. When McCombs, quite in despair, asked permission to release the Wilson delegates whenever it seemed advisable, Wilson consented with a heavy heart. There followed at once a furious telephone protest from McAdoo, succeeded by fresh cogitations and discussions at Sea Girt. The McAdoo side could put up solid arguments. The two-thirds rule had been deliberately retained, and not through Wilson's fault. Apparently the Speaker was the politicians' choice; but was there not ground for believing that the people preferred the Governor? Was not Bryan, the most influential man of the party, in a state of great disturbance over the "besmirching" of the Speaker by New York's support? Should Wilson disappoint the citizens who wanted him, abandon his plans for national service, and bring to nought the devoted work of all his friends, in order to be consistent, or to act according to party tradition, or to satisfy a scruple? The arguments prevailed. The message to McCombs was canceled; and three more ballots failed to break the deadlock.

Then Wilson moved shrewdly. Did not Mr. Bryan think, he asked, that since New York was apparently maintaining the deadlock in order ultimately to control the nominee, the candidates might be asked to refuse any nomination not made independently of New York? Bryan did something more effective still. Drawing on his dramatic talents to the full, he announced that, so long as Clark received the tainted New York support, he would give Wilson his vote. This time uproar became a brawl. Bryan's 1910 endorsement of Clark was painted on a banner and thrust before his eyes. Fists were shaken; police rushed in; and the Commoner's nose bled. Mr. Stanchfield of New York called him a "money-grabbing, selfish, office-seeking, favor-hunting, publicity-loving marplot." And if, as Clark and Carter Glass and many others were always to believe, Bryan was trying to prolong the deadlock in order to make himself the nominee, Mr. Stanchfield did much to block the move. "Colonel Bryan," he told the convention, "never intended to support the candidate of this convention unless that candidate should be Bryan himself." Whatever Bryan's intentions, he seems to have opened Wilson's path to the White House. Clark, to his stupefied indignation, stood tarred with the Tammany brush, over against Wilson, the progressives' Great Incorruptible.

The group at Sea Girt had now only to wait, as the votes for the Incorruptible mounted. He had one more decision to make. As a concession to the conservatives, he was asked for a promise that, in the event of his election, he would not choose Bryan as Secretary of State. With all his heart he must have longed to give it; but expediency, gratitude, and his general principle of refusing commitments as the price of office all commanded him to refuse. Already the rush for the "bandwagon" had set in. Even the big bosses of New York and Illinois were soon climbing on board, leaving no one but a group of sad Missourians behind. But what about harmony in the party Wilson was to lead? On the day after his nomination many of the important papers of the country printed a remarkable statement signed by Clark. It called attention to the fact that he had led Wilson on thirty ballots, and that on eight of these he had had a majority of all the delegates. It went on:

Nevertheless the nomination was bestowed upon Governor Wilson. . . . I lost the nomination solely through the vile and malicious slanders of Colonel William Jennings Bryan, of Nebraska.

The statement also contained Clark's promise to support the party's nominee with all his strength. But bitterness can curdle harmony.

CHAPTER V

Baltimore to Washington

———————◆———————

IT SEEMS ODD that someone with a taste for colloquialisms has not called 1912 the year of presidential "hijacking," or of alleged hijacking at any rate. Certainly the air of this country was never so full of charges that nominations for the presidency had been stolen from candidates well on their way to figure in the November balloting. Mr. Roosevelt, that expert in the gentle art of vituperation, taxed even his vocabulary to express in a fitting manner his belief (shared generally, but not universally, by disinterested persons) that the Republican nomination had been shamelessly stolen from him at the national convention by the supporters of Mr. Taft. Yet it is doubtful whether his bitterness in thinking about Mr. Taft equaled that of Mr. La Follette in thinking about him.

When, in the spring of 1911, the Republican Progressives had first organized to capture the Republican party and select the party's nominee, Mr. La Follette had, after due consideration, been chosen as their candidate. Some of the Rough Rider's closest adherents had helped to make the choice, since Colonel Roosevelt had said plainly that he would not run again. Mr. La Follette had visited the Colonel, just returned in triumph from African jungles and European courts, and pronounced him "the greatest living American." But both Mr. Roosevelt and Mr. La Follette changed their minds. Under solicitation from friends who loved and admired him, and who wondered whether the pride of Wisconsin was not too hostile to the East, too destructive and too bitter, to carry the Progressive cause to victory, Roosevelt's resolution wavered. Leading Progressives, including some whose campaign contributions would be very useful to the candidate, began to hint to La Follette that he should unselfishly make way for "the greatest living American." The Wisconsin Senator quite failed to see the point. The matter came to a head after Wilson and La Follette had addressed a great banquet of writers, editors, and publishers, gathered at Philadelphia as the Periodical Publishers' Association, in February 1912. Wilson, facing just the sort of audience which best suited him, talked progressivism on its highest plane, and kept his audience (which included Colonel Harvey) literally spellbound. La Follette, arriving late, and speaking under the strain of deep personal anxiety, let himself go in the kind of bitter denunciation which had been his great stock in trade. He talked so long and so repetitiously that a large proportion of the banqueters threw courtesy to the winds and left him to address their empty chairs. His failure was dramatically sudden and complete. Outside his personal following, the Progressives soon commenced to drift away from him as the banqueters had done.

Under increased pressure, Roosevelt "threw his hat into the ring." It was a bitter thing for "Fighting Bob" to see trusted supporters such as Senator Hiram Johnson pass over to the Roosevelt camp; to see his hopes of raising adequate campaign funds dissolve; but the chief wound to his pride was his belief that Roosevelt had used him as a mere "stalking-horse." In today's parlance, he was complaining of having been hijacked. And so, on the Democratic side, was Clark. In fact, almost everyone was using bitter words. Taft, while unwilling and unable to pay Roosevelt back in kind, made up for his deficiency in vituperation by acerbity.

But Wilson avoided personalities, kept cool, and talked of policies, of principles. He did so by preference and habit. His personal feeling was strong enough. "God save us from another four years of [Roosevelt] now in his present insane distemper of egotism," he had written before any of the three conventions had met. But he was literally "too proud to fight" as Roosevelt fought. And virtue had its reward. His clear, firm speeches were a relief from the Rough Rider's heat and violence. For the campaign from the outset was a Wilson-Roosevelt fight. Taft, annoyed by the complaints of his supporters that the only publicity he was getting seemed to revolve about his game of golf, pictured the situation with wry humor: "It always makes me impatient, as if I were running a P. T. Barnum show, with two or three shows across the street, and as if I ought to have as much advertising as the rest." For once the progressives of both parties had their day.

Sometimes a few sentences or phrases collected from the speeches and writings of a candidate are enough to give the whole tone of the campaign. For example these:

> Democracy means nothing unless the people rule. The rule of the boss is the negation of democracy . . . he is a foe to popular government who in any way causes the people to lose self-control and self-mastery whether from without or within. . . . The fight for progressive popular government . . . will certainly go on to a triumphant conclusion . . . irrespective of the personal success or failure of individual leaders.

And again:

> We need leaders of inspired idealism . . . who dream greatly and strive to make their dreams come true; who can kindle the people with the fire from their own burning souls. . . . It is little matter whether any one man fails or succeeds; but the cause shall not fail, for it is the cause of mankind. We, here in America, hold in our hands the hope of the world.

How excellently these words seem to express the attitude of Wilson. Yet they were not his words, but those of Theodore Roosevelt, spoken or written between the time of his return from Africa and Europe in 1910 and the presidential election more than two years later. They came from a man who had been lauded as a pioneer in attacking most of the evils on which Wilson was making war; who had led his country successfully through serious international crises, himself becoming an international figure; who, ranking with the manliest of Americans, had understood the *hearts* of his countrymen as none of his contemporaries had done or yet could do; and had been loved by his compatriots as none of his rivals had been (or would be) loved.

Since both he and Wilson were bidding for the progressive and independent votes, Roosevelt's chances of winning might have seemed excellent. "Roosevelt," Wilson wrote, ". . . is a real vivid person whom [the public] have seen and shouted themselves hoarse over and voted for, millions strong; I am a vague, conjectural personality, more made up of opinions and academic prepossessions than of human traits and red corpuscles." The Governor had reason to be doubtful of his success. If he had a great advantage in the fact that the whole Democratic party was interested in electing him, he was handicapped by the absence of a normal Democratic majority in the nation; by the resentment, not only of Clark's supporters, but of organization men in various States; and by his lack of all those political connections which Roosevelt had built up during his long years in politics.

With advantages balanced so evenly between the two more picturesque performers in a three-ring circus, and with so great a similarity in their offerings to the public, the contest became largely one of personalities. Roosevelt gave his estimate of his rival to Hiram Johnson when the election was over:

Wilson was from their [the Democrats'] standpoint the best man that they could have nominated. I do not regard him as a man of great intensity of principle or conviction, or of much reality of sympathy with our cause. He is an adroit man, a good speaker and writer, with a certain amount of ability of just the kind requisite to his party under present conditions. . . . In the campaign he talked ardent but diffuse progressiveness. He championed concretely a number of men or things for which we stand.

In its superciliousness and understatement of Wilson's good points, this portrait would have done credit to Henry Cabot Lodge. Wilson's "certain amount of ability" was later measured by Lloyd George as "supreme." But the passage is worth quoting. Take the two concluding sentences. It was true that Wilson "talked ardent but diffuse progressiveness," even to a point where his strongest supporters implored him to be more concrete.

Yet both they and Roosevelt overlooked one thing: Wilson had something in common with Jeremy Bentham. Each seized a yardstick of which the presentation might sound at first like "diffuse progressiveness"; but, by using it to measure actual conditions, each secured results that were perfectly concrete. Bentham had demanded "the greatest good to the greatest number"; Wilson replaced "good" with "power." And the motto of "the greatest power to the greatest number" (there seems to be no record that he ever actually used the phrase) was not only the lodestar of democracy, but could be used with dynamic force. One can test it in its application to the matter of banking and currency, rated by both parties as a question of first import. Wilson admitted that his knowledge of banking was rudimentary, but he could still apply his principle. The greatest power to the greatest number meant that the ultimate control of credit and currency was not to be in a small group of big bankers, who could use it for political or other selfish purposes, but in the people, through their elected representatives.

Thoughtful voters liked such concrete applications of general principles. Thanks to their use, there was an ordered reasonableness and a fine selection of essentials in what Wilson said. Roosevelt was apt to rush impetuously into details which might take the average man beyond his depth; but in listening to Wilson the average man could feel that his feet were on the ground. More essential, perhaps, in this contest of personalities was Wilson's ability to convince the better class of voters that he and his party were superior in integrity. In New Jersey he had seen to it that the party platform promised every reform for which there was crying need, and later, that the platform's promises were carried out with exemplary and quite unusual fidelity. Now, in the national contest, his party was bidding for votes on a platform more clear cut and more liberal than the one the Progressives had offered. Tariff for revenue, an income tax, the prosecution of trusts, presidential primaries, the direct election of senators, federal supervision of public utilities, constitutional amendment forbidding a second presidential term, and exemption of American ships from tolls in using the Panama Canal while engaged in coastwise trade were all promised.

It was not a platform that Wilson, if elected, could push through immediately. And it was distinctly not his platform. In fact, he was utterly opposed to the two provisions last mentioned. But on such crucial and pressing matters as the tariff and the trusts his position was as well known as were the courage, the honesty, and the independence he had exhibited in New Jersey politics. Neither on his party's offerings nor on his personal record could Roosevelt make the same appeal. The Progressive platform was built up of planks bewildering in number and often radical or even socialistic in aspect. It seemed like a program for the long future rather than for the immediate present. But its greatest weakness in the eyes of voters of Progressive views lay in two omissions that were striking. There were no promises of tariff revision or of really effective action against the trusts. In both omissions the sacrifice of Progressive principles to the need for enlisting Republican votes seemed clear; but the second was especially damning. For it was known that a plank in the platform adopted at the Progressive convention had promised drastic action against the trusts, and that this plank had been made almost meaningless after George W. Perkins of J. P. Morgan and Co., the greatest contributor to Progressive funds, had gone into private conference with Roosevelt. Wilson and other Democratic campaigners found "the missing plank" a choice target. Unfortunately for Roosevelt, too, they could point out that his surrender to Mr. Perkins was much in keeping with his record. The great corporations had played a major part in financing his campaign in 1904; and as President he had treated them with a discretion that had belied his "trust-busting" speeches.

In so far as cool reasonableness and a reputation for integrity could win votes, the odds were all on Wilson's side; but his helpers went through four unhappy months. The problem of McCombs, whom Wilson, through loyalty, and possibly with a touch of political astuteness, too, had refused to remove from his chairmanship after the nomination had been won, was increasingly serious. McCombs was sicker than ever, and in consequence more given to suspicion and jealousy. The way of his associates was hard. Only loyalty to their chief kept McAdoo and the other campaign leaders (Daniels, A. Mitchell Palmer, Joseph E. Davies, Senator O'Gorman, Reed of Missouri, and as many more) working under and with him. And the candidate himself was a problem. He dealt readily enough with the kind of malicious rumors which so often disgrace campaigns in great democracies: that he was bitterly anti-Catholic; that he was treacherously pro-Catholic (a member of the Knights of Columbus, so one rumor had it!); that he was anti-labor, anti-Negro.

But he did not then, nor ever, become the kind of "regular" politician who makes things easy for his managers. He did not seem to be of presidential timber when it came to "glad handing" voters, wearing Indian war bonnets or ten-gallon hats, slapping backs, kissing babies, or calling virtual strangers by their first names. It was impossible to photograph him driving a plow or milking a cow. In fact, he did not photograph well at all. As he said later, his "Presbyterian face" was better calculated to alarm his enemies than to increase the ardor of his friends. He was unwilling even to play the game in recognized fashion. He objected to long stumping tours for purely campaign purposes, to "back-platform" oratory, to constant interviews. He would not evoke cheers by making charges which no one could substantiate. He would not remove reproach from his party by blaming its rival for all its shortcomings. He would not even seek to win the press.

His sense of humor was apt to fail him when a cub reporter asked information usually possessed by high-school graduates, or when re-write men gave ridiculous headlines to reports of serious interviews. How could he tell amusing stories to illustrate his points, if he was to see such headlines next morning as "WILSON FEELS LIKE A FROG" or "WILSON ADVOCATES CHEWING TOBACCO"?

What was more serious, the inevitable but merciless intrusion upon his privacy, intrusion even upon the lives of the ladies of his family, which had now set in, was repugnant to his fastidious nature and to his sense of chivalry. He was in the broadest glare of publicity, without the protection which the White House would give him later on. Some representatives of the press felt that he blamed the whole fraternity for the thoughtless juvenility of a few; and on both sides a certain reserve was soon in evidence. His nerves, always more or less his secret enemy, were very much on edge; and as the weight of new publicity and new duty pressed on him a note of self-pity appeared in his letters.

> You cannot . . . imagine such days . . . an invasion by the people of the United States! I had . . . *dreaded* it, but of course had never *realized* what it was to be the principal victim.

And again:

> The life I am leading now *can't* keep up. . . . Not a moment am I left free. . . . I thought that last night I should go crazy with the strain and confusion.

Fortunately, his friends provided hide-outs; and his managers per-suaded him to stump the South and West. With the stimulus of seas of faces before him, and the conviction of speaking for righteousness within him, he could again be at his best.

This speaking tour produced nothing very illuminating with respect to Wilson's policies, but it did throw some extra light on Wilson's personality. There was really not much that he could say, except to ring the changes on his speech of acceptance, demanding the greatest power for the greatest number in all that touched the average citizen's welfare. But his tour was a success. With microphones as yet unknown, he now reaped full reward for the self-training of his youth in declaiming to fields and trees. His easy conversational talk, made more easy by the insertion of homely anecdotes, was heard on the outer limits of great gatherings. And his audiences appeared to be convinced. Perhaps, as

Mr. Baker has suggested, they were more converted to the man than to his reasoning; but the confidence of the public is no mean substitute for its intellectual concurrence or its love.

As the tour went on, Wilson seems to have made some almost pathetic efforts to create a warmer feeling by "talking down" to the voters. But in the main he was able to leave the popularizing of his campaign to Bryan, who has been credited with the amazing feat of averaging ten speeches a day for seven weeks. Consequently, Wilson was able to concentrate his fire on the points where his opponents were most vulnerable—on the questions of the tariff and the trusts. He was careful, however, not to alarm the business world too much. Business, he reminded his hearers, was "exceedingly sensitive"; and great harm might be done by "rash or hasty action." So the Democrats, in revising the tariff downward, would be practical, not like men "in love with a theory." His caution may have made it easier for Colonel Harvey to swing *Harper's Weekly* back to his vigorous support, but it did not alienate men of liberal views. Among the new and lasting friends he picked up at this time were Samuel Gompers and Louis Brandeis. All in all, he showed himself a keener politician than some of his support-ers had thought him. This came out in a tragicomic incident. When Roosevelt was wounded by the bullet of a lunatic, and Wilson accepted Tumulty's suggestion that he should refuse to go on speaking until his rival could do the same, a characteristic sense of fair play no doubt influenced him. But he realized how good a political move it was. "Teddy will have apoplexy when he hears of this," he chuckled.

When the campaign wound up at Madison Square Garden, with the collegiate shouts of "We want Wilson" that Princeton had interjected into it from the outset, the prospects that the "vague conjectural per-sonality" would defeat the "real vivid person" were promising. But it was not only Wilson, the Democrats, the regular Republicans, and the La Follette men who were hurting Roosevelt's chances. It was Roose-velt's own record, and, strangely enough, his vivid personality.

President Eliot, who had various affiliations with Roosevelt, and who never liked Wilson, explained privately to a friend why he could not support the former President:

Roosevelt has hold of a fact when he says that the machines have robbed the people of power which belongs to them; but he ought not to be so hot about it. . . . Nobody has ever made more brazen and effective use of officeholders and ex-officeholders to control committees and conventions.

Eliot went on with his analysis, in numbered sentences that cut like steel:

. . . (3) He was in no position to split the Republican party on the grounds he has alleged; because he has been an active participant in the sort of wrongdoing which he now denounces so violently; (4) he is responsible for the great fall in manners which marks the present presidential campaign; (5) his egotism, self-confidence, and personal ambition overwhelm his judgment and even his benevolence.

Probably Eliot did not hold Wilson (for whom he voted) entirely guiltless on all these counts, but he underlined sharp contrasts between the two rivals. La Follette, if one may judge from his *Personal Narrative,* left Roosevelt even less to stand on in the way of consistency and sincerity. The Colonel had reversed his stand on reciprocity with Canada. He had "turned sharp corners" on the tariff issue, highly praising (the *Outlook* was quoted here) the record-breaking protective schedule of the Payne-Aldrich bill. He had accepted all the partisan maneuvering, the obstruction and evasion of reform, for which the iron rule of "Uncle Joe" Cannon, as Speaker, had been responsible. He, the Progressive, had been careful not to disturb his pleasant relations with big business. He had consorted with Morgan and Frick and Harriman and Gould and others of the tribe. The trusts as a whole had multiplied their capitalization (far the greater part of it in watered stock) ten times over while he was President. He was nothing but an opportunist, La Follette charged, constantly doing things directly opposed to what he said. Perhaps no one but La Follette men, as bitter in frustration as their aggrieved leader, subscribed to these charges against the quondam "greatest living American" in their entirety. But there was quite enough truth in them to make Wilson's brief record at Trenton seem a glistening example of purity in politics.

And then Roosevelt's personality, his very picturesqueness, made him vulnerable to ridicule, the deadliest of political weapons. Wilson disdained personalities; but some of his supporters were less particular. Senator John Sharp Williams of Mississippi, who had admired Wilson's writings for many years, cheered him in his fight with Smith, advised him in his pre-convention campaign, and was now serving as a member of his executive committee in the East, adopted ridicule as the most effective medicine for Roosevelt's "disease." Carrying his campaigning into the Senate, he lightened dull hours with amusing doggerel:

> I'm twice as great as Washington
> I'm twice as great as Grant
> Because third terms they didn't get
> They needn't think I can't.

It was not long since the country would have resented such treatment of its Number One hero; but a change had taken place. Roosevelt himself sensed it when he wrote wistfully to William Allen White: "I think that the American people are a little tired of me." Yes, they were a little tired of him, tired of the big stick, of the vast exuberance, the vituperation, the nervous restlessness which had been so novel, so exciting, in the Rough Rider and the stentorian denouncer of the trusts. These had become a little threadbare, a little out of key, in the retired President, the elder (though not yet really old) statesman. It was rather nauseating to hear so eminent a man declare that the party badges of the President of the United States (incidentally an old friend and associate) were appropriately colored yellow. Novelty was now furnished by the crisp, alert Governor of New Jersey, who seemed to have the clean, compact utility of a brand-new broom. Wilson's intense idealism was not a factor with most of the voters. They saw him as a man who spoke clearly, meant what he said, and got things done, when he was given any chance.

The people whom Wilson's personality had impressed might have believed in him even more had they seen him on November 5, when all America was going to the polls, and excitement was running high. He seemed *par excellence* the plain citizen, waiting calmly to learn whether the people wanted him for their servant. He gave himself the luxury of sleeping rather late before he left the house on Cleveland Lane to cast his vote. Then he strolled about the town, showing the sights to Dudley Field Malone, and guarded by "Captain Bill," the huge "two-gun" Texas Ranger whom Colonel House had summoned for his protection after the attempt on Roosevelt's life. He had always got on excellently with Captain Bill, a man of simple tastes and thoughts, but with a reputation for killing that put Nick Carter or Jesse James to shame. Wilson's evening, by way of contrast, was spent with Browning, which Mrs. Wilson read aloud. As she went on quietly, the bell on Old Nassau commenced to ring, and kept on ring-ing "like a thing possessed" until, at ten o'clock, a telegram arrived. Then Mrs. Wilson had the joy and privilege of offering first congratulations to the man she had done so much to make famous.

In no time crowds of cheering undergraduates with torchlights, insistent on a speech, arrived. The President-elect obliged them from the porch, balancing himself precariously on a hastily brought out rocking chair. There was a reminiscent tone about the speech's opening, reminiscent not only of many Wilson speeches but of Gladstone's much-quoted words when Queen Victoria summoned him to become Prime Minister: "I have . . . a feeling of solemn responsibility. I know the very great task ahead of me." Slowly exact returns came in. Wilson had received half as many votes again as Roosevelt, and not far from twice as many as had gone to Taft. The next Senate would have a Democratic majority of six, and the House, already in Democratic control since 1910, would be more so in the next session.

Had Wilson persuaded the people to accept him for their leader? Had he been the people's choice—so much so as to carry his party to victory with him? Certainly he would want to think that it was so. Almost as certainly his belief in his own leadership, belief in his mission, belief in the people's wisdom, would help him to persuade himself that it was so, and to talk and act accordingly. On the face of it, such belief might easily have seemed justified. In a three-cornered race, a substantial plurality might be taken as clear evidence of popular favor. But it is an old and quite respectable maxim that voters cast their ballots against the candidates they do not want, more often than for the candidates they do. There is more than a little evidence that the maxim held especially true in the presidential election of 1912.

Mr. Taft, a competent judge of political developments, and as fair-minded as a man so deeply concerned could be, made a thoughtful analysis of the balloting:

I am becoming convinced . . . that the number of Republicans who voted for Wilson, in order to escape the danger of Roosevelt, reaches into the hundreds of thousands, and I must think, therefore, that Roosevelt drew a great many Democratic votes from Wilson of the labor, socialistic, discontented, ragtag and bobtail variety. Roosevelt had in addition the votes of the faddists, the radical progressives, the people with isms, the emotional clergymen and women, in states where women voted, and all the factional soreheads in the Republican party. . . . What I got was the irreducible minimum of the Republican party that was left after Roosevelt got through with it and after Wilson drew from it the votes of those Republicans who feared Roosevelt.

Mr. Taft had personal knowledge on which to base a part of his analysis. He had learned to his cost that "hardheaded businessmen," to whom Republicanism was a first article of faith, had been reluctant to contribute to his campaign fund because their first desire was to block the return of Roosevelt with all his "socialistic" projects. And for Roosevelt's defeat they had banked on Wilson, whether or not they had brought themselves to vote for him. Then with mingled disgust and amusement Taft had watched the blooming of a sudden friendship between those two political opposites, Senators La Follette and Penrose. Very boss of very bosses, the Pennsylvania Senator had delighted in taking lunch with "Bob," and planning the investigation of Roosevelt's campaign funds eight years before.

Yes, it was very probable that Wilson had garnered many votes from the Republicans, and by no means all of them because of admiration for his progressive leadership. As for the Democratic votes that he had lost, they may not have been so predominantly of the "labor, socialistic, discontented, ragtag and bobtail variety" as Mr. Taft surmised. Within his party Wilson was well supplied with enemies. He was not likely to find the leadership of the party, to say nothing of the nation, an easy task.

Ten days after the election Wilson, with his wife and two of his daughters, sailed for Bermuda, to take advantage of Mrs. Hulbert's thoughtful offer of her cottage for a month. They were very glad to get away. The house on Cleveland Lane had become bedlam. Friends and relatives, job hunters and publicity hunters, collectors of photographs and autographs, reporters and pseudo reporters, had battered at the doors. Thanks partly, no doubt, to a secret-service detail of guards (whom Wilson had vainly tried to send away), nearly all of them had been turned back. But the house was flooded with letters and telegrams, over which young secretaries worked feverishly; and which, a little later, would have kept the Americana section of Mr. Mencken's *American Mercury* more than supplied for months. The family found the still increasing publicity hard to bear. Mrs. Wilson, who for the short remainder of her life was called upon to mask her pride in her husband's rise to eminence and her distaste for all the pomp and circumstance that came with it, was very much harried.

She learned almost at once to buy things in New York for cash, in order to conceal her name; but even then she complained that she sometimes felt like an animal in a zoo.

Wilson, accustomed to notoriety by now, found certain compensations in the change. It was pleasant to be able to give his wife and daughters good clothes and even a little simple jewelry for the first time in their lives; pleasant to have a stenographic secretary who could help him through his correspondence with amazing speed; pleasant that the enthusiasm of old friends and Princeton undergraduates knew no bounds. Yet it was a vast relief to leave crowds and bands and intruders all behind, and to be treated by the Bermudians with respectful consideration for his desire to be left alone. He was ready for some diversions—family picnics, a little golf, and some evenings at a little theater, where a repertory company of small pretensions did its best. But his mood was very serious. Only a little later he disconcerted a clergyman at Princeton, overflowing with congratulations and good wishes, by the sharp query: "Don't you think you had better pray for me?" Not even the atmosphere of Bermuda could seduce him away from concentration on the tasks ahead.

He busied himself with masses of correspondence, and in planning for his Cabinet. His new friend, Colonel House, who had helped in the campaign by working to avoid breaks between McCombs and McAdoo, and between the national party organization and the chiefs of Tammany, had assisted him in drawing up a tentative list of Cabinet officers before he sailed, and was sending fresh suggestions and information to the Hulbert cottage. As his daughters enjoyed themselves on the island's beaches and driveways, Wilson solemnly drew up a sheet of paper for each suggested candidate, setting down the pros and cons in parallel columns. He was making his selection of persons as another man might have done of stocks or merchandise. But while Washington was mainly on his mind, New Jersey was not off it yet. There was unfinished business at Trenton, where the "castles" of the bosses, far from being "pasteboard," had already undergone repairs.

The unfinished business at Trenton was the question of the trusts. New Jersey enjoyed the reputation of being the "pioneer" among small States in enticing great businesses to make it their nominal headquarters, so that the incorporation fees and franchise taxes they paid might swell State revenues. Enticement was offered by removing restrictions on the formation of holding companies, interlocking directorates and monopolies, on stock-watering, and on other little practices which businessmen often found useful in mulcting the public. Corporations which had no intention whatever of operating within the State flocked joyfully to buy charters. Among them were some of the greatest in America. The condition was not only a disgrace to New Jersey, not only a sore temptation to business directorates, but detrimental to other States. The legislatures of some of the smaller ones, such as Delaware, Maine, and South Dakota, decided to offer similar enticements, and share the spoils. States which resisted temptation suffered.

Wilson had become especially sensitive about the corporations. During the presidential campaign, Roosevelt, accused of tenderness to big business, had scored by pointing out that Wilson had not redeemed the promise given in his inaugural as Governor to rid New Jersey of the corporation scandal. The reproach was ill deserved. In the session of 1911 there had been too much else to do. In 1912 there had been Republican majorities, thanks to the New Jersey rule of having annual elections for the legislature, and, apparently, to the desire of some of the Democratic bosses to check Wilson at almost any cost. But in 1913, when Wilson was President-elect, the time for dealing with the corporations had come at last. With his heart set on leaving a clean slate behind him at Trenton, he refused the demands for his resignation as Governor that the bosses made, and advanced against the corporations, armed with his new prestige as President-elect. During his last weeks at Trenton the passage of the "Seven Sisters" laws changed New Jersey from the blackest into one of the whitest sheep among the States in the matter of regulating big business. Wilson could depart in peace. It was not his fault that succeeding legislatures and governors, seeing corporation money that might have been New Jersey's flowing into other States, decided that purity was too expensive after all, and assassinated all Seven Sisters by the time Wilson's second term of office as President had reached its end.

While he was clearing his desk of New Jersey business, he was piling it up with the matters awaiting him at Washington. First and foremost came the selection of the Cabinet; but other matters were well in train. Prominent Democratic congressmen came to Trenton, by request, in order to talk over plans. Champ Clark arrived on Christmas Eve, to discuss "the state of public business in the House." Clark was in a savage mood. His smoldering anger at those who had "gouged him out" of the nomination at Baltimore had been fanned into flame by an editorial published in the very pro-Wilson New York *World* the day before. He had gone to Trenton, the *World* had claimed, to fight Bryan's appointment as Secretary of State. Years afterward Clark wrote, out of his undying bitterness: "I did not care a straw whom he appointed Cabinet members. . . . Two things I knew: First, no close friend of mine would be asked to sit in the Cabinet. Second, that Bryan would be in it." The meeting of the Speaker with the President-elect can hardly have been in the spirit of the season. Certainly it did not promise the sweetest harmony at Washington.

There was more cheer two days later, when Carter Glass of the House Banking and Currency Committee, and his expert adviser, Dr. Parker Willis, arrived. Though a cold had confined Wilson to bed at Cleveland Lane and forced the canceling of other engagements, the interview went through as planned. In an atmosphere of blazing logs, Christmas packages, and Christmas cards, the three men for two hours talked over the plans of Glass and Willis that were to underlie many features of the Federal Reserve system. Perhaps it would have been better if Wilson had had more interviews. For example, it was suggested that he should consult Mr. Henry L. Stimson, the Secretary of War, concerning developments in Mexico. But either he drew the line at taking counsel with Republicans, or else he felt that Mr. Stimson's views would be too militaristic for his own. Nor were most of the interviews he had—with Congressmen Burleson and A. Mitchell Palmer, Senators Culberson, Hoke Smith, Gore, and a few others— productive of the best results. Most of his visitors went away indignantly announcing that they knew no more than when they came. Wilson's tendency to hold himself apart from Congress was already evident. At any rate, he was studying the situation at Washington carefully, as the "lame duck" Congress went through the motions appropriate to making laws, and really did approve a separate Department of Labor and a Lincoln Memorial. It could hardly have been expected to do much more. Everybody at the Capitol was conscious that the approaching inauguration would be of no ordinary significance.

Just one week before the inauguration Wilson completed the selection of his Cabinet. He had done some unusual things by giving the country a Secretary of State who probably knew as little about foreign countries and foreign relations as any American in public life, and by urging a Quaker to become Secretary of War. But he had done his best, and had found the process of Cabinet making long and difficult. Doubtless he even found it painful; for it must have brought him the keenest realization he had had so far that politics, even when infused by idealism, remains the art of making the best of hard realities. Like most presidents, his desire had been to choose the best man possible for every Cabinet post. At Princeton he had shown marked ability in finding and enlisting the best men for his faculty. But the discovery and enlistment of first-rate Cabinet material, a far more difficult task than any academic one for any President at any time, held peculiar difficulties for a Democratic President in 1913. As Colonel House admitted sadly at the time, the party had been out of office for so long that few men of administrative experience could be found within its ranks. Democrats of executive capacity had often drifted over to the party that, best representing business, and being constantly in office, held out superior inducements, financial or political. The veterans among the faithful Democrats, being so long in opposition, had "developed critical rather than constructive faculties."

Nor was it easy to enlist the best men that the party could offer. Congress, imbued with the idea that economic equality is essential to democracy, had placed the salaries of Cabinet members at so low a rate as to make it difficult for any President to escape the undemocratic practice of recruiting largely from eligibles with private means. And since the chances of a Democratic victory in 1916 were more than dubious, men of the assured positions and incomes that went with competence to manage large affairs were not especially tempted by the offer of Cabinet posts. Some of the "rock-ribbed Democrats," as House called them, were ready enough to serve; but Wilson had little love for party stalwarts as a whole, and none at all for such of them as bore the taint of being machine men.

He must have found it trying to realize, as the weeks went by, how much his choice of Cabinet members was limited, and even in some measure shaped, by the exigencies of party politics. It was all very well for him to repudiate the spoils system, to keep in mind the ideal of making appointments on the basis of fitness, not of party services rendered. But the ideal had to be sacrificed, in appearance at any rate, on the altar of his own plans. He was determined that the national system of banking and currency should be reconstructed, the tariff cut down, the demand within the party for constitutional amendment forbidding a second presidential term disposed of tactfully, and a policy for the conservation of natural resources acceptable to Democrats in all sections of the country somehow worked out. But how were all these and still other things to be done, unless the party in Congress should give him strong support? And how could he hope for such support, unless he made concessions in his choice of a Cabinet to the party in Congress? Here was the rub.

The rub was almost personified in the benign if somewhat unctuous person of the "Peerless Leader," Bryan. Without the support of Bryan and his congressional devotees, the Wilsonian program would have little or no chance. Bryan inside the Cabinet was almost certain to be incompetent, perhaps ridiculous; but Bryan outside the Cabinet was almost certain to be dangerous. For the Peerless Leader, fully conscious of his past services and present strength, convinced as any man could be that to the victors belonged a division of the spoils, was naturally expecting a high post. Idealism in appointments was beautiful; but Bryan was indispensable. Unfortunately his appointment would still further narrow the field of choice. It would destroy Wilson's none-too-rosy chances of co-operation from the friends of Clark, and would be disliked by the followers of Underwood. Since Wilson needed a Cabinet of more or less progressive coloring in order to carry out his plans, the mere disapproval of right-wing party leaders (loyal Democrats first of all where voting was concerned) was not especially serious; but his advisers were troubled lest he should go too far to the left.

With advisers he was only too well supplied. Commencing even before the election, suggestions of every sort poured in from literally hundreds of quarters; and the small group of men entitled and qualified to be of help to him watched anxiously, and in varying measure gave advice. McCombs could hardly wait until the returns were in before presenting a list of faithful workers and of appropriate jobs for them. Wilson's stern refusal to proceed on any such basis wounded his feelings beyond repair. Bryan, on the other hand, showed surprisingly little disposition to interfere; but, the politician at all times, he urged the inclusion of a Catholic and a Jew. Thomas Pence, Washington correspondent of Josephus Daniels' paper, and one of Wilson's chief publicity men in the campaign, was able now and then to put in a word. So, apparently, was Cleveland Dodge, loyal and generous as ever, and now concerned to save Wilson from following politically dangerous impulses, such as the offer of a portfolio to Louis Brandeis.

But the people who really counted were House and Tumulty, and, almost certainly, Mrs. Wilson. House, now Wilson's one great intimate and confidant, appealed to her once at least. Tumulty, while possessing a shrewd appreciation of political forces, could not do much in rating candidates; but House, with his long political experience, his wide contacts, his discretion, his shrewdness, and his refusal to accept anything himself, was such an adviser as Wilson might have dreamed of, rather than hoped to find. Even before the election the Colonel had been on the lookout for material; after the election he helped to draw up lists, met and sized up candidates, sifted information concerning them, compiled a dossier for each important one, and suggested the political implications which any appointment might carry. By early January the list which Wilson had carried to Bermuda had been revised. A month later all appointments save those for the Interior, for War, for Commerce, and for Justice had been decided on; and several possible appointees for these four had been investigated and discussed. House must have been relieved as the end drew in sight, for he had been seriously worried.

The risk of antagonizing the party did not seem to worry Wilson; and his views and methods sometimes seemed to House imprudent and even dangerous. Party leaders in Congress grew bitter over their new chief's failure to consult them, over his determined reticence, over his giving House a monopoly of his confidence. In considering candidates, he seemed to care too little about their party "regularity," about political records which their appointments would bring under a spotlight. In some ways he was amenable enough. Almost at the outset he admitted that Bryan would have to have the State Department if he wanted it, no matter what ridicule and charges of political barter the appointment would entail. Nor did it take him long to see that Congressman Albert Burleson, as Postmaster General, would supply an indispensable liaison between the White House and the Capitol. Congress, denied its preference for ex-congressmen in the presidency and in most Cabinet offices, would be somewhat appeased by the appointment of this Texan with fourteen years of service in the House of Representatives. In fact Wilson seems to have given full value to House's advice, except as regards more openness with the party's leaders. The Cabinet that emerged was sufficiently regular to escape adverse comment; and if the demands of sectionalism were poorly met by the appointment of five Southerners among Wilson's chosen ten, the Texas colonel apparently felt no concern.

When, just prior to the inauguration, the membership of the Cabinet was disclosed, the Democrats could give it mild approval, but no more. Even House, who had worked so long and hard to make it, could not go further than to say that, "in all the circumstances," he and Wilson had "done well." Most Republicans merely scoffed; and their attitude has found echoes ever since. There was some unfairness about this—unfairness no doubt attributable in some degree to the presence of Bryan. The Great Commoner had been paid in full with the secretaryship of State, and, as House reported, was as pleased with his new dignity "as a child with a new toy." The Republicans were also smiling—for a very different reason. Bryan had certain admirable characteristics; but his love for bombast, his vast and complacent ignorance of almost all that lay outside his country and much that lay within, his intemperance in eating, his insistence upon inflicting his teetotalism upon even official guests, made him an easy mark for ridicule. His insistence on being allowed, for financial reasons, to combine Chautauqua lecturing with his duties as Secretary (he was reputedly well off) brought down a storm of ridicule. It did not add to the prestige of Wilson's Cabinet that its leading figure could be described as "a barnstormer, playing one-night stands, preceded by the magic lantern and followed by the hurdy-gurdy man and his dancing bear."

There were a few sneers, too, at Wilson's selection of Josephus Daniels for the Navy; but the other members of the Cabinet seemed merely undistinguished—until the time when some of them were able to prove their critics wrong. McAdoo went to the Treasury, Franklin Lane to the Interior, and D. F. Houston (called from academic life) to the Department of Agriculture. All three were to do the Cabinet credit. So was the Secretary of War, Lindley Garrison, whom Tumulty produced at the last moment like a rabbit out of the New Jersey hat. Wilson, who had failed to persuade two other men to take the post, appointed Garrison with such alacrity as to terrify Colonel House. The Attorney General, later Mr. Justice McReynolds, had won full recognition of his ability even then, though he was regarded in some quarters as too radical! The Secretaries of Commerce and Labor (the latter a former wage earner of the right wing) were competent at least. Unlike the jeering members of his party, Mr. Taft, who knew what it was to pick a Cabinet, decided that Wilson's was "about as good" as he could have formed. The verdict may well stand.

The inauguration was quite Wilsonian in its simplicity and in a certain seriousness. The weather had something to do with it. There was no rain; but there was not much sunshine, except on the face of Mr. Taft, who was beaming with friendliness and apparent relief to be through with a task which had never really suited him. Yet even he interjected a solemn note as he left the White House. "I'm glad to be going," he said; "this is the loneliest place in the world."

The new President made this Inauguration Day a rather somber one by insisting upon Jeffersonian simplicity and Wilsonian emphasis upon service plus family privacy. In fact, his insistence appears a little overdone. He gave the impression of regarding himself as a little holier than other presidents when he refused honorary membership in the fashionable Chevy Chase Club. He blighted the hopes of young people (including at least one of his own daughters), of dressmakers, of hotelkeepers, and of other business people in the capital by forbidding the customary vast and quite democratic inaugural ball. He struck the note of his whole attitude in the much-repeated phrase of his inaugural address: "This is not a day of triumph; it is a day of dedication." That "service" and "dedication" were perfectly compatible, even on the greatest occasions, with pleasure and emotional outlet; that they could, indeed, be all the better for being joyous seemed to be outside his ken. The official proceedings were devoid of any special incident. On the drive to the Capitol, Wilson shared a very decent amount of applause, as well as a four-horse carriage, with Mr. Taft. As he commenced to speak, the people in front of him broke the barriers and surged forward. This gave him, as it would have given almost any President, a welcome opportunity to show his feeling for them, by requesting that they should not be pushed back again. And perhaps it added something to the appeal with which he closed his speech: "I summon all honest, all patriotic, all forward-looking men to my side."

After the ceremonies at the Capitol came the great official luncheon at the White House. Mr. Taft, who had apparently defied precedent by accepting an invitation in advance, contributed a note of cheer; but when he left, things became more serious again. If one may believe "Ike" Hoover, the not-too-accurate major-domo of the White House,

General Wood, after more than once assuring an impatient President that they need be in no haste to leave for the reviewing stand, was virtually ordered to leave his lunch unfinished and start at once. The new Commander in Chief was teaching punctuality to a major general. After the review Wilson's desire for privacy was gratified. There was a family dinner (swelled to great proportions by the usual flock of relatives), and then the fun of excited exploration of the White House, of dividing up the living quarters, of planning ways of making them more livable. The ladies were still at it when the President returned from a Princeton smoker (possibly a less "democratic" affair, if one thinks of it, than the easily attended ball at the Patent Office would have been), and the fun continued till bedtime. There was a pause; then a jangling of several bells; then a President in his underwear, explaining to a startled doorkeeper that there were no night clothes in his room. Apparently even Mrs. Wilson could nod for once. When a trunk containing the night clothes arrived from the Union Station, the President was sound asleep. He slept easily and well; and he had learned never to stint himself in that respect.

CHAPTER VI

The President and the People

———————•◆•———————

IT SEEMS a safe assumption that no President in our history, even till now, has entered the White House with clearer ideas of what he wished to do, and how he proposed to do it, than did Wilson. All through his adult life he had been studying and thinking and writing about American presidents. In those thirty years and more, little that had happened at Washington could have escaped his eye. So his ideas as to what a President should do, and what a President could do, were fixed, until such time as personal experience might alter them. And no assumption is needed about the record he was to make. Authorities agree that, with the possible exception of Jefferson, no President up to his time (or for twelve years afterward) could boast of getting so much of the legislation he wanted through Congress. He repeated his record in New Jersey on a far grander scale, and under conditions very different, and in some ways more difficult. Considering that members of Congress are no more susceptible to idealism and altruism, and much more given to political bartering, than the rest of us; that they are naturally jealous of their claim to dominate, or even monopolize, the whole process of lawmaking; and considering again that Wilson was a newcomer to national politics—a rather austere and unapproachable one at that—this legislative exploit of his was in itself sufficient to elevate him into the company of the "great" presidents. It has been a small and select group. Theodore Roosevelt once anxiously inquired of a great authority on American history whether his place there was secure.

But there is a definition of greatness that has nothing to do with measured achievement, nor yet with fame. In a more philosophical or religious atmosphere than most of us live in, greatness is measured by giving, by service, by self-sacrifice. There seems to be no record that Wilson took thought as to whether he was "great" or not, still less as to whether others would call him so; but the greatness that he respected in anyone was always greatness in service. He had already preached unselfish service to any number of academic and political audiences. Now, as President, he emphasized it constantly. For example, in speaking of the men who fell at Vera Cruz:

They gave their lives for us. . . . That is the way in which men grow distinguished, and that is the only way, by serving somebody else than themselves. And what greater thing could you serve than a nation such as this?

The lifelong consistency of his preaching on this theme, and his equal consistency in living up to his preaching, forbid one to regard it as mere political stock in trade. Instead, it was the most vital article in his religion, even using the term religion in its narrower sense:

I am not fond of thinking of Christianity as the means of saving *individual* souls. . . . The only way your powers can become great is by exerting them outside the circle of your own narrow, special, selfish interests.

To Wilson, God was served, then, primarily if not wholly through man's services to men. Moreover, the very highest task that he or any other American could set himself was to serve the American people. For his Americanism had suffered no more abatement than his gospel of service. It had found one of its frequent expressions in his address on "The Heroes of Vera Cruz":

Notice how truly these men were of . . . our American blood . . . not drawn from any one country . . . free men everywhere have sent their sons and their daughters . . . to make that great . . . nation which consists of all . . . the best elements of the whole globe.

But a mere fusion of "the best elements of the whole globe" would not make true Americans. There must be unadulterated allegiance to the country. Some time before the assassination at Serajevo, and longer still before most Americans had begun to be troubled about "hyphenates," the President had denounced them. He did it at the unveiling of a statue of Commodore Barry:

John Barry was an Irishman, but his heart crossed the Atlantic with him. Some Americans need hyphens in their names, because only part of them has come over; but when the whole man has come over . . . the hyphen drops . . . out of his name. This man was not an Irish-American; he was an Irishman who became an American. I venture to say that if he voted he voted with regard to the questions as they looked on this side of the water and not as they affected the other side; and that is my infallible test of a genuine American.

Some of the party chiefs must have felt uneasy. The reasoning and conclusion were unassailable; but only a man too outspoken for his own good or the party's could have delivered such a speech. Senator Lodge may have made a mental note for future reference.

The fact that service to his people was a large part of Wilson's religion may account for a certain mystical quality with which he invested it; for some of his ceaseless activity in reform; and even in some measure for the role he was prepared to play in relation to Congress. The mystical quality came out in one of the occasional speeches in which he laid himself bare to the public in the way he often did to his correspondents, but seldom or never to individuals with whom he had official dealings. Talking to the National Press Club, about a year after his inauguration, he complained of the popular impression that he was "a cold and removed person" with a "thinking machine inside" which he would not "allow to be moved by any winds of affection or emotion . . . that [he turned] like a cold searchlight on anything . . . presented to his attention." Then came a curious avowal concerning his nature and his feeling for the people:

. . . if I were to interpret myself, I would say that my constant embarrassment is to restrain the emotions that are inside of me. . . . I sometimes feel like a fire from a far from extinct volcano. . . . In the position which I now occupy there is a sort of, I do not know how else to express it than to say, passionate sense of being connected with my fellow men in a peculiar relationship of responsibility, not merely the responsibility of office.

And he seems to have had something of this mystical relationship in mind when, referring to Lincoln and Jefferson, but almost certainly thinking also of himself, he spoke of the peculiar gift of a great popular leader:

A great nation . . . is led by a man . . . in whose ears the voices of the nation do not sound . . . accidental and discordant . . . but . . . reveal to him a single vision, so that he can speak what no man else knows, the common meaning of the common voice.

This was a heady doctrine, a rather perilous belief; for how would the arguments of other men prevail with a soothsayer such as this? It is said that on certain religious mystics and on certain idealists, religion or idealism may act as a flame does on a log—kindling it outside at first, but eating in until the flame from the log blends with the flame that kindled it; even burning on till the log is finally consumed. Perhaps in some measure his gospel of service to the people did this to him. Mystics and idealists may seem like other people in most respects, even to the possession of outstanding faults.

At any rate, Wilson continued to be a very human person, with a normal mixture of faults and virtues. The normality and especially the virtues were, as usual, evident in his domestic life. During his first weeks in Washington he found time to share the fun his wife and daughters had in the continued exploration of the White House; in unearthing neglected treasures, and finding obscure places for "white elephants"; in planning future improvements and future purchases. He sought relief from the "peculiar relationship of responsibility" to the people in snatching an evening for reading English classics now and then, in golf, in family gatherings, in the theater, and in baseball and football games, as weaker men have sometimes sought distraction in dissipation of some kind. It was not in his vibrant personality to take things serenely and evenly, no matter how imperturbable he might appear in moments of crisis. Probably in part because he and Mrs. Wilson were both conscious of the strain on him, and probably because there was something in him of the Scotch clansman, too, the presidential family in Wilson's time led an unusually domestic and even secluded life. Except when official entertaining was to be done, guests were usually from among the circle of family connections. And, no matter who was there, discussion of public matters was taboo. The result was politically unfortunate. In 1916 Walter Page, called over temporarily from London, reflected that there were two ways in which a President might live. He might live as Wilson lived, or he might summon men and women of affairs to his table, discussing serious things in easy and friendly fashion across the plates and cups. No one should have realized better than the former president of a university what advantages the second method offered.

In Wilson's case its value would have been especially great; for no one who had not seen the unofficial Wilson knew him; and few who saw the unofficial Wilson failed to like him. But he did little to dispel the popular impression concerning his coldness and austerity. Some of the politicians who came to the White House to talk business found the President less "regular" than was to their taste. He never smoked, and very rarely drank. The most a visitor could hope for was a possible cigar. All this makes his success in managing Congress the more remarkable. But more hospitality and "regularity" would have provided him with more friends to go wholeheartedly to his support in later times of need.

"The President closed his fingers into a sinewy fist. He leaned forward in his chair . . . as a man leans forward who is about to start on a race, his body taut, his muscles tense. . . . His eyes were narrowed, his lips slightly parted." As one would instantly surmise, it was a newspaperman and popular author who wrote that, Samuel Blythe. He had been given an evening interview in Wilson's private library and workroom; and, like many another person who had enjoyed, or would enjoy, a similar experience, had come away more than a little awed. The "tense" man in evening clothes who had sat opposite him had seemed so desperately in earnest about his convictions and responsibilities—convictions about, and responsibility to, the people. They had talked principally about Mexico (for this was in the late spring of 1914); but in a good deal of what the President had had to say he might just as well have been talking about his own country:

I challenge you to cite me an instance in all the history of the world where liberty was handed down from above. Liberty always is attained by . . . forces working below . . . by the great movement of the people.

I say to you that the old order is dead. It is my part, as I see it, to aid in composing . . . differences so . . . that the new order . . . shall prevail.

It was a Leader who was speaking, a man who believed, with desperate earnestness, that he was the people's chief interpreter and mouthpiece. Alleged belief of this sort has been the claim of many a soapbox orator, of men without knowledge or mental capacity to base it on anything but complacent certainty as to their good will, and firm conviction that they are not as other men. Hence they are usually as insignificant as what they call their arguments. But Wilson's consciousness of superiority was so well-founded as to be unavoidable; his sense of being a man with a "mission" to lead his countrymen was based in part upon his knowledge of American history and government, and also very much on his religion. During his pre-nomination campaign he had given to a Denver audience a strikingly frank avowal of the manner in which he applied his creed of service to himself. Because the day was Sunday, he had refused to make a regular campaign address, speaking extemporaneously, or almost so, on "The Bible and Progress":

A man has found himself when he has found his relation to the rest of the universe, and here is the book in which those relations [*sic*] are set forth. When you see a man going along the highways of life with his gaze lifted . . . to the sloping ways in front of him, then be careful of that man and get out of his way. He has seen . . . his relation to God . . . and therefore . . . his responsibility in the world.

The same warning, almost threatening, note appeared again later in the speech:

No man can sit down and withhold his hands from the warfare against wrong and get peace out of his acquiescence. . . . I will not cry "peace" so long as there is sin and wrong in the world. And this great book does not teach any doctrine of peace so long as there is sin to be combated and overcome in one's own heart and in the great moving force of human society.

His conception of himself as a man responsible to God and the people was avowed again, when, nine months later, he spoke in Chicago on Lincoln's birthday:

What produced the birth of Freedom in the modern world? It was the conception that every man stood naked and individual in his responsibility before his God . . . and so far as we have forgotten . . . it . . . we have gone astray and found ourselves in a jungle. . . . Therefore, I do not know of any better day upon which to explain what seems to me to be the duty of the Democracy than the birthday of Lincoln.

Roughly, what he said seemed to add up to this: that liberty was a gift from God to men, inherent in the proper relations of men to God and to their fellow men; that liberty had been obscured because so many men had forgotten this; that there were men, however, who remembered it, and were going forward with eyes fixed upon visions of true progress which realization of their responsibility to God and to their neighbors had given them. He had even warned his Denver audience that one could not with impunity block the path of men with such visions. Lincoln had been such a man; clearly Wilson intended to be another. To forget for a moment the nature and dynamic power of his religion is to ignore the ultimate force which spurred him on—the force which made him so idealistic, so courageous, so reckless, and even on some occasions so ruthless. It made him aggressive at all times. "I am sometimes very much interested," he told a Philadelphia audience, "when I see gentlemen supposing that popularity is the way to success in America. The way to success in this great country with its fair judgments is to show that you are not afraid of anybody except God and His final verdict." He always had been, and always would be, a warrior.

He was always the warrior, but always a Lonely Warrior, and, partly for that reason, never a Happy Warrior. Of course he had companionship, even deeper intimacies than are given to most men. Outside the close and affectionate family circle there were always a few intimates. There was nearly always one man, such as Mr. Hibben at Princeton and Colonel House at Washington, and there were always three or four ladies, such as Mrs. Hulbert (for some years Mrs. Peck) of Bermuda, and the wives of Professors Harry Fielding Reid of Johns Hopkins and Crawford Toy of Harvard. And only a little more removed were a number of men friends, acquired mainly at Princeton, as in the case of Cleveland Dodge, or in the South, as in the case of Walter Page. Yet, with this endowment, Wilson was unsatisfied. He confessed an intensity of yearning for more friends:

How few friends I have . . . partly because I am reserved and shy, and partly because I . . . have a narrow, uncatholic taste in friends, I reject the offer of friendship in almost every case; and then am dismayed to . . . see how few persons in the world . . . know me as I am . . . can give me sympathy and close support of heart. Perhaps it is because when I give at all I want to give my whole heart, and I feel that so few want it all, or would return measure for measure.

There was a disturbing amount of self-revelation in these sentences —revelation not only of a rather feminine strain unfitting to the man's general personality, but of self-deception, of flight from reality. He confessed on another occasion that at times his life seemed "rooted in dreams." Perhaps the life of any sensitive, imaginative, and precocious boy who grows into a supremely able man, inhabiting a world of thought, and sheltered by his family from the ruder contacts with reality, is apt to be.

In some ways his self-analysis seems correct enough. He had, indeed, an "uncatholic taste in friends." Instead of wanting friends who would give "measure for measure," he wanted friends who would give much more. For the real give and take of healthy friendship—the give and take of the frankest criticism, of affectionate and amused tolerance of obvious shortcomings and lapses, of utter disagreement on views of vital things, provided there is agreement as to what things are vital—for such exchanges he had small capacity. Only within noticeable limits was it permitted to his friends to criticize, to tolerate, to disagree on matters about which he cared deeply. Others might do these things with less offense, because, since they were not his friends, he did not fear their influence. Their influence on what? Apparently their influence upon his own inviolable mental processes.

Sonnino's coarse jest in Paris, in 1919, that Wilson, having lost his political virginity in the concessions he had made to France, was trying to regain it at the expense of Italy, struck at the essential egotism, the respect he had for his own idealism and his own thinking, the fear lest it be clouded by the influence of others, which limited Wilson's capacity for the best type of masculine friendship. It is doubtful whether he could give his "whole heart" outside his family; but he expected those he called his friends to give not only their hearts, but sometimes their convictions, too. And convictions in people of the better sort are usually linked up with principles. He never saw this because he never really saw his friends. He saw them, not as they were, but as he conceived that friends of his should be. His egotism was so frank and natural, so well glossed over by courtesy and dignity, as to be inoffensive except in times of stress; but it was too deep-seated to allow him to make the sort of friends he most needed.

If Wilson, in his years of public office, had possessed friends permitted to disagree and argue with him, privately and unofficially, on equal terms; to puncture some of his self-confidence; to teach him to laugh occasionally at himself, things might have been different for him, even possibly for half the world. But he had none. Most of his closest friends were women, to whom he was grateful, not only for their grace and charm and gaiety, not only for what he felt to be their "finer understanding" and "deeper sensibility," but for the sympathy, what he once called the "unarguing sympathy," they gave him. No doubt their sympathy greatly helped him, and thus materially contributed to what he did. Probably they were able delicately to argue with him more than he perceived. But their friendship should have been a complement to ruder male companionship, not a substitute. With increasing age, increasing prestige, and increasing devotion to his mission, he seems to have grown less capable of equality in friendship. For old friends who did not have to cross him, for Tumulty, the devoted subordinate, who could disagree but not resist, his affection did not wane; but his pride denied him friendship with any man who really obstructed him. His break with Mr. Hibben was one of the most revealing, as well as one of the saddest, incidents of his career. If by any chance it was not about that break that he wrote to Mrs. Hulbert in February 1911 it might well have been:

Why will that wound not heal over in my stubborn heart? Why is it that I was blind and stupid enough to love the people who proved false to me, and cannot love . . . those who are my real friends by the final, only conclusive proof of conduct and actual loyalty, when loyalty cost and meant something?

Again he was unconsciously revealing some of the worst of those faults of personality that flawed his indestructible greatness. However much Mr. Hibben may have allowed his opinions to be swayed at times by Wilson's foe, Dean West, he was not a man to "prove false" to his friends, to fail in loyalty "when loyalty cost and meant something." Perhaps the wound refused to heal because Wilson's stubborn egotism forbade him to admit that he had created in his mind a Hibben that did not exist. Apparently he felt betrayed because the real Hibben did not play the role assigned to the imaginary one.

Mr. Hibben had gone out of his life; but the sting of the breach, and the flaw in his character which made it lasting, were to do him poor service in the days to come. He would not only lack men around him who would wrestle with him when he was shortsighted or headstrong —he would show an inclination to distrust the motives of fellow countrymen and foreign statesmen who were ready enough to work with him. In this sense he was lacking in charity. But the weakest spot in Wilson's superb armor was his inveterate pride. It not only robbed him of the sort of friends he needed, but raised up enemies. What was more, it contributed to the exhaustion which wore him down and finally broke him. It may seem odd that his religion, deepseated and dynamic as it was, did not, until the very end, do much to correct the fault that was at the root of all his faults—the fault that was to be in great measure responsible for the most tragic of his failures. But even in his religion he was an individualist.

Lord Salisbury, that model of calmness and fortitude in affairs of state, once said that while he well knew the anxiety a man would feel in making a conscientious decision on some issue, he could not understand why one who believed in the divine ordering of affairs should be greatly troubled over what transpired. Salisbury could accept reverses serenely, even while he kept on fighting. With Wilson it was different. One of the most "liberal" of Presbyterians by now, he believed that Divine Providence held the ultimate ordering of affairs; but not, apparently, that immediate things were so ordered. Success or failure in any particular conflict was a trial of strength between him and the human forces of unrighteousness; so failure was hard to bear. For the people, on whose behalf the Lonely Warrior fought, would pay the price.

But Wilson, the dreamer and idealist, was also an audacious and resourceful man of action, who could draw on great knowledge of American history and politics in laying out his plans. No one knew better that the presidency was, in considerable degree, what a particular President chose, and was able, to make of it. The great question, of course, was that of the President's relations with Congress. Any thoughtful and aspiring occupant of the White House would seek to determine those relations according to his views about the presidency and in the measure of his strength of will.

What called in particular for decision was the part the President would attempt to play in the lawmaking process. Three former presidents especially stood out for their ability to stretch the presidential power beyond the ordinary limits of its exercise, by securing the legislation they wanted. Such stretching was apt to evoke complaints of "usurpation" at the Capitol, since a President who engaged in it was so using his constitutional right of recommending legislation as to take a guiding or directing part in it. Thus he was nullifying the supposedly sharp separation between the executive functions assigned to him and the lawmaking functions of the Senate and House of Representatives. Yet, be it noted, the three presidents who had been especially successful in doing this were famed exponents of democracy or progressivism: Jefferson, Jackson, and Roosevelt. They were alike in the fact that each had achieved success through the vigorous leadership of his party; but their records were different. Jefferson had been successful by using persuasion; by quietly or even, as Professor Corwin puts it, "furtively" winning consent to his plans from legislators, as individuals or in groups. Jackson, however, had defied Congress, and found his ultimate strength in direct appeals to the people. Roosevelt, possessed of remarkable ability to win the people's support, had developed a doctrine that the President possessed all powers of government which the Constitution did not specifically bestow elsewhere. The doctrine had been sharply but not conclusively attacked by Mr. Taft.

As to how Wilson would stand, no informed person should have had the shadow of a doubt. A President who believed himself to be the interpreter and mouthpiece of the people, who found the highest service to God in the service of his countrymen, and who saw himself engaged in a perpetual struggle on their behalf, would hardly stand aside when laws which touched their deepest interests were being made. Nor would the lifelong student of government, nor yet the ex-Governor of New Jersey. His speeches, his writings, and his record at Trenton had all showed that. So, incidentally, had the two-hour interview with Carter Glass and Parker Willis in his bedroom in Princeton. In fact, it is doubtful whether Jefferson or Jackson or Roosevelt had ever been as deliberately anxious to circumvent "the separation of the powers" as was Wilson. He had looked admiringly and longingly all through his adult life at the British system of combining supreme executive and legislative powers in the hands of a Prime Minister and Cabinet who ruled their party, yet were so responsible to Parliament and to the wishes and sentiments of the people that they could be expelled from office overnight. He was far too American to care a pin for the system because it was British; but it offered what he had found lacking in government at Trenton, and knew to be even more lacking at Washington: system and smooth efficiency in the lawmaking process, plus what he cared for even more—responsibility to the people. He showed his love for system even in small things: in his methodical tabulation of the merits and shortcomings of candidates for his Cabinet; in keeping one of the tidiest of all desks. He had not been long in the White House before the very drives he took were all laid out and classified, with deviation seldom permitted from a once-accepted route.

How much more did he wish to see a systematic route followed by the people's representatives in attending to the people's interests. But he did not find it in the prevailing legislative procedures he had attacked in his pre-nomination speeches. He did not find it in the introduction into Congress of a flood of bills, which might have been framed almost anywhere for almost any purposes. He did not find it in the subsequent handling of those bills. How could an integrated plan of legislation be worked out and carried through, when some hundred standing committees of the two Houses worked on the bills quite independently? In how far were the interests of the people safe in the hands of Congress, when the committees were presided over by men with no claim to leadership but the almost meaningless one of seniority at the Capitol; when they were sometimes "loaded" to represent some wing of the dominant party; and when they might be worked upon by the swarms of lobbyists who infested Washington? For of course the committees could virtually kill any bill, no matter how useful it would be to the people; and, in the last days of a session, they could sometimes persuade Congress to pass noxious bills which were never properly considered or discussed. They not only could, but sometimes did, do these things, as perhaps they do them still.

And how much was there in this procedure, Wilson asked himself, of that element so essential to democratic government—responsibility? He was in deadly earnest about the question of responsibility even, or rather especially, as applying to the President. In a famous letter to A. Mitchell Palmer, written a month before his inauguration, he denounced the way in which presidents had been allowed to influence the choice of their successors; denounced the practice of nominating presidential candidates in conventions, instead of by direct primaries; and insisted that some way of making the President answerable to the people, "either personally or through a Cabinet"; and perhaps answerable to Congress, too, would have to be worked out. The President should clearly be the people's (not the politicians') choice, and as clearly their servant. Like the British Premier, he should be the nation's Number One lawmaker, as well as its Number One executive. This would not only obviate most presidential vetoes and the obstruction they were apt to cause, but would make legislation more integrated and responsive to the people's needs.

Wilson was perfectly clear as to the position he was taking. In the same letter to Mr. Palmer he defined what he believed to be the proper position and functions of a President:

He is expected by the Nation to be the leader of his party . . . and
. . . play the part . . . successfully. . . . He must be prime minister, as
much concerned with the guidance of legislation as with the just and
orderly execution of the law. . . . He is the spokesman of the Nation in
everything . . . [and] is held responsible for what happens in Washington in every large matter.

But how could he meet such vast duties and responsibilities? Only
by gaining and holding the people's confidence:

    . . . so long as he is commanded to lead he is surely entitled to . . . all
the power he can get from the support . . . of his fellow countrymen;
and he ought to be suffered to use that power against his opponents. . . .
If we want our Presidents to fight our battles for us, we should give them
the means. . . . Strip them of everything else but the right of appeal to
the people . . . suffer them to be leaders.

"Battles" against whom? Presumably against congressional leaders,
perhaps even against some belonging to the party the President must
lead "successfully." One always comes back to Wilson's conception of
his duty, as President, to be the interpreter and mouthpiece and
champion of the people, should other organs of government fail them.
He pointed out that presidential power based on popular opinion
could hardly be abused, since the people would give their support
voluntarily, and withdraw it on the instant when it suited them. This
conception of the presidential office had not come to him as a result
of his election, nor even since his entrance into politics. He had outlined most of it in his *Constitutional Government,* written in 1908. It
is there one finds his much-quoted sentence: "His [the President's]
office is anything he has the sagacity and force to make it." There
was little doubt that Wilson would try to make it greater than it had
ever been. But he was not interested in power for its own sake. "I
want to be President of the people of the United States," he wrote
early in 1913.

Here, then, was the way in which he proposed to secure the passage
of an integrated plan of legislation, designed to meet the people's
needs. It was useless to think of checking the flood of bills, of doing
away with the standing committees, or even doing much to improve
them or their methods. But the President, given the functions and
power of appeal which Wilson claimed for him, could be a central
and directing force in lawmaking. He was, in fact, the only possible

central and directing force. In Wilson's phrase, his only was a "national" voice. But even though Roosevelt had accustomed Congress and the country to very much the sort of President that Wilson planned to be, Congress, at least, could not be expected to approve the Wilsonian conception of the presidential office. So Congress would have to be controlled, or "managed" to use a more polite word; and this could be done only if Wilson could make himself a successful leader of his party. Considering the divisions and the lingering resentments among the Democrats, even this task would not be of the easiest. But he was prepared to do his best, both because no one better understood the indispensability of parties in our political system, and because his own party had his firm allegiance, intellectually and otherwise.

Perhaps his attitude was best set forth in a Jackson Day address given at Indianapolis in 1915. The Republican party was a "covert and refuge" for the timid, usually taking its advice "from gentlemen old enough to be grandfathers." "Speaking as an historian," he could say that it had not had a new idea for thirty years. There were progressive Republicans, yes; but they counted up to only one third of the party; whereas among the Democrats the proportions were just reversed. It rested, then, with the Democrats to give the people the reforms they needed; but there would have to be "continuous and consistent teamwork." Only a party which could "hold absolutely together and march with the discipline and with the zest of a conquering host" could be of service to the nation. His tone grew menacing:

> If any group of men should dare to break the solidarity of the Democratic team for any purpose or from any motive, theirs will be a most unenviable notoriety and a responsibility which will bring deep bitterness to them.

His insistence on party regularity may have reflected some change of attitude that had come to him through experience. The apparent preference for "irregular" Democrats which, in Colonel House's opinion, he had shown in considering possible members of his Cabinet, had long since left him. He had found that when it came to getting things done, to pushing legislation through, some Democrats of independent views, who had appealed to him before he entered the White House by their apparent earnestness, displayed, in Mr. Milton's phrase, too much of a "prima donna" quality. But the tough veterans, friends of the organizations, who had no great liking for Wilson or his standpoint, had put their shoulders to the wheel in the good old party's interest. He made himself undisputed leader of the party. He controlled and used it in Congress in such manner as to give it an astonishingly creditable record. But his relations with it were never of the best. He loved it through loyalty to his upbringing, because of its comparative liberalism and blending of races, for great men it had produced, and for the opportunities it had given him. But it could not live up to his ideals; nor was its allegiance to him ever complete. There were to be times when Democratic chairmen of important standing committees would oppose him, and when he would need Republican help to carry measures through. And in various sections of the country the machine men had never accepted him, nor ever would. He must have realized that the party was not solidly behind him; but the party was only an instrument, after all. So long as the people believed in him, the party, and Congress with it, would have to toe the line.

"It has been a commonplace of recent American political history . . . that Mr. Wilson, more than any of his predecessors, has exerted an almost absolute authority over Congress." Professor Lindsay Rogers, who wrote this in 1919, found also that, during Wilson's presidency, Congress had passed legislation which "in importance, quickness of decision, and absence of partisan politics," was "without parallel in American history." Eleven years earlier Wilson had given what would doubtless have been his chief explanation of such phenomenal success if achieved by any President:

If [the President] rightly interpret the national thought and boldly insist upon it, he is irresistible . . . the country . . . craves a single leader.

In 1913 the single leader, faced with the immediate task of dominating an alert and sensitive Congress through his leadership of a none-too-united or enthusiastic party, had to do plenty of hard thinking and planning.

In some ways he was fortunate. The party had been out of power so long that its most influential figures in Congress had had little chance of developing their own leadership. And some of them were enthusiastic Wilson men. In the Senate, for example, that keen and caustic veteran, John Sharp Williams, was ready to maintain against the world that the country had not seen such a President since the time of Jefferson. In the House, Carter Glass was not only enthusiastic about Wilson's interest in currency reform, but remembered gratefully that the Governor of New Jersey had helped him, in 1911, to smash Virginia's Democratic machine. There were rising young Democrats, too, such as Cordell Hull, who regarded the new President admiringly. And of course Wilson's experience in putting through his legislative program at Trenton was a help. But his greatest asset was his knowledge of Jefferson's persuasive methods with individuals and caucuses, of Jackson's success in sheer boldness, and of what Roosevelt owed to publicity. Moreover, as Mr. Corwin points out, he was the first President who "knew something about the functioning of political institutions abroad, and who had the intellect and skill to apply his knowledge to the stimulation and enrichment of the political process in this country." By seeing to it that bills drafted by members of his Cabinet, who were responsible to himself, were introduced, he could come near to securing an integrated plan of legislation, and near to making the President, like the British Prime Minister, the Number One lawmaker of the country.

There were other ways of making the national government a little more responsible—such as bringing the chairmen of standing committees closer to himself and the members of his Cabinet, and himself closer to the people by addressing them, and securing their reactions, on great issues. He lacked Jefferson's persuasive charm in dealing with congressmen and Roosevelt's robust geniality in winning the affection of the public; but no one could be more convincing to congressmen or to the people, when it came to clear, terse argument. There was a reassuring firmness about him, too. Remembering that Mr. Taft, having made one concession to opponents of tariff revision, was driven into steady and disastrous retreat, Wilson refused to compromise on any great measure he had endorsed. It was the same with appointments. Feeling in the West could no more deter him from placing Mr. McReynolds on the Supreme Court than feeling in the East could dissuade him from putting Mr. Brandeis there. And not all the Thomas Watsons in America (and they seem to have been legion) could persuade him that Tumulty was a papal spy, laboring to import the Inquisition, and engineer a St. Bartholomew's massacre at Washington.

In Wilson's control of Congress there was something a little reminiscent of the Trenton days; but it was his effort to introduce system and responsibility that stands out. There were conferences with legislators (mostly chairmen of committees) on important bills; and although the President naturally did not attend caucuses where bills were formally adopted by the party, he had his ways of bringing influence to bear on Democratic lawmakers. Just as he had come to realize that the stalwarts of the party would do the most effective work, so he had to admit that intellectual persuasion required re-enforcement through less high-minded methods. Mr. Burleson proved "a past master at the combination of entreaty, cajolery, and command" required for managing congressmen, and "got enough jobs, campaign contributions, and other favors to keep them in the fight." Pressure was exerted, too, by a group of about thirty Democrats, mostly young, who met weekly to discuss the party's policies and activities, and invited three or four members of the two Houses to join in. What was more, they "put on the heat" at the Capitol, when the President needed help, and made themselves generally useful to their chief. Two prominent members were Franklin D. Roosevelt and Joseph E. Davies. And Wilson now fully appreciated the importance of the press. Shortly after his inauguration he had the problem of newspaper publicity examined, and a plan drawn up. As a result, regular presidential press conferences ("talking off the record") began in his first year of office. One may regard their institution as a mere party device; but there is everything to suggest that Wilson thought of these conferences as another method by which the people's leader could keep in touch with them. Even to the press, however, he would not be subservient. He risked disfavor by discontinuing the conferences after we went to war. He was afraid that they were giving aid and comfort, not only to the enemy, but to certain gentlemen whose chief interest was in the stock exchange.

But direct contact with the people by word of mouth was the indispensable weapon in his armory, as it had been at Trenton—always available, often visible, and sometimes used. "Strip [the presidents]," he had written, "of everything else but the right of appeal to the people." This was the way in which he could make himself "irresistible." He relied above all on the effects of frequent messages to Congress. With his own proviso that the President must "rightly interpret the national thought," his great weapon was a democratic one. He proposed to use it whenever it seemed to him that the politicians forgot the public's interests, and especially when economic and financial matters were to the fore. The "interests" were as much as ever in his mind. In an article he had published in the *Fortnightly* just before his inauguration, he had accused the Republicans of conducting the national government in accordance with the belief of Alexander Hamilton ("a great man, but in my judgment not a great American") that "the only people who could understand government, and . . . were qualified to conduct it, were the men who had the biggest financial stake . . . in commercial and industrial enterprises." He added dryly:

I suspect that the people of the United States understand their own interests better than any group.

But the people had to be informed and aroused by one who, like himself, understood "the common meaning of the common voice." Congress and the politicians were not likely to approve his course, but they would have to make the best of it. One of his interviewers asked him before his nomination whether "a strong executive" was not invariably charged with "interference":

"Invariably," the Governor replied. "I remember meeting a certain United States Senator on the train when Mr. Roosevelt was President . . . he said 'I wish the Constitution had not given the President the right to send messages to Congress.'

" 'It isn't that the President can send messages to Congress,' I said to him. 'The trouble, from your point of view, is that the messages . . . always reach the people.' "

He had added that, in his ability to send messages, any President possessed a "tremendous" power, which it was his duty to use carefully.

Well, the power was now his, and he soon showed that he knew how to use it to the greatest possible effect. Let danger threaten one of his favored measures in Congress, and the readers of all the principal newspapers of the country would find a message, usually brief and crisp, which gave an excellent presentation of his case and focused public attention on the issue. Moreover, he dramatized his leadership in a way which Roosevelt somehow had missed. Going back to very early presidential practice, he sometimes delivered important messages in person. The people saw Congress confronted, not with the words of a secluded chief executive, but with a vigorous man who seemed like an attorney pleading the case of the public.

Yet Wilson was not so foolish as to disregard the feelings of Congress. He spoke to the Houses in the tone of a partner. In the first of his special messages he asked the members to regard him as "a person . . . trying to co-operate with other human beings in a common service," not as "a department of government hailing Congress from some isolated island of jealous power." He sometimes went out of his way to present Congress with information and arguments on matters with which, constitutionally, they had no concern. Astute veterans, such as Senator Lodge, were not deceived; they could only bide their time. For five years and more Wilson's control of Congress was never lost. "Perhaps the greatest triumph that any American President has ever won in his relations with Congress," wrote Professor Rogers, "was the passage of his Selective Draft Act, when, at the time of the declaration of war, there was a clear majority in each House in favor of adhering to the voluntary principle." The end of Wilson's control was to come with the elections of 1918. As Antaeus drew his strength from contacts with the earth, so did Wilson from his contacts with the people. Both were destroyed when antagonists cut them off from the sources of their vigor.

CHAPTER VII

The People's Money

———◆———

Wilson had entered the presidency with clear-cut plans for exercising vast power. He had equally clear ideas as to the use he wished to make of it. As always, he was intent on getting more system and responsibility into the conduct of affairs. But his deeper desire was to get justice for the people, at the same time injecting more consciousness of their interests and more conscience into the people. He was looking at a complicated picture. The America of thirty years ago saw much the same conflicts of interests between capital and labor, between producers and middlemen and consumers of all kinds, as those we know. Moreover, then, as now, the country was a battleground of philosophies and theories about the proper relations of social groups, to say nothing of convictions bred out of partisan prejudice or mere self-interest, without benefit of philosophies, or even theories. The general atmosphere was at least as materialistic, as pervaded by the "profit motive," as that in which we live. Not the general good of society, but self-interest, especially of the financial kind, seemed almost everywhere the great motivating force. In many circles the rating of an individual's importance was almost as naturally preceded by the dollar sign as the estimate of his estate. So was the judgment of a man's "success." Popular novelists portrayed, and often admiringly, the "predatory" type in business and in politics.

Such an atmosphere of materialism was inevitably charged with suspicion and rancor. There were otherwise intelligent and well-meaning left-wingers who regarded the mere possession of wealth (outside their own circle) as creating a certain presumption of delinquency, which called for drastic remedies. There were otherwise intelligent and well-meaning right-wingers who suspected left-wingers of being motivated principally by greed, jealousy, and a realization of their financial incompetence. While the most provocative "isms" of our day were either unheard of or still remote, there were "isms" enough to fight about. Socialism, of course, had long been a familiar specter to many, a saving spirit to a few. Paternalism seemed to liberals or progressives a polite description of class domination to be achieved by the intrusion of big business into politics. Individualism, not yet "rugged" in common parlance at any rate, was coming to be regarded as a new name for the doctrine, long more elegantly designated as *laissez faire,* by which capital was "left to do" whatever it wanted, at the expense of ill-armed wage earners and the people in general.

Of course one could find in every community men and women who were tolerant, public-spirited, and accustomed to consult their consciences; but the American society which Wilson desired so fervently to benefit seemed generally wanting in moderation and morality. In some measure the want was likely due to the prevalence of still another "ism." Determinism was about in all its forms, economic and psychological and sociological. Darwinian ideas of development were being carried over into the fields of economics and politics. This materialistic atmosphere was repellent to Wilson, and not least in its deterministic trend. He must have realized that, when properly understood and prudently applied, belief that the development of social groups may be more or less "determined" by changes in economic organization, and the actions of individuals by the subconscious, need not lessen men's feeling of personal responsibility. But the discoveries or unproved theories of the determinists were constantly so misunderstood, exaggerated, and misapplied as seriously to threaten the functioning of conscience. There were people, it will be remembered, who developed brutal ideas of imperialism and conquest by mistranslating "the survival of the fittest" into "the survival of the strongest," and applying it to relations between great and small nations. It could quite as readily be made use of in business and finance.

Wilson, doubtless, had had this sort of thing in mind when he had complained in his sesquicentennial address at Princeton that scientific method, being given too great a place in other branches of study, had produced "agnosticism in the realm of philosophy, scientific anarchism in the field of politics." Now he was determined that conscience and morality should be given greater weight. The conscience of the people would support him, once he had reawakened it. So would consciousness of their real interests. He was planning for them a "New Freedom" (his admirers eagerly used the phrase)—a freedom from fetters which business had placed on them. Consciously, or more often unconsciously; by itself, or through its political alliances, business had been placing limitations on the opportunities for development of the masses. True, reformers of all classes, including many businessmen, were seeing this condition, and proposing remedies. The actual changes which Wilson had in mind were not especially individual. What marked his whole program was a consistent emphasis upon moderation and morality.

Of all the popular "isms" of his day, only individualism appealed to him; and his devotion even to that was not so great as it had been. Enough of it survived to make him impatient both of socialists and paternalists—even to serve him as a guiding principle. But he was fully persuaded that individual initiative should be kept within limits. His efforts to set such limits perhaps come more closely than any other single thing to supplying the keynote of his domestic policy. Individualism was to be cherished up to, but never past, the point where there was likelihood of its being used to the detriment of others. A recent valuable study of the development of his thought along these lines shows that his early devotion to the *laissez-faire* doctrine had begun to yield to a sobering realization of some of its defects before he left Johns Hopkins. It shows, too, how profoundly he was affected in the same direction by later reading. Whatever tendency he may have had to be a mere theorist on economic and social issues was corrected years before he went into politics. He had come to agree that theories and assumptions about human beings and their actions in society were no more than "skeletons," until they were clothed by "the flesh and blood of real conditions." One must have "an accurate view of human nature."

Being a man of the nineteenth-century way of thinking, and a historian to boot, Wilson sought a basis of reality in history. He believed in "progress" by an evolutionary process, but turned for confirmation to the story of mankind, not to the forced use (or is prostitution too harsh a word?) of Darwinian precepts. This belief in social evolution made him a reformer of the moderate type. He still had a place for Burke in his gallery of heroes, though Burke was now in the background. He was utterly inflexible in principle and resolve; but in shaping legislation he was willing to take all possible account of facts. The members of his Cabinet found him more than ready to consider new information and new arguments, even to change his mind when information and arguments were cogent—provided his principles were sustained.

The question of the Government's attitude toward big business, which in some form or other was always cropping up, gave him opportunity to show what limits he wished to place on individual initiative, in the name of moderation and morality. He stood by the position he had held for years. Where big business contributed to the public good, when it engaged in legitimate competition, as it often did, all power to it. But in spite of previous attempts of presidents and congresses and courts to keep it in order, it often misbehaved. It sometimes passed from free competition to "cutthroat" competition, and from there to actual monopoly. It sometimes cut down production costs at the expense of labor, and to the detriment, not only of labor, but of more conscientious competitors. It sometimes did all the wicked things forbidden by New Jersey's Seven Sisters laws. So the legislation imposing limitations and penalties on organizations that operated to the detriment of the public would have to be revised. But one point in particular was beginning to trouble him. The courts had decided that the principle of preventing any social group from acting to the detriment of the whole community should be applied impartially; but labor would not admit that organizations for the betterment of living and working conditions should be subject to the same restrictions as those organized for profit. So far Wilson had not shown labor the sympathy which it expected from a "progressive" leader of the Democrats. But Mr. Gompers had great hopes of him.

It took him two years of hard work, especially in the management of Congress, to see his principal plans for legislation on economic matters realized. "Our program of legislation with regard to the regulation of business is now virtually complete," he told Congress in December 1914. "The road lies clear and firm before business . . . the road to ungrudged, unclouded success." Almost needless to say, business, or most of it, did not agree. Neither did public men like Mr. Taft, who by that time had become convinced that the administration was killing prosperity, "surrendering everything to Gompers," but fortunately hanging itself in the process. Even Mr. Taft, however, expressed his admiration of the President's skill in handling the press and other "political instruments"; and everyone admitted that the legislative output of the two years had been at least remarkable. That of 1913 had been high lighted by the passage of the Underwood Tariff Act and the establishment of the Federal Reserve System, and that of 1914 by the setting up of the Federal Trade Commission and the enactment of the Clayton Anti-Trust Act. Combined with less famous measures, these four constituted a very thorough "regulation of business" indeed.

The President had carried through his program by unremitting work, by concessions to political realities which he disliked, by tact and patience when such qualities served, and by unrelenting pressure, broken by flashes of sheer audacity, when sterner qualities were required. Surveying the first year with cool British detachment, Mr. A. Maurice Low noted Wilson's success in taking advantage of our national taste for novelty, and dubbed him "a conservative iconoclast." But Mr. Low found the real secret of his success in the way he had seized the leadership and clung to it:

> From the first day he made his mastery felt. He spent no "honeymoon" weeks, hoping to win by amiability, and later, if necessary, to command.

All through the sessions, through long, hot summer weeks, his pressure was never relaxed. He was polite to Congress, even to a point resented by some of its members. One of his several breaches of precedents was in searching out senators at the Capitol, instead of summoning them to the White House, when he thought it would save time. He was always ready to consult with party leaders about the bills he had at heart, and to give way on what did not seem to him essential points. But he would not barter by using the threat of a possible veto; nor would he allow any "buck passing," any evasion of responsibility. Democratic senators and congressmen might receive personal assurances of the President's realization that they should let their consciences be their guides; but Wilson's general insistence on party discipline beneath his leadership, and his growing hold on public sentiment, made it impossible for a member of either House to show insurgency without running the risk of being branded as disloyal to his party.

Congress did not suffer this treatment gladly. Even during Wilson's first year of office there were angry murmurs that he was usurping some of its most important functions. But there was no revolt. A number of Democratic veterans in Congress fully sympathized with Wilson's plans; while those who did not follow willingly from conviction, did so in order to keep the party in office and have jobs to hand out. Mr. Taft later informed readers of the *Yale Review* that "twenty-five hundred nominations of [Wilson's] predecessor had been suspended by a Democratic majority in the Senate for the purpose of starting his administration well." Wilson's dislike of such expedients was extreme; but some of his closest advisers persuaded him that party loyalty might sometimes count for more than principles in getting essential legislation passed. Mr. Baker tells how Mr. Daniels dissuaded him from insisting that Senator Simmons of North Carolina should be kept out of the chairmanship of the Finance Committee, because he had voted for the Payne-Aldrich tariff. Reward came when Mr. Simmons stoutly championed the radical tariff revision which stood first on Wilson's program. So the veterans followed him. As for the large group of young Democrats, Wilson was a star of hope to most of them. Even some of the Republican Progressives soon found it difficult to withhold support from measures they had vigorously endorsed in principle. Mr. La Follette felt obliged in conscience to vote for the new tariff; and Mr. Beveridge's Progressive Republican circle showed distressed anxiety. For even if the people had not really chosen Wilson they were turning toward him more and more. He found time to appeal frequently for their support. He told a gathering of Philadelphians that he constantly felt it necessary "to come away from Washington and renew one's contact with the people . . . who do not ask for anything, but who do trust you." Otherwise, he would grow "weaker and weaker." In another speech he told of the efforts of the Government to give the people "their freedom, their right to lift themselves . . . and behold the things they have hoped for, and so make way for still better days for those .. . . who are to come after them." Some weeks previously he had demanded of Congress the people's "freedom" from the Payne-Aldrich tariff.

This, of course, is no place for any description or discussion of the new tariff schedules or the old—not even for more than mention of some leaders among all the men who helped in framing the new measure and steering it through the committees and Congress. Mr. Underwood was fortunately recognized as the leading Democrat, apart from the Speaker, in the House of Representatives; and, fortunately again, was unlike the Speaker in feeling no resentment against Wilson for what had occurred at Baltimore. An important section of the bill, establishing an income tax to supply some of the revenue that would be lost in customs duties, was drafted and principally defended in the House by Mr. Cordell Hull, serving on the Ways and Means Committee under Mr. Underwood. Even in those days his knowledge, skill, and democratic integrity stood out. Mr. McAdoo gave fine assistance from the Treasury.

There were many others who performed great service before the bill was placed before the President in early October. It represented the work of eight or nine months: weeks of hearings by both committees begun during the "lame duck" session; caucuses in which members of both Houses worked to arrive at compromises which would not be resented by the agricultural or industrial districts from which they came; more than four months of debate, during which the Republicans, especially in the Senate, used all possible tactics to delay action, and the business world cried out that uncertainty was proving ruinous; then, finally, the ironing out of differences between the Houses, as represented by nearly seven hundred suggested amendments.

What part had the President in all of this? Wilson had a decidedly minor part in the determination of the bill's provisions, and as decidedly a major one in protecting it against injury and in clearing its way to passage. When Senator Norris, resenting his legislative leadership, and noting his frequent conferences with the promoters of the bill at the White House and the Capitol, suggested that it was in reality his bill, John Sharp Williams was able to assure the Senate that the President had taken no part in decisions on the schedules except in the case of two items. One of these must have been sugar, for here the pressure, especially from Louisiana and Colorado, had been at its heaviest, and Wilson at his firmest.

Wilson's success in getting the sort of tariff he wanted falsified many predictions; but it was less striking than the means he used. Before his opponents had time to get well organized he made two sharp appeals to Congress and the people, dramatizing the issue, and enlisting the support of public sentiment. He began by calling a special session for early April, referring only to the tariff, though he had other things in mind. There was nothing startling about that. Then it was announced that he would break the precedents of over a century by appearing before Congress in person on April 8 to deliver a message. Presidential messages had long ceased to have much effect on anyone. Consisting too often of platitudes and abstracts of departmental reports, they had been "droned out to empty benches," and ignored by nearly all the newspaper-reading public. Now the President was to meet Congress face to face; and he was not the man to deliver himself of platitudes and abstracts. There was sharp reaction in the Senate when a resolution providing for a joint session of the two Houses to hear the message was introduced. Jeffersonian Democrats among the senators who, as Mr. Baker says, "believed in the 'separation of the powers' as they believed in Holy Writ," were on their feet to complain of this alleged imitation of the British speech from the throne, of this "cheap and tawdry imitation of the pomposities and cavalcadings" [either the Senator or the reporter must have been overcome by emotion at this point] of the European monarchies. But when the day arrived, neither "cavalcading" nor emotion was apparent in the President's address; instead, a certain friendly ingenuousness. This was the message in which he asked Congress to regard him as "a human being . . . trying to co-operate." There was moderation, too, in his promises that there should be no "reckless haste," no "revolution or upset or confusion," no cutting "at the very roots of what has grown up among us by long process." On the other hand, his speech, so brief and so concentrated on the tariff issue as to be sure of a wide circle of readers, left no doubt that his war on privilege and monopoly had begun in good earnest:

For a long time . . . we have sought in our tariff schedules to give . . . manufacturers or producers what they themselves thought that they needed in order to maintain a practically exclusive market . . . we have built up a set of privileges and exemptions behind which it was easy by any . . . forms of combination to organize monopoly. . . . We must abolish everything that bears even the semblance of . . . artificial advantage.

Among Democrats as well as Republicans there must have been senators and congressmen who felt anything but sure that there would be no "upset or confusion" in the application of this principle. But no one wished to appear as the advocate of what the President had denounced, and the applause from the floor and the gallery was so satisfactory that the President told Mrs. Wilson joyfully that he had "put one over on Teddy" by going in person to the Congress. Certainly the press, while in some cases critical, recognized the message's news value.

The early capture of the public's interest bore fruit when the House Ways and Means Committee reported out a bill, a fortnight later; and when, as the debates began, the lobbyists got down to work. The bill was not a free trade, tariff-for-revenue measure. But the protection that it gave was designed to balance the interests of producers and distributors and consumers, in fact, of the whole people. Just for this reason the bill, in slashing many duties, was of a sort to win more active foes than active friends. In the House, the administration's majority was safe enough; but in the Senate, protectionist by inclination, very sensitive about presidential leadership, and having only a slender Democratic majority, real danger could be foreseen. Would Wilson and his forces prevail? Everything possible was done to keep Democratic senators in line by personal conferences and letters. Efforts were made to persuade them to range themselves in caucus behind the bill, as the Democrats of the House had done. But the outlook seemed ominous. Pressure politics, never so active as when tariff measures are to the fore, threatened to ruin everything. Lobbyists, professional and otherwise, had arrived early:

Washington is fairly seething with tariff today (April 9, 1913). Hotels are crowded with businessmen from all over the country, attracted by the pendency of the tariff legislation. Wool men from as far west as Montana, fruit men from California, beet-sugar men from the West, and cane-sugar men from the South; New England manufacturers, woolen men from Pennsylvania, and representatives of many interests are on the ground to look after their own.

Of course it was impolite of the New York *Evening Post* to refer to all these eager visitors as "vermin"; but they did bear a certain resemblance to destructive insects of some kind, as they set themselves, group after group, to destroy one provision after another of the bill. Their efforts were supported by the customary deluge of telegrams, letters, and the memorials which people so often sign without much knowledge of underlying issues. The usual negotiations for various deals went on, with Senator A offering to demand higher rates for sugar if Senator B would reciprocate by coming out for higher rates on wool. The customary reports that the opposition would win and the bandwagon prove the safest place were set flying.

Senator Simmons put up a creditable fight; but there seemed every prospect that the lobbyists, expert in "panicking" politicians, would be too much for him. As usual there was no one to lobby for the consumers, for the people as a whole. At least there did not seem to be, until Wilson made his second dramatic move. He was thoroughly aroused. Not only was the tariff act itself in danger, but the pressure of the lobbyists struck at his own leadership, at his whole conception of the presidency, at his desire to bring system and responsibility into our legislative process. As Mr. Schattschneider puts it in his *Politics, Pressures and the Tariff:* "Unsupervised conduct in pressure politics means that the few will control the [legislative] process at the expense of the many." The situation was ideal for an expression of "the common meaning of the common voice." After the manner of good strategists, the President quietly "estimated the situation," and then, at the end of May, struck suddenly and hard. Through the representatives of the press he appealed to the nation:

Washington has seldom seen so numerous, so industrious and so insidious a lobby. The newspapers are being filled with paid advertisements calculated to mislead the judgments of public men . . . the public opinion of the country itself. There is every evidence that money without limit is being spent to sustain this lobby and to create an appearance of a pressure of opinion antagonistic to some of the chief items of the Tariff bill.

. . . the people at large have no lobby . . . while great bodies of astute men seek to . . . overcome the interests of the public for their private profit.

He appealed on behalf of Congress, as well as on that of the administration:

The Government in all its branches ought to be relieved from this intolerable burden and this constant interruption to the calm progress of debate. I know . . . I am speaking for the members of the two Houses. . . .

But he was not speaking for all of them. Some of them were incensed; and the "lobby" message was hotly debated in the Senate. There were demands that the President should make his charges specific or retract them; there were accusations that he was bullying his party. But, in so far as it is possible to judge, Wilson achieved his end. Lobbying, of course, went on; but his daring incitement of public hostility against the lobbyists seems to have made members of both

Houses wary about appearing to give their votes on the side of privilege and monopoly.

Wilson had no more spectacular moves to make regarding the tariff, but four months of persuasion and pressure lay ahead. For the most part, they were very hot and lonely months. Mrs. Wilson and her daughters went off to summer at Cornish, New Hampshire, among literary and artistic neighbors who delighted them. Fortunately, Tumulty, living at the White House, had a new ally in looking out devotedly for his chief. Dr. Grayson, who had been physician to Mr. Taft, and had been recommended by him in the warmest terms, was already beginning to play an important part in Wilson's private life, not only as a physician but as a friend. It was probably thanks to his influence that the President conscientiously put in an hour or so of golf daily, and did no more work on Saturdays than special emergencies required. Such strain as he felt came from worry, not from work:

It's the anxiety attending the handling of such "things" as that scoundrel Huerta [Mexico's newest dictator] and all other . . . matters [for] which your own judgments and principles furnish no standards.

But not so with the fight he was carrying on for tariff revision and a new banking law:

I of course find real zest in it all. Hard as it is to nurse Congress along and stand ready to play a part of guidance in anything that turns up, great or small, it is all part of something infinitely great and worth while, and I am content to labor at it to the finish.

Things were going well. "So far," he wrote, "my leadership is most loyally and graciously accepted." He was in a solemn, even exalted, mood:

These are stern days, and this all but empty house fits well with them.

Yet his sense of humor did not fail:

Every now and again, just to keep my hand in and feel natural, I break a precedent . . . today . . . I went to church in a white linen suit . . . I created a mild sensation . . . but that of course is what every public man wishes to do, at church or anywhere else.

No, it was not such a bad summer. He was able to make some short trips to Cornish; and he found Tumulty and Grayson "lovely fellows, both of them, and good company all the while." But really happy days arrived when the weather turned cooler, and the family came back, and the tariff bill, not just as he wanted it, but nearly enough, at last lay on his desk. "I have had the accomplishment of something like this at heart ever since I was a boy," he said.

Yet there was no suggestion of any pause for enjoyment of his success. In the same breath he went on:

. . . there is no use taking away the conditions of monopoly if we do not take away also the power to create monopoly. . . . The power to guide and direct the credits of the country is the power to say who shall and shall not build up the industries. . . . We are now about to take the second step.

Of course the second step was the establishment of the Federal Reserve System. To members of Congress this driving seemed hard. They, too, had gone through a protracted and exhausting session, through long, hot summer months. Why should not the President let them adjourn, calling them back earlier, if the passage of the banking bill was so pressing? But Wilson was as inexorable as fate. There should be no break at all. To deal with the banking system would probably be more difficult than lowering the tariff had been. In doing it the party would not be acting according to a long-established principle. It would not even be bound by such campaign promises of speedy action as in the revision of the tariff. Would it be wise to allow a break in the momentum that was carrying the great program through? Privately, Wilson seems to have suspected that the bankers might create a small panic, in order to block the bill, but he had enough arguments that could be used publicly. The new banking measure, already debated for months, was ready to go through its final stages in Congress. The public was on the alert— had, in fact, been so ever since a day in late June, when the President had fixed its attention on his "second step" in a particularly brief and incisive message to Congress:

It is absolutely imperative that we should give . . . businessmen . . . freedom of enterprise and of individual initiative . . . by removing the trammels of the protective tariff . . . the tonic and the discipline of liberty are to ensue . . . the control of the system of banking and issue which our new laws are to set up must be public, not private, must be vested in the Government itself, so that the banks may be the instruments, not the masters, of business and individual enterprise.

The words of that message were simple enough. Except for their precision and occasional beauty of diction ("the tonic and the discipline of liberty are to ensue"), they may have seemed commonplace to some. Others may have found socialism or state capitalism in them. But Wilson had no thought of government ownership, nor even of the regimentation of day-to-day business. On the other hand, there was to be an end of the "survival of the strongest" in finance. Instead, he wanted the application of his favorite principle—government regulation of the individual initiative of the few on behalf of the individual initiative of the many. He wanted to give the greatest power to the greatest number in business as in politics. And implementation of the principle was not to be based merely on theory. It was being based on long and thorough study of the working of banking systems in this and other countries; and the study was in the hands of men who consulted bankers at least as much as they consulted even the sort of books that governments and banks turn out. Mr. Low wrote that America's "most practical President" was the one in whom practicality was least to have been looked for.

"I know very well," said Carter Glass years later, "the chairman of the House Committee on Banking and Currency [himself] has been given an undue share of the praise [for the establishment of the Federal Reserve System]. But, gentlemen, the serious fact is that the master mind of the whole performance was Woodrow Wilson's. It was his infinite prescience and patience; it was his courage and wisdom; it was his patriotism and power—his passion to serve mankind—that gave zest and inspiration to the battle for financial freedom." Wilson himself had disclaimed such credit in writing to McAdoo in the autumn of 1914. He was referring to all that had been accomplished in the "regulation of business" since the time when he had taken office:

I do not know that any special credit belongs to me for the part I was privileged to play in the establishment of this new system . . . in it the labor and knowledge and forethought and practical experience and sagacity of many men are embodied.

Proud and egotistical as he was, a sense of fairness seems to have saved him from the vulgarity of conceit. Of the many men who had worked with him in the establishment of the Federal Reserve System, he would certainly have given first honors to Carter Glass. It was Glass's hand that he grasped just before signing the banking bill, on the evening of December 23, 1913, a year almost to a day since the two men had first discussed the matter at Princeton. The mutual tributes may well stand. Each man was the best possible judge of what the other had contributed. And both were more than ready to admit that much of the credit belonged to other men of the party, not only for hard work, but for pooling their views; which meant, of course, making concession to each other's points of view.

There were certain things on which all of them, and nearly all Republicans for that matter, could easily agree. Few people were ready to defend the existing law by which the amount of currency available in the country at any time was determined, not by the nation's commercial assets or needs, but by the amount of the nation's bonded indebtedness. Again, it was obviously wrong that money or credit available in the East should drop to a dangerously low level when the time came to pay for Western grain and cattle shipped to the Atlantic seaboard. It was clearly wrong, again, that when currency was abundant, money should pile up in the great banks of great cities, with New York at the peak of a sort of financial pyramid. Such accumulations could be, and sometimes were, used for speculation in stocks and in commodities. It was very wrong indeed that we should have to expect recurrent crises, and be dependent, as Senator Aldrich once remarked, on "a Mr. Morgan" for rescue. For years these faults had been pointed out by bankers and others. For years Congress had sought to correct them by setting up some system that would introduce more co-operation, more centralized control. The Republicans had held long hearings and investigations. They had set up a monetary commission, which had issued a valuable report. They had offered bills in three sessions. Senator Aldrich had put great knowledge and ability, to say nothing of time and work, into plans for a national bank. But Republican efforts had proved abortive largely because, in a country such as ours, there was inevitable conflict on two issues.

Now the Democrats had to face them. How much centralization and control should be imposed, especially by federal laws, upon free Americans who chose to embark their money and their energies in banking? For nearly a century, since the second Bank of the United States had been wiped out by the Federal Government, centralization and control had been kept down to a minimum, in deference to the individualism and independence of the American spirit. Everyone knew that the great bankers were often self-seeking and autocratic in their treatment of individuals and small banks. Wilson in 1911, it will be remembered, had indicted some of them to their faces in New York. Everyone knew that the small banks were often subservient or unsound.

But sentiment against government control, or the establishment of one great central bank, was still lively, especially in the more "liberal" sections of the country, such as the Middle West. It was especially hard to make the men and women of small towns see that government regulation which touched local banks and bankers (local places of investment and local friends) should be established in the interest of the people's own financial liberty and security. And given that more centralization and control must be set up, should it rest with the bankers or with the Government? Here distrust of too much governmental control, of too much bureaucracy, emerged; but the advocates of control by the bankers were not actuated purely by this worthy Anglo-Saxon instinct. Bankers have their normal share of human pride and selfishness, and often have friends in high political places. The Aldrich plan was popular in banking circles, but not with Congress or the public.

In 1913 Wilson and the Democrats faced this conflict of interests and principles. The party was ready to go to work. It had been busy, since gaining control of the House two years before, in pushing on the investigation of existing evils, and (thanks largely to the talents of Samuel Untermyer as counsel for the Committee on Banking and Currency) in exposing them to the public. Now, with a President of its own, and a small majority in the Senate, it could work constructively. The leaders were all agreed in their rejection of the Aldrich plan, but so much at odds in other ways that Wilson was to have full opportunity for displaying the patience, the courage, and wisdom to which Glass paid tribute. It would be difficult for him to make decisions. He had a good deal of the knowledge of banking and currency that a man may get from books and from consultation with ranking economists. But economists more than most people can disagree; and, what was more, Wilson had the practical man's distrust of specialists. He had warned even a class of midshipmen against adopting a "specialist" point of view. The men he would have to look to for advice, and for steering whatever plan might be agreed on through the committees and the Houses, were at least as practical as he; but they disagreed none the less. While no one of them could be classed as a pronounced conservative, their conflicting views reflected either deep devotion to the party's left wing or some sympathy with the right.

Bryan, alert as ever where the currency was concerned, wanted the bankers stripped to the last possible degree of power or even influence. Senator Owen, who would have principal charge of the projected legislation in the Senate, and who had studied the question long and thoroughly, was much of the same mind. So was Congressman Henry of Texas, chairman of the powerful Rules Committee of the House, and champion of agrarian interests. On the other side stood Mr. McAdoo, who had naturally seen a good deal of bankers, and still did. Not agreeing with some of McAdoo's ideas, but still to be classed as on the right, was Glass himself. Also very much in the picture (too much for Glass's taste at times) was Colonel House. He was the liaison man, the conciliator, as usual. He was always ready to work with Owen and Bryan, but equally ready to work with Glass or McAdoo. Moreover, he kept in touch with such great financial figures as Messrs. Morgan (the younger), Vanderlip, Frick, and Kahn. Through him Wilson could learn what "Wall Street" or almost any other interested group or individual was thinking. Outside the official family and House stood other helpers. Mr. Untermyer, to whom Wilson was still grateful for timely support at Baltimore, sympathized with the Owen-Bryan group. So did Mr. Brandeis, whose knowledge of the subject was impressive and whose views now carried increasing weight at the White House. The left-wingers were heavily entrenched. How was the New Freedom, with emphasis on moderation and morality, to show up in the outcome? The surprising thing about the outcome is not only that the Federal Reserve System probably worked as well as could have been expected of any previously untried plan, but that it was accepted at the time as satisfactory by all save extremists and diehards.

The Federal Reserve System was moderate and practical largely because Glass and Wilson were moderate and practical; and because the plan they first discussed at Princeton was thereafter treated as subject to modification, but in general holding good. There would be no more pyramiding of money in one or two great centers.

Neither would there be a national bank—a financial and political sovereign, controlled by financial and political junkers. Instead, the country was to be divided into twelve regions. In each there was to be a Federal Reserve bank, serving all national banks, and all other banks and trust companies willing to be bound by the provisions of the Act, in very much the way in which the member banks served their customers. So in every region of the country there would be an accumulation of resources through which credit could be distributed for the benefit of many banks. These regional Federal Reserve banks would naturally be run by bankers; but, since they would have such power over the handling of the people's money, they would be subject to inspection and control. But by whom? By a non-partisan Federal Reserve Board. There was precedent in the Interstate Commerce Commission. But who would appoint its members? Why of course the choice of the whole people, the President. The Board would see to it that every region was cared for financially; in other words, that the distribution of credit was on a national scale. According to Glass, the Board, the "keystone" of the structure, was suggested by Wilson. By accident perhaps, the plan offered, in economic matters, the elements of system and ultimate responsibility to the public that Wilson was trying to introduce in government. Of a certainty it curbed the individual initiative of the few in the apparent interests of the many. The other more flagrant evils of the old system were also to disappear. In future the currency would be elastic, based on the nation's commercial assets in gold and "liquid" paper. So far so good. To all of these features of the Glass-Wilson plan the party leaders might be expected to agree. But when it came to filling in the outlines of the plan, agreement vanished speedily. Should any bankers have seats on the Federal Reserve Board? Glass himself said "yes," but the Owen-Bryan group said "no." Should the Federal Reserve notes be issued by the banks? Wilson thought they should, but found Owen and Bryan opposed to him. And concessions were due them. Owen in his bill and Bryan in some of his platforms had called for a system by which deposits made in banks operating under the new law would be insured against bank failures. At the request of Glass, they had consented to drop their demand for the time being.

Dr. Parker Willis, the expert who had gone with Glass to Princeton, and whose advice was invaluable to Glass and to the President, declared later that it was a marvel, if not a miracle, that Wilson brought the Federal Reserve Act safely through all the currents and eddies which threatened constantly to wreck it. The American Bankers' Association, which, by supporting the Aldrich plan, condemned the administration measure from the outset, had great influence with conservative elements in Congress and outside. Later, the United States Chamber of Commerce lined up beside it. But, leaving aside his principles (which he would not do), Wilson could make few if any concessions to the conservatives. For the bill's passage, the votes of the liberals and agrarians, the members of the two Houses who followed Bryan, Owen, and Henry, were indispensable. And in this particular struggle his great weapon, appeal to the people, was of little use to him. He could, and did, ask public support in putting through a law which would remedy obvious evils and reduce the power of the great banks; but when it came down to details, the public could not be expected to understand the issues, and apply pressure. Little wonder, when even the American Economic Association refused to commit itself! All he could do was to find a basis of agreement between the party leaders, and then bring persuasion and pressure to bear on Congress.

In bringing the leaders together, Colonel House was of great assistance during the spring; but the greatest crises did not occur until after he had sailed for Europe, in May. On two occasions in particular Wilson had to take decisive action. In June, shortly before his sharp message to Congress, the question of allowing the bankers to have representation on the Federal Reserve Board had come almost to a deadlock. Wilson called Glass, Owen, and McAdoo to the White House, and announced his decision. The bankers should have no representation at all. It was hard for him to go against Glass, who had worked with him so loyally and so long, and who argued persuasively that the bankers were entitled, in the name of free initiative, to some share in the ultimate control of their business. But the Owen-Bryan group, supported by the opinions of Brandeis and Untermyer, stood firm; and Wilson apparently decided that they were right. Glass, who saw what bitter opposition to the bill the decision would stir up, made a final effort, and added some drama to the rather dreary struggle. He secured permission to bring to the White House a delegation of bankers belonging to the Currency Commission of the Bankers' Association. He later wrote an account of the meeting. Grouped around the President's desk, some of the bankers spoke sharply, as men with authority of their own, while others were all persuasiveness. The President heard them out, and then addressed them quietly:

"Will one of you gentlemen tell me in what civilized country of the earth there are important government boards of control on which private interests are represented?"

There was painful silence for the longest single moment I ever spent; and before it was broken Mr. Wilson further inquired:

"Which of you gentlemen thinks the railroads should select members of the Interstate Commerce Commission?"

The silence of the bankers could not be taken for consent; but Wilson had converted Glass. That must have relieved him; and all the more, perhaps, because he knew that he would soon have to take sides against Glass on the second of the two great disputed issues. In handling this second issue he found it necessary to be a little disingenuous. Should the Federal Reserve Bank notes be obligations of the Federal Reserve Banks or of the Government? The Bryan-Owen group was determined on their being government currency. But, as Glass vehemently protested, the coverage of the notes was in the assets of the Federal Reserve Banks and all the banks they served— even in the power of the Federal Reserve Board to withhold notes. Wilson privately assured Glass that he was entirely right—and forthwith announced that he was supporting Owen and Bryan. "The government liability is a mere thought," he said to Glass. But he went on: "If we can hold to the substance of the thing and give the other fellow the shadow, why not do it, if thereby we may save our bill?" He did not like such devious courses, but he did save the bill. Glass, sad but loyal, gave in.

When the debates in the House of Representatives began, Glass had reason to praise Wilson's "prescience." In spite of all the concessions made to Bryan and his friends, Mr. Henry and the extreme left-wingers cried out that "Wall Street" lurked behind the bill. For three months the struggle went on, with Wilson summoning the Banking and Currency Committee and various insurgent congressmen to the White House, and appealing to Bryan. Through most of August a caucus of House Democrats fought as to whether the party should endorse the bill. Endorsement was finally given when Glass produced a letter from Bryan, cutting the ground from under the insurgents' feet. But this was far from helping the bill in the Senate. There conservative forces, with strong outside support from the Bankers' Association, the Chamber of Commerce, and other business groups, kept the struggle going for six months. They relied especially on the familiar tactics of delay: demanding fresh hearings, flooding the floor with amendments, doing everything, it seemed, to kill the measure by producing sheer fatigue.

Wilson, having exhausted the possibilities of persuasion, and having won a convert or two in his own party, including Senator O'Gorman of New York, set his jaw, and encouraged the faithful to be steadfast in this endurance contest. Early in September he demanded that the Senate should have no adjournment for more than three days at a time. Already in this first session his attitude toward the Senate was hardening into something like hostility. In one private letter he protested against newspaper statements that he was "bending Congress" to his "indomitable, individual will"; and insisted that members accepted his "guidance" only because they realized his efforts "to mediate their own thoughts and purposes." Power lay "in one's capacity to . . . lead by reason and . . . co-operation." But only a week later he was taking a very different tone:

The struggle goes on. . . . Why *should* . . . senators . . . have to be led and stimulated to what all the country knows to be their duty! . . . To whom are they listening? Certainly not to the voice of the people. . . . They have strangely blunted perceptions, and exaggerate themselves in the most extraordinary degree. Therefore it *is* a struggle and must be accepted as such.

The strain was telling on him, but he was winning. House, now back from Europe, was helping Bryan and McAdoo in rounding up doubtful senators. Some of the bankers (subjected to Wilson's persuasive reasoning during interviews at the White House) were showing greater friendliness; and commentators were expressing such admiration as could not fail to affect the public. Colonel Harvey might be suspected of partisanship in writing that no President had "demonstrated greater capacity for true leadership"; but how could one answer that elder statesman among the Republicans, Chauncey Depew:

This man who was regarded as a pedagogue, a theorist, is accomplishing the most astonishing practical results.

The increasing swing of public opinion to the President was reflected in such elections as took place in that autumn; and even a senator of the most "blunted perceptions" was unlikely to overlook that. Opposition within the party was not dead. Senator Hitchcock, in particular, held out against the bill, and against the unusual attempt to have it adopted by a Senate caucus. But the caucus did vote against any Christmas holidays for the Senate unless the bill was passed by Christmas Eve. There is a limit even to the endurance of senators. In 1913 most of them got home to their native turkeys; and Wilson got his Federal Reserve Bill by a vote of fifty-four to thirty-four. The signing was an occasion for some ceremony. Fellow workers and "distinguished guests" formed a happy group. Mrs. Wilson, the Vice-President, the Speaker, Bryan, McAdoo, and Senator Owen were all there, to say nothing of Glass. There were congressmen of both parties, officials of the Treasury, reporters and attachés. The President signed with four gold pens. Three, which he had personally furnished, were presented to Glass, Owen, and McAdoo. Then Wilson, very happy, but showing fatigue as he had done for months, made a characteristic little speech. The Federal Reserve Act was to be "the first of a series of constructive measures." Then he and Mrs. Wilson left almost immediately for Pass Christian in Mississippi, to spend three weeks which covered his fifty-seventh birthday.

CHAPTER VIII

The Divide at Pass Christian

———————◆———————

Dᴜʀɪɴɢ the warm and sunny weeks at Pass Christian, health and vigor flowed back into Wilson. He felt gloriously relaxed, and so prepared to push ahead. But, as Mr. Baker has suggested, those weeks proved to be something of a watershed in his life. Things were never again to be as they had been in 1913. Long before another year was out he was to lose the first Mrs. Wilson, whose companionship, whose care for his every interest, whose political instinct and gentle, moderating influence had been of such inestimable value. The beginning of her fatal illness occurred, in fact, soon after their return to Washington. And Wilson's public life was to be different, too. For one thing, his relations with Congress would not be quite the same as in his great year of triumph. He would keep control, and see to it that more important legislation was put through; but his leadership would not be quite so willingly or completely accepted as it had been. He had taken Congress by surprise, much as he had taken the legislators at Trenton; but dissentient elements would now have had time to consider ways of obstructing him, or giving him trouble at any rate. Then, being a reformer, he inevitably trod on more and more toes. Even with the people he would not have quite the same success. The element of novelty would be lacking. And immediately in front of him lay the difficult problem of dealing with the trusts, made more complicated by the necessity of deciding in how far restrictions placed on their freedom of action should be applied to trade unions.

Other plans and problems stretched before him into the distance, like the wires of the telephone and telegraph systems which he once thought (though not for long) of trying to bring under government ownership. Woman suffrage, the choice of presidential candidates through primaries, conservation of natural resources, color segregation of persons in government service, better conditions for merchant seamen—all of these questions and many more were to be thought out. But it was not any diminution of his power or influence, nor any changes in domestic issues, that was to constitute the real divide. The great difference in the future was to lie in the increasing extent to which his thoughts and energies were to be diverted from domestic reform to foreign policy. Mr. Taft's administration had bequeathed to him a whole group of troublesome problems, relating mainly to our relations with Latin América, but also touching the Far East and our insular possessions and dependencies in two oceans. One of these questions, relating to affairs in Mexico, had engaged much of the President's attention before he went to Pass Christian; another, having to do with tolls in the Panama Canal, was to put his leadership to a severe test in the spring. All of them, but these two in particular, were to give clear indications of the nature of Wilson's foreign policy long before heavy guns began to thunder in Belgium. Yes, 1914 was to see Wilson increasingly forced to give himself to foreign policy. And he had provided himself with three advisers who were eager to assist him in formulating it when he had made Bryan Secretary of State; when he had sent Walter Page to our London embassy (after President Eliot and Richard Olney had declined the post); and when he had taken Colonel House into his heart and into his confidence.

It would be difficult to find a parallel to Wilson's friendship with House. Perhaps the most striking thing about it was not that the Colonel seemed almost ideally fitted to meet Wilson's needs, nor the coincidence that a man so fitted captured Wilson's confidence and affection at first sight, but that House was nearly as much in need of Wilson as Wilson was of him. His aspirations were in some ways very similar to the President's. He, too, was public spirited. He, too, was progressive in his viewpoint, but conservative by temperament. The political and economic credos of the two men seldom differed much in articles, although at the beginning they differed vastly in emphasis. Moreover, House, like Wilson, wanted to have an active, even a guiding, part in things. And he naturally preferred to be at the center of direction and of power. But in other ways (and here, apparently, was one of the secrets of a historic relationship) he was the very antithesis of Wilson. He possessed a gift for winning individuals, but no gift for winning the masses. He had neither capacity nor perhaps desire to play a conventional part in politics. He had no ability as an orator, none of the "regular" politician's stock in trade—not even a physical constitution that could be counted on to carry him through the wear and tear of politics. He could hope only to be a promoter, an adviser, an interpreter of men of his own mind, who had the gifts he lacked. Being a philosophical and well-educated man, he was probably content. There were plenty of cases in history where trusted advisers of rulers had been all the more powerful for being free from the obligations and limitations of office.

That the Colonel realized this seemed especially evident when Wilson, already beginning to lean on him, and grateful for what he had done in lining up Texas, converting Bryan, and helping in the selection of the Cabinet, asked him to take a Cabinet post. House gracefully excused himself as feeling unsuited to the task; but he later remarked confidentially that he would have disagreed so much with Wilson in Cabinet meetings that he would "not have lasted eight weeks." Considering that tact was one of the most notable of all the Colonel's gifts, the confidence must not be taken too literally. Yet he was right enough in apparently believing that he could do much more with and for Wilson out of office than in. He stood as a disinterested and devoted friend, untrammeled in his conversation and his activities by anything but the obligations of friendship and respect for the President's office. He was freer to argue, because he could not obstruct. No post could have suited him better. And the relationship was personally of the warmest. House and his wife were treated as close family friends. Wilson thoroughly enjoyed visiting the Colonel in his New York apartment and welcoming him to the White House. "You are the only person in the world," he wrote, in the summer of 1915, "with whom I can discuss everything." Since the time of his election as President he had signed himself "affectionately."

All circumstances had seemed to combine in fitting House for his task. Ample means made him independent of salaries or financial favors, and able to dispense liberal, and often useful, hospitality. A loyal Texan, he had finished his education at Cornell, and was quite at home in New York and generally in the East. In fact, his health made it desirable that he spend his summers in New England or in Europe. He was sophisticated, at home with people of all sorts. Everywhere he could pick up friends worth knowing; and his taste in friends, unlike Wilson's, seems to have been nothing if not catholic. In such circumstances many a man would have become a mere rover and a dilettante. But House was anchored by loyalty to his State, his party, his friends, his taste for politics, and his desire to be useful. So, long before his meeting with Wilson, he had become an expert politician, a dominating figure in three gubernatorial campaigns. In this way he had become one of those honorary colonels who owe their rank to governors. During the time of the Taft administration he had been on the lookout for a Democratic leader of sound and yet progressive views; and a meeting with Wilson in the last weeks of 1911 had clinched his conviction that he had found his man.

His allegiance, once given, was never withdrawn; and it was an allegiance such as few able and independent men would have been ready to offer. A man may satisfy his pride in being called on for advice by his leader; in taking the leader's place at important interviews; in being sought after as the leader's confidant or mouthpiece; in being used as a personal agent on confidential missions. House doubtless felt such pride. But he drudged unobtrusively for Wilson, too. He held no end of interviews with tiresome people who could not be offended or might possibly say something worth hearing, in order to spare his "Governor's" time and energy. With the same object he sifted masses of materials, so that he might offer computations and comments. He was usually in New York, but always prepared to start for Washington. Opinions as to the way he used his influence have differed. He has been accused of retaining his position as Wilson's confidant by being a "yes man"; of usurping Bryan's place as Wilson's proper adviser on foreign affairs, keeping the Secretary in ignorance of some of the things he knew and did; of acting abroad as Wilson's accredited agent when in reality he was an observer and reporter, and no more.

The validity of these charges seems to depend largely on the completeness of House's understanding of Wilson, and on the extent of Wilson's own complicity. House frequently disagreed with the President, and sometimes told him so. Very often he held his peace. A notably shrewd judge of men, he must have seen that Wilson would have no friendship on really equal terms. So he may well have decided that there were times when opposition, instead of doing any good, would put an end to whatever usefulness he had. Being less opinionated than Wilson, more capable of seeing both sides, he was less cer-

tain that he was right when their opinions clashed. Was he very
culpable in sometimes ignoring Bryan? The atmosphere of peace on
earth and of good will with which the Secretary flooded the Department of State was highly useful within limits; but it could not cover
up Bryan's lack of knowledge or competence in many crucial matters,
or his failure to keep confidential information from leaking out.
Moreover, Wilson, like most presidents, was always essentially his own
foreign minister; and House was unreserved with him where information was concerned.

Perhaps the Colonel did sometimes mistake the capacity under which
he went abroad before 1918. Mr. Baker points out how very personal
and noncommittal the President's few letters or cables to him were.
Perhaps House was wrong in often taking silence for consent. But
there is still a case for him. Wilson's messages, if noncommittal, were
cordial and grateful. And who was more justified in considering himself competent to interpret them than the most intimate friend of their
author? And was not Wilson rather disingenuous, if he allowed
House's standing to be misinterpreted by himself and by others? Disagreement about the extent and nature of the Colonel's influence is
still lively; but it was certainly the greatest influence exerted on Wilson by any man, from the time of his inauguration to that of his collapse. Moreover, since House had peculiar talents for seeing both sides
of a question, for smoothing down asperities, and for finding solu-
tions to situations that were embarrassing or worse, it must have been
very helpful. "Mr. House is my second personality . . . his thoughts
and mine are one," the President once said. Strange if egotism could
reach so far that a man could deny his "second personality" a considerable degree of influence.

"For Colonel House," writes President Seymour, ". . . foreign problems were always of the first interest and importance . . . all through
his varied activities as the President's adviser in 1913 there is obvious
the desire to free himself from the details of domestic politics and to
find time to help in the formulation of a positive foreign policy."
It was there, of course, that the great difference in emphasis which he
and Wilson originally placed on different aspects of public affairs
came in. House was shocked to discover that the President had been
content to let our new Ambassador to Great Britain sail without instructions, merely taking it for granted "that he would be diplomatic
and conciliatory." House wanted to see definite tasks assigned to our

envoys. Like so many people in the most recent years, he sought for an American foreign policy that would take account of the development of other important countries in this hemisphere, and of our increasing involvement in both hemispheres, through commerce, finance, and our considerable ownership or control of insular territories ever since our war with Spain. In years when our diplomatic agents all over Europe had to report on international crises which increased in frequency and gravity, it might even have been expected that the State Department would consider what should be our stand, apart from an almost certain proclamation of neutrality, should a major conflict break out. But House, like later seekers for a definite policy, found the cupboard almost bare.

There were certain elements which could be useful in making one. There was the Monroe Doctrine; and there was the evidence of history that we shared the British belief in arbitration as a valid method·of settling international disputes. There was an unavowed tradition of maintaining peace (no matter through how much bickering) with the British—a tradition based on the even less avowed advantages we had drawn from British naval supremacy, to say nothing of ties of blood, speech, and respect for law. There were also definite principles laid down in the President's speeches and writings. But elements and principles no more made a policy than swallows make a summer. Was there nothing definite? The people, if asked, would have said we should have no entangling alliances. That came from a Sinai shared by two early fathers of the republic (often misquoted textually and otherwise); and so, it seemed, must remain forever infallible, unmodified, no matter how much our strength and therefore our responsibility for the general welfare of humanity might increase; no matter how greatly new discoveries, in virtually decreasing distance, decreased also our security; no matter how much we became entangled through trade and money and "imperialism"; no matter, in fact, what you took "entangling" to mean—provided you took it to mean anything. Most Americans gave as much respect to this infallible pronouncement as they did to any commandment in the Decalogue; and few if any of the country's leaders saw reason to disagree with them.

Colonel House did not. But, no matter with how many elements and principles it might be combined, the Great Pronouncement was not enough for him. We needed a clear and consistent policy in dealing with Latin America; and we could feel our way to closer understandings in Europe without a suggestion of alliances. So we might promote one of our own interests—real peace, not armed peace shaken constantly by crises which could bring war overnight. Here indeed was a mission for America, altruistic, yet a matter of self-interest, too. Wilson, with all his idealism, his passion for service, and his power, would be an ideal man to take the lead, if House could persuade him to do it. The Colonel, who does not seem fully to have realized how constructive Wilson's principles were, was ready to try at any rate; and he knew that he had an enthusiastic ally in Walter Page.

The sending of Page to London was one of the most important appointments that Wilson ever made; and for at least two years the relationship between the President and the Ambassador was remarkably close and remarkably fruitful. They had enough in common to be able to work in sympathy, yet differed sufficiently to find stimulation in each other's views. Their similarity in outlook owed something to the fact that they were almost exactly the same age, and to their common upbringing in the South; but its real roots lay much deeper. Each man recognized in the other a man of public spirit, a man of ability, a man of letters, and, more than all, a man of ideals. When Wilson once remarked to House that Page's letters were, in so far as he knew, the best ever written by any man, he probably had more in mind than the sensitivity of impression, the humor, the rich tolerance, the charm of style, which have captivated countless readers.' The letters were packed full of liberalism, and of a liberalism which was Wilson's own. Among modern American statesmen, Page was the first, or among the first, to think and write constantly of the "forgotten man." Here, as in relation to all public matters, the intensity of his feeling was greater than Wilson's; but in ideals and ardent patriotism the two men stood much on common ground.

Page, like Wilson, believed with all his heart in the doctrine of service; and, like Wilson, coveted for his country the proud place of leader among all nations in the civilization of the future. As most men and women long to see the people they most deeply love earning respect and self-respect by altruism and scrupulous honor, so Page and Wilson were alike resolved that Wilson's administration should strike a new note in international affairs. Character, i.e., sheer honesty and even unselfishness, should prevail over nationalistic self-seeking in American foreign policy. And in their aspirations the United States was not merely to place herself and her own doings upon a higher plane: she was to be the example and the teacher of other nations. Page thought especially of the influence she could have upon England. Not that he regarded the British as more in need of teaching than other European nations: exactly the reverse was true. He felt that England could profit most by what America had to give, because the two nations were already so much at one that the British would come easily to the American point of view. But Page had little of Wilson's belief that teaching was done by clarifying and moralizing—even by resorting to pressure when it seemed to be required. The Ambassador sometimes preached to the British; but he preferred to do things by example, by persuasion, by the influence that can be exerted through understanding and friendship. Perhaps there was room for both methods where our relations with Britain were concerned. At any rate, the two men seemed united in desire for diplomatic relations based upon honor and upon reciprocity in friendliness.

No American Ambassador could have been better fitted to deal with the British Government by friendly persuasiveness. From the time of Page's arrival in London relations between the American Embassy and Downing Street became rapidly more friendly. Not that Page was under any illusions where the British were concerned. Some writers, struck by passages in his warm and impulsive letters, in which he praised the best of what he saw in the British ruling classes unrestrainedly, have received and given the impression that he saw nothing else. It would be quite as easy, and quite as accurate, to select passages which would make him seem an Anglophobe. He was weighed down in England by what seemed to him the omnipresence of the forgotten man. He felt that England, while a genuine democracy from a political point of view, was anything but democratic socially, or in her relations with less advanced peoples. He had no hesitation in telling the British to their faces that he could find among them no such opportunities for the wage earners, no such equalities in education or in access to the higher walks of life as he had known at home. One even wonders whether he did full justice to Mr. Lloyd George's remarkable new deal. He found the British dull and unreceptive where new ideas were concerned; he found the working classes deplorably servile, not taking sufficient account, perhaps, of the fact that ingrained class consciousness is one of the most difficult of all social phenomena to overcome.

Yes, he railed against the British, time after time; but all the same he loved them for their past, and for the virtues World War II was to make so evident. He regarded them as superior to all people save his own, and was earnestly intent on persuading them to adopt new and better courses. In the future, as he saw it, Britain and America should share the leadership of the world—but always with America ahead. Again and again he used the phrase, "the future of the world is ours." And the British, despite the frankness of his criticisms, took him quickly to their hearts. He was exactly what they liked in an American. He made no attempt whatever to be British; he was transparently honest; he had that hallmarked courtesy that comes from tolerance and modesty and kindliness; and, quite frank about what seemed to him their faults, he was always ready to see the best in them. They even listened to his criticisms, perhaps even pondered them. His presence was felt wherever he appeared; and Mrs. Page, who shared to the full the affection and admiration which he won, found her tea table surrounded by some of the greatest public figures in England.

No wonder the President wrote that he could not be glad enough that he had put Page where he was; that Page had taught him that real information about other peoples and their aims and policies was to be had at dinner tables and house parties, rather than in diplomatic documents. No wonder he wrote: "You are a lamp to my feet." At one of the most critical periods in world history Page was building a bridge between the two greatest English-speaking capitals, and above all between the President and Sir Edward Grey.

One needs to know but little of Grey to understand why his relations with the American Ambassador passed rapidly from liking to friendliness and from friendliness to intimacy. For Grey, though on one or two occasions driven to subterfuge in the interests of his country, was as honest and direct as Page. And, like Page, he was a friendly person, who found it a relief to know an ambassador with whom he could discuss the most difficult questions as man to man. His liking for America seems to have resembled that of Page for Britain; and the ideals of the two men for their countries were never far apart. Similar tastes in books and recreation helped to cement the tie. When they talked of Wordsworth now and then, at times when things were difficult, they were showing mutual realization that an *épanchement de cœur* is sometimes to be reckoned among the authentic processes of superfine diplomacy. The relation was a thoroughly two-sided one; but Page always felt that he was initiating Grey into the American viewpoint. Wilson was informed of all this at frequent intervals; and his reaction seemed one of genuine pleasure. Considering how reserved he was, it is notable that he should have written the Foreign Secretary to express the hope that Grey would look upon him as a friend.

Unfortunately, Page's relations with the State Department were almost as unhappy as his relations with the Foreign Office were pleasant. To some extent this was his fault, to some extent Bryan's, and to a large extent the fault of no one in particular. Politics had placed the Great Commoner in a post he was anything but qualified to fill; and politics, combined with practice, and with Wilson's conception of the presidency, gave him power to irritate ambassadors but not control them. Bryan had certain endowments as Secretary of State, especially from Wilson's point of view. For one thing he worked. Moreover, his genuine benevolence was an asset. Arbitration had no greater protagonist. His great aim was the conclusion with as many other states as possible of treaties calling for impartial investigation of all disputes between nations which arbitration failed to settle; and for agreement that no hostilities should commence until this "cooling" period (perhaps a year) was at an end. Wisely, the states were left free to take such action as they might choose later. Moreover, Bryan concluded or renewed arbitration treaties which would rule out hostilities at any time or stage. Nearly all the principal states signed the "Bryan" treaties; but Germany, to her own vast detriment, refused.

Wilson, full of belief that the world was rapidly on the way to better things, adopted Bryan's policy as his own: Page, while so much closer to *Realpolitik,* had neither reason nor occasion to oppose it. But Page found the State Department's methods of conducting diplomacy intolerable. For no matter how much Wilson might decide on policies, revise dispatches or even write them, it was the State Department with which Page had to deal. Dispatches had to go to it; instructions came out of it; and information was supposed to issue from it, too. Perhaps Page, an idealist and something of a perfectionist as well, was more impatient than he need have been; but his annoyance was not primarily personal. His pride in his country was hurt by seeing in what estimation America's "foreign minister" was held abroad. It is within common remembrance that even on this side of the water the air was full of such stories as that Bryan did not know that Francis Joseph was addressed as Emperor-King, and had sent an urgent request that all discussion of religion and national churches be eliminated from deliberations on Balkan problems! Page was jarred constantly by official bad manners, by Bryan's carelessness in acknowledging or in rejecting international courtesies, by unconventional and unnecessary harshness in the phrasing of our notes, by the State Department's failure to give him information even on the most vital matters during his first months in London. He had no idea whether his dispatches were ever read, or whatever became of them. He complained that the most confidential letter he ever sent the President had "disappeared" in Washington, though he had good reason to conclude that it had reached Bryan's desk. Even that was not the worst. At least three times during the early period of his embassy he had to apologize to Grey for the release to the American press of confidential communications made to him.

It would not be worth while to pay so much attention to Page's success in London had it not become of such vital importance after the outbreak of war, or to dwell on his tribulations and protests if they did not underline House's complaint that Wilson paid too little attention to foreign affairs before 1915. The President showed no concern over the State Department's shortcomings. He laughed over "the well of silence" in the State Department's building, and encouraged Page to keep in direct touch with him. He must have realized that not even House was giving him more devoted and admiring service. And Page, at least as much as House, was trying to draw him, and through him the nation, into greater participation in world affairs. Such differences as there were between House and Page reflected their temperaments. House, always cool and judicial, calmly concluded that Wilson could benefit other nations and ourselves, too, by formulating and following a policy of greater "neighborliness" toward Latin America, and of using our friendly offices to reduce the causes of acute friction in Europe. Page, deeply reflective, but imaginative, impulsive, and ardent, leaped to the idea of our world leadership, with Britain as a junior partner. Both were tugging insistently at Wilson.

No one is likely ever to succeed in making Wilson picturesque, as a statesman at any rate. His policies were almost as sober and conventional as the gray suits he preferred to wear. In handling foreign questions during his first term, his touch seemed less certain than when domestic matters were to the fore; and instead of the insistent drive to get things done as fast as possible, he showed that attitude of "watchful waiting" which some people were to find so exasperating during the period of our neutrality. But there was the same inflexible determination about principles, the same insistence on moderation and morality. Mr. Notter sums up much of his attitude in a sentence:

This man . . . saw America as an expression of moral, Christian impulse, and American greatness as shown in the way she used her power.

If Colonel House and Mr. Page had made a close study of Wilson's speeches and writings over many years, they would have seen that he was quite ready to play the role they had assigned to him, whenever domestic questions were not too pressing. If foreign statesmen had done the same, they would have been better prepared for his attitude when we were still neutral, and even for his policies at Paris. He stood for "America First" in nobility of service. But what could America do to serve the world? Why, she had a "manifest destiny" to promote world peace; that, and to make herself the pattern and patron of self-government. Nations as well as individuals had claims to full opportunities for development. We should have no right, of course, to interfere with another nation's internal affairs; but (and here Wilson faced but could not solve an inconsistency) we could use influence, even a little pressure, for another nation's own good.

Some peoples might not be ready for self-government, but they should be assisted in getting ready. There were, for instance, China and Santo Domingo; and there were our possessions and dependencies: Hawaii and the Philippines and Puerto Rico. Cuba, it seemed, was already prepared. Again, we should see to it that the money power had no more influence in our foreign than in our domestic politics. Here, too, materialism, monopoly, and privilege were to be excluded as far as possible. As for our relations with other great Powers, we should always remain quite independent, free to act as we chose; or rather, free to lead. But complete isolation was no more feasible than it was morally justifiable. We should co-operate in good works with other Powers. In particular, we should co-operate with Britain, since she agreed with us that the rule of law—natural, civic, and international— was a first essential of peace and order. And she, too, preferred evolution to revolution. Our best opportunity to show our sincerity in applying these principles would be found in our dealings with Latin America. Wilson's beliefs had, in fact, been applied to half a dozen concrete problems before the end of 1913, but especially to the questions of Mexico and of tolls charged in the Panama Canal.

Mexico has often stirred the sympathies and puzzled the brains of

Americans; but never more so than in the first years of Wilson's presidency. In 1911 the long dictatorship of Diaz had come to a violent end.
Diaz had given the country unaccustomed order and unaccustomed
material prosperity; but two of the conditions he left behind were to
trouble Wilson sorely. Foreign capital had poured into the country,
bringing with it, as usual, the danger that its owners would urge pressure, or even intervention, if their investments were threatened. And
prosperity had not touched the masses. Nearly all the good land was
in great estates. The peasants, often peons, toiled along in poverty
and illiteracy, having little if any idea what democracy, political or
economic, might mean.

The revolution of 1911 had seemed to produce nothing but confusion
worse confounded, blood-spattered, and offering no promise of real
leadership. Madero, who had overthrown Diaz on the pretext of making the government more "constitutional," and of distributing some
of the land, had opened the floodgates of violence. He was overthrown
and shot in cold blood by a bandit named Huerta little more than a
fortnight before Wilson had been sworn into office as President. But
within four days another contender for power, Carranza, had appeared,
claiming to be a reformer in the Madero manner. Foreign investors, in
great alarm, were soon appealing to their governments. In the amount
of investments in Mexico and the number of citizens domiciled there
this country stood easily first. But Britain stood easily second; and hers
was no small stake at a time when the importance of oil was just being
recognized.

Sir Edward Grey regarded Huerta with disgust; but the good, old-
fashioned custom of all governments had been to let the Latin-
American republics stew in their own juice, and give recognition to
whoever rose to the top. Grey compromised by recognizing Huerta
provisionally, keeping his hands free to reverse his action later. Would
Wilson give recognition of any kind? Recognition was very important
to Mexico's murderer-dictator. On it hinged his ability or inability to
borrow money. It also seemed important to people who had investments in Mexico. It would help Huerta to maintain "order," partially
by means of borrowed money. Certain businessmen made their desires
known at Washington. What especially troubled them was the fear
that Britain was stealing the game. They pointed out that the British
Ambassador to Mexico, Sir Lionel Carden, was notoriously anti-
American; and they claimed (though on what evidence does not ap-

pear) that he was supporting Huerta in the interests of a British oil
magnate, Lord Cowdray.

Wilson, after considering the possibility of following Grey's example,
had decided to give no recognition, even if, as actually occurred,
Huerta manipulated his own "election" to the presidency. He had
found the man's very claim to office insupportable. In his annual message to Congress, at the beginning of December, he had used language
seldom applied to even the *de facto* head of a friendly nation:

> There can be no certain prospect of peace in America until General
> Huerta has surrendered his usurped authority. . . . Mexico has no govern-
> ment . . . the attempt has broken down. . . . Even if the usurper had
> succeeded . . . he would have set up nothing but a precarious and hateful
> power.

But Wilson's objections went far deeper. There was to be an end to
"dollar diplomacy," which Mr. Bryan neatly defined for him:

> The financiers charge excessive rates on the ground that they must be
> *paid* for the risk that they take and as soon as they collect their pay for
> the risk, they then proceed to demand . . . that the *risk* shall be elimi-
> nated by governmental coercion.

He himself had told a public gathering, back in October, that dollar
diplomacy was a denial of equality, and so of essential friendship,
between American States:

> You hear of "concessions" to foreign capitalists in Latin America. You
> do not hear of concessions to foreign capitalists in the United States. They
> are not granted concessions. They are invited to make investments. . . .
> We must prove ourselves . . . friends [of the Latin-American coun-
> tries] . . . upon terms of equality and honor.

Wilson would have none of the argument (endorsed by Mr. Taft) that
the working of concessions might be good for the "less advanced"
countries. In spite of his summer outburst, his "own judgments and
principles" were supplying him with "standards." There should be no
recognition of Huerta, nor intervention either. "Wilson's refusal to
intervene by force of arms in Mexico for the protection of American
lives and investments," wrote President Eliot to Lord Bryce, "seems to
me the best thing that has been done for the peace of the world by any
government—ancient or modern." But deepest of all, perhaps, in Wil-

son's mind lay his desire to do something for the Mexican people. It came out a few months later in his interview with Samuel Blythe:

My ideal is an orderly and righteous government in Mexico; but my passion is for the submerged 85 per cent of the people of that Republic who are now struggling toward liberty. . . .

The President showed some naïveté in believing that he fully understood the Mexican problem, and especially in thinking that Carranza, or even Villa, Carranza's insubordinate lieutenant, was more "constitutional" than Huerta. But Huerta was the immediate obstacle to better conditions, and at least as undeserving of American support as any of Mexico's would-be rulers. Wilson had taken steps to weaken him before going to Pass Christian.

Huerta's fate was sealed when such support as he had secured from the British was withdrawn; and it is commonly said that Wilson secured the withdrawal by a "deal" with the British Government concerning the Panama Canal tolls. The question of the tolls was simplicity itself as compared with the other. The British, who had had some real claims to participation in the construction and control of the Panama Canal, had finally relinquished them in the Hay-Pauncefote Treaty of 1901, on condition that the vessels of all nations should be treated equally. But after it had been decided that tolls should be charged for use of the Canal, Congress, in the summer of 1912, had passed a bill exempting American vessels engaged only in coastwise traffic from their payment. The vote had been non-partisan. The grievance this created concerned all other countries; but it concerned Britain first of all. Moreover, men high in the councils of both the Democratic and Republican parties regarded the act as a breach of faith, and so a blight upon our record as a strictly honorable nation.

Among the Democrats, House and Page were strongly of this mind. Bryan was not, though he was willing finally to advocate the dropping of the exemption in the interests of international harmony. Wilson had told House of his opposition to the exemption nearly six weeks before his inauguration, but he had been in no hurry to press the matter. The formal opening of the Canal was still some distance off; his first interest was in the passage of the tariff and banking bills; and the question of the tolls was bound to be so contentious that he would do well to establish his leadership before referring the matter to Congress. The exemption had been endorsed in both the Democratic and

Republican platforms of 1912. Yet an understanding between Wilson and Grey concerning its repeal, and about the situation in Mexico, had been reached before Wilson had gone to Pass Christian.

In London, Page had worked unremittingly. House, visiting England in the preceding June, had informed Grey authoritatively of the President's personal attitude and intentions concerning the tolls. Grey had been quick to reciprocate. His Ambassador to this country not being in good health, he had sent his own able secretary, Sir William Tyrrell, to Washington in the autumn, to discuss the two pending questions with the President. Tyrrell was astonished at the President's candor. "If some of the veteran diplomats could have heard us, they would have fallen in a faint," he said to House. What struck him most of all was the paternalism toward Latin America which Wilson had revealed. "I am going to teach the South American Republics to elect good men," he had declared! An understanding had been reached; but the term "deal" seems rather harsh. It is true that Wilson coupled the two questions when asking the Senate Foreign Relations Committee to support him when he brought the tolls question before Congress, but he had made his decision regarding the tolls before Huerta had seized power, and Grey had always been reluctant to give even provisional recognition to Huerta. At any rate, by the time Wilson went to Pass Christian, it remained only for Grey to move Sir Lionel Carden to Brazil, and for Wilson to ask Congress to reverse its action in the matter of the tolls. Grey straightway carried out his part of the bargain, thus helping to procure the downfall of Huerta in the following July; though not before an unfortunate brush had cost the lives of American marines at Vera Cruz. That was easy enough for him to do. But it also remained for Wilson to persuade Congress to go back to a strict interpretation of the Hay-Pauncefote Treaty; and that was sure to put a heavy strain upon his leadership.

The avoidance of long quotations is a wise and accepted practice, but it seems worth while to make an exception in the use of certain passages from the book Mr. Tumulty wrote about the President, when all the storms of Wilson's life were past:

The first word I received that the President contemplated addressing Congress, asking for the repeal of Panama Tolls, came about in this way: I was notified after dinner one evening that the President wished to confer with me in his study. When I arrived at the White House Mrs. Wilson met me and informed me of the plan which the President had in mind with reference to this matter and of his decision to issue a statement that night which would be carried in the newspapers the following morning, and of his determination to address Congress. . . . Mrs. Wilson showed considerable excitement over . . . the matter. . . . She said she had argued with the President . . . that if he intended to do so unusual a thing that now was the inopportune moment for it for the reason that it would create a party crisis and probably a split, the result of which we could not foresee. When I went into the President's study, he read me the announcement he had prepared for the papers.

Tumulty himself was much alarmed:

Frankly I put the whole political situation in the country before him as it would be affected by his attitude in this matter, saying to him that the stand he was about to take would irritate large blocks of Irish, Germans, and other anti-British elements in the country, and that we might expect that the leaders in our own party, the heads of the various committees, like Fitzgerald of Appropriations, Underwood of the Ways and Means, and Clark, the Speaker of the House, would be found in solid opposition, and that, at a time when we needed every bit of strength to put our party program of domestic legislation into effect, it seemed to me unwise to inject this matter, which could only be a disturbing element, into our party's councils.

But Wilson would not budge:

In discussing the matter with me . . . he said: "I knew the view you would take of it, but, unfortunately, every argument you lay before me in opposition . . . is purely a partisan one. . . . I am the trustee of the people and I am bound to take cognizance of the fact that by reason of our attitude on Panama Tolls . . . we are looked upon as a nation that does not live up to its plighted word. We may have made a very bad bargain with England on Panama Tolls, but it will be all the more credit to us if we stand by an agreement even when it entails a sacrifice. . . .

Still Tumulty argued, warning the President of the effect his action might have upon the congressional elections in the autumn. Wilson answered that he had considered all possible effects, but was obliged to think first of America, and could not have "her word questioned in every court in Europe." It is very possible that Mr. Tumulty's account of the conversation was given from memory, and that, even considering how much a conversation of this sort must have impressed him, he went wrong in some details. But certainly in all substance his story stands, and is of marked significance. The "large blocks of Irish,

Germans, and other anti-British elements in the country" were to give Wilson constant trouble all through the period of our neutrality in World War I, and to bear some part in defeating his plans for an enduring peace.

The Irish block was easily the most dangerous. It did not, of course, include all Americans of Irish extraction or Irish birth. There were a considerable number of whom it could be said, as Wilson had said of Commodore Barry, that they were not Irish-Americans, but Irishmen who had become Americans; that they would vote according to the way things looked in this country, not abroad. But the "hyphenate" element (blissfully unconscious for the most part of being hyphenate) was probably preponderant in numbers, and certainly preponderant in strength. It was largely concentrated in great cities; it was organized in a network of societies, of which some were not in purpose at all political; and it was so hot with passion (even as anti-British political groups have been inflamed against each other in Ireland itself) that it could easily be swayed by orators to a point of insensibility to the sort of cool reasoning that was Wilson's chief asset.

Politicians had soon learned to capitalize on the undying hatred of most Irish-Americans for the British and all their works. Britain's treatment of Ireland had been the worst, the almost inexplicable, blot upon her record as the pattern and patron of freedom in Europe; and the orators often made a black record seem blacker still by adding fables to facts. It was, of course, among the Democrats, less associated than the Republicans with the employer class, and more receptive of immigrants, that the greater part of the Irish-Americans had found their political home. Democratic state and municipal machines had come largely into their hands. It was no uncommon thing to hear Irish songs sung at Democratic rallies, as though the party had somehow stemmed out of Erin.

Between Wilson and this powerful element of his party there was a great gulf fixed. Tumulty, as good an Irish Catholic as the best, and as competent to speak of Wilson's views on this question as any man, has borne evidence that Wilson was fully conscious of all that the Irish had suffered at British hands, and was deeply sympathetic with their efforts to regain full self-government. In New Jersey there had been a group of men of Tumulty's type who had worked with and for him steadfastly. But Wilson was ardently, invincibly American—too much so to tolerate people whose allegiance to America was not entire. The "hyphenates," as he had styled them, would have been genuinely astonished and hurt to find their patriotism questioned. America had been a land of hopes and dreams to most of them and their forebears. Thanks to their capacity and willingness to do the hardest work, and to their flair for politics, they had made some of the hopes and dreams come true. They had no desire to live in any country save America. But they saw no reason why they should not use their political power to shape our foreign policy for the special benefit of Ireland, and to oppose any friendly relations between the American and British governments. It did not seem to occur to them that the Government at Washington would be in hard case indeed if citizens stemming from each of the nationalities blended into the American people should follow their example. It did not seem to occur to them that international usage no more allowed our Government to interfere on behalf of Ireland than of Alsace-Lorraine, or Russian Poland, or Croatia. In fact (for degrees of "advancement" do not count in such matters) Britain would have had equal right to interfere on behalf of the Philippines. Nor did it seem to occur to the Irish-Americans that American unfriendliness toward Britain might not be in the interests either of America or of world peace.

But these considerations counted tremendously with Wilson. In handling foreign policy, as in handling the tariff, he felt himself to be the trustee and representative of the people as a whole, not especially of those who had come from Ireland or any other place. He had much the same feeling toward lobbyists for the Irish or any other nation as toward lobbyists for the sugar interests. No people were to feel his detachment more acutely than did the British and their American friends between 1914 and 1917. But the Irish-Americans were not temperamentally fitted for detachment and reasoning in politics. So the gulf between them and the President remained unbridgeable to the end, no matter how party leaders succeeded in screening it at times.

It first came into view on the Panama tolls question, as Tumulty had foretold. The President had, in fact, needed no warning. He had been especially anxious about the attitude of Senator O'Gorman of New York, as a member of the Senate Foreign Relations Committee. Rightly or wrongly, he saw the Senator as a man who "constantly [regarded] himself as an Irishman contending against England, rather than as a United States senator upholding the dignity and welfare of this country." House reported that the Senator's son-in-law, Dudley Field

Malone, had promised to reason with him. The whole committee having been brought to the White House for discussion, and converted to some extent at least, the President followed his usual tactics by delivering a brief message to Congress and the public on March 5. Asking for the repeal of the act of 1912, as a "contravention" of the Hay-Pauncefote Treaty, he went on:

> Whatever may be our differences of opinion concerning this . . . measure . . . outside the United States . . . the language of the treaty is given but one interpretation, and that interpretation precludes the exemption I am asking you to repeal.

Tumulty was startled by the almost minatory tone of other parts of the message:

> No communication I have addressed to the Congress carried with it graver or more far-reaching implications as to the interest of the country. . . .
> I ask this of you in support of the foreign policy of the administration. I shall not know how to deal with other matters of even greater delicacy and nearer consequence if you do not grant it to me in ungrudging measure.

It was a daring demand. Senator Lodge thought the matter should be arbitrated; and arbitration would apparently have satisfied Sir Edward Grey. But Wilson, no lover of half measures, preferred to wipe the slate immediately.

The nationalist-isolationist and flatly anti-British elements were up in arms. Senator Borah, arguing in lawyer parlance that we were entitled to any advantages under the Treaty which we had not specifically renounced, would not "by a damn sight" see the exemption given up, and was prepared for a "last-ditch" fight. There was, to quote Tumulty, "a shower of personal abuse and vituperation from Irish organs and from a group of newspapers that were presently to appear as the chief supporters of Germany." Though Burleson and McAdoo worked desperately to keep the party in line, veteran Democrats in both Houses deserted the President. He was saved by the younger men of the party, and by the help of some Republicans. Mr. Elihu Root, then senator from New York, made a brilliant speech in support of the message; and Senator Lodge both spoke and voted in its favor. Wilson had won; but he had learned what to expect from certain elements of his party when it came to foreign policy. Neither was there much if any evidence that the people had hearkened to his voice. He must have been relieved in turning back to his domestic program, by taking the trusts in hand.

Wilson had of course been thinking about the trusts for a full year, to say nothing of some twenty previous years at least. He had hardly settled into his offices at the White House before he had set the Departments of Justice and Commerce the task of finding what the trusts were doing, and what they were capable of doing. The Sherman Anti-Trust Act of 1890 was much better than nothing, but not nearly good enough. It had been all very well to forbid every "combination . . . in restraint of trade . . . among the several states or with foreign nations," and to decree heavy penalties. But loose phrasing had given the courts great latitude in interpreting the act; and the penalties had not had much effect. Juries, it seemed, were unwilling to convict in individual cases, knowing that the acts which they were punishing were common practice. Moreover, as Wilson was fond of pointing out, the punishment of a corporation was felt by a mass of generally innocent stockholders, in so far as it was felt at all. Wicked directors got off too easily.

And big business had grown bigger and bigger. Ten years after the Sherman bill was passed, United States Steel organized the first billion-dollar corporation in the country. Mr. Taft had instituted impressive proceedings against American Tobacco and Standard Oil; but still the trusts insisted upon flourishing. In the 1912 campaign all three parties had promised to take them in hand; and the Democrats had promised specifically to make war on interlocking directorates, stock watering, price discrimination, and other undesirable corporation practices. The principal author of the Seven Sisters laws in New Jersey was more than ready to carry out these campaign promises.

Occupied as he had been with the tariff, with banking and currency, with portents of trouble regarding Mexico, with questions upon end, Wilson had been gathering information and opinions about the trusts since his first weeks in office. Information had come from the Departments of Justice and Commerce, and from Joseph E. Davies, as head of the Bureau of Corporations. For opinions the President had relied especially on Mr. Brandeis. The preparation of anti-trust legislation had devolved mainly on Henry·Clayton, chairman of the House Committee on the Judiciary. Some members of the Cabinet, feeling that Congress and the country were getting out of breath, counseled delay.

Early in 1914 they were re-enforced from an unexpected quarter. The papers carried the news that certain financial magnates, headed by Mr. Morgan and Mr. George F. Baker, were resigning from various directorates. Though the magnates directly or indirectly retained widespread power in big business, the papers talked of an "epoch-making event"; and a writer in *Harper's Weekly* used the occasion to stress the President's ascendancy:

He dispenses the high and the low and the middle justice. . . . He is, indeed, chief magistrate to the uttermost fringe of his authority.

Wilson was pleased by the resignation of the magnates. He was willing to give them credit for sincerity. But he was not willing to take chances. The legislation concerning the trusts should go forward as planned.

On January 20 he addressed Congress benignantly, expressing the happy belief that antagonism between business and Government was at an end; and that Congress, in dealing with the trusts, would merely give expression to "the best business judgment" and the "business conscience and honor" of the nation. These, it appeared, demanded action against interlocking directorates and holding companies, and called for a federal trade commission which could direct the dissection of productive industries which had "passed the point up to which combination may be consistent with the public interest." The President also asked that power be given the Interstate Commerce Commission to regulate the issue of securities by the railroads. The message breathed a beautiful optimism which the sequel did not justify. There was fiery discussion in Congress when the new proposals, put concretely in the "Five Brothers" bills (so dubbed in delicate compliment to the Seven Sisters), were presented to Congress. In the party there was obvious restiveness, disinclination on the part of some members to vote.

But Wilson, using much the same technique as in 1913, eventually got his way. The Five Brothers, reduced to three in the Clayton Anti-Trust Act, the Trade Commission Act, and the Rayburn Act, were slowly pressed through. The condemned practices of great corporations were all forbidden; and the language of the Sherman Act in banning "every" combination restraining trade was corrected by the exclusion of labor unions, agricultural organizations, and other bodies operating outside the strictly business world. The Federal Trade Commission of five members, well paid and rigidly non-partisan, was given power to investigate trade, to report, to make general rules, to issue injunctions, but not to punish. In fact, the new legislation placed less emphasis on penalties than the Sherman Act had done. To use the words of a recent special study, the trust was "no longer an ogre . . . to be bludgeoned into submission with . . . a dissolution suit, but rather the result of a number of malignant growths each of which must be cauterized." The three acts were pressed through; but at the last minute Congress refused to pass the Rayburn Act, giving the Interstate Commerce Commission power to regulate the issue of securities by railroads. It refused because the investment market was so upset by the outbreak of World War I. Wilson's reform campaign was checked by what he regarded as the criminal stupidity of European governments. He was angry with them, one and all.

CHAPTER IX

Keeping the People Out of War

THERE is a story that before our entrance into the war one of Wilson's daughters impulsively expressed some admiration for the qualities of the French people, and then, checking herself, asked repentantly: "Oh dear! Was that unneutral?"' It is as well authenticated as such stories can be, and seems entirely plausible. A dutiful daughter may well have taken seriously the President's much-quoted appeal to the nation on August 19, 1914:

> We must be impartial in thought as well as in action, must put a curb upon our sentiments . . . this great country of ours . . . should show herself . . . a Nation that neither sits in judgment upon others nor is disturbed in her own counsels.

House declared himself delighted with the message; but some people read it with astonishment. It was self-contradictory, for one thing. It contained the admission that "the utmost variety of sympathy and desire" among the American people, intense desire that one side or the other should be victorious, was "natural and inevitable."' But in the next breath Wilson seemed to·say the inevitable must be averted somehow. And then, how could a man who had proved, to his own cost, his deep attachment to morality in foreign relations, now ask his countrymen (who knew, among other things, what was happening to Belgium) to refrain from sitting in judgment? In other words, not to exercise any moral sense. And how could he ask this of them without asking it of himself? Yet the plea became something of a *leitmotiv* in his speeches. As late as January 1916 he begged a Pittsburgh audience to be "neutral in spirit and in feeling." Almost everyone agreed, in the first months at least, that we should be neutral; but why so astringent a neutrality? Even though "benevolent" neutrality, allowing some favoritism in action, was obviously impossible in view of public sentiment, indication of some sympathy with the French or British could have been given in the tone of notes sent to them, or in the extension of certain courtesies. Nothing of the kind appeared. Some of the reasons for Wilson's attitude are plain enough. Others are matters only of guesswork. Among these must be placed the circumstances under which the appeal of August 19 was issued.

On August 1 Germany declared war on Russia. On August 6 Mrs. Wilson died at the White House. The President had apparently given up hope about a week before. During the weeks that followed he bore up bravely, working incessantly, and bringing in relatives to help him tide over the shock. But to those with whom he was most intimate he sometimes revealed himself as a distracted and sometimes almost despairing man. The future must have looked very bleak.

Mrs. Wilson had managed to make even some of the rooms in the White House homelike; but without her the very essence of home life would be gone. It had been such a relief on some evenings to close a door, forget that he was President, stretch out on the hearthrug before the fire, and recite poetry to his wife, or listen while she read to him. It had always been a relief, an adjustment of perspective, merely to meet her when he came home. Even when they had talked of politics and affairs of state, she had always been soothing and helpful. She had remained a keen but sympathetic critic of all his speeches and writings, a complete and utterly trustworthy confidante. Her devotion to service, both through her husband and along her own special lines, had been shown in many gracious ways. Congress, informed that she was sinking, had quickly passed a bill for slum clearance in Washington, which she had very much at heart, so that she might be told before her final lapse into unconsciousness. From Murray Bay, where he was summering, Mr. Taft wrote very understandingly:

> Mrs. Wilson was a very sweet woman and offered an antidote to his [Wilson's] somewhat angular disregard of other people's feelings. . . . The White House will seem very solitary to him without her, for . . . there is a splendid isolation about it that makes sorrow keener.

The Mrs. Wilson of early days had lived on to the end. To the outward world she had managed, as she said, "to make believe very hard" that she was "a different kind of woman" from what she had been in the early Princeton days; but to the President she and all that she stood for had been the same. Now she would be gone. He would not even have his three daughters around him, for within the year one of them had become Mrs. Sayre and another Mrs. McAdoo. He was the last man to let private grief interfere with public duties, yet it does not seem an entirely unwarranted guess that his private distress of mind helps to explain the self-contradictory and unrealistic features of his first appeal to the people concerning the world war. But it could have had nothing to do with his recurrent appeals for neutrality "in spirit and in feeling." Those, it seems, were nothing more than rhetorical efforts to keep the fires of passion in America banked down as far as possible.

One certain determinant of his first reaction was his surprise and shock in realizing that war had come. As Page had hoped so ardently, he had been prepared to help, all in good time, in making America serve as the pattern and patron of all freedom-loving nations in the twentieth century, much as Britain had done for Europe in the nineteenth. As House and Bryan had so desired, in their different ways, he had been ready to help other nations to find enduring peace—when he should have time to do it. But now, while he was still occupied with his first task of making America a better place for Americans, he found himself facing a war which seemed to him as stupid and unnecessary as it was bound to be harmful. It would not only hurt all the participants, but hurt his fellow citizens in their unity and their prosperity. It would interfere with some of his plans for them. It was hard for him to cope with it, because he had no clear idea as to what it was all about. Before his inauguration he had known almost nothing of European countries by personal observation or contact, and little more about their relations than other Americans of good education and intelligence. During the time of his presidency he had become more interested and a good deal better informed. Colonel House, by going abroad and picking up acquaintances, had secured some understanding of the danger that had been keeping every foreign office and commander in chief in Europe on the *qui vive* for years.

House had considered the possibility of reducing the danger by some kind of understanding between this country, Britain, and Germany, with France and Japan as other possible participants. He had talked with Page and Grey. Grey had been more than ready to let him try his hand. In the autumn of 1913 Sir William Tyrrell, of course with Grey's consent, had encouraged House to see what he could do at Berlin, especially by a private interview with the Kaiser. House was to stress the increasing cordiality of Anglo-American relations, and suggest that Germany should share in this spirit of good fellowship. So the way to a limitation of naval armaments might be made easier. Wilson, then much more interested in the Federal Reserve Act, had seemed "almost" enthusiastic about the plan; but his first annual message to Congress, on December 2, 1913, had shown him curiously blind to the increasing number of cumulus clouds that were piling up over Europe. He had spoken of a "cloud" over Mexico; but, he had told Congress:

> many happy manifestations multiply about us of a growing cordiality and sense of community of interest among the nations, foreshadowing an age of settled peace and good will.

The context suggests that he was pinning his faith to a future in which "Bryan" treaties would cover the earth. However, he had encouraged House to continue his soundings, and to sail for Germany in May 1914. At Berlin, House had been startled by finding "militarism run stark mad" and by the bitterness of von Tirpitz toward the British. But the apparently more receptive attitude of the Kaiser and the German Foreign Office had encouraged him. So had Grey, when they met again in London.

Even after the assassination at Serajevo, the Colonel, still hopeful, had written the Kaiser, to assure him that the President and Grey were in deep sympathy with efforts to bring the three nations into closer touch. Before sailing for home he had had many conversations with members of the British Cabinet about international collaboration, especially in developing the "waste places" of the earth. He sailed for home just as the Austrian ultimatum went to Serbia, and just two days before Germany declared war on Russia. There have been differences of opinion as to what his mission might have accomplished had the assassination at Serajevo not occurred, and as to the President's real interest in it. But the point here is that House's hopeful letters must, if anything, have increased Wilson's horrified surprise in learning that war had come. Moreover, Wilson had not only been shocked, but probably rather chilled. Offers of assistance in averting war, made by the State Department and by Page just before hostilities commenced, had been "gratefully" but firmly declined by Grey. Considering the delicacy of the situation and Mr. Bryan's unfortunate and exaggerated reputation for ineptitude; considering Grey's passionate desire for peace, and the endorsement of his answer by men as well qualified to judge as House, Page, and Richard Olney, it may be judged that the British Foreign Office had acted wisely. But Wilson, very sensitive in his patriotism, was presumably irritated by the British refusal of these offers. Nor could his cordiality toward any of the belligerents have failed to suffer somewhat by the complete failure of an offer of mediation which he made to all the Powers on August 4.

And his Americanism gave him an even more direct grievance against all the belligerents. He always saw himself as the representative and mouthpiece of a substantially united people. And now, almost overnight, the people had become divided as never since the Civil War. Almost everyone agreed upon neutrality; but when it was realized that, should America become involved, it would almost inevitably be on the side of the Entente, nearly all Americans more or less took sides with one of two groups, each a conglomeration of diverse elements. Between these groups a struggle of opinion soon flamed into passion. The flare-up over the Panama Canal tolls had been no more than a light breeze which heralded this and ensuing storms. On one side was a group which stood for peace at almost any price. Its center was composed of men and women who hated or merely disliked Britain. There was a certain element of humor in the make-up of this core. It was rather amusing to see Irish and German hyphenates, very active and often noisy, as fellow workers with quiet Yankees, whose attitude was governed by what they believed to have been the issues in our Revolution and in the War of 1812. Often distinct from, but working with, the Anglophobes, were isolationists and pacifists. In cities such as Boston, where people of relatively recent Irish or German origin were numerous, you met people of the group at every turn; in some cities of the Middle West, where isolationism blended with hyphenism, it was not always comfortable to be outside the ranks. Before long, too, this group was drawing influential allies from people of the farm belt and cotton-growing states, who saw their incomes dwindling, thanks to the British blockade.

Wilson, who had singed his fingers in the Panama Canal tolls affair, had to be careful. The group comprised a large section of the public he so deeply wished to serve; and the large majority of its members were persons to whom a Democratic President, much in earnest about reform, would naturally look for votes. He had far less political affiliation with most of the people on the opposite side: men and women who loved France as a fountainhead of culture, or Britain as a wellspring of constitutional government; bankers and businessmen who had a financial stake in an Allied victory; and a great mass of lovers of constitutional government, who hated on principle all that was militaristic and authoritarian in Germany and Austria, and saw what they hated horribly exemplified in the rape of Belgium.

In the reaction of postwar days it became the fashion to set down the leaders of this second group as equally hyphenate with the first, or as mainly actuated by a lust for war profits, or even as warmongers. As applied to any but small elements, these charges do not stand. Most of its members adhered to it on principle; and a number of them were eminent. President Eliot, for example, was certainly not a profiteer, not a warmonger, nor yet a hyphenate. But during the first five months of our neutrality he pointed out that the Central Powers were a threat to world peace, in encouraging beliefs that the greatness of a state lay in its military strength; that treaties were not to be taken too seriously; and that armies, bureaucracies, and diplomatic corps might function secretly and outside popular control. He called attention to the great part that the fears the Powers had had of one another had played in bringing on the war; and how little commercial jealousy between Britain and Germany had had to do with it. But, irrespective of the virtues or vices of the groups or their leaders, the war was dividing the people, and greatly irritating their somewhat puzzled President.

Wilson's appeals for impartiality in thought, for a curb on even sentiment, for neutrality "in spirit and in feeling," brought him some abuse and ridicule; but no one can take them seriously now. He was merely working to keep the people as united and as cool as possible. He intended to keep the country out of war, because he was sure that our neutrality would be best for us and for all the world; and because he hated war on principle. The more detached and impartial the people were, the easier would be his task. But he could hardly have expected the people to live up to his preaching; because he failed signally to live up to it himself. House recorded in his diary a conversation he had with Wilson before the war had been on a month:

I was interested to hear him express as his opinion . . . that if Germany won it would change the course of our civilization and make the United States a military nation . . .

He felt deeply the destruction of Louvain, and I found him as unsympathetic with the German attitude as is the balance of America. He goes even further than I in his condemnation of Germany's part in this war. . . . He was particularly scornful of Germany's disregard of treaty obligations.

House's evidence by no means stands alone. Wilson's Attorney General, Mr. Gregory, told of a Cabinet meeting in which Wilson, facing protests that he was not showing sufficient vigor in resisting British encroachments on our rights as neutrals, answered that "the ordinary rules of conduct did not apply; that the Allies were standing with their backs to the wall, fighting wild beasts." One doubts whether the President really went as far as that. Tumulty's quiet testimony carries more weight:

> Witnessing from day to day the play of his feelings . . . I am certain that had he been free to do so he would have yielded to the impulse of championing a cause that in his heart of hearts he felt involved the civilization of the world . . . the idea of trusteeship . . . held him in check . . . the consciousness that . . . he had no right to permit his own passionate feelings to govern his public acts.

He did not find it easy to keep himself in check. He more than once referred to his efforts not to "see red." He confessed in Chicago that he was "careful to refrain from reading the details in the newspapers" [of what was happening in Europe]; and, while he assured Pittsburghers that he had tried "to hold off from every passion," he did not boast of success. Kansas City was informed that he "would not draw a passionate breath," for fear of disturbing "the nice equipoise" in America. Yes, the idea of trusteeship ruled him as usual; but it was beginning to expand from an idea of trusteeship to America to that of trusteeship to humanity through America. House and Page were ready to urge him on. "Be ready," Page wrote in August 1914, "for you will be called upon to compose this huge quarrel."

Irritated, disillusioned, lonely, but increasingly exalted, the President set the course that America was to follow until the day, two years and eight months later, when he asked Congress to recognize that we were at war. Good or bad, it was his course. Professor Lindsay Rogers brought this to the attention of the readers of the *Quarterly Review* more than four years later:

> Our proclamations of neutrality, our silence over the rape of Belgium and succeeding violations of International Law so far as they did not affect

our rights, and the policy pursued toward England and Germany which aimed at persuading them to abandon their restrictions upon American commerce, represented the will of an executive head who was not responsible to the Legislature.

He emphasized how determined Wilson had been to keep us out of war:

> He could have led the country into war when the Lusitania was sunk; the crime of the Sussex in April 1916 could likewise have been made a *casus belli* that would have been approved by the American people. The proposals of peace in December, 1916, were sent without consultation except perhaps with a few intimate friends.

Even the terms of peace which we were to support, the "Fourteen Points," while communicated to the Senate as "associated" with the President in determining our obligations, were all Wilson's. In the end, he broke relations with Germany, and armed our merchant ships, on his own responsibility.

It is generally agreed that he acted as the majority of the people wished him to do. But that is not to say that he merely *followed* the wishes of the majority. Just as he had attempted to shape public sentiment about the tariff and the Federal Reserve Act and our relations with Latin America and the Panama tolls affair, so he worked to keep it in line with his own ideas concerning our neutrality. It is impossible even to guess how much effect he had on popular feeling; but it is his intention which counts in any estimate of his statesmanship. This country was not to be involved in the European struggle, no matter what course that struggle took, unless and until Wilson felt that we were intolerably insulted, even attacked. As Mr. Bailey says: "The leading American . . . non-interventionist—was . . . Woodrow Wilson." His motives? Who ever really knows the motives of a statesman, living or dead? Who ever knows what part, for example, patriotism or egotism has played?

In considering this period of Wilson's career it is especially difficult to know. One may spend days and weeks in vainly searching his speeches and his policy during the time of our neutrality for evidence of his usual clear thinking and consistency. But it is easy to sympathize. The conflicts and confusion that one sees in him were those of the country. Only a few Americans, all or almost all of them people who knew Europe, or had given long consideration to foreign policy, were then able to point out considerations which are commonplaces now. Wilson, like the nation as a whole, was too baffled by the complexity of immediate problems to look much into the future. Like most people, he was apt to confuse three separate things: the origins of the war, the manner in which belligerent governments conducted it, and the probable effects upon the future of America and of the world in general, which the victory of one or other of the groups of belligerents would entail. The fact that it was too early to be sure about "war guilt" apparently seemed to him, the apostle of morality, an excuse for keeping silent about the Germans' treatment of Belgium. He would admit privately to House that a German victory "would change the course of our civilization and make the United States a military nation"; but he would never hear of our intervening to prevent a German victory.

Instead, he was eager to secure a negotiated peace on the basis of the *status quo ante,* not troubling himself about the fact that the *status quo* would provide no real peace, but an armed truce which any crisis might shatter. True, he was beginning, under strong promptings from House, to feel, as Grey did, that there should, in future, be an international organization to prevent war. But what chance would the old conditions have afforded for a successful organization of this kind, especially since not even House believed that this country would or could take part in it? Wilson seems to have based his ideas upon that vision of "an age of settled peace and good will," of which he had spoken in his message to Congress; and to have clung desperately to some of them, even when the mirage had disappeared. He was an ardent democrat, and, in the milder sense, a pacifist. He showed this in pronouncements seldom made by historians. Possibly forgetting the American Revolution for a moment, he told a New York audience that "force will not accomplish anything that is permanent." And more than once he was insistent that always "rulers," and never peoples, had been responsible for wars. So, regardless of facts or arguments, he clung to non-intervention and peace based on the *status quo.* And, persistently, he molded public sentiment along these lines, even while he threatened the Reich with war.

There will always be difference of opinion as to the President's wisdom; there can be none about his continuing desire to keep in touch with the people, to serve them, to represent them, to the best of his ability:

I would a great deal rather know what they are talking about around quiet firesides all over this country than what they are talking about in the cloakrooms of Congress. . . . There is only one way to hear these things, and that is constantly to go back to the fountains of American action.

He was always interested in knowing what foreign policy real Americans, not hyphenates or partisans, wanted. But he seemed more anxious to lead than to follow. "I am more interested," he once said to Tumulty, "in the opinion the country will have of me ten years from now than the opinion it may be willing to express today." It was not inclusion among the lists of "great" presidents that he wanted, but the approval of a nation he idolized and idealized:

I like that expression of Henry V . . . "If it be an offence to covet honour, am I the most offending soul alive," [*sic*] and I believe that could be said of America.

As usual service was to be the test:

Our whole duty . . . is summed up in this motto, "America first." Let us think of America before we think of Europe, in order that America may be fit to be Europe's friend when the day of tested friendship comes.

For America's cause was "the cause of humanity itself." And why not? "In the plenitude of its power and the unrestricted area of its opportunities," our nation "had nothing to covet." So we Americans were "a body of idealists more ready to lay down our lives for a thought than a dollar." And our service to a world at war? We could render that best by staying out. The wheels of commerce had to be kept going; the want and destruction that were piling up could not be met except through our riches; and our own calm, impartial judgment would be more needed still. A peace policy was what the people most desired:

If there is one passion more deep-seated in the hearts of our fellow countrymen than another, it is the passion for peace.

Just one thing might come even before peace—the preservation of our honor. By the beginning of 1916 Wilson, taking a "swing around the country" in the interest of preparedness, was warning audience after audience that the time might come when even peace would have to be sacrificed to that. He told a Chicago audience that we must maintain our position as "the moral trustee of the world," and a Des Moines gathering that we were "looked upon to sit in a sort of moral judgment upon the processes of war."

All this was very patriotic and pleasing. But a number of thoughtful Americans, while quite agreeing that the only possible policy for the immediate future was that of neutrality, were not sure that we could emulate Henry V, "be fit to be Europe's friend" when the day of testing came, or act as "moral trustee of the world," if we allowed the Central Powers to win. Senator John Sharp Williams, who, gratefully recalling bright student days at Heidelberg, loved the German people, warned that there were elements in Germany which dreamed of dominating the world; and that should the Allies go down to defeat, we Americans would have to resist German interference in South America, and build ourselves the greatest fleet in history. Long before the outbreak of the war Mr. Lewis Einstein, even then an experienced and much-traveled American diplomat, had pointed out that a German victory might lead to German attacks on Canada and on Caribbean islands; force our Navy to defend us (if it could) in two oceans; and leave us "confronted by an Empire supreme on land and sea." Hence, "the disintegration of the British Empire would be a defeat for America."

Other authorities, such as Mr. Root, who had noted evidences of German official hostility to us since the time of our war with Spain, were apprehensive, too. Theodore Roosevelt was so prophetic as to declare it "quite in the cards to see Germany and Japan . . . join together against the United States and any other Power that stood in their way." In varying degrees President Eliot, Colonel House, Mr. Gerard, and Mr. Lansing felt the same; and so, of course, did our Ambassador to Britain. Page often sat through the late night and early morning hours in a little room high up in the embassy, pondering how America might be first in the world under Wilson's leadership. With a close vision of the war, such as no one in Washington could share, he grieved deeply over the loss and suffering, and longed to see peace brought back as soon as possible. Both from British and from German sources he heard that there was likely to be a long stalemate. Something should be done to break it. But it seemed to him that if peace was to be lasting, German militarism would have to be put down. Why should not this country bring pressure on the Germans to make peace on terms that would remove the menace of their army from Europe, and do justice to Belgium? The President could warn the

German Government that in case of its refusal to make such a peace we should supply the Allies with everything they might need, even possibly with American warships, officered and manned by British crews.

Page should have realized, of course, that public opinion would never have allowed the President to follow such a policy; and that to suggest it to Wilson, once Wilson's mind was fixed, was only to court rebuke. For the President, while privately denouncing the Germans for their conduct in Belgium, and declaring that their victory would bring danger to America, agreed with most of the policy of his Secretary of State, who saw no moral issue; believed there was no danger; wanted to see a negotiated peace as soon as possible; and felt that we should offer equal resistance to British interference with our commerce and Germany's submarine campaign. As Mr. Van Alstyne points out, in his *American Diplomacy in Action,* this policy, carried to its logical conclusion, would have meant war with both Britain and Germany, or submission to both of them; and either war or submission would have given the Germans victory. Wilson differed from Mr. Bryan on one essential point: there was to be no war with Britain, not even a diplomatic break. But he could not announce that to the British people or to his countrymen.

Since the Germans did not begin to threaten American lives and property for half a year, the State Department commenced by devoting all its energies to the British. It had no light problem on its hands. Like the President, it intended to demand the last jot and tittle of our rights as neutrals in trading to the Continent. Wilson had reasons in plenty for demanding all that established rules of international law gave us: his trusteeship of our commercial interests; his desire to remain a mediator acceptable to Germany; the undesirability of giving the Anglophobes an excuse for making trouble; the interests of his party and the reform measures which he still expected it to carry through. But the British, whose great weapon against the Kaiser, especially in those opening months, was the blockade, quite naturally stretched their belligerent rights to the utmost possible limits. Moreover, their naval officers were tactless and peremptory. Unfortunately, international law, being a mere codification of established usage, left large areas in which the two sides could make conflicting claims—a sort of no man's land, which both sides wished to capture, and which was swept constantly by claims, protests, and arguments. During our own

Civil War the situation had been similar, with the British insisting on the rights of neutrals, and Washington on those of belligerents. But the conditions in 1914 were far more difficult, because the methods of warfare, the very nature of warfare, were being revolutionized.

Even thirty years ago war was commencing to be war between populations, not merely between armed forces. The Zeppelins, dropping their bombs on London, high lighted the change. The alterations that new methods of warfare were making in international usage are best exemplified in the matter of contraband. It had been easy in the old days to list absolute contraband—to set down the articles which armed forces used in fighting. It had not been too difficult to agree about conditional contraband, goods subject to confiscation only when intended for the use of armed forces. But now raw materials to be made into arms and munitions had become as important as arms and munitions themselves; and rapidly the lists of such materials grew longer. There was rubber, there was copper, and, above all, there was cotton. Its use in the making of high explosives had been developed just before the war broke out. England was consequently straining to expand the list of contraband to cover almost everything; while the State Department, in the interests, and under the pressure, of our producers and exporters, was straining as hard to keep it within bounds.

And what about food? The German Government controlled and allotted all that entered Germany; so how, asked the British, could any of it be distinguished as conditional contraband? Thus the two governments struggled. Old usage conflicted with such recent usage as that of the Russo-Japanese war; and even recent usage could be treated as inapplicable to changes still in progress. Even older usage could not give our State Department a clear case. The government at Washington had treated cotton as contraband in the War Between the States, since it was then used as currency.

The same struggle went on over the methods which the British used. Old methods of blockading having become impossible, thanks to mines and submarines, the British had closed all water lanes to Germany and her immediate neighbors. American merchantmen were informed that they would be guided through. Of course they were searched, especially after it was found that quantities of contraband were omitted from their manifests and ingeniously concealed. No real searching could be done at sea, especially not with submarines about, so our ships were taken into British ports. And the British were so slow in dealing with them that even Page was frequently angry.

Here in America the prices of our commodities and the volume of our exports both shot up. Yet murmurs against the British became a roar of protest that penetrated the State Department, the Capitol, and the White House. The protests mounted as the war went on. There was deep resentment over British seizures of American exports to Germany's neutral neighbors—neighbors from which she bought large quantities of these American goods. The British claimed that it was proper to keep these neighbors down to the figure of prewar imports from America. They insisted that our exports were none the less exports to Germany because they were landed in a Dutch or Scandinavian port, and sent on by rail or ferry to the Reich. And here again they found us vulnerable. No courts had more strongly upheld this doctrine of so-called "continuous voyage" than our own, when, during our Civil War, Federal warships had seized goods sent from Europe to Mexico for re-export to the Confederate States. But what attention would our producers and exporters pay to that? What interested them was the widespread belief that Britain was more particular about rationing Germany's neutral neighbors when it came to America's exports than to her own. They were still further enraged by British interference with our mails, and the report that British manufacturers were profiting at our expense from trade secrets which the censorship disclosed. They did not know, or did not care to know, that contraband was being sent by mail, and that information of great value to the German Government was relayed from Britain to Germany by way of this country. How could they know or weigh either facts or law? So all that many of them saw in British practices were new instances of British arrogance.

Since the War of 1812 (which was forgotten in Britain), any question that had to do with "visit and search" had touched a particularly sore spot in America. Our producers and businessmen had some genuine grievances in British procrastination and in that stretching of international law to which belligerents (which have so much more at stake than neutrals) are always given. But their sense of grievance apparently far outran realities. The British spent great sums in buying what they seized; and Mr. Van Alstyne has pointed out that "after the war, when the question of claims arose, it developed that, with very few exceptions, the 'American' cargoes about which the State

Department wrote profuse notes of protest to London were not American-owned but German-owned." But the position of Wilson and the State Department was very difficult. Although our grievances were vastly exaggerated, thanks largely to stimulation coming from various anti-British groups, the feeling about them was genuine and natural. So the barrage of notes went on; and Sir Edward Grey wrote his Ambassador at Washington in deep distress:

> What is felt here is that while Germany deliberately planned a war of pure aggression, has occupied and devastated large districts in Russia, Belgium and France, inflicting great wrong on innocent populations, the only act on record on the part of the United States is a protest singling out Great Britain as the only Power whose conduct is worthy of reproach.

British sentiment was also in error; but it was shared in more or less degree by great numbers of Americans. There was another no man's land in this country, raked by the recriminations and protests of the pro-Ally and anti-British groups. The White House and the State Department received the fire of both.

Sympathy for the President and the State Department is increased by remembrance that both groups of combatants in Europe, assisted by eager friends in America, were drenching the people with propaganda, legitimate and illegitimate, true and false—with the British holding distinct advantages in every way. But it is somewhat diminished by a certain lack of realism in the position they took up. They knew full well how hard it had always been for neutrals to persuade or force belligerents to live up to rules accepted in times of peace. In 1914, when conditions of warfare were altering so rapidly that a belligerent naval Power such as Britain was sure to demand the utmost indulgence in the application of old principles, it might have seemed the part of wisdom merely to demand that the British Government should show as much respect for rules to which it had already bound itself as changing conditions made reasonable. Unfortunately, Wilson, the ardent American and the perfectionist, and the State Department, in the hands of men more given to legalism than to the give and take of traditional diplomacy, did not regard this as enough. Five years before an international group of experts, gathered in London, had issued a "Declaration," codifying what seemed to them the best procedure of the time. The Declaration had never been formally accepted by our Government, and had been specifically repudiated by the British, as placing too severe restrictions upon the rights of a belligerent conducting a blockade. Yet in 1914, of all times, the State Department demanded that the British should accept the Declaration, and should live up to it. There is no space nor need for following the ensuing controversy in detail. Grey, feeling it impossible to comply, and yet unwilling to refuse outright, attempted to compromise; and, whether from preoccupation or intention, appeared to play for time. In the end our demand was dropped. It had ill served Wilson's wishes. It had not made him a particularly acceptable mediator in British eyes, and it had quickened passions here in America which he had tried to moderate. But before the Declaration was forgotten, these had flared up to new heights with the inauguration of Germany's submarine campaign in February 1915.

In this age of horrors it is difficult to realize that the German proposal to sink Allied merchantmen without warning, and without provision for the safety of crews or passengers, seemed to many people like sheer piracy. It was, according to existing codes, which here again had not caught up with twentieth-century inventiveness. The danger to which a submarine exposed itself, in surfacing to give warning to a probably armed merchantman, was not accepted by such people as an adequate excuse. Neither was the impossibility that submarines should take prizes into ports, or find accommodations for more than a few prisoners.

German sympathizers in this country and some of their auxiliaries were satisfied with the German case. They found justification in the Allied "starvation" blockade, as murdering vast numbers of civilians slowly and painfully. There was, of course, no starvation in the early period of the war, but the cry made effective propaganda with many humane people. They found further justification in our exports of munitions to Allied countries, despite the fact that we were acting according to an accepted code of which Germany had frequently made use. But in essence the dispute boiled down to one question: was or was not the taking of civilian lives, and especially of American lives, to be treated as something very different from interference with our trade? Senator Lodge put it concretely enough when he once asked whether a bale of cotton bobbing in the water should seem to us as much a matter of concern as a drowning child's head.

To Wilson, deeply angered with the British as he was, this question of human lives placed Germany's proposed action in an utterly different category from British sins. It also seemed to him no mere stretching, but a flagrant violation, of America's acknowledged rights. The Germans had warned that, since the Allies were making use of a traditional but objectionable *ruse de guerre* by hoisting neutral flags, neutral as well as Allied merchantmen would be in danger. The German proposal, he decided, would have to be resisted, immediately and consistently. The decision took courage. If he persisted, sharp dissent was to be expected from large elements of his party in the nation and in Congress. It was to be expected from his Secretary of State and from Mr. Kitchin, majority leader in the House. But he did not hesitate. As the dispute continued, he removed or waved aside extraneous arguments. He proposed that the submarines should let merchantmen alone, provided the British let food shipments through. Germany's refusal to agree to the suggestion robbed the "starvation" argument of much weight. As for our sale of munitions, he had only to point out that any change by the United States "in its own laws of neutrality during the progress of a war" would be an unneutral act.

Meantime, he had been dealing with the principal issue. As soon as the German Government's intention had been announced, he had issued, on February 10, the first of that long series of notes to Germany by which he tried so desperately to keep us at once in self-respect and out of war—notes which brought him such praise, such abuse, and even such contempt, as few presidents have known. The German Government's war-zone proclamation, said the note, would constitute "an act so unprecedented in naval warfare" that our Government was reluctant to believe its issue possible. Then came a very stern warning. If German submarine commanders were to mistake an American for an Allied merchant ship, to destroy it, or to take the lives of American citizens,

the United States would be constrained to hold the Imperial German Government to a strict accountability . . . and to take any steps . . . necessary . . . to safeguard American lives and property . . . and the full enjoyment of their acknowledged rights on the high seas.

This, of course, was a threat of war. But the Germans were not worried. Knowing Wilson's passionate desire to keep us neutral, and how fully Congress and the nation were in accord with it, they could afford to go ahead. Expressions of regret and monetary compensation should be enough to avoid a break when American lives and property were destroyed.

For three months and more their confidence was justified. Incidents such as the torpedoing of an American tanker, with the loss of three American lives, might have been made the basis for vigorous action; but Wilson worked as hard as ever to keep things quiet on the diplomatic and home fronts. "When you are right you can be calm," he told a religious conference at Washington, in March. No one would be allowed to "rock the boat." In April he begged the ladies of the D.A.R. to "preserve the judicial temperament"; and promised the Associated Press that the world "would someday turn to us for . . . cooler assessment of the elements engaged." Moreover, the State Department seemed to be using its sharpest pen for dispatches to London. Franklin Lane offered a tribute to the impression of impartiality which the administration was giving:

We are being generously damned by the Germans and the aggressive Irish for being pro-British, and the British press people and sympathizers in this country are generously damning us as the grossest of commercialists who are willing to sell them into the eternal slavery of Germany for the sake of selling a few bushels of wheat.

"The boat" seemed quite steady until on May 7 it was rocked violently by the torpedoing of the *Lusitania* off the coast of Ireland, with the loss of one hundred and twenty-eight American among nearly two thousand civilian lives.

People still argue as to whether the Germans had justification in the character of the vessel and her cargo; and whether Americans who traveled on her, despite a warning published in the American press immediately before she·sailed, were entitled to the protection of our Government. At the moment most of the nation was in no mood to argue at all. Horror and indignation were so general that, had Congress been in session, Wilson might not have been able to keep us at peace with Germany. Here was a case in which the people, not the "rulers," were ready to press for war. But Congress was not in session, and Wilson could have his way. Most of his advisers believed that the end of neutrality had come, or was very near. House, traveling at the time between Berlin, Paris, and London, in the hope of finding some basis on which peace negotiations might commence, felt that

Wilson had only the alternatives of obtaining a cessation of the German submarine war on all non-combatants or of joining the Allies:

America . . . must determine whether she stands for civilized or uncivilized warfare. We can no longer remain neutral spectators. Our action in this crisis will determine the part we will play when peace is made.

But with House far away it was apparently to Mr. Tumulty that Wilson unburdened himself most freely.

Tumulty's account of Wilson's talk may lack textual accuracy, but it seems completely in character. As usual, he was "the trustee of this nation." He could easily understand the people's "emotionalism," since he would "see red" himself, if he thought about the published details. But with "so many conflicting crosscurrents of national feelings in the country," would the whole people move against Germany with enthusiasm? Would the prevailing mood last when the "horrors and bloody aftermath" of war appeared? Would it last even until Congress could take action? And then came the reason of reasons: America must be free to offer herself as "the only mediating influence" in making peace. Wilson became prophetic then:

What I fear more than anything else is . . . world chaos and bankruptcy . . . the distempers, social, moral, and industrial, that will flow from this world cataclysm.

Since the Germans were evasive, Wilson sent three notes about the *Lusitania,* allowing the controversy to drag on for months, and obtaining no substantial satisfaction in the end. He tried very hard to observe the old *fortiter* and *suaviter* motto. Remembering Belgium, people must have found curious his acknowledgment, in the first note, of "the humane and enlightened attitude hitherto assumed by the Imperial German Government in matters of international right." But he sounded firm enough when he rejected in advance "expressions of regret and offers of reparation"; and especially when the third note declared that acts of commanders of German vessels in contravention of the rights of American citizens would be regarded as "deliberately unfriendly." In diplomatic phraseology, the term carries, of course, the most serious possible warning.

Judged by the notes, Wilson had gone as far as House or most of the other men whose opinion he respected had desired. People like Mr. Theodore Roosevelt demanded the seizure of all German ships in American waters and an embargo on commerce with Germany. People like Mr. Taft and Senator Williams wanted a break in diplomatic relations, but no war, unless Germany made it unavoidable. But Wilson's course won general approval from the nation after the first excitement had died away. Even in Britain, no influential person seemed to feel that he had been under obligation to go further than he did; though there were sharp comments in France. But would he stand by his demands and warnings? Berlin was ready to bet that he would not, and to base its gamble on evidence more specific than its knowledge of his general attitude, and of feeling in Congress and among the people. Three days before the first *Lusitania* note was sent Wilson had made one of the most pacifistic of his speeches:

The example of America must be a special example . . . the example of peace because peace is . . . healing and elevating . . . and strife is not. There is such a thing as a man being too proud to fight. There is such a thing as a nation being so right that it does not need to convince others by force.

"Page and all of us are distressed," House wrote; but the Germans must have read the speech with very different feelings.

Their optimism was soon re-enforced. Before the sending of the second note, Mr. Gerard, entertaining Herr Zimmermann, the Under-Secretary for Foreign Affairs, at lunch, had heard him, "after his customary two quarts of moselle," assure the American wife of a German that she need fear no diplomatic break, since the President was not in earnest. Calling on Zimmermann later, to request an explanation, he was shown a cable from the Austrian Ambassador, announcing on the authority of Mr. Bryan that the President was bluffing! Mr. Gerard had, of course, to send the information unofficially, by way of Colonel House. Whatever the degree of Bryan's guilt (and if he was correctly reported his conduct is better left without comment), the Austrian Ambassador's report is entirely plausible. For Bryan had wished Wilson to send an unofficial letter, asking the Germans not to take our Government's official communications seriously. No wonder the Germans continued to be evasive and to take American lives from time to time on the high seas.

The *Lusitania* episode had one tangible result—the departure of Mr. Bryan from the Cabinet. Bryan had never agreed that our disputes with Germany called for sterner notes or measures than our differences with Britain; and the *Lusitania* sinking brought matters to a climax. Though Germany, like Japan, had singled herself out by refusing to sign a "Bryan" treaty, the Secretary demanded that we should offer to arbitrate our differences with her concerning her submarine warfare. He insisted that Americans should be prevented from traveling on belligerent merchantmen. He refused to sign the second *Lusitania* note, lest it should lead to war. He departed benignantly, expressing his belief that he could "help the President more on the outside." His ways of doing it included attempts to destroy the effects of some of Wilson's speeches and to organize a revolt in Congress, aimed at his leadership and his control of policy. But all that lay in the future. Wilson accepted Bryan's resignation with every appearance of regret. But he had been advised, not only to accept it, but thank God for it, by a lady whom he was hoping to marry, Mrs. Norman Galt.

The President, in this spring of 1915, had fallen suddenly and very deeply in love. Some people blamed him for finding consolation so quickly, not sufficiently considering, perhaps, that his very devotion to his dead wife, combined with the isolation his position imposed on him, had made him intolerably lonely. And few people realized his lifelong need for sympathetic feminine companionship. Mrs. Galt must have appealed strongly to all that was romantic in him. A beautiful and gracious woman, in her early forties, she represented the oldest of old Virginia, even to descent from Pocahontas and John Rolfe. But she was no languid Southern beauty, of the kind so often pictured against backgrounds of pillared porticoes and magnolia trees. Since her husband's death in 1908 she had had an active part in carrying on his jewelry business in Washington, and had found time to do a good deal of traveling in Europe. She understood the arts of living graciously, entertaining charmingly, and dressing exquisitely. Franklin Lane, in describing his young daughter's pride in a new evening cloak, spoke of her as feeling that "Cleopatra and the Queen of Sheba and Mrs. Galt had nothing on her."

Mrs. Galt was also cheerful, self-confident, and adaptable. She could throw off cares and enjoy the good things of life in a way the academic and rather ascetic President had never learned to do. She could not only draw him out of his depression and his loneliness, but draw him into pleasures and relaxations of which he had never had enough. Later, they would often be together on bridle paths and golf courses and in theaters. Having had little formal education, Mrs. Galt was more interested in people than in books; but she was not a woman to be satisfied with brightening up the President's leisure hours. She had strong likes and dislikes, and was by no means ready to take Wilson's friends on faith. She also had decided views; and was so sure that the President was right in almost everything he did that it was her habit to urge him on, not to suggest caution or compromise. Men near the President were to become increasingly conscious of all these things.

The courtship of a President must always be difficult, to the point of being almost ludicrous. His visits to private homes are not only chronicled, but almost excluded by official etiquette. On drives, he not only has the company of six or eight burly guards, but, if a lady is along, must be as carefully chaperoned as was a nineteenth-century debutante. Nor can the frequent visits of a lady to the White House escape notice. Considering all the difficulties, Wilson's second courtship seems nothing if not impetuous. He first met Mrs. Galt toward the end of March; he asked her to marry him during the first week in May. Then a considerable pause ensued. They both realized what comment there would be; but the President, having made up his mind, was prepared to defy everyone and everything. Mrs. Galt, more sensitive and sensible, demanded time; and it was not until September that their engagement became a fact. Wilson seemed rejuvenated by his love affair. Mrs. Galt was showered with flowers and letters and telephone calls on a private wire. There must have been a small boom in the production of purple orchids for the Washington market. If one may believe "Ike" Hoover, even official business suffered; and the President's friends became anxious. It was apparently a relief when the announcement came that the wedding was to take place a week before Christmas. Thanks, apparently, to Wilson's taste for simplicity, it was to be an evening wedding in Mrs. Galt's small house.

For so solemn an affair the wedding had its humorous aspects. Wilson's people were democratic and liberal in their gifts:

Every manufacturer, producer, and merchant seemed to feel he was privileged to send a sample of his wares. Soap of every description, toilet preparations, perfumes, brooms, brushes and dusters, pieces of furniture, mineral waters of all kinds, candy by the crate, and cakes in large box lots, much handiwork of good housewives, a barrel of sugared popcorn and enough fruit and vegetables to open up a large market—these were but a few of the gifts.

Purple orchids and Scotch heather (perhaps the florists were unaware that the President preferred to speak of himself as an Irishman) featured the decorations; and a mirror "enabled the President and his bride to see all the guests as the service was being performed." When the time for going away arrived, perhaps one of the maddest dashes made by a wedding car in history occurred, as the President's limousine attempted to outdistance all the press cars. The chauffeur was so successful that he managed to lose nearly all the reporters, the police escort, and, almost, the secret-service men, in a dash of twelve or fifteen miles. After that there was a train journey and blessed quiet. In January Mrs. Wilson, settled into the White House, assumed the task of arranging documents for the President's signature, and shared with the famous typewriter the privilege of bearing him company in his most secluded hours. Their mutual and lasting devotion, and her equally lasting solicitude for his health and happiness and success, were evident from the first; and she rapidly became the closest of all his confidants, closer than Tumulty, closer even than Colonel House. Any new intimacy such as this is apt to have a relaxing effect on older ones. The period of Wilson's deepest intimacy with Colonel House, for whom Mrs. Wilson seems never to have greatly cared, apparently came to an end within a year or so of the President's remarriage. But House still retained first place among his men friends and trusted counselors.

CHAPTER X

Ballots Against Bullets

———— ✦ ————

Soon after the President and Mrs. Wilson returned from their honeymoon, Theodore Roosevelt, the Great Progressive, sat down to write confidentially to Senator Lodge, his standpat Republican friend:

Apparently the Republicans are expecting to beat Wilson by keeping as neutral as he is as regards international duty, by supporting him in his sham-preparedness program, and letting him pose before the country . . . as the champion of preparedness, and by then trusting that on the tariff and by some more or less secret understanding with the German vote they may be able to replace him by someone to whom the Germans won't object, and who has not declared himself in any way that will hurt anyone's feelings on any of the questions that are of . . . vital concern to this country.

Roosevelt could not stomach that. He regarded Wilson as "conscienceless"; but he had no greater respect for Republicans whom he believed to be playing politics quite as unforgivably:

It may be that such a course is the one most certain or most likely to result in replacing Wilson in the White House by a Republican. From my standpoint it would make it a matter of entire indifference whether under such circumstances Wilson succeeded himself or a Republican succeeded him. Such tactics may be politically sound . . . they are bad tactics from the standpoint of the country.

Wilson would doubtless have been immensely interested in that letter. Preparations for the presidential election of 1916 were already under way, and the Rough Rider had touched on some fundamental issues.

For Wilson, the situation was very different from that of four years before. This time there was no question at all as to his nomination. The single-term plank of the Democratic platform of 1912 had long since been buried. But there was at least an average amount of doubt as to the election's outcome. It depended on so many things. If Roosevelt came out again to head a third party, Democratic chances should be excellent. But supposing the Republicans and Progressives should agree upon a candidate, what then? Would the record of Wilson's administration give the Democrats the majority, by attracting enough independent and progressive votes? It was certainly an impressive record; and one calculated to appeal to all voters who held progressive views. But it had raised up some powerful enemies. It had apparently alienated most of the business world. Many Democrats must have agreed with Mr. Taft that the Underwood tariff (which never had a fair tryout, thanks to the war) would be ruinous to industry. The labor vote was a doubtful quantity, since much of it might be attracted to the "full dinner pail," held out invitingly by Republican speakers. A good deal could probably be done in the current session to please wage earners and farmers, too; but, on the other side, there was the resentment of food and cotton producers about Wilson's failure to deal more effectively with the British blockade.

But all guesses based primarily on past or future domestic issues were rather futile. For questions raised by the war had pushed themselves into first place. In a way, the war was helping Wilson's chances. As some of the Republicans noted mournfully, the Democrats might profit from the high prices of nearly all commodities. But then, as Franklin Lane had said, the administration was being damned on the one hand for being pro-British, and on the other for being so commercially minded as to be practically pro-German. The hyphenates offered a special problem. Wilson's attitude toward them had been made clear enough in a number of speeches; and Roosevelt had condemned them, too. But the regular Republicans, even when they accused the President of allowing the Germans to play fast and loose with him, had been very discreet in speaking about citizens of German or Irish blood. Hence Mr. Roosevelt's bitter complaints about Republican campaign plans, based on "some more or less secret understanding with the German vote," on "keeping as neutral as [Wilson] is as regards international duty," and "supporting him in his sham-preparedness campaign." Preparedness was the issue of the moment, as Roosevelt was writing, and as an apparently rejuvenated Wilson was plunging into a mass of unfinished and new business. But the extent and character of our preparedness depended, or should have depended, on our relations with the belligerents, and especially with Germany. Never for a week, nor even a day, had Wilson failed to find those relations difficult.

One of the things which made it especially hard to deal with Germany was that no one could be sure, not even Mr. Gerard himself, just who was in control there at any particular time. The Foreign Office made great protestations of wanting to remain on friendly terms with us; Count Bernstorff made even more. But Wilson doubted the sincerity of both, and suspected that the German Navy was ready to torpedo ships on its own responsibility. Our Government's confidence in the good will of the Central Powers was not increased by Gerard's reports of the way we were hated in Berlin; nor yet by the fact that Wilson had to demand the recall of the Austrian Ambassador and of two German attachés (the now illustrious von Papen being one of them) for complicity in a campaign of sabotage against our industries. All of this formed a menacing backdrop before which the long drama of Wilson's attempts to keep the use of submarines within what then seemed the limits of decency continued to be played out.

After the *Lusitania* dispute, the next act had centered about the torpedoing, in August 1915, of the liner *Arabic*. There was no warning; the ship was bound for America, hence carrying no contraband; and two American lives were lost. Though Count Bernstorff had apparently urged his government to satisfy our State Department's demands that the sinking should be disavowed and a promise given that no more such sinkings should occur, it had not been until the beginning of October that the Germans had given way. And even then Wilson's undoubted diplomatic victory was discounted within a month or so, when the *Orduna* was torpedoed by an Austrian submarine. Privately, Wilson declared that "no decent man, knowing the situation," could fail to be "heart and soul for the Allies"; but publicly he kept on "waging peace" by diplomatic notes. Determined as ever on nonintervention and on mediating the whole conflict, he wrote plaintively that he could not decide at what point patience ceased being a virtue. Even House was losing patience:

I am surprised at the attitude he takes. He should have determined his policy when he wrote his notes of February, May, June and July . . .

in the long run, I feel the nation would suffer more in being supine than in taking a decided stand.

The Colonel wrote very frankly to the President, advising diplomatic breaks with the Central Powers on the *Arabic* and *Orduna* sinkings, even at the risk of war. But he merely wasted time and ink. It is no great wonder that an increasing number of Americans, especially in the Eastern States, went from impatience to irritation, even to feelings of humiliation and disgust.

It is still less wonder that the British, who could never realize that this nation was not overwhelmingly Anglo-Saxon; who did not understand the reasons for our isolationism; and who were now desperately afraid of a German victory, felt even more deeply still. Suffering on the battlefield, by submarines, and by Zeppelin raids; knowing how gladly their government would have escaped involvement in the war, they were hurt and puzzled and angered not only by Wilson's patience, but by evidences of anti-British sentiment among the American people. It was a sentiment that sprang from a dozen tangled roots, and crept like a vine through most sections and classes. Sometimes it showed itself unpleasantly. There had been the case of the ship *Dacia,* transferred from German to German-American ownership, and dispatched to Germany, specifically in the hope that its seizure by some British warship would create a diplomatic incident. The incident would probably have been only too real, if Page had not suggested to Grey that the French should make the seizure. Since the French made it, there was no outcry. House, taking note, urged that more French and Russian ships should be used in the blockade.

Even Grey might wonder at such favoritism. Grey did wonder; and so did that great and informed friend of America, Lord Bryce. He found it strange that America should fail to realize how great a danger to herself, as well as to civilization generally, a victorious and militaristic Germany would prove. And all the while the tension between Washington and London was growing, as the British tightened the blockade on Germany's neutral neighbors, and prepared to declare cotton contraband. The State Department sharpened its tone in protesting about the blockade to Grey.

More than ever Wilson was walking a tightrope. House warned him that to use all the pressure on England which he had it in his power to use might earn British resentment which would last over into the

Peace Conference. It was at this time that Page performed his greatest services, and began to receive increasing censure, not only from Wilson but from House. Even yet he was not blindly Anglophile. He still wrote bitterly of British bungling. The much-repeated charge that he helped Grey to answer a dispatch from his own government has little weight when one remembers that the British Ambassador at Washington did the same, and that such procedure is not unusual with envoys. There was little if any difference between the British viewpoint and his own; but there is no proof that he did not reach his own quite independently. More serious was the fact that he showed no appreciation of American public sentiment, and far more serious a disinclination to carry out instructions of which he disapproved. But, with it all, Page's services are difficult to exaggerate. Somehow he and Grey managed to smooth differences and soften asperities. The British were able to keep up the blockade until the time when we joined them in maintaining it; and Wilson could honestly point to his insistence on the acknowledgment of our neutral rights. The Germans were not deceived. "Nobody in Germany believes in the impartiality of the American Government," wrote Bernstorff. Gerard described himself as "a present object for concentrated hate."

It is easy enough to sympathize with Wilson's efforts to keep the people out of war and our Government in a position to mediate; but, considering his distrust of the Germans and his knowledge of their feelings, his attitude toward preparedness showed him unrealistic and stubborn. Not from tenderness toward the Allies so much as from mere prudence, a number of distinguished Americans had been urging, since 1914, that we should make some preparations to defend ourselves. It is not impossible that Wilson's attitude would have been different, had the advocates of preparedness been different people. Army and Navy men, having a sense of responsibility for the nation's safety, were naturally for it; but Wilson had as yet little use for "specialists" —especially perhaps when they wore uniforms, and most particularly when they busied themselves with anything that touched upon his policies. And the great Army advocate was General Leonard Wood, a former Chief of Staff, and also an admirer and close friend of Theodore Roosevelt. Of civilian advocates, Colonel Roosevelt was by all odds the most active, and the most abusive in commenting on Wilson's stand.

It was possibly unfortunate, too, that most of the demands for improvement in our defenses came from Republicans. Wilson had received invaluable Republican support in Congress, especially from Senator Lodge, in the Panama Canal tolls affair, and (with some reservations) in his Mexican policy. He had expressed his gratitude. But the war and the approach of another presidential election had changed all that. The rift with Senator Lodge, that was to prove so fatal, soon appeared, and widened rapidly. If the 1916 elections were to send Wilson and the Democrats back to the place where they belonged, all possible criticism must be brought to bear on them. And Lodge believed sincerely that the administration's policy toward the war was unrealistic and unworthy of the nation. Wilson's dreamed-of role as the great mediator made no appeal to him. Neither did the icy impartiality, the apparent indifference to moral issues, which Wilson felt it his duty to preach and ostensibly to practice. As little did Wilson's attitude on preparedness. So through all of 1915 Lodge had attacked Wilson publicly, frequently, and bitterly. Some of his charges had been preposterous. He had represented Wilson's opposition to Huerta as mere personal vindictiveness toward an individual who had refused to bow the knee. Sometimes the Senator's opposition seems to have been well based. But his tone and bearing were unfortunate; and the antagonism between him and the President grew apace. The fact that he stood shoulder to shoulder with Roosevelt on preparedness not improbably contributed to Wilson's stubbornness.

The best that can be said for Wilson's attitude is that it corresponded with the general sentiment, both of the people and of Congress. But Wilson helped to create the sentiment. He did it all the more effectively by dissociating himself from the extreme pacifists, and from the absurdities of their campaign. He had his way. As a result, we entered the war almost totally unprepared in so far as the Army was concerned; were consequently responsible for some prolongation of its miseries; and might well have been involved in an Allied defeat. One cannot even dismiss Colonel Roosevelt's contention that, had we armed in time, we need never have been forced into war at all. House wrote in his diary:

The President has never realized the gravity of our unprepared position. I have urged him from the beginning. . . . If war comes . . . it will be because we are totally unprepared and Germany feels that we are impotent.

Gerard's reaction was the same:

The people here [in Germany] are firmly convinced that we can be slapped, insulted, and murdered with absolute impunity, and refer to our notes as things worse than waste paper.

Both these comments were written in July 1915. Thanks to Mr. Daniels and his nautically minded friend and Under-secretary Franklin D. Roosevelt, the expansion of our inadequate fleet was under way; but, so far, Wilson had been opposed to any strengthening of our Army. The Army had not much more than 50,000 men available, after posts and coast defenses had been provided for. Yet Wilson had repeatedly threatened Germany with war. One cannot help feeling that there was coming to be something of a *fiat* attached in Wilson's mind to Wilson's will. We were to remain at peace; but a great nation which had learned to hate us, and which Wilson thoroughly distrusted, was to stop when he held up his hand.

Even at that, why no preparedness? The fact that its principal advocates were, as he once said grimly, "no great friends" of his, may have been contributory to his attitude, but could not have been more. True, the Anglophobes and isolationists were on the alert, and the pacifists active. It was the time of the Ford "peace ship." But when, at Princeton, at Trenton, or at Washington, had Wilson, wanting anything, been stopped from trying to get it, even by opposition far more serious? Against the opponents of preparedness he could always have appealed to th people. He did appeal to them; but he influenced public opinion against preparedness in so far as the Army was concerned. In his message to Congress in December 1914 he had denounced the idea of "a large *standing* army" [italics inserted]—as though anyone had ever suggested that. He had talked of "a reversal of the whole history and character of our polity"—as though that had been suggested, too. He had spoken touchingly of lads spending "the best years of their lives making soldiers of themselves." Mr. Bryan could hardly have improved on that part of his message. Along with similar presidential utterances, the message must have been scanned with interest at Berlin.

In the late summer of 1915, when Mr. Bryan had left the Cabinet and the Germans were creating the suspicion that lip service was all they intended giving to the *Lusitania* notes, Wilson apparently commenced to realize that in foreign relations his fiat was not enough.

We might—though even to admit the possibility came hard—we might conceivably be forced to fight. So he began to think over possible methods of preparedness, but only in terms of pure defense, and in the spirit of his message to Congress. His reluctance to give the least encouragement to military preparations was very obvious. He refused to visit Plattsburg, where patriotic college lads, all volunteers, of course, were receiving a whole month's R.O.T.C. training. The reason he gave—his fear that his visit would be attributed to partisan motives —was far from convincing. As for the scheme of military preparedness he was about to advocate, the best commentary ever made on it lay in the fact that he was one of the first to consign it to oblivion as soon as he realized that we should almost certainly be forced into war.

Mr. Baker has pointed out that he moved "with profound hesitation," and that his speeches on preparedness, before 1916, had not been received enthusiastically. How could the people have been enthusiastic when Wilson's own reluctance and hesitation were so plain? In so far as the public knew, hesitation and reluctance were the last qualities to be looked for in him when he believed in anything. It is true that he felt it necessary to tour the Middle West, in order to smooth the way through Congress of the more-than-modest proposals he was prepared to make. It is true that Mr. Bryan followed in his footsteps, crying "peace." But either Mr. Bryan's dove of peace was as easily frightened as any hummingbird, or Mr. Bryan was thinking of a coming war of ballots, not bullets. He often did.

When Wilson propounded his scheme for military preparedness to the Middle Westerners, he impressed upon them that the time might come (and if it were to come, it would come soon) when peace would have to be sacrificed to the upholding of America's honor. Privately, he was telling of his fear that he would wake up some morning to find we had been forced into war. Yet his scheme for preparedness was no more than a gesture. He offered an increase in the regular Army too small to be significant, and the creation of a "continental army" of 400,000 men. The figure looked imposing; but it was the quality of the new army that would count. It would need good organization; and it would need considerable expert training, if it was to function as anything but a home guard, recruited to meet invaders who were as likely to come from Europe as from Mars. The kind of warfare that was going on in Europe was new and, for those days, very technical. Moreover, military men agreed that infantry must be so disciplined by continuous training as to give automatic obedience to commands. Only this would take all the men of a unit "over the top."

But what was the President's "continental army" to be like? It was to consist of volunteers. It was to reach full recruitment in about three years. It was not to be "organized." It was to receive training for "very brief" periods in each year; and it was to get its training largely from the National Guard. Yet the National Guard, as events would amply prove, varied in quality from State to State, knew nothing whatever of current methods of warfare, and had never had opportunity to learn automatic obedience. The Secretary of War, Mr. Garrison, as much a civilian as the President, but convinced that soldiers knew more about soldiering than did civilians, protested against the lack of organization and the inadequate provision for training; against the proposed reliance of the nation "upon a military force that it does not raise, that it does not officer, that it does not train, and that it does not control." He even showed some sympathy with the idea of conscription, which Wilson was to insist upon a year later. The President admitted that the Army should be "federalized"; but after months of consideration, during which war had come appreciably nearer, he declared that his mind was open to suggestions of any sort. Garrison, able, tactless, and impatient, had been out of sympathy with other of Wilson's policies. This was the last straw. His resignation, together with that of the Assistant Secretary, reached Wilson early in February; and Mr. Newton Baker, whose views and ways corresponded much with the President's, soon occupied his place. With Garrison went whatever small hope of real military preparedness there had ever been.

Yet Wilson stood as firmly on his insistence that the American people's rights should be respected as though the nation had been ready to go into action at any time. He had to meet what he would have called two "acid tests" in the early months of 1916. The first came more from Congress than from Berlin, involving an attempt by pacifist elements among the Democrats to deprive him of some of his initiative in foreign relations, and so to repudiate his leadership. An old issue came suddenly to be dangerous. The British had for some time been arming their merchant vessels. At the beginning of February 1916 the Germans (who had never really complied with our notes concerning the *Lusitania* and the *Arabic*) announced that their submarines would treat all armed merchantmen as warships. This touched off an inflammatory condition in Congress. In January Senator Gore, a leading Democrat, having consulted Bryan, had introduced bills to forbid the issue of passports to Americans planning to travel on ships owned by belligerents. In effect, he was proposing that Congress should partially nullify the President's notes to Germany, and make itself the judge of the propriety of claims we might make upon the Reich. Wilson's party was splitting on the issue; and the split was weakening his position in Europe and in Congress.

The President, insistent as ever on what he regarded as the people's rights, used conciliation as far as it would go. Numbers of senators and congressmen were summoned to the White House; the British were asked to disarm their liners and merchantmen, on condition that the Germans should observe the old rules governing visit, search, and capture. But the British and Germans would neither trust one another nor be persuaded that they would gain by the bargain. Would Wilson then adopt the Bryan-Gore position—a position which was to seem reasonable to nearly all Americans in the next world war? He would not. In refusing to disarm their merchantmen, the British were within the rights that international law gave them, no matter how desirable a change in the law might be. So Germany must still be held to the existing code.

The crisis shaped up rapidly. On February 16 the State Department informed the German Foreign Office of the administration's stand. On the day following Congressman McLemore of Texas, a Democrat working in connection with Bryan, introduced the first of two resolutions that Americans should be warned not to travel on merchant ships of the belligerents. Nine days later Gore offered a similar resolution in the Senate. Meantime Wilson, having consulted the chairmen of the Senate and House committees that dealt with foreign affairs, and having been told that the McLemore resolution would pass by a majority of two or three to one, had made one of his famous appeals, in a published letter. He began by telling the people of his confidence that he could keep the country out of war, pointing out that Germany's announcement. was contrary to assurances that she had given us and insisting that no nation had the right, after war had begun, to alter or disregard accepted principles of warfare. Then came the appeal:

I cannot consent to an abridgement of the rights of American citizens. . . . The honor and self-respect of the nation is [*sic*] involved. . . . To forbid our people to exercise their rights for fear we might be called upon to vindicate them would be . . . acquiescence in the violation of the rights of mankind everywhere . . . a deliberate abdication of our . . . proud position as spokesman even amid the turmoil of war for the law and the right.

When even this letter did not stem the revolt, Wilson made public another, addressed to the ranking member of the Rules Committee of the House:

The report that there are divided counsels in Congress in regard to the foreign policy of the government is being made industrious use of in foreign capitals . . . it cannot fail to . . . expose the country to the most serious risks.

At the same time he took the offensive in action, by urging that the resolutions should come up at once for vote. His perfect presentation of his case, and his aggressiveness, gave him one of his outstanding victories in all his dealings with Congress. In both Houses all but a small section of the Democrats turned back to him. Aided by half of the Republicans, they crushed the McLemore-Gore-Bryan revolt. The victory was won shortly before the sinking of the *Sussex* produced the second great test.

The State Department's famous note on the sinking of the *Sussex* (a Wilson note, somewhat strengthened, on the insistence of Lansing) summarized to perfection the reasons why the sinking seemed so great an atrocity and so flagrant a disregard of the warnings given regarding the sinkings of the *Lusitania* and the *Arabic*:

The *Sussex* had never been armed; it was a vessel known to be habitually used for the conveyance of passengers across the English Channel; and was not taking the route followed by troop ships or supply ships. About eighty of her passengers, non-combatants of all ages and sexes, including citizens of the United States, were killed or injured. . . . The *Sussex* was torpedoed without warning or summons to surrender.

The note, traversing the background of the incident, contained one indisputable statement: "The Government of the United States has been very patient." At the time it was being too patient to please great numbers of Americans, including Lansing and ·House. Mr.

Daniels gives an account of a Cabinet meeting at which opinion was sharply divided:

I took the ground that, aside from other questions, if Wilson brought on war with Germany except after exhausting every possible means to avert it, the country would rise up against him in the 1916 election.

That was hardly the kind of argument that appealed to the President, except perhaps in touching his desire to stay in office to do the things he planned on doing for America and mankind at large. But he seemed as sure as ever that the longer he could stave off war, the greater contribution he could make. And the majority of the people, especially west of the Mississippi, still wanted peace.

Lansing and House believed that only a diplomatic break could put an end to the German Government's evasiveness; but Wilson, determined both to have no war and to bring Germany to terms by threats of war, decided to risk fresh ridicule and abuse by continuing his barrage of notes. But the note on the *Sussex* sinking was not couched, as the earlier notes had been, in terms menacing but general. It was an ultimatum of the milder sort. Unless the German Government should "immediately [Lansing was responsible for that word] declare and effect an abandonment of its present methods of submarine warfare," diplomatic relations would be broken. Wilson gambled; and Wilson won a rather surprising victory.

The Germans battling the French at Verdun, and watching the British gathering up their power at last, did not care to take chances. The required promises came from Berlin, and were fairly well lived up to for nine months. The President and Mrs. Wilson celebrated the German concession by playing golf, attending a circus, and going on a week-end cruise. But Wilson was planning future moves—mediation and an international organization to keep the peace. His first appearance as an internationalist came on May 27, in a speech he made at Washington before a meeting of the League to Enforce Peace.

The circumstances were long to be remembered. For his fellow internationalist that evening was Senator Lodge. Although the Senator had backed the President in opposing the McLemore and Gore resolutions, the relations between the two men had become more unfriendly than ever. In March the Senator had confided to the *Springfield Republican* his conviction that Wilson's administration, if not the worst in history, was the worst since Buchanan's at any rate. The platform greetings must have been very cool. In view of later developments, Lodge's was the more historic of the two speeches:

> The limit of voluntary arbitration has, I think, been reached . . . the next step . . . is to put force behind international peace, an international league or agreement, or tribunal, for peace. . . . I know how quickly we shall be met with the statement that . . . no nation can submit to the judgment of other nations . . . the difficulties that arise when we speak of anything that seems to involve an alliance.

The passage immediately following is at least as well worth remembering:

> But I do not believe that when Washington warned us against entangling alliances [Lodge properly substituted "permanent" for "entangling" when the speech was printed] he meant for one moment that we should not join with other civilized nations if a method could be found to diminish war and encourage peace.

The Senator was taking no new stand. A year before he had told a commencement gathering at Union College that peace could "only be maintained by putting behind it the force of united nations." Now, in 1916, he was singing a duet with Woodrow Wilson. Wilson offered a more specific plan. If we should ever have the privilege of initiating a movement for peace, he was sure the people would wish its Government to favor, among other things,

> an universal association of the nations to maintain the inviolate security of the highway of the seas . .·. and . . . a virtual guarantee of territorial integrity and political independence.

There they were already: "the freedom of the seas," which was to give no end of trouble in the armistice negotiations; and the fatal Article X of the Covenant of the League, which Senator Lodge was to oppose with all his might. But Senator Lodge was probably in no mood to be critical in May 1916. The opening of the Republican and Progressive conventions in Chicago was only a few days off.

Different as were the conventions and election of 1916 from those of 1912, it would again be difficult to say that the people made Wilson President because they agreed with his convictions and his policies. In large measure the people who voted for him probably did. But the Republicans and Progressives, while not nearly so helpful in his second election as in his first, did help to some extent. And it is hard to see how he could have secured his slim majority without Bryan's appeal to pacifists and isolationists with whom Wilson by no means saw eye to eye. From this distance, at least, the attempt of the Republicans and Progressives to get together by holding their conventions simultaneously at Chicago, and agreeing upon a candidate, suggests a curious degree either of optimism or of inadequate planning. It seems strange that the Progressives could have hoped to pour new wine into the old Republican bottle; and to do it by securing the acceptance of Roosevelt as the Republican leader. Had they succeeded, Wilson would have had little or no chance.

But the Republicans saw no reason to pay so high a price as that for victory. Roosevelt, they announced, as the Progressive convention opened, was the one man they would not have on any terms. Then came the most inconsistent of all Roosevelt's inconsistencies—his amazing suggestion that the Progressives should nominate one of their most inveterate and outspoken enemies, his good friend Senator Lodge. In the stupefaction produced by the Rough Rider's message, the Progressives threw all thoughts of reconciliation with the G.O.P., all reflection, all control aside. Roosevelt was placed in nomination by Bainbridge Colby and Hiram Johnson, and was called upon to show his loyalty by leading his party, as he had done in 1912. Peremptorily, he declined. Mr. Bowers, in his great life of Senator Beveridge, has described the outcome in unforgettable language:

That day, too stricken to leave town, Bainbridge Colby shut himself up in his room at the hotel. At his feet lay a crumpled telegram from the New York World asking for an expression on the future. Finally he recovered it and sent a reply. The purport was that the army had been deserted by the General, and that real Progressives would have to determine their course. Many were to go over to Wilson, Colby among them. Many, a bit bedraggled, dragged themselves like poor relations back to the party they had left four years before. The great adventure was over.

It was perhaps a little harsh to say that the General had deserted; it was perhaps unfair of Tumulty to say that Colonel Roosevelt refused to go on splitting Republican votes because of his hatred of Wilson. He was not physically fit for a campaign such as that of 1912 had been; and he had written Lodge some time before that he had disqualified himself by his attacks upon the hyphenates. What Wilson gained or lost by the death of the Progressive party one can only speculate; but he was able to make good use of some of the votes it had released. On the whole, he was fortunate, too, in the Republican choice of Mr. Justice Hughes.

It is difficult to decide in how far Wilson was responsible for the fact that the Democratic convention and the campaign which followed it were carried on to the insistent chant of "He kept us out of war." Bryan, who realized the value of the slogan, and perhaps hoped that its use would bind the President later, branded it on both convention and campaign. But House certainly approved it soon after the convention, and certainly intended (whether or not the intention was carried out) that he and the President "should aid in preparing the keynote speech." The convention was something of an oratorical debauch. Mr. Bryan, excluded by the liquor interests from the list of delegates, appeared in the press gallery, and was given so long an ovation that he had to go into hiding. Then came the keynote speech of Governor Glynn of New York:

[The President's] policy may not satisfy those who revel in destruction and find pleasure in despair . . . but it does satisfy . . . the mothers of the land at whose hearth and fireside no jingoistic war has placed an empty chair. It does satisfy the daughters of the land. . . .

Governor Glynn was sure that it was equally satisfactory to the fathers and the sons, though these would fight, of course, if Reason and Honor and Justice ever commanded it. No wonder Mr. Bryan wept openly with joy. He must have been almost equally pleased with the words of Senator Ollie James of Kentucky, the permanent chairman:

Without orphaning a single American child, without widowing a single American mother, without firing a single gun, without the shedding of a single drop of blood [the President], has wrung from the most militant spirit that ever brooded above a battlefield an acknowledgment of American rights and an agreement to American demands.

And then, of course, Mr. Bryan was forced to speak:

I join the rest of the nation in gratitude that at a time like this we have a President who is trying to keep us out of war.

"His eloquence and Glynn's and James's," writes Mr. Daniels in *The Wilson Era*, "reached the heights—a trinity rarely equaled." So Wilson's campaign was shaped. He and the members of his Cabinet were scrupulously careful to make no promises. He had already said repeatedly that peace might very soon prove impossible. But wishful thinking somehow translated "has kept" into "will keep" in the consciousness of many voters.

Meantime, the congressional session was wearing on, and neither neutrality nor the coming of the elections did much to divert Wilson's interest from domestic problems. The war itself had been creating new ones. Our industries and foreign trade were booming; the incomes derived from business swelled correspondingly; labor, never before in quite such great demand, was organizing, under Samuel Gompers, to claim its share of war prosperity; and the farmers, also prospering, were anxious to buy more land. Ever since his inauguration Wilson had wanted to help the farmers. Now their time had come. About the middle of July the Farm Loan Act gave them banks of their own in each of the Federal Reserve districts, with a Federal Farm Loan Board to watch over the system as a whole and advise the Government regarding any required changes. In future, tenants who wanted to become landowners could get money at moderate rates, and even assistance in arriving at the proper value of the land they wished to buy.

In September came labor's turn to benefit. The brotherhoods of railroad men demanded an eight-hour day. The managers of the railroads at once refused. The brotherhoods threatened a strike, which would have paralyzed the country at a time as critical for the Allies as for American business. The exemption of unions from the restrictions of the Clayton Anti-Trust Act had made governmental coercion impossible, even had the administration favored it. Wilson suggested arbitration. The brotherhoods declined. At the end of August, just a week before the strike would have begun, Wilson asked Congress to put his program for settlement into effect by the passage of the famous Adamson Law. Not only was the eight-hour day to be granted, but the Interstate Commerce Commission was to have power to establish a relation between the rates charged by the railroads and the value of their properties. On the other hand, there were to be no more strikes until proper investigation of differences between railroad managers and employees had been thoroughly and publicly worked out. Should they occur, the Government was to have power to take over the railroads. Opposition was naturally bitter, but the law was pushed through just in time. Unfortunately, as it seems, Congress refused to accept the President's recommendation for the handling of strikes, leaving the new law more one-sided than Wilson would have had it. But everyone saw its significance for the future of labor as a whole. Also in September came legislation which grieved many people of large incomes and large estates. Surtaxes were to be paid on incomes exceeding $40,000, and on the profits of munition makers in particular; heavy inheritance taxes were laid on millionaire estates. The Northeast grew increasingly resentful of the "radical," the "socialist," in the White House, as the presidential campaign went into high gear.

As compared with its predecessor, the campaign was sobriety itself; but the rather humorous conditions that surround most campaigns were not lacking. As usual, the efforts of both sides were concentrated on certain doubtful States; as usual, it was the votes of doubtful voters in these doubtful States that had especially to be fished for; and, since the wishes of these doubtful voters were no secret, the rival fishermen offered baits of considerable similarity. It seemed imperative to promise that everything possible would be done to keep America at peace, and simultaneously to see that American rights, interests, and honor should stand unimpeached. Whether and how it would be possible to achieve both these aims, well, discussion on that point was to be avoided as much as possible. It was better to stick to "Americanism," which offered safe ground, so long as the term was not too much defined. Even on domestic issues, divergence was limited. The tariff issue was naturally whipped up; but Republican orators could not say much against the Federal Reserve system or most of the main features of the Wilson legislative record. President Eliot found "no difference between the two great parties in their truckling to Labor." He noted the same "non-resistant" attitude of the two candidates on woman suffrage, except that Mr. Hughes "gave such bad reasons for succumbing."

Even the personalities of the two candidates coincided more than usual. Both were men of dignity, common sense, and self-restraint. Both attempted to convince by reasoning. But Wilson was much the better campaigner for all that. He could put point and fire into his speeches—even some charm. Mr. Hughes was so legalistic that at least one eminent Republican was afraid to vote for him, lest he should break with the Allies in the matter of the blockade. He was hampered, too, by party instructions, especially about tenderness to hyphenates. Wilson was under no such restraint. His well-known rebuke, delivered through the press, to an Irish hyphenate who threatened him with defeat, is still worth quoting:

I would feel deeply mortified to have you or anybody like you vote for me. Since you have access to many disloyal Americans and I have not, I will ask you to convey this message to them.

The rebuke had probably better news value than any other incident in the campaign; and since the Irish-American votes were lost to Wilson anyhow, its effect in an election based on "Americanism" was probably excellent. Only just before the election did Mr. Hughes follow suit; and it was not in him to lash the offenders as the President had done.

Wilson's campaign was pressed on with great zeal. Colonel House was apparently the master strategist, an expert in finding the doubtful votes in doubtful States, and surprisingly prophetic in deciding which States were, and which were not, worth trying for. The general plan was to concede to Mr. Hughes all that lay east of the Mississippi and north of the Ohio (secretly of course), and concentrate on the South and West. Tactics were more the business of the new campaign manager, Mr. Vance McCormick, a liberal Pennsylvania Democrat. Thanks partly to the efforts of Mr. Bernard Baruch, long since an ardent Wilsonian, Mr. McCombs had been persuaded to withdraw, once the convention had ended.

Many special contributions to success were made by other leading Democrats. Mr. Bryan campaigned with astonishing vigor in the West. It is claimed by one of his biographers that Wilson lost only one State which the Great Commoner entered. The *Chicago Tribune* complained that he was the most powerful man in the country, and more responsible for Wilson than in the 1912 campaign. Mr. Daniels went as far afield as Kansas and Rhode Island, and was very helpful in securing published endorsements from the country's leading inventor and leading industrialist, neither one a Democrat. His position had brought him into contact with both of them. One of Mr. Edison's phrases especially took the voters:

They say Wilson has blundered. Perhaps he has, but I notice that he usually blunders forward.

Mr. Daniels was also of great value when the Democratic campaign chest ran dry, as usual. He approached Mr. Ford at a small lunch party, where the great industrialist and the great inventor held a contest as to which could outkick the other, with the globes of a chandelier as a target. Mr. Ford said he did not believe in campaign spending, and would not give a cent. To the consternation of Mr. McCormick, Mr. Daniels said he quite agreed that much campaign spending was a corrupting influence. But what about legitimate publicity? Mr. Ford thought that over. He would see, he said, that the reasons why Wilson should be elected were "presented in papers of large circulation in the pivotal states." In the end, as Mr. Daniels says, "he had kicked higher than Edison," who had been the victor in the chandelier contest.

But Wilson's campaign managers were worried, and justly so. So many forces were working against their candidate, especially in such great pivotal States as New York, Pennsylvania, and Illinois. The Irish-American vote was hopelessly lost, and much at least of the German-American vote (even normally Republican) with it. Great numbers of voters either felt that Wilson should never have shaken his fist at Germany at all, or else that, having once shaken it, he should have brought the Reich to terms. The Adamson Law seemed to have been doubtful, if not bad, politics. Even former Progressives, like Beveridge, used the alleged bullying of the railroads to increase the resentment of businessmen and stockholders. Mr. Daniels thought that labor was grateful; but Mr. Tumulty did not. The liquor interests were displeased with Mr. Daniels for drying up the Navy. The effect of Wilson's second marriage was feared. Before it had occurred, Mr. Daniels had been deputed to ask the President to put it off; but neither he nor anyone else had dared.

Maine still held its reputation as a barometer; and Democratic morale suffered badly in September, when Maine went strongly Republican. The sky darkened over New York, deemed almost indispensable for a Democratic victory. Tammany, without loving the party less, seemed to hate Wilson more. And well did Wilson know it. He seems to have been particularly moody and nervous all through, telling House, in May, that defeat would be a relief, and that a second term might be "an anticlimax." He must have been in a curious mood indeed when he wound up his own effective speechmaking (mostly "front-porch," since "firesides" call for radios) in the Empire City.

McCormick and House had planned everything in meticulous detail; but, as House recorded, nothing seemed to please Wilson:

> It was the most acrimonious debate I have had with him for a long while. He did not like the New York program, he did not like the Republican expenditure to defeat him, as evidenced by the full-page advertisements in the morning papers. The Republicans had sixteen columns to our one and a half. He thought New York "rotten to the core," and "should be wiped off the map."

House and McCormick argued that only through the practice of advertising in opposition papers could the Democrats get into the more powerful Republican press at all, and that the President had as many friends in New York as anywhere. But they were accused of "New Yorkitis," and the tirade went on:

> The campaign should be run from elsewhere. He was absolutely certain of election without New York . . . organization amounted to nothing . . . the people determined such matters themselves. . . . To hear him talk you would think the man in the street understood the theory and philosophy of government as he does, and was actuated by the same motives.

And within a week Wilson was showing such imperturbability under apparent defeat that everyone around him wondered!

Not for the first nor the last time Republican strategy apparently helped to defeat the Republican party. It was based almost wholly on the idea of attacking the administration's record. As to what should have been done, as to what incoming Republicans would do, their orators were noticeably reticent. With a candidate less honest or less dignified than Mr. Hughes, the strategy might have worked better. But Mr. Hughes neither could nor would appeal to passion. Neither was he resourceful in evasion when questions proved embarrassing. The story that when asked what he would have done about the *Lusitania* had he been President, he merely "coughed," hits off the situation well enough. Doubtful voters in doubtful States demanded more than that. Everyone knows of the strange outcome: concessions of Hughes's election by even the New York *World* on election night; the Democratic banquet at the Biltmore ("never such a morgue-like entertainment in the annals of time"); then, as the night drew on and late returns from the West came in, increasing doubt, reviving Democratic hopes. And, finally, California. Mr. Daniels believes that the deciding influence in California was his policy, as Secretary of the Navy, in paying long-overdue attention to the Pacific coast. However that may be, Wilson's loss of California would have made Mr. Hughes President by a margin of two electoral votes. The closeness of the election was hardly more remarkable than Wilson's calmness. He seemed almost incredibly unconcerned. When, on election night, the presidential family was too agitated even to drink the customary bedtime milk and orange juice and ginger ale, the President went off to sleep as usual. It was thirty-six hours before he knew definitely that California had saved him. In the meantime, he had seemed more interested in the baptism of a Sayre grandchild.

CHAPTER XI

From Mediator to War Lord

H<small>E KEPT US OUT OF WAR</small>" had been an excellent campaign slogan; but, for all that, the number of really firm non-interventionists had been decreasing since the summer. At that time Professor Bliss Perry, giving commencement addresses in Iowa and Nebraska, and stopping over in Chicago to observe the Republican and Progressive conventions, had not heard a single person west of the Hudson, "except one redheaded Canadian Pullman conductor," say that we should go into the war. Among his Boston friends the feeling was very different; but his Yankee farmer neighbors in Vermont kept saying: "We don't know anything about the right and wrong of it." Perhaps in November he would have heard the same people say the same things; but through the country as a whole apprehension was increasing, and with it antagonism toward the Germans. For only the hyphenates wanted Germany to win; and Germany, now definitely under the control of her military and naval commanders, gave good promise of winning. France and Britain had had greater casualties than they could afford at Verdun and the Somme; the Somme operation had been disappointing in the extreme; Russia's army had been checked in the "Brusilov" offensive, and was becoming demoralized; Rumania, with its oil and wheat resources, was being rapidly overrun; and U-boat sinkings, already dangerous, would be far more so in the spring.

So there was increasing worry and dissatisfaction on the part of the many Americans who had been willing enough to let the Allies fight their own way to victory, or to a negotiated peace; but who felt that we could not, in the interests of our own security, allow Germany to dictate peace terms. Naturally, perhaps more naturally than justly, there was growing dissatisfaction with the way in which the President allowed the German Government to string out negotiations, instead of bringing it to time. Wilson himself was strained, nervous, and worried. He could not tolerate the thought of our entering the war; but neither could he tolerate the thought of German victory. Ergo, he *must* bring the war to a close at the first possible moment.

He had never really stopped trying to end it. He had made or, as some think, merely encouraged, two particular efforts, early in 1915, and again at the beginning of this, the election year. In each case Colonel House had gone to Europe, in the hope of carrying olive branches between Paris or London and Berlin. But, as he was forced to realize during his first mission, he needed the wisdom of the serpent as much as he did the gentle qualities of the dove:

> Unless one has undertaken such a job himself . . . he cannot possibly imagine the pitfalls that lurk on every hand. . . . If I succeed in doing no more than keeping out of trouble, I shall consider I have been fortunate.

The story of the two missions has, of course, more to do with House than with Wilson; but it cannot be omitted from any account of Wilson's long effort to seek peace and ensue it for the world.

The first trip was finally decided on during a twelve minutes' conversation between the President and the Colonel early in January 1915; but a good deal of preliminary work had been done in the preceding months. Wilson readily subscribed to House's idea of persuading the belligerents to make peace on the basis of the territorial *status quo ante,* general disarmament, and the evacuation and compensation of Belgium. He also hoped that House, by going to England, would be more successful than his Anglophile Ambassador in clearing up disputes concerning the blockade. In fact, he may, in his own mind, have regarded discussions about the blockade as the Colonel's primary mission, for there was scant reason to hope that the peace effort would succeed. Page and Gerard wrote that Britain and Germany were both determined to fight through to victory. Mr. Gerard jocularly warned House that the Germans would not be satisfied unless "we joined them in war, gave them all our money and our clothes and the U.S.A. into the bargain." The Entente and German ambassadors at Washington were equally agreed in predicting failure.

Wilson seemed hopeful and eager. He assured House that they

"were of the same mind"; gave him a letter to be used in any capital, offering himself, not as a mediator, but as a channel of communication between the belligerents; and took time to see him off at the station in Washington. Apparently he did not realize—nor did House until he learned by experience—the enormous difficulty of stopping twentieth-century war. He did not appreciate that neither side dares to make the first move, so long as the outcome is doubtful, for fear of giving an appearance of weakness and pessimism to the other side, still more to neutrals, and most of all to its own peoples. Peoples buoyed up by promises of victory and great national gains to endure terrible loss and suffering will not easily endure being told, while a spark of hope remains, that the promises cannot be kept. For the same reasons, neither side cares to bind itself to peace terms which the other can be expected to find acceptable.

House learned fast enough. Arriving in England early in February, on one of the *Lusitania*'s last crossings, he soon won Grey's sympathy and confidence. Wilson's wisdom in the choice of his agent is attested by Grey's tribute to House, written long afterwards:

> I found combined in him in a rare degree the qualities of wisdom and sympathy. . . . It was at once a relief, a delight, and an advantage . . . to talk with him freely. . . . His criticism or comment was valuable, his suggestions were fertile.

But the Foreign Secretary was apprehensive of a German trap and of the "storm of disapproval" that would be produced in England by any immediate peace moves. When Gerard outlined to House by letter the hard terms which the German Government might agree to accept, provided the Entente should offer them secretly and immediately, House saw that the game was up. In order to keep contacts established, in view of possible future missions, he went on to Berlin. His visit there was "exceedingly trying and disagreeable in many ways." The sinking of the *Lusitania* dropped the curtain on the whole futile episode.

The second House-Wilson attempt to find the way to peace, an attempt which took House back to London in the first week of 1916, was not conceived in that spirit of absolute neutrality for which the President was still publicly pleading. The general idea, it will be remembered, was that we should not only offer diplomatic help to the Allies in stopping the war on terms acceptable to them, but hold out to them a virtual promise of our military intervention on their side, in case Germany either refused to discuss peace, or proved too exacting at the peace table. In October 1915, only five months after the failure of the first effort, and while our negotiations with Berlin regarding the *Lusitania* were hanging fire, the suggestion had been made to Grey by House, in a letter revised by Wilson, word for word. We should "probably" go in with the Allies, said the letter, in case the Germans proved obstructive or unreasonable. Since the power to make war belongs to Congress, the insertion of the word "probably" was unavoidable; but it cannot be said with any certainty that Wilson had nothing but the Constitution in mind when he inserted it.

Grey, to whom the war was a perpetual agony, seemed attracted, and immediately asked and received assurance that the establishment of a League of Nations would be included in Wilson's peace terms. But, on behalf of all the Allied governments, he also asked for a more definite proposal, and for more definite assurance of our military intervention, in case the Germans proved recalcitrant. Virtually everyone in Britain expected that they would. On the other hand, Gerard reported that the German industrialists, unlike the Junkers, were becoming war weary. It is hard to decide just what Wilson was thinking, except that the idea of our involvement in the war was about as repugnant to him as ever. He wanted House to go back to England; but again he was thinking largely, and perhaps primarily, of securing greater concessions regarding the blockade. The Colonel carried no instructions, beyond what he regarded as assurances that his ideas and the President's were in complete accord, when he and Mrs. House sailed for England in an unwelcome floodlight of publicity.

Again he and the President were soon made to realize the difficulty of persuading angry belligerents to accept a negotiated peace. In London he was, as usual, treated with the deepest consideration by everyone, and invited to enlarge on his project. He told the members of the Cabinet that Wilson would favor the restoration of Alsace-Lorraine to France, the handing over of Constantinople to Russia, reparations to Belgium and Serbia, and the establishment of a League of Nations. Sometimes he got into discussions on more contentious points, such as Wilson's desire for "the freedom of the seas." This was a ticklish subject, especially at a time when the State Department was making demands about the blockade which neither Grey nor any other Foreign Secretary would have been able to concede without being driven from office. Nor were the Colonel's chances of carrying through his great project increased by British irritation over these demands, and by something like contempt for Wilson's willingness to go on arguing with the Germans about the *Lusitania*. The latter, according to Page, had deprived every member of the Government of "any confidence in the strength of the President for action."

House pressed on busily and hopefully with his "unofficial" talks. During a visit to Berlin he discovered that even von Bethmann-Hollweg was so far from favoring reasonable peace terms as to believe that his country would be entitled to an indemnity. But probably this seemed to him an additional reason for urging Britain to take advantage of the President's plan. At any rate, he tried the use of a little pressure on the British, warning them that they could not hope for American aid if they did not take advantage of Wilson's offer before their military position had become very serious. He came home in March 1916, believing that they would do it whenever they had success enough to avoid the appearance of weakness. He was able to present the President with a memorandum drawn up by Grey, putting the proposal on record. The memorandum also contained the British Government's noncommittal answer that it could "say nothing" until after it had consulted its Allies—at some future and more propitious time. This seemed a meager reward for a venture which had cost House much effort and some risk. If Wilson had really pinned any hopes on House's mission, Britain's coolness may have helped to harden his heart against the Allied governments.

But was it strange that the Allied statesmen, bent on teaching the Germans a lesson, bound by innumerable promises to their people to carry on till victory came, did not find the Wilson offer worth while? They dissected it in the light of long diplomatic experience, and of reports on America's President, her Congress, and her people. If the President called a peace conference, and the Germans refused to enter it; or if, having entered, they were unreasonable about terms, America would "probably" join the Allies. The Allied statesmen knew that the insertion of the word had been obligatory on Wilson; but, all the same, it constituted an enormous loophole through which the President or Congress would find it easy to escape. There was little or no doubt that Congress, backed by public sentiment, would make use of the loophole, unless the President stopped it up. Presidents can produce situations in which Congress cannot in decency or honor avoid war. But could Wilson produce such a situation on Germany's mere refusal to discuss peace, or agree to terms which he favored? No President would risk the disaster of defeat on an issue of this kind.

Wilson would have to use subterfuge, by producing a break on the submarine issue. But would he? After issuing some of the most solemn warnings which the diplomatic vocabulary offered, he had allowed the Germans to argue about the *Lusitania* almost *ad nauseam*. He was still publicly urging neutrality in thought and in spirit; he was opposed to any real military preparation; and he was promising to use every possible means to keep the country out of war. The Allied statesmen also knew that a presidential election was coming on. Probably Grey, and perhaps some of the others, realized that Wilson was not a man to break his word, or to barter convictions against ballots. But it was hard to say how far his *personal* commitment to overlook the "probably" went; and it was harder still to reconcile his speeches and his attitude on the expansion of the Army with any definite promise. And supposing Germany *was* brought into a conference with Wilson in the chair, what sort of peace could the Allies expect? According to House, the Germans would be compensated for restoring Alsace-Lorraine to France, remaining substantially as potent for mischief as before. Or what would Wilson do about "the freedom of the seas," and other such issues, which the Germans would hardly fail to raise?

The Allies, deeply convinced of their own rectitude, were far from pleased with Wilsonian pronouncements as the year went on. In October 1916 the President declared that the war had been caused by 'nothing in particular." Two months later he observed that, judging from the public statements made by the governments of the belligerents, "the objects which the statesmen . . . on both sides [had] in mind . . . [were] virtually the same." This was literally true; but Wilson was widely credited with having said that the war aims of the two groups of belligerents seemed identical to him. This last observation was made in the course of a third and last effort, this time official and quite his own, to bring about a negotiated settlement.

Now, he merely asked the belligerents to state the specific terms on which they would be willing to end the war, and what they were willing to do about providing for peace in the future. The situation of the British, as described by Mr. Lloyd George later, might well have made him hopeful that they, at least, would be very moderate:

Ministers who had held key positions in the Cabinet . . . were advising their colleagues that we could not carry on the War for many more months. Our principal naval adviser could see no remedy for the submarine attack. Discontent was spreading rapidly in our workshops. The pacifist movement was growing in the country . . . statesmen like Lord Lansdowne . . . were advising an early settlement.

But the British were as dogged then as they proved themselves four years ago; and the French were under worthy leadership. So, to Wilson's disappointment and surprise, the Allied peace terms bore a family resemblance to those which a defeated Germany faced later at Versailles. The German terms, refused at first, but finally given to the President in a letter from Bernstorff to House on the last day of January 1917, were even more those of conquerors.

A week before receiving them Wilson had shared his own opinions on the subject with the Senate. In view of the speeches he was shortly to make to America-at-war, his address to the senators, like his statement that the war had been started "by nothing in particular," will bear remembering. It was the last of those honest but rather ill-judged speeches that caused so much heartburning in Allied capitals. It was the last time he would offer himself as the impartial mediator between the quarrelsome nations of Europe. No lasting peace, he said, could issue from "peace forced upon the loser, a victor's terms imposed upon the vanquished." The peace must be one "of which the very principle [was] equality and a common participation in a common benefit." So he came to the phrase that was to stick: "It must be a peace without victory." And he used another phrase, less quoted, yet very characteristic in showing his inability, during the time of our neutrality, to disentangle facts from ideals. "I am seeking only to face realities," he said. *Realities,* when, after all the efforts he and House had been making for more than two years and a half, neither side had shown the slightest willingness to consider "the very principle" of equality! *Realities,* in talking about "peace without victory," while he had in his pocket Allied peace terms realizable only through complete victory, and when he could hope for no terms of any different nature from Berlin!

It was fine idealism to believe that, once the guns stopped shooting, and men stopped dying, there would be "common participation in a common benefit" from the kind of governments then existing at Berlin and St. Petersburg; but had even this much discoverable connection with realities? Wilson was not long in finding out. On the very day when House, in New York as usual, received Germany's peace terms from Bernstorff, the State Department was informed that Germany would begin "unrestricted" submarine warfare, not in a week nor in a month, but on the following day. She withdrew all undertakings that she had given; defied all the President's protests and warnings; and even went further. Not merely merchant vessels known or believed to be of Allied ownership, but all neutral merchantmen apparently bound for Allied ports were liable to be sunk without warning, and without regard for the lives of those on board. Germany would *permit* our neutral and sovereign Government to send one passenger vessel to and from Europe every week, provided it bore the markings, and followed the routes, which Berlin specified! The Germans naturally believed that they were provoking us to immediate hostilities. The President disagreed.

Various people have written of Wilson's amazement at Germany's step, despite the repeated warnings he had received. They have written of his "gray" face and hard-set jaw. But a sufficient account of his reactions in the tense days that followed is supplied by the single pen of Colonel House. The Colonel reached the White House on the following morning.

The President said he felt as if the world . . . after going from east to west . . . had begun to go from west to east, and that he could not get his balance.

After some hesitation and discussion Wilson agreed that Bernstorff should get his passports at once. But,

He reiterated his belief that it would be a crime for this Government to involve itself in the war to such an extent as to make it impossible to save Europe afterward. He spoke of Germany as "a madman that should be curbed." I asked him if he thought it fair to the Allies to ask them to do the curbing without doing our share. He noticeably winced at this, but still held to his determination.

Such "realities" as those created by the German announcement were difficult for him to face:

> The President nervously arranged his books and walked up and down the floor. Mrs. Wilson suggested golf and asked whether I thought it would look badly. . . . The President at last suggested that we play a game of pool.

Two days later Wilson explained the diplomatic break with Germany to Congress. He condemned the German Government's "sudden and deeply deplorable renunciation of its assurances"; but informed Congress that nothing save "overt acts" could persuade him that it meant to carry out its threats. He added that the nation stood true to "the immemorial principles of our people . . . the bases of peace, not war."

He acted in the spirit of his speech. Everything possible was done to quiet the people and the press. House even assured a delegation of extreme pacifists that the President "was quite as anxious to keep out of war" as they were. The President was, in fact, making some last desperate efforts to arrange a negotiated peace that would have allowed us to gloss over Germany's obliteration of all neutral rights. Meantime, Wilson's people were in a state of sore perplexity. They had been accustomed to receive leads from the White House; but in this desperate crisis no lead came. What crystallized public sentiment was the alertness of the British in discovering and publicizing a very natural move made by Herr Zimmermann, now German Minister for Foreign Affairs. A government on the verge of war will seek allies. Germany's logical choice was Mexico. A bribe was needed. What would appeal more to the Mexicans than the promise of Arizona, Texas, and New Mexico, in case of victory? But what could have roused the war spirit so effectively in every State of the Union as the news that Germany was willing to hand over three of them to our neighbor? Nearly all Americans were excited. Among those who seemed least excited was the President.

Wilson seemed calm; but his state of mind must have been pitiful. He was going through some of those pains of frustration by which idealists pay for the good they do. He was suffering in this way far more than in his last years at Princeton, though less, perhaps, than he was to do after the war. With nearly all his advisers, a decided majority in Congress, and the far greater part of the nation ready for war at last, he seemed more of a pacifist than he had ever been. In persuading the nation for two years and a half that war would be a "crime," he had persuaded no one more than himself. And the closer war came, the more vivid his anticipation of American casualties. Probably, too, his obstinacy made him the more insistent on preserving peace, as he felt that some people, the Germans in particular, were determined to force us to take up arms. When it was pointed out to him that the nation now favored war, he, who had always expressed such confidence in the people's judgment, remarked that the people were sometimes wrong. His sense of personal responsibility had never been more acute. When men around him spoke of the humiliation of America, of the contempt that other nations would feel toward us if we backed down under the extreme of outrage and insult, his answer was that *he* would personally take all the blame!

In his travail, he shut himself up, as he was to do at Paris later. Bliss Perry, spending the later winter and spring in Washington, found that friends with even greater claims upon the President's attention than his were refused access. All alone Wilson was battling with the problem of defending our neutral rights against a Power which had wiped them out, and would hear no argument but that of force; and at the same time of keeping us at peace, in order "to save the world."

But that did not mean that he had lost ability to strike swiftly and hard. He decided that our merchant vessels should be armed; and had a bill empowering him to arm them prepared and introduced. Both Houses approved it overwhelmingly. But a group of eleven men, representing the familiar Anglophobe-pacifist tie-up, and led by Senators O'Gorman, La Follette, and Norris, decided to make use of the Senate's strange and unfortunate lack of any rule to prevent even three or four members from defeating the wishes of the people, as expressed by their elected representatives in both Houses of Congress. No one knew better than Wilson that these "filibustering" groups are not only irresponsible in any proper sense, but often bring our Government into contempt. No one could have been more irritated and humiliated than Wilson was in watching them drone on, hour after hour, day after day, reading newspaper files, poetry, anything that would keep their voices going, and prevent one of the world's greatest legislative bodies from functioning. No one was better fitted than the President to see that their procedure is somewhat comparable to the *liberum veto* practice which helped to ruin old Poland, but like nothing else in any great government of our times.

The eleven senators killed the bill for the arming of merchantmen, but they did not daunt the President. Discovering that he possessed, in fact, authority to arm the ships without authorization from Congress, he did so immediately. Meantime, as in the days when tariff lobbyists threatened the people's interests, he called the attention of the country to an abuse which even today awaits a remedy. On March 4, just after he had been sworn in for his second term, he gave the press a statement on Senate filibustering:

> In the immediate presence of a crisis fraught with more . . . possibilities of national danger than any other the government has known within . . . history . . . the Congress has been unable to safeguard the country or to vindicate the elementary rights of its citizens.

He pointed out that, in the session which had just closed, appropriations and a number of important bills, approved by large majorities of both Houses, had been blocked by this preposterous filibustering. A few opinionated senators had produced "a complete paralysis alike of the legislative and of the executive branches of the government." Toward the end of the statement came the best-known passage:

> A little group of willful men representing no opinion but their own, have rendered the great Government of the United States helpless and contemptible.

As usual, he declared his confidence that the people of America would "draw the moral." He had used, of course, too contemptuous a tone toward men of whom some had achieved distinction and were acting in all sincerity. He was imprudent, too, in his implied indictment of the Senate as a whole. But his pride in America was touched. He knew how important it is that the people of a democracy shall respect their government. Perhaps he knew that it was not, and is not, unheard of for college undergraduates to read the *Congressional Record*, merely as offering more absurdities than the comic magazines.

Wilson's struggle to keep us out of war ended on April 2. By that time "overt acts" by German submarines had piled up; Russia, by the first of her 1917 revolutions, had saved us from the prospect of having to co-operate with one of the world's most autocratic governments; and some measures of preparation for hostilities had gone quietly forward. The enlisted strength of the Navy had been increased; and Admiral Sims had been sent, incognito, to consult with the British Admiralty on measures for insuring the safety of American merchantmen. The whole country felt that the end had come when, on March 21, Wilson called Congress to meet in special session on April 2, to "receive a communication by the executive on grave questions of national policy." But the people did not know the President. He was still reaching desperately for expedients that would allow him, without loss of honor, to avoid war. On the night before he was to address Congress, Frank Cobb of the *World,* now deeply in his confidence, received an emergency call to report at the White House. Arriving at one o'clock on the morning of April 2, he found the President "uncanny." At this eleventh hour Wilson declared that "he'd never been so uncertain about anything in his life" as about his decision to ask Congress to declare a state of war. He seemed distraught.

Yet, facing Congress, eighteen hours later, he not only presented an excellent case for war, but showed that he had been planning the way in which war should be carried on and the sort of peace he would now demand:

> The present German submarine warfare against commerce is a warfare against mankind. . . . The challenge is to all mankind. . . . We will not choose the path of submission and suffer the most sacred rights of our Nation and our people to be ignored or violated.

Such language was certainly to have been expected; but Congress may well have been startled when the President, advocating an immediate increase of the Army by at least half a million men, declared that they should be "chosen upon the principle of universal liability to service." Nor could anyone who had not been in Wilson's confidence have expected the pronouncement that peace in future could be secured only through "a partnership of democratic nations," since "no autocratic government could be trusted to keep faith." This led up to the keynote sentence: "The world must be made safe for democracy." Unless one takes it that Wilson believed peace in the present for America more important than peace in future for the world, it is hard to reconcile this with the efforts he had just been making to arrange a negotiated peace, in which the "autocratic government" of the Second Reich would have been counted upon to enter the "partnership" and "keep faith." And Frank Cobb may have wondered what had gone on inside the President since their early-morning talk, when he read the closing sentence:

America is privileged to spend her blood and her might for the principles that gave her birth and happiness and the peace which she has treasured. God helping her, she can do no other.

Perhaps he realized that Wilson was never a man to do things by halves.

The speech was well received. Within four days the two Houses passed the war resolution by something approaching unanimity. The only serious opposition came up in the Senate, where the woes of Ireland were once more interjected into American foreign policy, and where the curiously unrealistic theory that the power of money had played a dominant part in bringing us into the conflict was first revealed. Senator Norris could see no reason for our participation, save the desire "to preserve the commercial right of American citizens to deliver munitions of war to belligerent nations." His oratory became Bryanesque as it reached its peak: "I would like to say to this war god, You shall not coin into gold the life blood of my children." The idea, offspring of a materialistic age, was to become an obsession with a certain section of congressmen and a certain school of writers. But it has not appealed to those who have given close observation to Wilson's record and papers; nor, for that matter, to people who have studied the *Wall Street Journal* and the *Journal of Commerce*. Congressmen and writers have apparently found the heights and the evidences of Wilson's purity of motives inaccessible.

People who had deplored Wilson's cautious hesitancy and the lack of consistency or realism in some of his policies as long as we remained neutral, were pleasantly surprised when he turned out to be a very good war President. Almost overnight he appeared his confident, clearheaded, hard-driving old self again. For the pre-1914 Wilson had had many of the qualities of an effective war leader: concentration on the job in hand, swiftness and decisiveness when his mind was once made up, a taste for organization, an inclination to cut red tape and sweep obstacles aside. His ability to appeal to a nation at war and his capacity to pick and make full use of good helpers were, if less pronounced, at least quite adequate. The change in his bearing was a natural result of the removal of many repressions and tensions. At last he could give full vent to his feelings about the German Government and its militarists, outdistancing House and Senator Williams, at least equaling his Ambassador in London. He could do it without fear of injuring either his foreign policy or his leadership in Congress. Even Mr. Bryan offered his services to the war effort in any capacity, "until called to the colors."

In the war fervor that took hold of the nation, the President seemed more than ever The Leader, the "common voice." Union for victory was the common desire; and no one was more set on the success of our armed forces than was Wilson, so long as the kind of peace he wanted was unobtainable. Even in war he wanted to see "America First." Late as it was, he could push a program of real preparedness, with little to fear from congressional leaders. Then there was blessed relief from disputes about submarine warfare and the blockade. Our Navy would join in hunting the U-boats, and (under some rather transparent disguises) in making the "illegal" blockade tighter than it had ever been.

The President would not even have to trouble himself about getting "peace without victory." His only great concern would be in seeing that we (or he) should have a dominant influence in the decision as to when and on what terms the enemy could have peace. Even outwardly the war-making Wilson seemed different from the neutral one. For a long time he had obviously been tired and strained. Now, although he had never been so busy, he appeared happy and very fit. Some of the credit went to Mrs. Wilson and Dr. Grayson. They saw to it that he spent two or three evenings of every week at the theater, and that he got enough rides and walks and golf. But, as usual, his health responded to his spirits. He was obviously enjoying the exhilaration of the wartime atmosphere; and, probably quite as much, the expansion of his power.

"Wars cannot be waged by debating societies," wrote Professor Lindsay Rogers; "one man or one small group of men must have the power to make decisions, to change regulations." Lincoln's wartime government had been a sort of temporary dictatorship, based mainly on his "Commander-in-Chief" powers. Wilson made use of those powers, too, not only in such matters as deciding that an expeditionary force should go to France, but in creating a Committee on Public Information, with authority over censorship, and a War Industries Board, with the duty of "co-ordinating" private industry. In general, however, he relied as usual on his legislative leadership in Congress. Unfortunately, this did not comfort some of the senators and congressmen. It irked them to realize that they themselves had to give him the right to interfere increasingly with the activities and the fortunes of civilians. Every law they passed on such matters as food and fuel control, shipping and shipbuilding, involved the creation by the President of new governmental machinery under his personal control. In view of possible emergencies, the powers given to the President had sometimes to be very broad. Witness the fact that he had only to sign a paper, in order to make himself, in December 1917, the tsar of all the railroads. Congress could investigate and criticize to its heart's content, but it could not do much more. Stopping appropriations and impeaching high officials are not safe practices when a war is on. There was plenty to investigate and debate—inefficiency or worse in the production of ordnance, merchant ships, and, above all, aircraft. But Wilson could not be greatly blamed.

It is true that he was "much more interested in the *originating* than in the *directing* function"; but it is also true that he "had more duties to discharge than any one man could adequately perform." And he made his work even heavier than it need have been. In almost everything but military and naval matters he reserved all important decisions for himself. What is more, he resisted every effort made by Congress to diminish his responsibility and authority. He opposed the creation of a committee of the two Houses to supervise expenditures, of a war cabinet, and of a ministry of munitions. He fought a proposed transfer to the Inter-State Commerce Commission of some of his power to control priorities. And in every case he won. There was never a chance of overriding his veto. He even demanded and secured the power to abolish any bureaus or commissions or agencies of which he did not approve, and to distribute powers among all those that remained. He would not have liked being called a "war lord," but he wielded all the powers of one. It was not until after his return from Paris that Congress had its day.

The people seemed willing to let him have all the power he wanted, more because they were angry and determined and impatient of long wrangles in Congress than because he was especially successful in appealing to them. Except for occasional phrases in some of the later ones, his speeches had little or none of that gripping quality which one feels even in reading the war addresses of Chatham and Lincoln and Mr. Winston Churchill. There was too little heart in them. There was too much idealism. Or perhaps the idealism was pitched too high. Thus to the Confederate Veterans:

> We are going to lay all our wealth, if necessary, and spend all our blood, if need be, to show that we were not accumulating that wealth selfishly, but . . . for the service of mankind.

Or, again, in his appeals for gifts to the Red Cross:

> You cannot take very much satisfaction . . . in lending money to the United States, because the interest you draw will burn your pockets . . . give . . . all that you can spare, and do not consider yourself liberal. . . . If you give with self-adulation . . . you are giving to your own vanity.

It would be difficult for any people to reach up quite so far, or, at any rate, to enjoy being preached to in such terms by its elected servant.

If the people were not deeply stirred, those of them who carried his earlier speeches in their memories must sometimes have been startled at the change which had come over him. His Flag Day address in 1917 contained what House regarded as the sternest arraignment of German militarists and the German Government yet heard. It reads like some speech delivered during the present war. The war had been begun by "the military masters of Germany," who had never regarded the peoples of the world as "of like blood and frame as themselves." On the basis of "concrete plans" and "well-advanced intrigues," they had tried to carry out a design "which compassed Europe and Asia, from Berlin to Bagdad." The German Government was ready to make peace while it still held advantages with which it could buy its "pound of flesh." If the "military masters" could get such a peace, they would be entrenched in power; should they fail, "a government accountable to the people themselves [would] be set up in Germany":

> If they succeed they are safe and Germany and the world are undone; if they fail Germany is saved and the world will be at peace.

Then the well-known peroration:

> This is a Peoples' War . . . for freedom and justice and self-government amongst all the nations of the world. . . . For us there is but one choice. We have made it. Woe be to the man or group of men that seeks to stand in our way.

In this and in the Allied countries the speech was well received. In Germany, it was asked just how and just when the President had

learned of the military masters' vast intrigues. Some Americans wondered about this, too—remembering that the President had recently
said that the war had been caused "by nothing in particular," and
that there must be "peace without victory."

Later, people in the Allied countries noted something else. They had
been fighting hard, and suffering much, for more than thirty months.
Thanks to our military unpreparedness, it would still be long before
we should be able to give their armies any real relief. In Britain and
France the governments had insisted from the outset that they were
fighting for much the same objects as those which Wilson was setting
forth. But one would hardly have judged from his speeches that the
Allies knew anything about courage and sacrifice and suffering, or that
some of the Allied leaders also had ideals. We Americans, it seemed,
were to be freedom's chief, if not first and only, champions.

In this way, in several ways, Wilson claimed for us the position of a
separate and chosen people among all the belligerent nations. He was
speaking from full conviction; but was he contributing to the ends he
had in view? He was certainly not educating the American people in
the belief that we should be able to co-operate wholeheartedly with the
other great democracies at the Peace Conference and afterward. Of
course he was all for close co-operation in the war. Walter Page was
instructed to point out to Sir Edward Grey how much congressional
argument against the war resolution had been based on England's
treatment of the Irish, and that the establishment of "a satisfactory
method of self-government for Ireland" would remove the only obstacle to close relations between Westminster and Washington. A mission, selected by the President, and including Elihu Root, John R.
Mott, Charles Crane, and Cyrus McCormick, started for Russia, to
prevent "the socialist element" in the new government from putting
an end to joint operations with the Allied armies. The President, invited to a "Made-in-Japan" banquet, found the festival very timely
"in this critical hour when the United States takes its place alongside
of Japan in the battle for righteousness and civilization."

But even in co-operating we should still be separate. We were not to
be one of the Allies, but an Associate. Wilson deprecated the sending of
Allied missions to Washington, lest it should seem that we were being
led. And apparently Mr. Walter Lippmann and his associates of the
New Republic were really suspicious that Mr. Balfour and his mission
planned to drag us into a secret alliance of some sort. Even in fighting

we were to act as independently as possible. Our slowly forming Army at first got little training in the kind of warfare that had been going on in Europe for three years. The President's opposition to the sending of American officers to Britain or to France for observation and training was apparently in some degree responsible. Not General Pershing, but Wilson, first decided (wisely enough, perhaps) that our Army, when it did reach the combat area, should always retain its identity as "a separate . . . component of the Allied forces."

But even more in making peace than in making war was our privileged position to be emphasized. Wilson's desire for international leadership was already strong. Perhaps Frank Cobb of the *World* helped to re-enforce it, by having a presidential address translated into German, so that French aviators could scatter copies along the German lines. At any rate, the President was convinced that our stand at the Peace Conference would have to be a separate one. Mr. Balfour told him about the secret treaties between the Allies, and furnished the State Department with copies of nearly all of them. Against the advice of House, who feared trouble, the President discussed war aims with the heads of the Allied missions, and had a brush with M. Viviani about France's views. Complaining later to House of the imperialistic aims of the Allied leaders, he added a sentence which would have disturbed them mightily: "When the war is over we can force them to our way of thinking because by that time they will, among other things, be financially in our hands." He was preparing not only to lead the other nations into righteousness, but to club them into it. He was not a Calvinist for nothing.

CHAPTER XII

The Peoples' War

In an "APPEAL TO THE PEOPLE," made a few days after we entered the war, Wilson had demanded that Americans should "all speak, act, and serve together." The nation was quite ready. Some Republican leaders talked of a party truce; and there were suggestions that we should have a coalition Cabinet. The President did not agree. He knew that coalition Cabinets are usually troublesome; and he had no intention of allowing his authority or his leadership to be challenged. Moreover, as Mr. Root said, the Republicans were ready to do their utmost to forward the war effort in any case. But outside the Cabinet, Wilson was more than ready to make use of them in positions of great influence. Three assistant Secretaries of War and two assistant Secretaries of the Treasury, the majority of the members of the Council of National Defense and of the War Trade Board, were of the G.O.P. So were the heads of the Red Cross, of the Aircraft Board, of the Emergency Fleet Corporation, and of the National War Labor Board (the last mentioned being Mr. Taft). When the Aircraft Board, which at first functioned miserably, was accused of inefficiency and corruption, the President, by way of staving off senatorial action, placed the investigation in the hands of Mr. Hughes.

Of course no decent President would have thought of parties when it came to choosing commanders of the armed forces; but since some charges of partisanship were brought against Wilson by friends of Colonel Roosevelt and General Wood, it is worth noting that General Pershing, Admiral Sims, General March, our Chief of Staff, and other high commanders were all Republicans, in so far as military and naval officers could be reckoned party men. Nor can any charge of partisanship be entertained on the basis of the Roosevelt and Wood incidents. The former was annoying and rather preposterous; the latter was deplorable. Colonel Roosevelt, after visiting Germany in 1910, had brought home a photograph of the Kaiser and himself on horseback, inscribed by his imperial host: "The Colonel of the Rough Riders lecturing the Chief of the German Army." Mr. Roosevelt had thoroughly enjoyed the joke; but his actions in the spring of 1917 suggest that he had not taken it at its full value.

He not only asked that he should be authorized to raise, train, and take to France a division of volunteers, but that certain officers of the regular Army should be assigned to it. When his military standing was questioned, he informed the War Department that, as a former President and therefore Commander in Chief, he was eligible for any command! He wrote Senator Lodge that, in his opinion, General Pershing should have equal rank, and that their two divisions, with a third, should form an army corps under his great friend, General Wood. He also confided in the Senator that he was moderating his attacks upon the President, until the matter had been arranged. Remembering that he was no longer physically well, one would gladly pass over his speeches and letters and activities at this and later times, if their effects had not sometimes been serious for Wilson. So innocent were we Americans of any knowledge of modern warfare in those days that a respectable minority in the House of Representatives and a respectable majority in the Senate voted for an amendment to a bill expanding the Army which specifically endorsed the Colonel's plan. There were people (and Clemenceau, curiously enough, professed to be of their number) who thought that Roosevelt's position, record, and great enthusiasm would make him a morale builder for the wearied troops of the Allies.

The decision lay with the President. He realized that to let the ex-President have his way would seem generous, and would therefore be popular. He knew that he was almost certain to be accused of partisanship if he refused. But Roosevelt's proposal lay entirely outside the plan of the War Department and General Staff. What sort of discipline would have obtained in the A.E.F., with a divisional commander who was a rank amateur in real soldiering, but never forgetful that he had once been able to give orders to every general in France? Wilson left the decision to Secretary Baker; but it does not seem possible that he would have allowed Roosevelt to go to France. A good deal of the inevitable abuse poured in on him; and Mr. Roosevelt's attacks upon his administration and his policies became more vitriolic than before, if possible. They were the more effective because there was real ground for criticism in the treatment of General Wood, the Rough Rider's friend. Neither Wilson nor General Pershing thought that General Wood's presence in France would be conducive to the best of discipline; but they had apparently nothing to do with the fact that the General, after being allowed to prepare a division for overseas service, was detached from it and ordered to stay at home, immediately before it was to sail. In this case, army routine was responsible for a clumsy and painful blunder.

Wilson had to take most of the blame when things of this sort occurred; but in point of fact he interfered very little with his Secretaries of War and the Navy, or with the armed forces. When Mr. Baker presented the names and records of six possible commanders of the A.E.F., Wilson told him to make the choice. The recommendations of the General Staff met little or no opposition at the White House. Except when blasting at the British Navy for what he regarded as its lack of initiative, demanding that the submarines should be attacked like "hornets" in their nests, and giving his views on the proper methods by which vessels should be convoyed, he now seemed willing to let uniformed "specialists" have their way.

All the same, it seems surprising that even before we went to war he agreed readily with the General Staff that the new "national army" divisions should consist of conscripted men. Conscription had no more nor less to do with a "standing" army or a reversal of all our "national polity" than it had had in December 1915, when he had told Congress that volunteering offered the only proper method of recruiting in America. If he had ever regarded his "preparedness" program of 1915–16 as more than a gesture, he had performed as much of a *volte face* here as in his views on the war's origin and the undesirability of victory for either side. At any rate, he argued convincingly that every young man was under obligation to defend his country, and that it was the Government's duty to place him where he would be of the greatest use. He did not even approve of the exemption of conscientious objectors, lest the "unconscientious," the shirkers, should take refuge under it. But neither, for that matter, did Mr. Bryan!

It cannot be said that the President's advocacy of selective service was a matter of expediency; for the "War Army Act," introduced on

April 5, and endorsed by Secretary Baker and the General Staff as well as by himself, severely tested his leadership. The House Committee reported out the bill with an amendment that the selective draft should be resorted to only in case there should not be enough volunteers. Even at that, the chairman refused to sponsor it, and the task fell to the ranking Republican of the committee—who happened to be of German birth. Mr. Kitchin, the majority leader, was opposed to it. The Speaker, Champ Clark, said that Congress would never accept the selective draft, since the words "conscript" and "convict" had the same significance for Americans. Things went better in the Senate; though here the majority of the opposition was composed of Democrats. The President was firm, and the President was confident. As Congress debated the bill, all the forms necessary for its execution were quietly printed, so that recruiting should be carried out with the least possible delay. The President's pressure, exerted by the usual methods, gave him what Mr. Lindsay Rogers called "perhaps the greatest triumph that any American President has ever won in his relations with Congress" in the space of about a month. On June 5 nearly ten million men were registered for the draft. Meanwhile, the executive offices of the White House were humming with activity.

It has been said that only a "superman" could have handled efficiently the multiplicity of tasks that added themselves in 1917 to the ordinary duties of the President. Merely to set up all the new boards and commissions and agencies which were needed would have been a sufficient tax on any busy President's executive ability. But that was only a beginning. Demands, disputes, and protests crowded in from every side. There were questions of desperate urgency to be met. Admiral Sims and Mr. Page kept cabling from England that a situation of extreme peril had arisen out of the success of the German submarine campaign and Britain's consequent lack of food. That meant, among other things, the sending overseas of all anti-submarine vessels that could be spared, the greatest possible acceleration of our shipbuilding program, and the establishment of priorities in the handling of freight by our railroads. Then came news that the British, who had made liberal loans to their allies, had now reached the end of their resources in making purchases abroad. Unless we should extend large credits, they could no longer supply their forces with American munitions that were indispensable. French needs were similar. That meant, among other things, successive arrangements for loans to the Allies and the enlargement of our war loan drives.

At the same time, the administration had to be thinking about our own war activities: the dispatch of Pershing, with his token force; plans for the training and transportation of the real A.E.F.; consideration of General Smuts's suggestion that our greatest contribution would be in furnishing the Allies with sufficient planes to give them the mastery of the air; devising ways by which, without too obvious a right-about, we could tighten the blockade against which we had protested for so long. This last task was difficult. But by joining (instead of opposing) the British in blacklisting neutral firms which traded with the enemy; by refusing to coal vessels engaged in trade which benefited the Central Powers; by virtually abolishing the distinction between absolute and conditional contraband, to say nothing of issuing lists of contraband about as comprehensive as could be conceived; and by giving out that we were merely attempting to prevent the escape of submarines, when we helped to make the North Sea a vast mine field, the administration managed to tighten the blockade without too much loss of face. But handling such questions took time and energy. And all the world, or most of it, seemed out of joint. The State Department was especially occupied with Mexico, disorderly and unfriendly to us, as usual; with Russia, where our mission found the Army disintegrating, German propaganda increasingly effective, and "the socialistic element" gaining; and with Japan, even then insisting on special rights in China which we could not recognize. Our difficulties in dealing with these and other countries had been accentuated by our entrance into the war. The President, feeling it his duty to make all important decisions, was again subjecting himself to serious strains.

At home the difficulties multiplied. Since few even of our regular Army officers had much idea of the nature and importance of intelligence in twentieth-century warfare, it was not surprising that even the *New York Times* complained constantly that news was kept from the public; and that the introduction of the administration's "Espionage" bill raised a storm of protest. The bill provided for the punishment of persons who violated regulations laid down by the executive, to prevent the publication of information about our defense measures which might be useful to the enemy. With the press up in arms, Republicans and Democrats joined in refusing to approve even the mildest censorship provisions that could be devised. The bill, as finally passed, strengthened the hands of the administration in guarding our security in such ways as the exclusion of seditious matter from the mails; and the Government's relations with the newspapers were made easier by the creation of the Committee on Public Information, headed by Mr. Creel. But the gentlemen of the press remained discontented, as they will always be, perhaps, until editors who function in wartime are given some elementary instruction in naval and military intelligence.

There was also much delay and trouble about food control. Herbert Hoover, after remarking (as Leon Henderson has reason to remember) that "the man who [accepted] such a position [would] die on the barbed wire of the first-line entrenchments," did great service by bravely agreeing to become Food Administrator himself. It was the beginning of his close connection with Wilson, a connection founded on deep mutual respect. But food control was established only after another row of first-rate proportions in Congress. Senator Sherman denounced the Food Control bill as "foolish, autocratic, confiscatory, unconstitutional, and idiotic." He was sure that labor unions so controlled the administration that no union member would ever see military service in France against his will.

The President's hope that Americans would "all speak, act, and serve together" was not being too well realized. Difficulties about sedition were constantly coming up. Citizens were apt to pass the limits of propriety or even loyalty, officials those of justice or even common sense. To add to the confusion, the "suffragettes" were pushing their campaign in the streets. And over all domestic issues loomed the relations between capital and labor. Either strikes were unusually frequent, or the effects they had on the country's war activities made them seem so. Great efforts to prevent them had been made. Mr. Gompers had urged capital and labor to postpone, for the duration, "any plans for changes in labor standards"; and the administration had provided new and ample machinery for the arbitration of disputes. These were the bases on which Wilson took his stand, a stern and even minatory stand, throughout. Perhaps his position was best set out in an address to an A.F. of L. convention in November 1917:

While we are fighting for freedom we must see . . . that the conditions of labor are not rendered more onerous . . . also . . . that the instrumentalities by which the conditions of labor are improved are not blocked or checked. . . . I have taken pleasure in conferring from time to time with your president, Mr. Gompers . . . I like to lay my mind alongside of a mind that knows how to pull in harness. The horses that kick over the traces will have to be put in corral.

The "horses" which showed inclination to "kick over" might, of course, be offspring either of labor or of capital, since "nobody [had] the right to stop the processes of labor" before exhausting "all the methods of conciliation and settlement."

The President had found labor "reasonable in a larger number of cases than the capitalists"; but, no matter which side was at fault, it was essential to bring the two face to face. On this the Government would "insist." With mine operators and manufacturers Wilson had already struck a harsher yet more idealistic note:

> I hear it insisted that . . . it is necessary to pay very liberal and unusual profits in order to "stimulate production." Do [the people who say this] mean that you must be . . . bribed to make . . . a contribution that costs you neither a drop of blood nor a tear, when . . . men everywhere depend upon . . . you to bring them out of bondage and make the world a fit place to live in again . . . that you will . . . drive a bargain with the men who are enduring the agony of this war on the battlefield . . . with the bereaved women and the pitiful children?

Those who had fixed excessive maritime freight rates, in spite of the fact that extra hazards were covered by war-risk insurance, "had taken the most effective means in their power to defeat the armies engaged against Germany." Wilson was equally ready to apply the whip to any labor organization that misbehaved. Witness his speech to the brotherhoods of carpenters and joiners:

> No body of men have the moral right in the present circumstances . . . to strike until every method of adjustment has been tried to the limit. If you do . . . you are undoubtedly giving aid and comfort to the enemy.

He was not increasing his popularity with either side; but, as he thought at least, he was helping the nation to win the war.

"Woe be to the man . . . that seeks to stand in our way," Wilson had cried, in his Flag Day address. He talked in that tone to the representatives of capital and labor; and, being no respecter of persons, he did not hesitate to administer something like a snub to no less a person than the Pope. Handicapped as he was by feeling against his Church which was almost as universal as the Church itself, and by the unsatisfactory relations of the Vatican with the Italian and other governments, Pope Benedict XV had now become the logical mediator, if not the only possible mediator, of the world war. In August 1917 he took up the task which Wilson was no longer able to perform. He asked the belligerents to come together for the discussion of peace terms. The general principles which he suggested as a basis for the discussion were decidedly Wilsonian: the displacement of "the material force of arms" by "the moral force of right"; a "simultaneous and reciprocal diminution of armaments"; the settlement of international disputes by arbitration, "subject to . . . sanctions to be determined" against any State refusing to arbitrate or accept an arbitral award; "the true liberty of and common rights over the sea"; and the "reciprocal restitution of territories." All questions of frontiers were to be worked out at the peace table, due weight being given to "the aspirations of the populations." The appeal was very gently and persuasively worded. But the President, so long the great advocate of mediation, answered it, on behalf of the Allies and their great Associate, in terms that clearly constituted a reproof:

His Holiness in substance proposes that we return to the *status quo ante bellum*. . . . The object of this war is to deliver the free peoples . . . from the menace and the actual power of a vast military establishment controlled by an irresponsible government which . . . secretly planned to dominate the world . . . without regard to the sacred obligations of treaty or . . . long-cherished principles of international action and honor. . . . We cannot take the word of the present rulers of Germany as a guarantee of anything that is to endure.

It was just seven months since Wilson had made his "peace-without-victory" speech; and there had been no essential alteration in the German Government or in its principles—or lack of them. The Wilson of August 1917 seemed to be reproving, not merely the Pope, but the Wilson of seven months before. The peacemaker had seemingly been transformed into a war lord. Yet this was more true in appearance than in reality. Even in the first months of the war, the President's thoughts had turned constantly to peace. It was not to be a papal peace, nor peace along the lines proposed by peace societies in this country and Britain. Their program he professed to find too definite. Still less was it to be the sort of peace which the Allied governments had in mind. No, the peace was to be a Wilson peace. With the war once over, he would force the Allied governments "to our way of thinking."

As the summer of 1917 passed into autumn and the autumn into winter; as young Americans trained for overseas service; and the new boards and agencies learned by trial and error to do efficient work, Wilson found himself facing a question that would have taxed the wisdom of Solomon—the question of dealing with Russia. No American really understood the situation there, or could be more than merely lucky in predicting the outcome. Outside old Russia, most of the divisions of the former empire, in both Europe and Asia, had either declared independence or were more or less in revolt. No one could be sure that they would ever be subdued again. Even at Petrograd and Moscow the Bolsheviks were able to rule only by a reluctant alliance with the terroristic Social Revolutionaries. In other countries they were generally regarded as a mere faction, and an odious faction, which might be put out of power at any time. The army having almost completely broken down, troops of the Central Powers were supreme in the Ukraine; while the Turks were joyfully reclaiming their ancient sovereignty in the Caucasus. As a whole, the more or less liberal Russian middle class was waiting for redemption from its communist oppressors, even at German hands.

Lenin, very conscious of his party's insecurity, was for peace with the Central Powers at almost any price. His peace policy had been a major element in giving the Bolsheviks their mastery of the country. Without peace he could not hope to make it communist. He would even let the Germans keep control of the Ukraine, would even pay an indemnity in food and war supplies, it seemed, if those were the lowest terms on which they would make peace. Trotsky did inquire what Allied aid would be forthcoming, if the Bolsheviks refused the peace terms which the Central Powers were offering; but there is no reason for believing that Lenin would have carried on the war, no matter what promises might have been made to him at Paris, London, and Washington. And no promises whatever were made. The French detested the Bolsheviks as men who had betrayed and endangered France, by allowing the Central Powers to concentrate their armies on the western front, and by furnishing supplies which reduced the effectiveness of the blockade. Nearly all Frenchmen suspected the Bolshevik leaders of being German agents, or "collaborationists." The fact that the Germans had sent Lenin back to Russia gave the suspicion much plausibility.

And what was "bourgeois" France to think of men who were

determined to rob her, by repudiating all foreign indebtedness, except only to the Central Powers; who proclaimed, even through the unusual medium of diplomatic notes, their desire to see capitalism abolished everywhere? What were religious and moral Frenchmen to think of men who were aggressive atheists; and who, as the first "totalitarians," were already displaying a ruthlessness and brutality toward internal enemies which modern civilization had supposedly debarred? Instead of helping this pestilential Russian faction in establishing itself, to the detriment of Russia and all the Western world, the thing to do was to make common cause with all elements in Russia which were prepared to reverse the Bolshevik policies, domestic and foreign. These elements, it was believed, might even succeed in restoring the eastern front.

There were two excuses for intervention of some sort. Large stocks of war matériel, supplied by the Allies to the Tsarist Government, were lying at Murmansk. The landing of Allied forces there and at Archangel would at least prevent the German use of these supplies on the western front. The other possible bridgehead for intervention was at Vladivostok. There the excuse was the appealing one of protecting the 50,000 Czechoslovaks who, captured as prisoners, had reorganized within Russia to fight the Central Powers; had drifted into hostilities with the Bolsheviks; and now, strung out along the trans-Siberian line, had become an important element in the anti-Bolshevik movement. They were brave and capable fighters; and they had been trying to girdle the world in order to fight the Germans, their oppressors for centuries.

The British point of view differed in few particulars from the French. The British Government was no better informed as to circumstances and prospects. Even Lord Robert Cecil, Balfour's Under-Secretary at the time, was reputedly among those who found it difficult to believe that the Bolshevik leaders were not German agents. Bruce Lockhart, stationed at Petrograd and later at Moscow, saw much closer to the truth. But Lockhart's obvious sympathy with some Bolshevik ideals made him more or less suspect in Downing Street. So the British, while apparently more troubled than the French by the idea that intervention without an invitation from responsible leaders was an infringement of the very principles the Allies were fighting for, swung over more and more to concurrence with French policy.

Wilson's dealings with Bolshevik Russia constituted only one of his many world war activities; but it is difficult to think of another so well worth following. For it tested him in more ways than one; and, as some of the Allied statesmen may have realized, offered more than a suggestion of what was to be expected from him at the Peace Conference. He acted under great handicaps: inadequate or false information, conflicting influences, and arguments. Even without these, things would have been hard enough. He was trying to stick to his liberal principles in a world where his type of liberalism was already in eclipse. He was trying to get them adopted in a country where they were understood and subscribed to only by a powerless and terrorized minority. As a result, his policy was sometimes unrealistic almost to the point of absurdity. But he could follow no other, without denying the most fundamental article of his political beliefs—the ability of the people almost everywhere to give themselves free government. This faith of his had greatly developed with the years. In 1901, when reflecting on problems of government as a professor at Princeton, he had published in the *Atlantic Monthly* an article setting down "the necessary conditions precedent to self-government." They included:

> The slow growth of the sense of . . . community and of fellowship in every general interest; . . . the self-restraint of give and take; . . . the patience and intelligence which are content with a slow and universal growth.

But in 1917 and 1918 he talked with apparent confidence of the immediate establishment of self-government in Russia! The people there would win their way to freedom and world fellowship if treated generously and sympathetically; if given material relief, and subjected only to a minimum of pressure.

Either he utterly misconceived conditions, and above all the political immaturity of the Russian masses, or his mystical belief in the people had made him one of those idealists with fixed ideas who bruise or smash themselves in contact with reality; who often do much temporary harm in the process of doing lasting good. He detested the theories and the methods of the Bolsheviks. Moreover, he had great sympathy with certain of their victims and their enemies. He was once observed with tears streaming down his cheeks, as a Russian lady of the old regime poured out to him the horrors experienced by her and by so many of her kind. He felt as deeply as anyone for the valiant Czechoslovaks. But he was on guard against emotionalism as usual; and somewhere between the old Russian government and the new lay "the people." He seemed to feel that even the Russian masses would somehow hear his voice, and respond to his hopes for them. This placed him, as usual, apart from the Allies. In fact, both he and the country seemed to stand more and more apart as the first spirit of camaraderie died down and old or new causes of ill feeling thrust themselves in. Wilson believed that the Allied governments wanted to "scoop everything" in the way of imperialistic gains before the Peace Conference could meet. And even in the spring months of 1918, when it was a question whether a sufficient number of our troops would get to France in time to prevent an Allied debacle, the eternal jealousies between American and British commercial interests poked up their heads.

Within this general setting Wilson applied himself to the task of dealing with the Russian riddle. On March 11, 1918, he addressed a message to "the people" of Russia, expressing his hearty sympathy with their desire "to free themselves forever from autocratic government." There was no way of sending it except through the Congress of Soviets. Since "the Russian people" could hardly answer him, the Bolshevik leaders did. Side-stepping the autocratic government issue, as well they might (having used Red troops to disperse the constituent assembly two months before, when only one third of the delegates proved to be of the true faith), they expressed thanks for the sympathy, but also the fervent hope that the happy time was not far off when all peoples, of course including Americans, would "throw off the yoke of capitalism" and "establish a socialistic state of society which alone is capable of securing a just and lasting peace." There was really nothing that the President could say to that.

When, on the day following the dispatch of Wilson's message, the Bolshevik Government signed the Treaty of Brest-Litovsk, the Allied governments protested vigorously. Wilson, acting independently as usual, seemed to go as far as even he could do in sheer defiance of realities. He would not protest the treaty. The treaty did not exist for us, he said, since we had not recognized the Bolshevik Government which made it. "There [was] in fact no Russian government to deal with." So "the Russians" were still allies, and still at war. Whatever we should do would be done in a spirit of friendliness between co-belligerents. This sounded delightfully humane and brotherly. But Wilson had to deal with the interventionists in Allied countries and at home. He had, as at Paris later, to reconcile his principles in so far as possible with facts, and with demands from Allied leaders that were difficult to refuse.

The question of action at Vladivostok was the most critical. Wilson at first opposed any American participation in a suggested Japanese landing. But slowly he gave ground. The Supreme War Council of Allied statesmen and their military advisers, formed in November 1917 to secure unity of action, urged our participation vigorously; and the President was much interested in hearing of "nuclei of self-governing authority" in Siberia. He was so poorly informed as even to wonder whether we could legitimately assist General Semenov, who, according to Lockhart, was "a Cossack general waging a brigand warfare against the Bolsheviks" from within the Chinese border. During the spring and summer of 1918 the pressure steadily increased. Mr. Balfour argued that action against Germany from the east was much needed, and might help to rescue Russia, Bolsheviks and all, from Germany's clutches. General Foch supported him. Our minister in China wired that our representatives in Siberia believed that only intervention could stop the Germans even there. Reports came in that the movement in Asiatic Russia against the Bolsheviks was growing. At the same time, Wilson was being urged to send at least a token force to Murmansk. Mr. Lansing and General Bliss, the latter acting with the Supreme War Council, thought it would be worth while.

The President was sorely perplexed. How could he tell whether "the people" of Russia were really friendly or hostile; how much attachment, if any, they had to their Bolshevik masters; whether intervention would be welcomed as assisting them to liberate themselves from a government they had certainly not chosen, or would be resented as an inexcusable violation of national sovereignty? Wilson's principal advisers were wary of direct and immediate intervention at any rate. Mr. Lansing suggested asking Mr. Hoover to head a relief mission to Russia, and delaying action until he could report on what he found. Colonel House, after consultation with Lord Reading, made the more subtle suggestion that the mission should be given such "military assistance" as it might need in order to function effectively. Perhaps the idea was that a mild measure of intervention, baited with and cloaked by benevolence, could be adjusted to conditions on the ground.

Under all this pressure Wilson publicly announced his policy in July 1918. It seems worth noting that his friend and admirer, Mr. Justice Brandeis, believed that this was the first of a series of mistakes which the President was to make under a strain which was too much for his nervous system. The Government, said Wilson, saw justification for aiding the Czechoslovaks in their plight, but only "in the interest of what the Russian people themselves" desired. It would therefore be willing to collaborate with the Allies for this one object; but would give no countenance to any interference in the internal affairs of Russia, or to any dimunition of her territorial integrity. It would also yield to the judgment of the Supreme War Council by sending a small force to Murmansk. Wilson had yielded against his better judgment. In fact, Mr. Newton Baker revealed that he agreed to action in northern Russia only because he had already denied so many Allied requests. He had assumed that he knew how the Russians felt; and had showed his suspicion of some of the Allies.

He had attempted a compromise, but the compromise brought him no peace. The British commander in northern Russia attempted to make the Allied forces there and in Siberia into an eastern front against the Germans, with the Czechoslovaks as a connecting link. The Czechoslovaks seemed unwilling to desert their anti-Bolshevik Russian friends. Mr. Balfour stated that the British general in the north had taken unwarranted action; but not before Wilson had bitterly complained of the "utter disregard" of the conditions he had attached to the intervention of our troops. "Strongly as our sympathies constrain us," he wrote, "to keep the country on the Volga front out of the hands of the merciless Red Guards," he would insist upon adherence to the terms he had laid down. So matters drifted on to the autumn, when the collapse of the Central Powers diverted attention from Russia. The whole episode had been unfortunate. But Wilson had done his best, in an impossible situation, to show some regard for international usage, and yet to conciliate the largest number of people. He had shown his sympathy with the prevailing sentiment in this country; horror at Bolshevik brutality, desire to see self-government in Russia, and sympathy with the Czechoslovak legion. He had tried to give encouragement to Russian liberals. He had made as many concessions to the Supreme War Council as his principles and the opinions of his military advisers would allow. As a result, he had not pleased anyone, either in this country or abroad.

Nor had the Russian imbroglio been of good omen for the approaching Peace Conference. The Allied statesmen had found the President unrealistic and stubborn: he believed that he had seen in them new

evidence of untrustworthiness. He was probably confirmed in his resolution to "force them to our way of thinking" when peace was being
made. "Our" way of thinking had been laid down in the "Fourteen
Points" address and in subsequent speeches.

Probably few people remember the resourcefulness shown, at a certain embarrassing moment, by Mrs. John W. Davis, whose husband
became Ambassador to Great Britain, when, in 1918, Mr. Page sacrificed his life to his duties. During a lull in the conversation at an official
dinner party everyone was staggered when a British general with a
booming voice asked Mrs. Davis what meaning she attached to "the
freedom of the seas." Mrs. Davis was afraid that she didn't know very
much about it, but thought it "had something to do with mixed bath-
ing, hadn't it?" Next day her drawing room was filled with flowers by
the Embassy's grateful and admiring staff. There was to be far more
serious embarrassment, before and during the Peace Conference, because no interpretation of the Points was forthcoming until a beaten
Germany had offered to accept them as a basis for the negotiation of
peace. At least some of the blame was due to Wilson's insistence upon
holding himself and his country so much apart; to his apparent lack
of any desire to come to an exact understanding on peace terms with
the Allied statesmen.

After our entrance into the war he had gone on secluding himself.
Bliss Perry, knowing the strain it was placing on him, and remembering how he had formerly found relief, suggested to Jusserand that "he
should stroll over to the White House some evening, and talk Wordsworth":

The ambassador's face changed sharply. "He doesn't want to see any
of us," he remarked; and at that we joined the ladies.

No understanding about the Points was reached.

None was necessary on most of them. Except that the one calling
for the establishment of Italian boundaries "along clearly recognizable
lines of nationality" was in sharp conflict with the promises the Entente
governments had made to Italy when, in the anxious spring of 1915,
they had been bidding against the offers of the Central Powers for
her entrance into the war, the Points concerning territorial settlements
were strikingly similar to a set of proposals which Lloyd George (to
Wilson's obvious annoyance) had published a few days before the
Fourteen Points speech was made. With some of the general principles

laid down, concerning "open covenants openly arrived at," "freedom of the seas," removal of economic barriers, disarmament, the adjustment of colonial claims, and the establishment of an association of nations, the case was different. All but the three first mentioned had been included in proposals offered by the British Premier. But the three afforded legitimate ground for disagreement; called for sacrifices on the part of subscribing Powers; and should have been clarified. Even where American and British principles appeared to be the same, interpretations might differ. Was it to be expected that the French and British in particular would accept whatever the President's idealism decreed for them? Before we should be able to give effective help to their armies in the field they would have endured all the perils and miseries of the war for well onto four years. Their casualties would almost certainly make ours look insignificant. Neither would the ruin of France's best industrial region, the sinking of Britain's merchant fleet, the bombings of London and Paris, be lost sight of.

But Wilson, determined that we should "save the world," even in spite of itself, did not see things in this light. Material losses, even casualties, could be regarded as passing things, especially when one's own people had suffered only a minor share of them. But a new order, based on the proper principles, would endure, to prevent fresh casualties and losses. Not long before we entered the war, the *Volkszeitung* of Cologne, speaking in anything but a friendly spirit, had described the President's attitude with great accuracy:

Mr. Wilson has the burning ambition to step forward as the leader of a new humanity and to create for his country an authoritative influence in world questions. . . . No chief of state has ever before addressed other powers in a tone resembling his. Mr. Wilson has chosen a forum from which he sees all the nations of the globe assembled as his hearers. He speaks . . . in the capacity of the preacher of a new system of justice and freedom.

Yes, he saw "all the nations of the globe assembled as his hearers." Consequently, he addressed their governments in a tone which the *Volkszeitung* found "bordering closely on the limits of the endurable."

He went on speaking in that tone. In September 1918 he talked to a New York gathering in support of the fourth Liberty Loan. Beforehand he told Tumulty that the Allied statesmen would not like some of the things he planned to say. "We must be brutally frank with friends and foes alike," he said. In his speech he was fiercer than ever in his denunciation of autocratic government and militarism, of the lack of respect for either honor or justice displayed by the rulers of the Central Powers. But, all the same, he insisted that the peace settlement would have to be one of "impartial justice in every item," as applied even to nations to whom we should not wish to show justice. The settlement should not accord privileged treatment, economic or otherwise, to any country or group of countries. He went on to promise that America would bear her full part in the projected association of nations, and to repeat his demand that economic barriers between the nations should be removed as much as possible. Here the question of interpretation came up immediately, not in Britain, France, or Italy, but in America.

World peace was important; but one had to think of the immediate future of American business, even though, in the long run, business is apt to suffer heavily from war. Only a month after his fourth Liberty Loan speech the President found it necessary to assure the country, in a letter to Senator Simmons, that the removal of economic barriers would not prevent any nation from setting up as high a tariff as it saw fit, provided the tariff should apply equally to imports from all countries. That point was settled; but some thoughtful Americans must have realized that the removal of economic barriers, like all the other general proposals contained in the Fourteen Points, could be carried out only through the adoption of the last—the one demanding the establishment of an association of nations. If there was really to be open diplomacy, it would have to be practiced by all governments. It would be much the same with disarmament, colonial adjustment, and the freedom of the seas, whatever that might mean. But the Allied statesmen did not appear to be disturbed. The Fourteen Points speech was magnificent propaganda. It has even been called the most effective of the whole war. The Points could be interpreted, and, if need be, modified, when the time came. The time came sooner than they expected; and Wilson had played a considerable part in advancing it.

By 1918 the President had settled into the business of running the war; but outwardly there was nothing whatever about him to suggest the temporary dictator, much less the war lord. The people sometimes got glimpses which showed him to be the kind of homely, democratic chief of state that such a country as ours appreciates. On a Sunday morning he might be seen walking to church with Mrs. Wilson, like any ordinary citizen. Once a group of people standing on the platform at Manhattan Transfer caught a glimpse of him in the presidential car, holding out a skein of yarn for Mrs. Wilson to wind up. And, just as of old, men and women who went to him privately with grief in their hearts found him full of sympathy. When he received a delegation representing the oppressed nationalities of Austria-Hungary, Paderewski came away in tears, while Masaryk declared him "the most intensely human person" he had ever known, "actually incandescent with feeling." Amid all these cares, his sense of humor had not deserted him. When Dr. Grayson persuaded him to wear a white glove to prevent the infection of a burned hand, he wrote his daughter, Mrs. Sayre, that he felt as though he ought to be "handing things."

The great role he was playing, and expected to play, in world affairs had seemingly produced no personal conceit. There is no reason to question the sincerity of a letter in which he thanked the authorities of Cambridge University for the degree they were conferring on him. He could not see, he wrote, that he had ever done more than follow the path of plain duty. He would not hear of allowing the great Muscle Shoals Dam to be named after him. A pleasant note of easy informality veiled his authority even in his conduct of the war.

There was now a group of men referred to popularly as the "War Cabinet": Messrs. Hoover and Garfield (controllers of food and fuel), Baruch (raw materials, minerals, and metals), Hurley (shipping and the emergency fleet), Vance McCormick (War Trade Board), and McAdoo (Treasury and railroads). Every week they met the President informally in his own study, sitting and smoking at their ease. Wilson never allowed the conversation to stray far from the point; but he would relieve the seriousness now and then by telling one of his stories. The nation as a whole, looking on, approved.

Of course the slanders that are spread about men in public life were current, as usual. Without the slightest foundation Mrs. Wilson was reported to be pro-German; and the fable that the President (of all people!) had brought us into the war under Wall Street influence was spreading, like a drop of oil on a blotter. Wilson was always sensitive to evil-speaking about himself, and still more about the ladies of his family; but he claimed, at least, to be unable "to take the malignancy too seriously," and to have "steeled" his heart to endure whatever people with evil tongues might say.

As for the international situation, his attitude was unchanged. He insisted that we should hold ourselves apart as far as possible from the Allies. But he was giving them the kind of aid they needed most. Even London's ultra-conservative *Morning Post* admitted that we had made the blockade more effective than it had been before; that our generous financial help had been a determining factor; and that the effort we were making to pour troops into France showed a certain fine unselfishness. It was only about the disposition of these troops that any particular disagreement appeared. Nearly everyone, through recollection or through reading, knows of the long and troublesome dispute that went on in the spring of 1918 between General Pershing and the French over the use of our forces to strengthen the weakest points in the French and British lines. Pershing was as anxious as any man could be to give the Allied forces effective aid. But he had instructions that his forces should serve as a component unit; and, like all our higher officers, he felt keenly that the honor and prestige of our Army would be best served by keeping our expeditionary force intact and separate. Only in that way could the staffs acquire the experience they were going to need for the greater tasks ahead. Foch and the British were insistent; and the fact that British tonnage was transporting most of our troops gave them an added argument. Wilson showed up well. He patiently considered all the arguments; he firmly supported the American High Command; but he urged Pershing to view the Allied demands "as sympathetically as possible." His influence probably had weight in the arrangement of a compromise which pleased no one fully, but worked out well enough. All the time his fervor was rising. When Lord Reading, at the end of March, explained the dire need of reinforcements on the western front, he received the well-known reply: "Mr. Ambassador, you need say no more. I will do my damnedest." Speaking early in April, in support of the third Liberty Loan campaign, he declared himself as ready as he had ever been for "a fair and just and honest peace"; but, since the Germans demanded terms we could never grant, he could see only one answer:

Force, Force to the utmost, Force without stint or limit, the righteous and triumphant Force which shall make Right the law of the world.

It seemed a far cry back to the days when he had been declaring that force never settled anything. But what he was advocating, in his own mind at least, was the use of force by a policeman against its use by an outlaw. This was to be a peoples' war to secure the peoples' peace.

CHAPTER XIII

Rehearsing for Peace

WE SOMETIMES HEAR that Wilson "lost the peace" largely because there had not been sufficient "preparedness" for the Peace Conference. Certainly a closer preliminary agreement on the "war aims" of the victors, at any time before the Conference opened, would have helped. Such an agreement might perhaps have been reached, if the great Associate had seen reason to become a co-belligerent, and so to gain the full confidence of the Allies during the earlier stages of the war. It is possible that greater progress might have been made even in the time there was, if Wilson had established more intimate contacts with Allied statesmen, recognizing that they and their peoples were also anxious to see the world run on better lines. But we have been learning that agreements on war aims are not to be had for the wishing; and, looking back, it seems that the preparations made for the Paris Peace Conference add up to a very respectable total.

The Allied governments had made preparations of two kinds; and we have sometimes given too little attention to the second kind in our inclination, whether justified or not, to be virtuously indignant about the first. It has been the custom to regard the network of secret treaties and agreements concerning the division of territories which were to be taken from Germany and her allies as more wicked than they really were. Mr. Bailey has reminded us that secret treaties were not regarded as immoral until Wilson declared them so. These particular ones violated in greater or less degree the principles of self-determination and self-government; but they were made under the stress of what seemed necessity or dire need, and probably saved the world from the disaster of a victory by the Central Powers. Such things are often done in war. At the present moment we and the British can no more afford to insist that our greatest ally shall be observant of self-determination and self-government than the French and British were able to do with regard to Italy in 1915. Other treaties and agreements of World War I, including the promise that Japan should fall heir to Germany's islands in the Pacific north of the equator and to her powers and interests in China, were impossible to square with Wilson's points and principles. Neither did they square with either the declarations or the desires of the British and French governments.

But much sounder preparations had been going forward on territorial questions. In Britain, a group of able scholars and foreign servicemen, who knew the continent at firsthand, had long been engaged in a study of all the territorial issues that were likely to be raised. Its work was comparable to that carried on in this country by scholars carefully combed in 1917 out of our best universities and colleges. These men of "The Inquiry," as it was called, had furnished preliminary reports to Wilson when he was working out his Fourteen Points, and were to receive the highest praise at Paris for their ability and their thoroughness. The French had made some study of the subject, too, though it has been felt that their interest had been a good deal concentrated upon their country's special needs.

A second kind of preparation for the Conference had been going on in Britain and in France as well as in America. It will be remembered that a league or association of nations had been one of Mr. Lloyd George's "points"; and, whatever his personal convictions regarding it may have been, Englishmen were as much interested in the idea as Americans. Sir Edward Grey, Lord Bryce, Lord Robert Cecil, and some of the leading Fabians were enthusiastic advocates; and, well before the armistice, reports reached Washington that the demands of Englishmen in general for a league had reached the proportions of a "flood." There was a flourishing League of Nations Society in Britain; and various schemes had been drafted—one of them, under government sponsorship, by a committee which took its name from its presiding officer, Lord Phillimore. A similar though less vigorous and popular movement was going on in France, with Léon Bourgeois as one of its leaders.

Here in America the League to Enforce Peace had been promoting, since 1915, the formation of an international organization which would settle international disputes through a council of conciliation or a court, according to their nature. Its members generally favored the use of force, if need be, to compel the submission of disputes before recourse was had to war. The United States was to be a full participant. Mr. Taft took the lead. Closely associated with him were other Republican leaders, such as President Lowell and Mr. Root. Senator Lodge, it will be remembered, had spoken for the League on the same platform with Wilson in May 1916. This and related peace organizations, such as the World Peace Foundation, the American Peace Society, and the World's Court League, were busily organizing meetings and circulating literature. According to all the evidence there is, the great majority of Americans were strongly in favor of our membership in some international organization of this kind. Wilson, it seemed, would have difficulties about the secret treaties and agreements, but could expect strong backing, at home and at the Conference, in seeking a peace that would embody most of his principles—for future use at any rate. But he needed the official concurrence of the Big Three in Europe, the support of his own people, and the submission of the German Government.

Germany's apparent willingness to make the sort of peace that the President wanted took everyone off guard. Her own new Chancellor, Prince Maximilian of Baden, was startled by the sudden insistence of the High Command that an armistice must be sought at once; and complied reluctantly. But the Germans, in asking Wilson to bring the belligerents together to discuss peace on the basis of all his points and principles, as laid down especially in the Fourteen Points and fourth Liberty Loan speeches, had no intention of surrendering. If it seemed that they would be able to get satisfactory peace terms, all well and good; if not, the armistice would give them time to reform and revitalize their armies. Insistence by America and the Allies on stiff terms would not only put new fight into the army, but rouse the populace, even to a possible *levée en masse.*

That the Germans appealed personally and only to Wilson was natural. Their introduction of peace terms into negotiations for an armistice was unusual and very shrewd. They knew that, for half a dozen reasons, they could expect our Government to be more lenient than the governments of the Allies. As the *Volkszeitung* had shown a year and a half before, they understood Wilson's determination to claim the dominant place for himself and for his country in the settlement. They knew that he would stand firmly on points and principles.

They knew that the Allies were in no position to break with us at a time when our armed forces were practically indispensable.

But there were two other considerations to which they may have failed to give due weight. If Wilson moved under competent advice, and moved slowly, as he was wont to do, deterioration in Germany's position might force her to accept military and naval terms that would make her renewal of hostilities impossible. And Germany's military and civilian rulers may or may not have taken serious account of a third of the President's speeches defining his position on war aims, the so-called "Four Points" speech, delivered on the preceding Fourth of July. In approaching Wilson, they made no specific reference to it, as they did to the Fourteen Points and fourth Liberty Loan speeches. Yet they had no reason to quarrel with demands for "the reign of law," the application of private standards of morality to international affairs, and a peace settlement "upon the basis of . . . free acceptance . . . by the people immediately concerned."

Point I, however, may have caused wrinkling of brows at the Wilhelmstrasse. It called for the destruction or "reduction to virtual impotence" of "every arbitrary power" that could "of its single choice disturb the peace." Any German ministers who had kept count of the President's utterances may have found it unpleasantly reminiscent of the passage in his 1917 Flag Day speech, in which he had promised that if the "military masters" of Germany failed to get the sort of peace they wanted, they would have to give way to "a government accountable to the people themselves." And he had gone on, it will be remembered, to say that only when Germany had had such a change of government could the world look for peace. But probably the German authorities did not realize how much his hopes had now become focused upon an association of nations, or how much he had come to regard himself as the champion and interpreter of all peoples to whom self-government was denied.

The arrival of Prince Max's note, on October 6, must have seemed to Wilson like the glorious fulfillment of a dream. It gave him the complete freedom of action that he wanted. He could take the matter up with the Allies, or reject the appeal, or carry on negotiations by himself, just as he chose. Under such circumstances, heads of states are wont to consult their allies or "associates." House suggested this course, and advised that he himself should be sent immediately to Europe. But the President neither approached the Allies, nor sent the

Colonel to consult with them, nor asked his Cabinet's advice, until he had practically brought the matter to a conclusion by an interchange of notes with the German Chancellor. He worked long and anxiously over the notes he sent. He discussed them with House and Tumulty and naturally with Lansing and Polk. But they were his notes, the expression of his policy. Hardly anyone was pleased.

Apparently most Americans regarded the German appeal as nothing but a trap, and would have had the President reject it out of hand. They were for unconditional surrender, and a march to Berlin, too. General Pershing agreed with them; and General Bliss would have preferred German surrender on stated terms. Most of the leading papers took the same tone. At various stages of the negotiations, leading Republican senators, including Senator Lodge, introduced resolutions demanding that there should be no bargaining with the Germans until they had laid down their arms. Colonel Roosevelt asked his friends in the Senate to repudiate all the President's vague points and principles, the "freedom-of-the-seas" point in particular. Mr. Taft was much upset at Wilson's acting independently of the Allies:

> He recognizes no obligations of partnership or of decent courtesy. He thinks he is running the whole show himself. . . . The German peace offensive . . . appealed to his vanity. . . . It was to be his peace and nobody else's peace. Sometimes I feel like bursting, but as Theodore does the bursting, perhaps I can pursue some other function.

Needless to say, the Allies quite agreed with him. Thanks to a French interception of Germany's appeal, they had its text as soon as Wilson did. They were naturally resentful of his failure to consult them, and as naturally nervous lest he agree to conditions, political or military, which they could not approve. Foch and other high officers worked out military and naval terms; and repeated warnings were sent to Washington that the Germans should not be granted an armistice that would leave them in a position to resume hostilities. In Berlin it was simultaneously decided that Germany should accept no armistice that would not.

And the Allies had much more to say. The British pointed out that the Allied statesmen had never bound themselves to the Fourteen Points. They forwarded a statement of objections to at least four Points, and tried (unsuccessfully) to get the President's definition of "the freedom of the seas." It was high time, they urged, that our Government reached an understanding with the Big Three on these matters. Would not the President send over someone enjoying his full confidence?

The President was willing to send House—when the time should seem to him opportune. He was ready to come to an agreement on peace terms—provided they were his own peace terms. And his determination did not stop there. At least as early as the time of House's second mission to Europe, in the winter of 1915–16, he had thought of himself as presiding at the final settlement. If the vision had ever grown dimmer, it was now sharp enough again. Hardly more than a week after the arrival of Germany's first note, House told Lansing that the President was thinking of attending the Peace Conference. But in the meantime he still had to secure German submission to his peace program, Allied concurrence, and the backing of his people. The first item on the docket was the handling of the Germans.

It is, of course, impossible to tell to what extent he had planned, or even hoped, to be able to bring such pressure as he did upon the German Government. He may have hoped for, but could not have counted on, its increasing inability to resist. Other unpredictable factors now entered the situation, such as the strength of American public sentiment in favor of stern treatment for Germany, and the senseless crime committed by a German submarine commander in sinking the *Leinster,* on October 12. Yet his whole conduct of the negotiations suggests a consistent plan; and, thanks largely to Professor Rudin's masterly treatment of the whole question of the armistice, one may make a reasonable surmise as to what it was.

The President intended to bend the Germans to his will. He told House that they would have to accept any terms they could get if they really were beaten; and that he did not care to negotiate with them if they were not. So long as he could bend them to his will, he was anxious to have the armistice negotiations succeed. He was sure, so he told Tumulty, that the German appeal represented the people's wishes, though it came from a source so "odious and hateful" as the Kaiser's government. The idea of a march to Berlin did not appeal to him at all. The armies making it would be "stained" by devastation of the Fatherland. Moreover, according to Tumulty, he calculated that it would cost a million American lives.

He wanted an armistice; but he did not want one that would leave Germany quite helpless. He told House—and here the authentic Wilson touch came in—it should be "as moderate and reasonable as possible," since "too much success or security on the part of the Allies" would make it difficult if not impossible to secure "a genuine peace settlement." The Allies, like the Germans, would have to be subjected to pressure. Never since the old days at Trenton had he quite given up the practice of having a pistol in a holster, to be brought into view when people threatened to resist his work for righteousness, and to be used in cases of necessity. The first German note reached him on October 6. Two days later his reply was on its way. It was rather a startling note. It was natural for him to demand a definite acceptance of his peace program and the evacuation of all territories occupied by German troops. But who could have expected him to inquire whether the request for an armistice came from "the constituted authorities" of Germany, which had "so far" carried on the war?

Prince Max chafed at such unheard-of interference in Germany's internal affairs; but, since the High Command was still presenting a black picture of the Reich's prospects, he accepted the demands, and soothingly assured the President that a large majority of the Reichstag and the people were back of the armistice appeal. Wilson, with House beside him, put in three or four days of thought and work on his second note, while belligerent senators and editorial writers fulminated, and Mr. Balfour sent anxious messages from London. The note gave a sharper turn to the screws he was putting on the German Government than anyone had looked for. After making it clear that American and Allied officers would handle the military and naval terms, he returned to the subject of Germany's rulers. He must call attention to the fact that his "Four Point" speech had demanded the destruction or "virtual reduction to impotence" of every arbitrary power that could disturb the peace. He must be frank enough to say that Germany's existing government was "of the sort described." He must also point out that the "process of peace" would depend upon its being definitely and satisfactorily altered.

Prince Max was staggered. In the language of the *Volkszeitung*, "the limits of the endurable" had been far overrun. But what was he to do? When Ludendorff declared that army morale was improving, Scheidemann answered that civilian morale was deteriorating, thanks largely to lack of food. And the German people, whose political education had been much assisted by the knowledge they had gained of Wilson's points and principles, could not be roused to desperate resistance by his condemnation of "arbitrary power." It seemed that the only thing to do was to keep the negotiations going until Wilson furnished better reasons for a break. So on October 21 the President was informed that Germany's people had been given responsible government, and that the Reichstag would soon have the power of decision regarding war and peace. It was at this point that Wilson sent House to Europe, and first consulted his Cabinet.

While House was on the water, the President's third note was sent off to Berlin. As a communication from the government of one great Power to that of another, it is rather a "museum piece":

> The nations of the world . . . cannot trust the word of those who have hitherto been the masters of German policy. . . . The Government of the United States cannot deal with any but veritable representatives of the German people. . . . If it must deal with the military masters and the monarchical autocrats of Germany now, or if it is likely to have to deal with them later . . . it must demand, not peace negotiations, but surrender.

Give up your power to men who can be trusted, give it back to its rightful owners, the people, if you want the sort of peace terms you are asking for: keep your power, and you will have to surrender without assurances of any kind. That, in substance, was what the former President of Princeton wrote to a successor of Prince Bismarck.

Though it was impossible to say that Wilson was demanding the Kaiser's abdication, his notes immensely stimulated the growing demand for it in Germany. The German Cabinet was divided. The High Command, insistent that negotiations with Wilson be broken off, appealed to the army against the civil government.

Ludendorff was dismissed; but his dismissal did not solve the Chancellor's problem. As Mr. Rudin says, "he found himself in the dilemma of having to choose between the army that would not fight if the Kaiser went and the people who would not fight if the Kaiser remained." And fighting of any kind was going to be increasingly difficult, thanks to the collapse of Germany's allies. Bulgaria was already out of the war; Turkey and Austria were about to follow her. Germany, able only with difficulty to hold one front, would soon have to be holding two. One answer after another to Wilson's third note was drafted, each softer than the one before. The last was well calculated to appeal to the President's sensibilities. The peace negotiations, it said, were being conducted by "a government of the people." And this government of the people awaited "a peace of justice," such as the President had offered. The Germans were apparently obeying the injunctions of the peoples' advocate. On the night of November 8 the Kaiser, yielding to irresistible pressure, consented to abdicate as German Emperor. His abdication was no doubt partly responsible for a passage in the speech which the President made to Congress on the original Armistice Day:

Armed imperialism such as the men conceived who were but yesterday the masters of Germany is at an end. . . . The arbitrary power of the military caste of Germany . . . is discredited and destroyed.

But the last of Germany's pre-armistice notes had also expressed confidence in Wilson's ability to secure "a peace of justice." In the interval since receiving Germany's last note, he had done his best to be worthy of the confidence. On the day before the note left Berlin, Colonel House had presented himself to the Allied statesmen.

House's famous encounter with the Allied statesmen at Paris, in the last days of October and the first ones of November, was a fitting curtain raiser to the coming drama of the Peace Conference. Except that Wilson's part was played by his understudy, all the great actors were there. The hero, very pleasant but very firm, and somewhat exalted, too, made his entrance, holding a plan that would, he hoped, give justice in the present and peace in the future to everyone. He asked for its free acceptance by the other principals. The other principals, more worldly wise, more realistic, and tied by inexorable forces in rather the manner of Ibsen characters, raised objections of various kinds. The hero, a rich and powerful man, who could make serious trouble for all of them, and had foreseen resistance on their part, proceeded, with great dignity and politeness, to make threats. The threats brought concessions to most of his demands; but these concessions, being made under duress, lacked the moral force of a contract in the fullest sense. The transaction had something of the character of a shotgun marriage. No amount of threatening could secure real consent. For one thing, the hands of the other principals were tied. The irony of the situation at Paris in October 1918 and in the following spring was that the peoples who had fought what Wilson called the Peoples' War would not have allowed any representatives of theirs to make what Wilson would have considered a true Peoples' Peace.

Wilson was the leading man, the hero, the Galahad, the leading exponent of high ideals; but the three great Allied prime ministers were very far from being villains, from being exponents of all that was reactionary and unjust. They were the responsible heads, and worthy heads at that, of the three greatest democracies in Europe. Lloyd George was Celtic, impressionable, skilled in the technique of smart lawyers, a practiced politician, and quite markedly a weathervane. But there was still in him some of the quality that had made him a pro-Boer, a little-Englander, a moderate pacifist, and a man accused of "socialistic" leanings. His budget of 1909 constituted a bolder attack on the sacred rights of property than any Wilson had made; and he had borne a great part in giving the then United Kingdom a "new deal," with which, in some respects, we are still catching up. Years and the war had certainly made him more conservative; but in achievements for "liberalism" he could be ranked as the President's greatest rival. Clemenceau remained what he had always been, a "radical" in the French sense, and a friend of the people; although his burning devotion to the security and the interests of his country had latterly diverted him from internal reform. Orlando was able, liberal, tolerant and friendly; a lawyer and, like Wilson, a former teacher.

And yet between these three and Wilson there was a great gulf set. It was not so much a gulf between good and evil as a gulf created by circumstance—by that, by Wilson's purer idealism, and by Wilson's belief that his own people, sharing this idealism, should have the moral leadership of the world. He was treading a dangerous path, most dangerous of all, perhaps, in the temptation that constantly assailed him to think of himself as the world's great moral arbiter, and to discount both the good intentions of European statesmen and the difficulties they faced. He would have been a man of rare humility if he had not yielded now and then, as his critics accused him of doing constantly. But this shortcoming, such as it was, shrinks to something like insignificance when measured against his inveterate courage, his readiness to sacrifice political prospects, health, and even life itself, so long as he might execute his mission as America's mouthpiece and generalissimo in the conduct of world affairs.

He had reaffirmed his faith, during the preceding July, by a message delivered on his behalf to a convention of teachers:

The children should come to see that it was . . . the providence of God that the United States and Germany, the one the most consistent practitioner of the new creed of mankind and the other the most consistent practitioner of the old, should meet in battle to determine whether the new democracy or the old autocracy shall govern the world. . . . [They should see] the stern duty and the supreme privilege which belong to the United States of being chief interpreter to the world of those democratic principles which can rid the world of injustice and bring peace and happiness.

If he magnified his personal responsibility, account must be taken of the sort of messages which were reaching him. Clemenceau, from whatever motives, had written him a year before, as "from man to man":

You did set us such a magnificent example that we need only follow you and you may be assured that we will spare nothing to do as well as America is doing.

Bergson had addressed him in terms calculated to turn the head of any man:

Tell the President that he is our Pope. Where we used to look to Rome for spiritual leading, now we look to Washington.

Mrs. J. Borden Harriman, who delivered the message, reported that Wilson's eyes filled with tears. From England, too, had come messages. There was Miss Margaret Bondfield's: "All we ask of our government is that it follow Woodrow Wilson." And there had been one from Walter Page, whose irritation during the days of our neutrality had not destroyed his admiration or his loyalty:

As leader and spokesman of the enemies of Germany—by far the best trumpet-call spokesman and the strongest leader—your speeches are worth an army in France and more, for they keep the proper moral elevation.

It would have been hard for Wilson not to feel that he and his country were coming down from Sinai to give a set of new commandments to an errant world.

The three Allied Premiers who confronted Colonel House in the last days of October 1918 could not have been expected to enter into Wilson's feelings. Long careers in politics, involving the holding of high offices, had given them a feeling of trusteeship for their countries' immediate interests. It had made them watchful, too, both of potential foes and of apparent friends. Ideals appealed in varying degrees to all of them; but hard facts claimed their attention first. The peoples, who had long been nervously conscious of living very near to Germany, whose belief in the sole "war guilt" of the Central Powers was absolute, and whose sufferings had been intense, were much more ready to applaud Wilson's points and principles in the abstract than to see them applied impartially.

Again, the treaties made by the governments which the premiers represented, both with one another and with Japan, could hardly have been repudiated by men who had made capital out of Germany's "scrap of paper." Wilson was for the abrogation of all of them. The French Government was at one time ready to oblige him; and the British would probably have been willing to do the same, provided some arrangement could be reached about the promises it had made to Australia, New Zealand, and South Africa. But Italy and Japan had paid for their promised acquisitions in advance. Who would drive the Japanese out of the Shantung Peninsula and the German islands which they had occupied; or how would the Italian *people* receive the news that they were not to get territories for which they had paid with such great loss of life?

How, for that matter, would the French people accept Wilson's ideas as to what was necessary for their future security, or the British people a "freedom of the seas" which, as they thought at least, would deprive them of their great weapon, the blockade? France, her streets filled with cripples and mourning clothes, her churches with mourners; France, with her wrecked mines and industries, with her farms and orchards, with whole towns and villages laid waste; France, convinced beyond argument that all this death and misery and desolation was the fruit of unprovoked attack by a greedy, ruthless, and far-too-numerous foe, wanted the greatest compensation that could be had, and the greatest possible security from fresh attacks. Many Frenchmen wanted actual revenge. The British, having less reason, were somewhat less bitter; but what they wanted was in essence much the same. Italy had mourners and misery, as well as her set of promises. Had the Premier of any of the three countries consented to such peace terms as Wilson had in mind, it is virtually certain that he would have been replaced at once by a man of less yielding type. Of the Big Four at Paris, only Wilson had fixed tenure.

So a gulf lay between him and the Big Three, dug partly by his idealism and his pride in his own people, dug partly by circumstance. The only possible bridge across it was that of compromise. Later, the Germans were to claim that they had been tricked by Wilson into making peace on conditions never carried out. Many people in other countries were to agree. There was no *voluntary* bad faith on Wilson's part; and it would be hard to show that there was any on the part of the principal Allied statesmen. They were forced by an idealistic American into outward acceptance of conditions which they did not approve, and which neither they nor any men in their places could have persuaded the angry and victorious peoples of three great democracies to accept. Wilson's critics in Germany and elsewhere would have done better to count up what his idealism and courage had accomplished, both for the immediate and for the distant future. The basic elements of the whole tragic affair were in clear evidence during the armistice negotiations at Paris.

Nothing was more evident than the President's determination to force the Allies, as he had forced the Germans, to adopt what he regarded as better ways. It will be remembered that he did not want military and naval terms that would give the Allied governments "too much success or security"—in other words, too much ability to resist him in the making of the peace. He was determined that, in spite of the objections they had made to some of the Fourteen Points, while he was negotiating with the German Government, they should now swallow down the lot. House encouraged him in feeling that if he did not succeed, the Germans would be able to accuse him of bad faith. Since no armistice had yet been made; since Wilson had never been entitled to speak for any country but his own; since the Point dealing with the future of Austria's subject nationalities had already been altered, and that dealing with economic barriers reduced to something approaching nullity, House's position seems extreme.

What it apparently comes to is this: he was as determined as his chief that the peace should be completely a Wilson peace. The official interpretation of the Fourteen Points was to be the President's. Walter Lippmann, secretary to The Inquiry, together with Frank Cobb, drew up a document interpreting all the Points, which the President approved. That such dictation to statesmen who were trustees for their countries, and had ideas of their own, was none too tolerable, did not apparently trouble House. Infomal conversations with Allied leaders and reports of stormy sessions in the British Cabinet left him unmoved. His approach, no doubt agreed upon with Wilson, was gentle to the point of being rather disingenuous. The President, he told the Allied statesmen, wished to know whether they were ready to make an armistice leading to a peace based on the President's peace program, as the German Chancellor had asked. They were, of course, free to decide. Any illusions they may have had about their freedom were soon dispelled.

The Allied statesmen, having undoubtedly anticipated House's move, were ready with their replies. Sonnino, the Italian Foreign Minister, a hard and able man to whom idealism made no appeal, protested that peace terms should not be interjected into negotiations for an armistice. Lloyd George asked whether the Allies, by making an armistice on the terms proposed, would not bind themselves to acceptance of the Fourteen Points. The Colonel thought they would. Clemenceau remarked that he had never endorsed the Fourteen Points, and inquired whether Lloyd George had. Lloyd George had not. The Points were then read, and the Lippmann-Cobb interpretations offered. The interpretations were reasonable; but the Allies were restive under the obvious pressure that Wilson was using, and made objections to various points.

Colonel House put on the screws. If they were not prepared, quite voluntarily of course, to agree with the President's program, the President might have to ask Congress whether the United States, having attained its own war aims, cared to go on fighting for those of the Allies. When Clemenceau inquired whether this would mean our making a separate peace with Germany and Austria, the Colonel thought "it might." Apparently enjoying himself immensely, he cabled Wilson of "the exciting effect" which this produced. Colonel Bonsal pictures Mr. Lloyd George as leaping to his feet, with flashing eyes. There were probably many Americans, in and out of Congress, whose reaction would have been similar. As the German High Command pointed out to the Chancellor at about this time, Germany's military prospects would be not at all hopeless should Wilson take America out of the war. The consequences which the withdrawal of America's armed forces would produce, even the immediate effects that the President's appeal to Congress would have on the morale of both sides, were impossible to calculate. There was no more talk of a general rejection of the Fourteen Points.

But demands for alterations or different interpretation of certain of the Points made trouble for several days. Three stood out in particular. The Italians naturally objected to the Point relating to their boundaries; since the Lippmann-Cobb interpretation frankly admitted that it would give them less than they were entitled to by treaty. The French wanted a very clear understanding regarding the reparation Germany was to make for damages done to their country. The British would not accept Point II, which called for the "freedom of the seas." It was over the British objection that the longest and sharpest tussle came; and it was in this tussle that the President's methods of getting the kind of peace he wanted came most clearly into evidence. From first to last Lloyd George was firm. The navy was the one great fighting arm which Britain always had in readiness; and without the blockade it had imposed, defeat of the Central Powers would seemingly have been impossible. The Lippmann-Cobb interpretation correctly said that Point II was to be linked up with the establishment of the League of Nations. In that case, said Lloyd George, Britain would have to see the League of Nations first.

Colonel House and the President tried to supply interpretations that made blockade and the freedom of the seas compatible; but it seems as impossible now, as it did then to the British Premier, to concede that they made their case. Persuasion failing, threats of various kinds were made to Lloyd George, Lord Reading, and Sir William Wiseman. On the basis of the curious assertion that British navalism was essentially the same as German militarism (Wilson must have known that Britain had no naval junkers acting in virtual independence of her civil government), the British representatives were told that neither this nor other countries would submit to a continuation of Britannia's rule over the waves. Never again should we or other neutrals tolerate such interference with commerce as the British Navy had practiced. Rather than allow this, we should provide ourselves with a greater fleet and army than the British could keep up. Having more natural resources, more men, and more money, we could certainly do it.

For days House continued to engage in our rather national habit of lecturing. "If the British were not careful they would bring upon themselves the dislike of the world." In a future war they might well find us among their enemies. Germany had come to grief thanks to her army; and he believed it "inevitable," so House warned, that Britain would have cause to regret her arbitrary attitude on the freedom of the seas. Sometimes the envoy outdid the President (who was delighted with his methods); and sometimes the President outran his envoy. House did not reveal that Wilson threatened to appeal to

Congress on this issue alone. But, in general, the Colonel was the most compliant of agents. Though he considered Anglo-American friendship all-important, he seems never to have reminded Wilson that British "navalism" had been an important element in Germany's defeat, or that it had worked greatly to our advantage over a long period of our history.

Mr. Lloyd George was accustomed to weathering storms. Even when Clemenceau, probably tongue in cheek, urged him to accept "the principle," he refused. And he produced an argument so valid that even House had not much more to say:

> It's no good saying I accept the principle. It would only mean that in a week's time a new Prime Minister would be here who would say that he could not accept this principle.

He would agree to discuss the freedom of the seas at the Peace Conference; but that was all. The President, under House's persuasion, gave in. The Germans were informed that the Allied governments would give them an armistice, while making reservations on two of the Fourteen Points. They reserved to themselves "complete freedom" at the·Peace Conference regarding the freedom of the seas; and they would require from Germany reparation for "all damage done to the civilian population of the Allies and their property by the aggression of Germany by land, by sea, and from the air." Sonnino fought hard for a third reservation on Italian boundaries; but Orlando, who at first supported him, gave in. After all, Italy's acquisitions on the continent were to be at the expense of Austria; and the armistice already granted to Austria could scarcely be regarded binding as to·the Fourteen Points.

The struggle was at an end; and House warmly congratulated the President on what was certainly a substantial victory. What mental reservations the Allied statesmen would allow themselves, in virtue of the pressure placed on them, only the Peace Conference would show. But resentment, and more than resentment, lurked. As good an example as any was seen in a discussion of the British leaders with the Dominion premiers. In the interest of their future security, South Africa had been promised German South West Africa; Australia and New Zealand, Germany's insular possessions in the Pacific south of the equator. Canada's highly respected Prime Minister, Sir Robert Borden, who, like Wilson, had nothing to demand for his country, was insistent that these promises should be carried out, despite anything the Fourteen Points might say concerning colonial questions. It was only one of many signs that Wilson was to have no easy time in carrying through his peace program. What proved to be a far more serious portent occurred on November 5, the day when Wilson's victory over the Allied statesmen was achieved. It was the day when the congressional elections were held.

On October 25 Colonel Roosevelt had written to Senator Lodge another of those letters which make one feel that sickness and perhaps frustration had brought all the worst of him to the surface:

I am glad Wilson has come out in the open; I fear Judas most when he can cloak his activities behind a treacherous make-believe of non-partisanship.

He was referring, of course, to Wilson's appeal to the people on that same day to see that the new Congress should have Democratic majorities in both Houses. The President had taken some pains to meet the inevitable criticism in advance:

I have no thought of suggesting that any political party is paramount in matters of patriotism.

His plea was reasonable, from his own point of view. The Republican leaders, as he said, had been unquestionably "anti-administration," despite the fact that they had been "pro-war." A month earlier he had written a member of the great Scripps newspaper family that Colonel Roosevelt's son-in-law, Nicholas Longworth, had supported the war in such a way as to bring the sharpest criticism to bear on his administration, and to show an obvious desire to take the conduct of affairs out of the administration's hands. Now, emphasizing that it was a time of crisis for America and for the world, he urged the necessity for "undivided support to the Government under unified leadership." And he added an argument which was incontestable:

The return of a Republican majority to either House of Congress would . . . certainly be interpreted on the other side of the water as a repudiation of my leadership.

He made the appeal, not only under the increasing pressure and increasing anxiety of his own party and its candidates, but in view of the bitter campaigning of his opponents, and of Colonel Roosevelt in particular. Six months before he had told Congress that politics were "adjourned," and that the fall elections would go to those who thought least about them, and were able to show superior records. If he had been in earnest then, he had soon changed his mind; but his declaration on the "adjournment" of politics was remembered—to his later cost.

Was Wilson's appeal to the people one of his major blunders, as has been so often said? Did it mark the deterioration of his power to exercise sound judgment? And, if so, what was happening to him? None of these questions, when one thinks of it, can be answered with any degree of certainty. That there was a deterioration, many agree. But when did it set in? Judge Brandeis, it will be remembered, thought that it had been apparent a good deal earlier than this; but men who were closer to the President saw no particular change until after his illness during the Peace Conference. Mr. Bailey, who has recently considered all the evidence, dates the appearance of "a different Wilson" as of October 1918. What happened to the President? Did success and adulation go to his head? Were the labor and responsibility of making all Europe submit to his plans for world betterment too much for a man who had never been robust in physique or nerves, and was already worn down by the crushing load of work and anxiety that he had been carrying? Both things no doubt contributed; but Wilson's comparative freedom from personal conceit, and the relentless way in which his conscience, his idealism, and his pride in America drove him on, suggest that what Mr. Bailey calls "the strong wine of victory" was only a minor element.

Whatever in him did change, those three driving forces were to go with him through collapse and illness and apparent failure up to his death. No other statesman of his time, save only perhaps Lenin, seems to have worked under such compulsion from within. Was his appeal to the people evidence that his power of judgment was failing? It was made on the advice of such experienced politicians as Tumulty and Burleson. His appeals to the nation had been very successful in the past; and there was more precedent for this than there had been for some of them. It had been supplied especially by President McKinley and by Colonel Roosevelt on McKinley's behalf, during our war with Spain. But the people, naturally, had little interest in precedents; and Colonel Roosevelt did not find it necessary to remember them. Wilson, he declared, might as well have denied the right to vote, even the right to discuss public questions, to all Republicans—

denied it, in fact, to people of both parties who were unprepared to take a "rubber-stamp attitude of complete servility." But Wilson had found Republicans "good enough to spill their blood like water overseas under the flag." The President, he shouted, preferred anti-war Democrats to pro-war Republicans at the Capitol. Mr. Taft gave the lie to Wilson's charge that his opponents had tried to take the conduct of affairs out of his hands; accused him of extreme partisanship in appointments; declared that only public opinion had forced him to bring the German Government to its knees; and promised that a Republican victory would end the dangers of there being a "negotiated" peace. Mr. Hughes did his bit, by promising that his party, in control of Congress, would make Wilson the leader of the nation, not merely of the Democrats! None of them, of course, mentioned the President's struggle to give us moral leadership, and Europe a just and lasting peace. All's fair, it seems, in love and politics.

Was Wilson's appeal, and the ammunition his opponents were able to make out of it, responsible for the fact that a decided majority of the electorate turned their backs on him at the polls for the first time since they had made him President? No one can say whether the results of the election would have been more favorable or less favorable to the administration if there had been no appeal. Too many other considerations entered in: the inevitable enmities that any reforming, low-tariff administration would have made; the resentment of hyphenates, pacifists, and isolationists against a President who had taken us into war; the harsh tone Wilson had used to capital and sometimes to labor; the reaction of congressmen and their friends against his wartime "dictatorship"; the richly furnished campaign chest on which the reunited forces of Republicans and Progressives drew; the anger of some industrialists at getting no war contracts, and of others at being milked by taxes on excess profits. And then, as Mr. Milton says, there was "the general irritation of a civil society unaccustomed to the straitjacket of war"—the dislike of meatless days and war loan drives and government control of our railroads. The irritation was largely unconscious, still more unreasonable, and yet potent. We had not been long enough or deeply enough at war to realize the necessity for inconveniences. And now that the war was obviously over, it seemed safe to make a change.

However the outcome was determined, it was terribly serious for Wilson. The fact that the new House of Representatives would have a small Republican majority did not matter greatly in itself. But two things did matter. It appeared, in Europe as well as here, that the President had asked for the endorsement of the people, and had been refused. Colonel Roosevelt made use of his international renown to see that Europe did not miss the point. And then there was the Senate of the new Congress, the Senate that would deal with the treaty. So close was the race that the election of Mr. Henry Ford in Michigan, running as a Wilson candidate, would have produced a tie in the Senate, a tie which would have given Wilson a majority, had all Democratic senators supported him, through the Vice-President's casting vote. Mr. Ford was defeated by Mr. Truman Newberry. The *American Year Book* for 1919 contains an interesting passage:

On March 29, it was announced that a Federal grand jury at Grand Rapids . . . had indicted Truman H. Newberry and one hundred and thirteen other persons for corruption, fraud and conspiracy in connection with the election of Senator Newberry. . . . The claim was that between $500,000 and $1,000,000 had been expended. . . . Immediate investigation was entered upon by the Elections Committee of the Senate, but no report was made by it at the end of the year.

Eventually the scandal forced Newberry out; but in the meantime the Republicans, thanks to Mr. Newberry, controlled the Senate. Hence the Foreign Relations Committee to which the peace treaty was referred was headed by Senator Lodge, and packed with inveterate foes of Wilson, his Treaty, and his League. Yes, it does seem that all's fair in love and politics.

CHAPTER XIV

Mobilization for Peace

F ROM NOVEMBER 5, 1918, the day doubly marked by Wilson's success in getting his peace program accepted by the belligerents in Europe and by his apparent failure to secure endorsement from the American people, one can picture him as campaigning on an eastern front with headquarters in Paris, and on a western front with headquarters at Washington. His opponents on both east and west were for the most part honest and well-intentioned men. Their range of vision had never equaled his; and probably their faith in ideals had grown weaker with age and with long immersion in politics, national and international. Wilson appears to have so misread the situation on both fronts as to convince himself that he should take and keep control in the east, attending to the west later. The American people, he was sure, would always hear his voice and follow him. But the Allied statesmen, as he told his advisers and experts on the *George Washington,* en route for Brest, would have to be dealt with firmly. Not only would they, unlike the American delegates, be working for nationally selfish ends, but they would be misrepresenting their own peoples!

The President's faith in the masses everywhere was magnificent; but it was so mistaken as to be tragic. As General Smuts wrote, soon after the Peace Conference, the shortcomings of the Treaty were to be traced more to the Allied peoples than to the men they had sent to negotiate for them at Paris. Not that they were bad peoples. They were merely intoxicated by exhaustion, by fears and grief and victory and promises. The adoption of propaganda (true and false) as a normal weapon in twentieth-century warfare had helped to make it impossible that the peoples should emerge in any reasonable state of mind. They wanted a better ordered world; and many of them had an almost pathetic confidence that Wilson could do more than anyone in producing it. But all the while their passions ran unchecked. The only possible check would have been a religious one; and religious influence had for a long time been giving ground, in a deterministic and materialistic atmosphere.

There was to be evidence of this at Paris, when attempts were made to establish some link between religion and the establishment of peace. A Portuguese delegate received little or no sympathy in his protest that even the Treaty of Berlin had been made in the name of God; and a religious clause inserted by Wilson in his first draft of the Covenant was dropped, as a way, it seems, of meeting Japanese resentment over the refusal of the Conference to declare for racial equality! At any rate, the passions of the peoples were a determinant. The Allied representatives at Paris were alert enough in reaching out for what they thought would serve their countries' interests; but where they failed to represent their peoples was in demanding too little, not too much.

Wilson's opponents on his western front came gradually to be a conglomeration of groups, representing points of view sometimes so different as to be contradictory. A nineteenth-century British statesman once described a similar conglomeration as "a fortuitous concourse of atoms." Some of Wilson's antagonists damned him for interjecting too much idealism into the Peace Treaty, others for his failure to inject enough. But the solid core of the combination was simply partisan. There is no condemnation in the adjective. Along with the crowd of men bred by parties who merely love the game of politics, or love the spoils, or act from unthinking loyalty, there is always a sincere and thoughtful element. Perhaps Republicans are more apt than Democrats to believe (as did the British Whigs of old) that they have given their country the best of what it has, and are its proper guardians. For reasons of differing validity, the Republicans, from 1918 to 1920, were eager to eject Wilson and his party as soon as possible, and on any plausible pretext.

Since success in creating a better world order would offer the Democrats superb campaign material, some Republican leaders decided, as soon as peace was in the air, to blunt this Democratic weapon by at least reshaping any peace treaty that the President might bring home with him. The fact that he had angered them unnecessarily, and was to go on doing it, gave added zest to their effort. That was in the natural run of politics, since foreign policy was normally treated as a partisan issue. Again, it was natural that hyphenates and isolationists should line up with partisan antagonists against a President who had led the country into war and had become an ardent "internationalist." Still, the "concourse" looked unusual. There was a suggestion of miscegenation of some sort in warm co-operation between Senators La Follette and Johnson, and Senators Knox and Lodge. And who would have expected to find Senator Lodge as the hero of most of Boston's "Irish" citizens?

What was far more "fortuitous," and tragically so, was the final presence in the anti-Wilsonian group of left-wing liberals who were genuine idealists. It was the old story of liberals forgetting that true liberalism involves concessions to circumstances and to other points of view; the old story of perfectionists preferring to see people starve rather than help in giving them half a loaf. One of the most curious things about the *Senate Documents* relating to the Treaty is the insertion of editorials from our most liberal weeklies by senators to whom those weeklies must in general have been anathema. The editors, engaging in some armchair diplomacy, excommunicated Wilson for his failure to force the Allies to live up to all his points and principles. He could never have done that at the height of his health and strength, at the peak of his national and party leadership. There must have been times when he felt, as he had done in the old Trenton days, that every reformer should put on his desk a card inscribed: "DON'T BE A DAMNED FOOL."

Unfortunately, he sometimes showed poor judgment in estimating and dealing with his potential opponents here in America. Thanks to his appeal for Democratic majorities in Congress and the skillful use that had been made of it, the Republicans were in an ugly mood. Moreover, his relations with the Senate, where so many G.O.P. leaders sat, had become more and more unsatisfactory. The breach was fundamentally political; but it was also a good deal Wilson's fault. He did not like the Senate; and his incidental indictment of the whole body, when he condemned the filibustering of "the little group of willful men," had been only one of various utterances which had made his feeling all too plain. Now he was to give the whole body, and its Republican members in particular, some tangible causes for complaint.

He was to do it in his preparations for the Peace Conference. He had decided to go to Paris, and to go as one of America's five Peace

Commissioners, in spite of all that close friends and members of his "war cabinet" could say. Arguments that he would be all the more influential if he remained in aloof majesty, speaking by cable as an arbiter, not as a combatant, did not shake his resolution in the least. No more did pleas that his countrymen, and especially his party, both needed and wanted him at home. He could argue plausibly on the other side; and there are good judges who hold even now that he was right. If he hesitated at all, a cable he received from House, telling him that Clemenceau, Lord Reading, and Sir William Wiseman (to say nothing of nearly all influential Americans in Paris) thought he should return to America before the actual opening of the Conference, doubtless determined him once and for all. He replied reprovingly and angrily:

> The suggestion that I should not sit as a delegate . . . seems to me a way of pocketing me. I infer that the French and British leaders desire to exclude me from the Conference for fear that there I might lead the weaker nations against them.

Colonel Bonsal, behind the scenes at this time and throughout the Peace Conference, wrote that "the illusion under which the President labored that all the European Powers were banded together against America was . . . to become . . . an obsession."

House, who also thought it would be unwise for Wilson to remain for the Conference, but could not say so without giving ground for suspicion that he wished to play the leading part himself, was able to hope that the President would not stay long in Europe after all. There was to be a preliminary conference, at which a preliminary treaty, covering military and naval terms and such general conditions as the establishment of an association of nations, would be negotiated by all the Peace Commissioners. Wilson might sign the preliminary treaty, size up the people and the situation, and then come home, to negotiate detailed terms of the Treaty by cable, and look after his fences in America. A cable that he sent the Colonel suggested that that was what he had in mind. Apparently even House did not fully understand the President. But who did, or, for that matter, ever has or ever will?

One thing is sure: Wilson was going overseas, to take charge of the campaigning on his eastern front, at a time when the home front was showing signs of giving serious trouble. Already the war drums of certain anti-League senators were throbbing. And the man who first sounded them was not from Harvard and Massachusetts, but from the University of Kansas and from Idaho, that able and inveterate isolationist, Borah. Borah, who had refused to be a Progressive because political sense told him that third parties in our system will not do, was as honestly and fearlessly progressive within the Republican party as any Progressive who had broken away. Naturally, he had approved and supported much of Wilson's domestic program. But he often justified Senator Williams' remark that he was like the man who said he was going home to lunch, and if lunch wasn't ready, he was going to raise Cain; and if it was, he wouldn't eat a bite of it. What was more, everything predisposed him to be an isolationist: his Bohemian-German-Irish ancestry, his life in the Middle West, and very obvious limitations in his knowledge of Europe and of its history.

It is easy to understand Borah's narrowly nationalistic point of view; it is more difficult to explain how so honest a man could distort and misrepresent Wilson's plans for a League, as Borah did from first to last. Perhaps long and successful practice as a lawyer had given him the habit of using questionable evidence and unwarranted but plausible arguments to support a case. Lawyers are said to be capable of imposing even on themselves. It was reported that Borah's eloquent misrepresentations drew tears of joy from Senator Lodge, who presumably was not given to weeping. And they were soon being improved upon by Hiram Johnson and other senators. They found much natural response from plain men and women who cherished isolationism both as a tradition and as sound policy. Senator Lodge did more than weep. At just what point he had then arrived in his journey from the position of a leading advocate of our participation in an international association to see that peace was kept, to that of the most influential enemy in America to the League of Nations as agreed upon at Paris, is doubtful. But there is no doubt at all of his desire to use what opportunities the gods offered of freeing the country from Democratic rule, and especially of Wilson, whom he detested from the bottom of his soul. This personal animus was reciprocated in full measure.

The struggle between the two men was to be as historic as that between Gladstone and Disraeli, despite Senator Lodge's inferiority in position and in intellect to the great Conservative imperialist. Beneath the surface each of them must have recognized that there was much to be said for the other. Wilson knew that Lodge was an asset to the Senate in point of education, experience, and quite superior ability; that he had done some useful things for his country; that he possessed the esteem and friendship of distinguished people; and that at least many of his avowed convictions were honest ones. But it is not difficult to see why he seemed to the President a sinister figure when it came to politics. It was not the antagonism of a "Celt" who lacked a distinguished American pedigree toward a man of pure Anglo-Saxon and colonial forebears, as the late Bishop Lawrence maintained in his biographical eulogy of the Senator. Wilson saw in Lodge a combination of two elements in American life which had irked him for many years: a man who, himself most privileged, favored privilege of every kind, and was at the same time a politician, inveterate and unscrupulous. He was not likely to forget that Lodge, possessing all the advantages that American life could offer, had condemned and yet supported Blaine; or that he was ready to "talk Irish" (he of all people!) to the hyphenates, so long as he could hope to down the Democrats. Wilson was partisan enough himself; but there were things at which he had always drawn the line.

Nor could the President, none too tolerant of dissent, accept the Senator's views and record on many past and present issues: his high protectionism; his eagerness to get us into war with Spain; his insistence on a rigid separation of powers in government; and his belief that a senator or congressman's duty was not to represent the current wishes of his constituents, but to exercise higher judgment. Wilson's dislike of Lodge had deepened all through the period of the war. Though Lodge was on record as agreeing with Webster that "party politics should cease at the water's edge," no one had assailed the administration's foreign policy more bitterly. No one had sneered more (and Lodge was an adept at sneering) at Wilson's unfortunate "too-proud-to-fight" remark, or had been more contemptuous of "the bloodstained thing that is called peace in Mexico." Lodge's already obvious desertion of his former internationalism seemed the last straw. There were many people to whom the Senator's ways in this matter were to seem devious. "To have followed the trail of Lodge in that Treaty battle," a Texan friend of House's later remarked, "would have broken the back of the most supple rattlesnake." Since the time in 1884 when Lodge had brushed aside the injunction of Carl Schurz (the immigrant) that a man in politics must think first of his country; when he had parted from distinguished Massachusetts Republicans who were old associates by his insistence on supporting Blaine, the Senator had been in the most extreme sense a party man. Not only was his motto "My party right or wrong," but he observed few limits in referring to its rival. In 1912 he had described the Democratic party in its historical alignment as "standing for slavery, secession; repudiation of the public debt; fiat money; free trade; free silver; the overthrow of the courts and government ownership." It was a bitter thing to him that the people had brought this party back into power, after wisely excluding it for sixteen years.

Nor had Lodge ever felt much respect for the party's new leader. There was probably something more than humor in his remark to Colonel Bonsal that the language in which the Covenant of the League was drawn "might get by at Princeton but certainly not at Harvard." The Senator, whatever his virtues, notoriously made an art of superciliousness. But of course his feeling had far deeper roots. This newcomer to politics, who had benefited by Republican divisions to bound into the highest office in the country, was full of wrong ideas about government, about the tariff, about all sorts of things. What was more, he had dared to be arrogant, to be autocratic, to aspire to leadership of the whole nation, to bear down upon Congress. Not even to the Senate had he shown due deference.

Then, during the 1916 campaign, the feeling between President and Senator had become more sharply personal on both sides. On no better foundation than smoking-car gossip Lodge had told two public gatherings that only the resistance of the Cabinet had prevented Wilson from informing the German Government that he had not meant what he said in his first *Lusitania* note. Wilson had been irritated for some time by the Senator's attacks; but such an assault upon his honor, and the fact that it was made in the course of a political campaign, would, by themselves, be sufficient to account for the brusqueness of his published reply: "The statement made by Senator Lodge is untrue." Lodge had publicly to retract. To whatever extent partisan or personal feeling may have swayed him, this advocate of the League to Enforce Peace began to endorse Borah's isolationist speeches before our entrance into the war. In the year and a half that had intervened before the armistice he had done much to justify

Wilson's charge that his party had managed to support the war, while indicting the administration constantly.

Wilson's dealings, or lack of dealings, with the Senate, from the time of the armistice on, seem to offer better evidence than his pre-election appeal to the voters that his political judgment was no longer what it had been. Ten years before, in writing his *Constitutional Government,* he had pointed out the difficulties a President was likely to meet in making treaties, should the opposition party be in control of the Senate. He had gone on to suggest that a sagacious President would "establish intimate relations of confidence with the Senate on his own initiative . . . [by] keeping himself in confidential communication with the leaders." In this way he might not only avoid trouble, but get useful advice. Wilson had even pointed out that a President's power of appeal to the people would be less potent in dealing with the Senate than with the House, since the Senate was less "sensitive to opinion," and even "apt to grow, if anything, more stiff" under "pressure of that kind."

But he seemed to have forgotten all of this by November 1918. He made no effort to enlist the co-operation of the senators, or to find out what objections on their part he probably would have to meet, by telling them what sort of international organization he had in mind. He had some excuse for this, in the fear that premature opposition by such men as Lodge and Borah would weaken his position at the Conference; but it seems impossible to find anything but a flagrant error of judgment in his selection of the four men who, with himself, should act as Peace Commissioners. Among the five, there was only one Republican; and he, while possessing an admirable record in diplomacy, was neither a party leader nor a senator. Since Mr. Lansing was the one man in America whom it was necessary to appoint; and since Colonel House and General Bliss and Mr. White could all have been with him and given him the benefit of their wisdom and experience without acting as Commissioners, there was room for three Republican leaders, in particular Mr. Taft. It would have been the part of wisdom to take two at any rate.

The Senate would probably have been placated, had appointment to the Commission been offered to one or more of its members. If, as Wilson contended, there was impropriety about involving senators in the making of a treaty on which they would later have to pass, he might, it seems, have allowed the Senate to decide on that point for itself. Mr. Bailey points out that he could not have passed over the senior Senator from Massachusetts, as ranking Republican on the Foreign Relations Committee. That raises a number of interesting speculations, such, for example, as to whether Lodge would have been more dangerous in Paris or in Washington. The reasons for Wilson's selection never having been clear, the general assumption has been that he wanted fellow Commissioners who would give him no trouble. One thing certain is that he made the Republicans, and especially their senators, much more hostile than before. If Colonel House had been in America, Wilson might have acted more wisely; but Colonel House was in Paris, preparing for the Conference.

The Allied leaders were preparing, too—preparing with what must have been mixed feelings. Lloyd George wrote later that they were intensely curious to see the President. He himself had quizzed men near him, who had been to Washington, as to every detail of Wilson's personality and views. All three Allied Premiers were ready to be friendly and co-operative, in some degree, perhaps, because Wilson's influence with their own electorates was an undetermined quantity, but certainly in the main because they all lived within the liberal faith. But their friendliness was inevitably tempered with doubt and caution. It was impossible to know how much of a doctrinaire Wilson would show himself; how far he would yield to their arguments or their necessities; or what pressure he would attempt to bring. His tussle with the British, during the armistice negotiations, over the freedom of the seas, had served warning that they might find him very difficult. So they awaited his coming with curiosity and with some trepidation, too. Already Clemenceau had gained an important victory for France. Before House had sailed, Wilson had suggested that the preliminary Peace Conference should convene at Lausanne, where the people would be friendly and quiet, and the hotel accommodations adequate. House had differed only in preferring Geneva; and had discovered that Lloyd George and Orlando agreed with him. It seemed at first that the French Prime Minister, who was demanding that Versailles, which would virtually mean Paris, should be chosen instead, would have to give way. But Wilson in some manner became persuaded that in a Swiss city the delegates would be exposed to the activities of "poisonous" (presumably pro-German and Bolshevist) agents. Reluctantly, House had to tell the British and Italians that the President was all for their meeting at Versailles.

Lloyd George resisted; but House was so faithful an envoy that, even in his realization of the mistake his chief was making, he turned to the British Premier's bitter enemy, Lord Northcliffe, for help. Lord Northcliffe's *Times* came out for Versailles as the meeting place. Apparently that settled it. And probably it helped later to settle other things. Mr. Harold Nicolson has made the point that holding the Peace Conference at Paris was rather like trying a murderer in the house of his victim, with the victim's family looking on. Wilson, always thin-skinned, was to find this out when the Paris press, probably the most expert in the world at throwing darts, found occasion to turn on him. Also, the choice made Clemenceau the presiding officer, with some power to control debate. Wilson had not thought of that. House had to break the news.

Professor Carlton Hayes once pointed out that there was something tragic in Wilson's attitude toward all that lay before him when he and Mrs. Wilson boarded the *George Washington* for Brest on December 2. The war had not shaken him out of that conviction, so widespread before 1914, that the dawn of a new day was just breaking. People were going to be more reasonable and kindlier than they had ever been; progress along the lines of nineteenth-century ideals was sure. The President was especially confident about the triumph of self-determination and of the movement toward international co-operation for preserving peace, though he expected that he would have to fight for it. The trip promised to be a delightful one in every way. The ship was slow; but a man so tired as Wilson (he slept for two full days) had no fault to find with that. There were good company and good conversation to be had. The French and Italian Ambassadors to Washington were on board with their wives; and so were John W. Davis, on his way to succeed Mr. Page at London, Mr. Lansing, and the charming Henry White. There were two moving-picture projectors, one for the people in the staterooms and one for a body of troops below decks. In the evenings, after dinner, the President and Mrs. Wilson went down to the lower one, where they could join in singing "Over There" and "Pack Up Your Troubles" and all the other favorite war songs. They attended the Sunday service for the soldiers, too; and every doughboy came up to shake hands with the President. These, not the occupants of the staterooms, were "the people." No matter how exalted the President's mood, he had no desire for personal grandeur. Mrs. Wilson tells of his annoyance on discovering that a special chef from the Belmont Hotel had been brought on board to cook the presidential meals.

But if Wilson was resting, he was not loafing. And he had with him on the *George Washington* most of the men and the materials he needed in preparing for the Conference. In his pocket he had a well-developed scheme for a League of Nations, worked out since the preceding summer with House's help, and owing much to the favorite British draft. In the ship's staterooms were a regiment of experts and advisers, one hundred and fifty of them from The Inquiry, loaded with their books, maps, and charts. One of the ship's big lounges had been fitted up for their use; and in the mornings the President was apt to work with some of them.

He also had with him a carefully worked out plan for procedure at the Conference, delivered to him by the French Ambassador. Being French, it was very logical; and it might have been expected to appeal to him even more in other ways. For it provided that all matters for negotiation were to be approached in the light of the pre-armistice agreement, and especially of the Fourteen Points. What was more, it suggested the wholesale abrogation of the secret treaties and agreements, and the denial to Britain of any sizable reparations, except for the sunken merchant fleet. But in Wilson's eyes it had the defect of giving precedence, and hence emphasis, to the wrong matters. The League seemed to be relegated to a secondary place. He might, it seems, have tried to get it amended to suit his tastes. Instead, he put it aside, substituting merely a list of general topics to be taken up, in the order which appealed to him. He seemed to be displaying, in a different way, some of that impatience with any attempts to guide him that had apparently contributed to his imprudence in dealing with the Senate.

The belief that he was about to reshape the affairs of Europe in conformity with American ideals seems to have put him into an exalted and startlingly prophetic mood. Notes taken by Dr. Isaiah Bowman on his talk in mid-ocean to the experts bear ample evidence to this. Elaborating on his belief that the peoples who looked hopefully to the Peace Conference would have no proper representation from their delegates, he went on:

Unless the Conference was prepared to . . . express the will of the people rather than that of their leaders at the Conference, we should be involved in *another breakup of the world,* and . . . *it would not be a war but a cataclysm.*

The American delegation would have to fight (apparently against all the other great delegations) for a proper League, for a new world order abolishing "the balance of power." It would fight as agreeably as possible, *"but disagreeably if necessary."* If it failed, the Peace Treaty would not work; and in that case the world would *"raise Hell."*

The President's meeting with the delinquent Allied leaders promised to be interesting. Preparations for it had been made in much detail. At about the time Wilson addressed the experts, a message arrived from Colonel House, setting out the arrangements for his first contacts. It gave a timetable of the festivities which were to mark his reception in Paris; it informed him that he would be expected to spend about three days in viewing France's devastated areas and visiting some of the Allied troops; and it earmarked about the same amount of time to be devoted to visiting the Italians. Three days after New Year's official discussions would commence. The President was probably none too well pleased. Some festivities were inevitable; and Mrs. Wilson, whose pleasure he kept much in mind, would doubtless enjoy them. With the rest of the program it was different. He was eager to get to work; and he never liked to have things laid down for him. But he could not be bound to anything beyond the opening ceremonies; so there was nothing to be disturbed about.

He might have been upset, though, a little later, as they were approaching Brest, had broadcasting been well developed in those days. For he might have heard Mr. Lloyd George delivering a speech in his "khaki" election campaign. The Prime Minister, subtly guarding himself with reservations which could later be referred to in a printed text, but which no excited crowd or casual readers would notice, was apparently telling a delighted British electorate that Germany should and could pay the whole cost of the war. It seemed that his views concerning the pre-armistice agreement were rather different from the President's. But Wilson, not hearing the speech, was able to sail into such a welcome as no American in Europe had ever had, feeling as exalted and confident as ever. In Paris, the palatial residence of Prince Murat was all in readiness. The speeches of welcome, and, what the President doubtless found more important, the ovations on the boulevards, were all that could have been desired. Paris seemed to have taken him, the incarnation of American ideals, to its very realistic heart.

"Ike" Hoover, brought over from the White House to take charge of presidential housekeeping in Paris, at first found the Murat palace, with its unaccustomed arrangements and foreign staff, decidedly bewildering and difficult to handle. Wilson must have been in a somewhat similar frame of mind. The festivities worked out perfectly, with the President appearing every inch the dignified but democratic statesman expected from America, and Mrs. Wilson all queenly graciousness. First contacts with the French and Italian leaders (Lloyd George's election was keeping him busy in England) went off smoothly, though there was perhaps a touch of acid in the French Premier's remark that the President did most of the talking. Wilson was not, apparently, much troubled at finding Clemenceau rather doubtful about the working of the League, or at failing to convince Orlando and Sonnino that they should "lessen their holds" on the Treaty of London. The League could and should smooth difficulties at the Conference and later.

Behind the scenes he and House were soon at work again upon the Covenant. In general, there was little conflict between the American and British plans; but Wilson had his own favorite article. The independence and territorial integrity of member states should be guaranteed. He had expounded the idea on the same platform with Senator Lodge, before the League to Enforce Peace, in the late spring of 1916. He had emphasized its importance in talking to his experts and advisers on the *George Washington*. He was never to give it up. As Article X of the completed Covenant it was to be the focal point in his battle with the Senate. So he worked with House on the Covenant when he was not talking with Allied statesmen or receiving all the hospitality and the honors that the French showered on him.

Apart from arrangements for the first festivities, the program laid down in House's message did not long survive; but the President did do some touring. He went to England, and then to Italy, probably much less interested in making contacts with royal and other official personages than in coming face to face with "the peoples" of whom he wished to be the true representative. But, as House mournfully noted, while Wilson was away, the peoples, while showing all respect for the twentieth-century Moses from America, were giving evidence that they had other gods than his. The "khaki" election gave a smashing victory to Lloyd George, thanks largely, it appeared, to his subtly guarded promises and the quite unguarded promises of certain of his political adjutants. The electorate expected that the last possible pfennig would be squeezed out of Germany as indemnity, or as "reparations," if the President of the United States preferred the word. House, having personally argued this matter in the pre-armistice negotiations, appreciated the portent. Moreover, being as enthusiastic as Wilson himself about the League, he grew more pessimistic still when, four days after Christmas, Clemenceau got a great vote of confidence in the French Chamber on what was clearly an affirmation of faith in the value of "power politics."

What was more, the principal change which Wilson made in the plans for his touring, and some of the incidents his touring produced, soon made it obvious that he had no real understanding of the peoples' mood, and so of the way to win them to him. Before getting to principles, it was necessary to give them praise, and, more still, to show them sympathy. Wilson refused to visit France's devastated regions, for the time being at any rate, because, as he declared, the French were at the game of trying to make him "see red." However right he may have been as to the motives of those who had planned the visit, he would have done well to think what effect his refusal might have upon French sentiment. Having time to spare, he accepted urgent invitations to go to Britain and to Italy. Considering how much outside the whole European picture he was, his decision had much to commend it; but it must have been hard for the French to understand why he would not take a couple of days to see what the Germans had done to them. Nor did his visits to the other two great Allied countries work out as well as they might have done. In Britain the fault was the President's; in Italy it was his hosts who were to blame.

The British, who appreciated the American war effort, were much more sympathetic with Wilsonian ideals and plans than the other great Allied nations; and felt even then that cordial Anglo-American relations were a first essential to their foreign policy and to a better world order, spared nothing to show appreciation and friendliness to their guests. Their mourning and their privations were put aside. The arrangements went far beyond royal honors, which were naturally accorded everywhere. A public holiday was decreed, to give vast numbers of procession-loving Londoners a chance to see and cheer the President. American soldiers, with wounded men in front, were packed into the courtyard of Buckingham Palace, to offer a greeting from home, when the carriages drove up from the station. Before long the President was addressing a London crowd from the balcony where royalty usually appeared. Inside the palace, and at Marlborough House, where Queen Alexandra was living, the President and Mrs. Wilson were treated as familiar and cherished friends. Wilson, meeting the heads of all the three political parties at a lunch given by the Prime Minister in Downing Street, was asked to unveil a portrait of George Washington, hung in the dining room. Mrs. Wilson was quite carried away by the warm thoughtfulness and informality which she and her husband met everywhere outside the state functions. She was also very much aware of some of the hardships which the royal family had shared with the people. She shivered in the unheated palace; and found Princess "Pat" in ecstasies over her recent engagement, the Wilson visit, and her first pair of new slippers in four years.

Unfortunately, the President made speeches calculated to chill the marrow of any people emerging from more than four years of desperate and costly war. In replying to the King's toast at the state banquet (the most magnificent ever given, within the Premier's memory, at least), he talked of America's unselfish love of freedom, and the privilege he was to enjoy in helping to bring "moral judgments" into the settlement. He seemed to be delivering a sermon, almost a sermon of warning. It would now be for the victorious nations to show whether they understood the meaning of words they had been using, such as "right" and "justice." It "would take more courage to resist the great moral tide" now in flood throughout the world, than to go with it. But it was the omissions which hurt most. Wilson had not a word to say about the courage and endurance of the British, or the achievements of their armed forces; not a word of sympathy for the relatives of well onto a million men of the Empire who had given their lives. He was not unsympathetic: his single-track mind, and perhaps his fear of emotionalism, prevented him from reaching out to the people with whom he so much wanted to make contact. His speech was so unfortunate that Sir William Wiseman and House's son-in-law, Gordon Auchincloss, secured his permission to insert a saving paragraph in the version given to the press. But it was hard for him to mend his ways. At the Guildhall, on the following day, he did refer with some admiration and gratitude to the fighting men of all Allied and Associated countries; but the speech was mainly a cold homily on the League. In two speeches at Manchester he showed something of his old ease and humor; but even there he did not give the British people what they wanted. So he did not win British hearts.

Nor did he win French ones either. The French were deeply hurt when he postponed his visit to the devastated areas; and some of them must have been annoyed when a part of one of his Manchester speeches seemed a clear rebuke to Clemenceau for his attachment to "power politics." The President was to make some amends early in February, when he received the unprecedented honor of being invited to address the French Chamber of Deputies. There he referred to "the appalling sufferings, the terrible tragedy of France." But French and other Allied statesmen and delegates to the Conference may have heard or read the peroration (italics inserted) with mixed feelings. Suggesting that the American peace delegation might paraphrase General Pershing's "Lafayette, we are here," he went on:

We [Americans] might, if we could gain audience to the free peoples of the world . . . say "Friends, men, humble women, little children, we are here; we are here as your friends, as your champions, *as your representatives. We have come to work out for you* a world in which all countries can enjoy the heritage of liberty for which France and America and England and Italy have paid so dear."

If Wilson had heard and remembered the quip that the British never believe that you can do anything to them, or the French that you can do anything for them, he might have altered his phraseology. But probably ardent patriotism, combined with fixation on his peace program, would in any case have been too much for him.

Rome received the President and Mrs. Wilson by hanging out, not only its flags, but its emblazoned tapestries; and cascading its guests with mimosa and violets. The Quirinal proved to be more magnificent than Buckingham Palace, and the Italian royal family as friendly and informal behind the scenes as the British had been. Wilson was pleased to find the crowds dense and demonstrative; pleased again when he received the freedom of the city, with the right to say *"Civis Romanus sum."* But the visit was sadly marred by an incident related at some length, and with some variation in details, by Mrs. Wilson and by Gino Speranza, son of a professor of Italian at Columbia University, and attaché to our Embassy in Rome. There was a serious background to the incident. The Italian ministers, uneasy over the conflict between Wilson's "Point" concerning Italian boundaries and the terms of the Treaty of London, were anxious to come to an understanding during the President's visit. At that time agreement might have been possible, since the Cabinet had not yet taken a definite stand and the people were not as yet alive to the issue. Wilson said quite truthfully that he had not studied the matter sufficiently to negotiate on it; but the Italian ministers suspected that he was avoiding discussion because his mind was already made up. They were doubtless made more suspicious still when he gave private interviews to two prominent left-wing leaders, enthusiastic supporters of the Fourteen Points, one of whom had just resigned a Cabinet post.

This probably had much to do with the Italian Government's decision to prevent the new *civis Romanus* from satisfying his heart's desire by addressing his fellow citizens in the streets. A passage from Speranza's diary seems worth quoting:

I wish I could record . . . all the obstructive measures taken by the Italian Government to prevent the President from speaking to the people. . . . The officials in charge of the visit even lied to him. They told him that on the way to the Chamber of Deputies, his motor would stop in the Piazza Venezia, so that he might speak to the people, but instead they whisked him off to Montecitorio. When he asked if it were there that he was to speak to the citizens, they replied, "No, it is now too late." Meanwhile the Ambassador in his car and thousands of persons were waiting in the Piazza. Even the plan for the President to stop a moment in the Piazza on his way to the reception at the Capitol was frustrated; and finally, on the evening of his departure, as he started to go out on the balcony of the Quirinal, from which it had been arranged for him to say a few words, he was informed that there was no audience—quite true, for a cordon of troops on the Piazza in front of the palace prevented anyone from coming into it. After the President left Rome, the Government circulated reports that Wilson had a *fobia* for crowds; also that it feared someone might throw a bomb. All rot. The people really trust Wilson, almost too much, I think.

Mrs. Wilson describes the President as "blazing with anger," and adds: "He expressed himself in no uncertain terms both to the press and to the officials who tried to explain." Wilson made a number of speeches before he left Italy, at Genoa, Turin, and Milan. From a balcony he told forty thousand Milanese, packed into the great square, that he had "never known such a greeting" as theirs, and that it had brought tears to his eyes. But he was not the sort of man to forget the incident at Rome. One may imagine that his jaw was firmly set when he got back to Paris on January 7. A week and a half would still elapse before the opening of the Conference; but that would be well occupied in deciding such delicate questions as the number of delegates to be allowed to the smaller Allies, and how much publicity there should be. To the President it meant primarily a chance to work away at the drafting of the Covenant.

Wilson's part in the Peace Conference has become an oft-told tale. All the books on the making of the Treaty and the League Covenant, all the published letters and diaries of great participants, all the official publications that have poured out since Mr. Baker put so much thought and labor into his study of Wilson's work at Paris have made it additionally easy for all of us to follow the President's activities in the greatest of his ventures. Recently, Professors Birdsall and Bailey have reviewed the material with such meticulous care and keen insight that, in an attempt to give a homespun account of Wilson's career within defined limits, one is tempted to pass over the Conference, in order to get more space for consideration of the forces which produced disaster on Wilson's western front. But something must be said about the facts that underlay Wilson's other tragedy: the transformation of that admiration and confidence which European peoples offered him when he sailed into Brest in December 1918, into anything from disillusionment to the bitterest hostility.

The alteration in feeling was not confined to men and women who could not have much information about the facts; nor yet was it restricted, in the circles of the well informed, to people wedded to old ways, or disappointed in hopes of what their countries were to gain. One of the most venomous and unjustifiable of the attacks made upon Wilson's work at Paris, upon his public and even upon his private character, came from the lips of one of the most eminent of England's left-wing liberals. A number of liberal armchair diplomatists in Europe and America turned on the President because he made concessions on reparations, on European boundaries, on mandates and sovereignty in Africa and Asia. It seemed to mean nothing to them that the problems of the Conference were too vast for any man to understand, especially since much thought and study were impossible during a desperate race for time against the spread of destitution and border wars and Bolshevism and anarchy. It was nothing to them that the force of nationalistic influences, both in Allied countries and in America, combined with the impossibility of shelving, as scraps of paper, treaties signed and sealed by other governments, gave Wilson only two possible courses of action.

He had to choose between leaving the Allies to make a far worse peace, or bringing home with him the one he did, trusting that our vast influence as a member of the League would be used to set things right. His liberal critics made no allowance for the superhuman labor on behalf of what he regarded as American ideals that broke him as the Conference went on. They concentrated on his concessions and his failures, overlooking his firmness and his successes. Some of them went so far as to demand our rejection of the Treaty, League and all, on the ground of Wilson's faithlessness to his ideals. The cool appraisal of historians has destroyed their case. In Mr. Birdsall's words:

A careful study of the record reveals an extraordinary consistency in Wilson's fight for his program under overwhelming difficulties, as well as a high degree of political intelligence in translating the abstract principle of his program into concrete details of application.

He would have found it so much easier and more popular to surrender on everything except Shantung; even to throw his influence toward the making of a covenant too innocuous to form a good target for his adversaries in Washington.

Only small sections of informed and high-minded people in the Allied countries of Europe would have cared much if he had put the soft pedal on all his points or principles, so long as he helped to create some sort of league. The vast majority wanted lasting peace; as much security as they could get, in case another war should come; as much in the way of reparations as they could extort; punishment for nations on whom they placed the full blame for the war; and the checking of the Bolsheviks. Desire for sheer revenge or "loot" was neither general nor lasting. These peoples respected and admired the President, though how much on account of America's contribution to victory, and how much for his idealism, it is impossible to tell. Probably they liked his idealism well enough in the abstract; but, being like most of us, were less pleased when it became concrete. It was soon evident that they would not willingly allow it to stand in the way of their satisfying what seemed to them quite natural desires. And their delegates, being replaceable whenever they failed to respect the wishes of their electorates, had their parts laid out for them almost as clearly as Wilson had laid out his. Conflict was unavoidable.

CHAPTER XV

Action on Both Fronts

———————◆◆◆———————

PEOPLE who have analyzed the proceedings of the Peace Conference have naturally concentrated on conflicts about "war aims," mistakes in organization and procedure, and the detection of "second-
story" work. But most of the men who were present and saw the proceedings at close range seemed at the time more impressed by the
immense burden of work that lay on them, the need for haste, and the
difficulty of evolving order out of what threatened to be chaos.

Mr. Ray Stannard Baker, who was director of the American Commission's press bureau, has stressed those elements in a way difficult to
forget:

At Vienna, a hundred years ago, they danced their way to peace. . . .
But in Paris in 1919 no one danced. At Paris they worked. . . . I can
never at all get the pleasing picture . . . of Four Olympians dominating
the course of the world. . . . I can recall only the groups of hard-pressed
and harried human beings—the Four most of any—struggling under tasks
too great for them, and smarting under the unrelenting attacks of . . .
public opinion. . . .

There was never enough time, nor tranquillity either:

. . . the councils at Paris were . . . constantly agitated by cries of
hunger . . . coming up from Vienna or Armenia or Russia, or alarmed
by the noises of new wars broken out in Poland or the Balkans or distracted by the fierce uprisings of peoples, as in Hungary, too miserable,
cold, hungry, hopeless, to await the orderly processes of the peace. And
at all times . . . there rose the specter of Chaos.

Wilson, who perhaps loved too few individuals, but loved the peoples of the world exceedingly, and who saw happiness for mankind only in the framework of order, must have been especially sensitive to these alarms and cries.

As for the confusion, he himself is often held accountable for some of it, in having put aside the French plan for the Conference. But there would have been a good deal in any case. The number of problems to be handled was as unexampled as the number of States (more than thirty Allies if the British Dominions were counted) which would presumably have to be satisfied. Each of the great Powers had a regiment of experts, advisers, executive officers, pressmen, and photographers. Americans attached in some way to the Conference numbered thirteen hundred; the British filled five hotels. Within the national contingents there was fair order. In fact, our contingent was like a political G.H.Q., complete with staff officers (intelligence officers in particular); its own couriers and its own post; its own telephone and telegraph services, carefully protected against tapping by the agents of any other government; and a printing press, turning out a *Summary of Information,* as the presses at Chaumont had so lately done.

Doubtless all the great delegations were well organized; but around them eddied such a conglomeration of "pressure groups" as even Washington had not dreamed of. Obscure peoples and minorities of all sorts, scouts and lobbyists for special interests, were forever passing from delegation to delegation; forever trying to buttonhole influential people; working incessantly to secure private interviews, in which they might get inside information, and would at least be able to set out their arguments. Some of these pressure groups were American. The most active and persistent, especially in the later stages of the Conference, was that of Ireland's friends.

At the Crillon, where American G.H.Q. was installed, the rooms in which the mighty people of our own and other delegations usually came together were those of Colonel House. In view of his previous relations with the President and with the Allied statesmen, it was natural that the Colonel had the position and responsibilities of a chief of staff. But it was unfortunate that the President never even thought, as Mrs. Wilson testifies, of the feelings of his Secretary of State. Mr. Lansing was the "foreign minister" of the United States; and at the Conference the foreign minister of each government ranked second to the delegation's head, becoming chief *pro tempore* in the head's absence. Mr. Lansing did not conceal the fact that he regarded the establishment of the League and the realization of other Wilsonian ideals as "insignificant" in comparison with the formulation of concrete peace terms.

Considering the opposition to the administration and some of its objectives that was piling up in Washington, the President would have been wiser, as well as kinder, if he had enlisted his Secretary of State's support, by asking his advice, and giving him as much official precedence as possible. Instead, he at first allowed the meetings of the five Commissioners to take place in House's rooms. And our newspaper correspondents, finding direct access to the President impossible, took the cue, and went to House instead of Lansing for their material. The President, who had been merely thoughtless, remedied this condition by making Mr. Baker the channel of communication between our Peace Commission and our press. It was Mrs. Wilson, informed by Mr. White, who told him how deeply hurt Lansing was. Mrs. Wilson believed that the Colonel had deliberately attempted to impress the American public with his importance in this way. Perhaps her personal feeling misled her. For the accusation does not seem to fit in at all with House's character. Mrs. Wilson apparently did not know that the Colonel himself had suggested to the President that it would be better to have the Commissioners meet sometimes in Lansing's office, or in the offices of White and Bliss. But the situation was never essentially changed, nor was the Secretary of State appeased.

The matter may seem trivial, but its consequences were not. Had Mr. Lansing been more tactfully treated, and taken into the President's confidence; had Wilson discussed with him his aims, his difficulties, and the reasons for the decisions that he made, Mr. Lansing might not have been, in effect, a valuable witness for the prosecution when the Senate Foreign Relations Committee in August 1919 indicted the President and the Treaty before the people. All the Commissioners save House were in general ignored. House, sharing Wilson's hopes, and well acquainted with the Allied statesmen, was of great use to him. Except on certain special matters, the others, or so he thought, were not. As his responsibilities, especially for getting a satisfactory constitution for the League incorporated into the Treaty, weighed more and more on him, time became more and more precious. So he withdrew himself from people whose help seemed unimportant, taking House, whom he regarded as almost an *alter ego,* along with him.

On the other hand, he was more than ready to make use of his experts when he needed them. The late Professor Haskins, anything but an undiscriminating eulogist, decided that "none of the chief delegates was more eager for the facts . . . and none was able to assimilate them more quickly or use them more efficiently in the discussion of territorial problems." What it came down to was that the President often sought information, but rarely sought advice. He knew exactly what he wanted; he knew, or thought he knew, what obstacles he was facing; and he had no time or vitality to spare for discussions that seemed to him needless. It had been different at Washington, where his patience with the slower, and even the tedious, members of his Cabinet had been notable. Now he was too keyed up, and too conscious of the need for haste, to show much patience with anyone. He was ruthless with others; but he was even more ruthless with himself. Lloyd George, himself a titan for work, was amazed at the burdens which the President assumed.

In some ways he seems to have burdened himself needlessly. Perhaps by this time the habit of drafting things in his special system of shorthand, and typing them out himself, was too strong to be broken; but it called for unnecessary expenditure of time and energy. And many of the interviews he granted seem to have had little point. A glance at the page from his list of engagements which his great biographer has reproduced leaves one puzzled. Why, when every minute was precious, should he have found it necessary to see a delegation wishing "to explain the humitarian and sanitary program of the National Union of French and Belgian Railway Men," or one from "The Celtic Circle of Paris, to present a national anthology of bards and poets"?

It is easier to understand how delegations from small, oppressed peoples or minorities—peoples and minorities of whose homes and histories he had little or no knowledge—were able to gain access. But what good did it do? The delegates who secured appointments were apt to find him cold. He had laid down in speeches the principles that were to be applied to all peoples for their greater freedom and happiness. Surely that was enough. Was he to help them in getting this or that valley or ridge or group of mines, when his principles had been made clear, and his experts could show on maps just how they should be applied? And yet, instead of asking Colonel House or someone else to sift the list of those who wanted to see him, and dispose of the unimportant, as the Colonel had done in America, he let these people draw on his time and energy. Why? Presumably because he thought they should have contact with their true representative.

But by far the greatest strain that he put on himself was in getting the kind of league he desired. The delegates to the Conference soon found that the only way in which they could hope to deal with all the problems before them was to parcel out the work between commissions and committees. There were some sixty of these before the Treaty was finally drafted; and the most important was the Commission created to draft the League Covenant. For any of the great leaders, membership in this meant a heavy additional burden. Since they would have to keep themselves free in the daytime for discussions and interviews of all kinds, and since the drafting of the Covenant required close attention and a good deal of argument, they could serve on the Commission only if it met in the evenings. Neither Lloyd George nor Clemenceau cared enough about the Covenant to commit himself to such long working hours; but Wilson and Orlando did.

The President did not dare to let the Commission work without him. For it was soon apparent that French ideas as to the kind of league that was needed were very different from American and British ones. So there was only one thing for it: Wilson, with House beside him, would have to steer the drafting of the Covenant himself. What his decision cost him, one can only guess. The meetings of the Commission were apt to last until midnight, and sometimes even later; his preoccupation with its proceedings prevented him from giving as much attention to other matters as he would have wished; and French acceptance of his plan had later to be paid for.

Nor can one decide how much he got in return. Some of his critics have claimed that his insistence upon having the Covenant drafted before other matters were seriously taken up, slowed up the Conference. Mr. Bailey has pretty well disposed of them. Others have agreed with his bitterest opponents in the Senate, that the Treaty should have been made first and the Covenant later. David Hunter Miller, who was at least as good a judge as anyone, set down his opinion on this point, after having had eight years to consider it:

. . . if not written in 1919 as a part of the Treaty of Versailles, no Covenant would have been written at all, no League of Nations would have existed . . . in our time.

Of all the silly comments about the Conference of Paris . . . the most inane is that it would have been better to write the agreement about a League later, when there would have been time for calm reflection . . . for there has been no moment since 1919 when either that agreement or any other agreement whatever could have been reached . . .

The wisest of Wilson's many wise decisions was to put and keep the League in the Treaty of Peace.

Perhaps the only remaining contention is as to whether Wilson might not have been better advised to insist that the original idea of concluding a preliminary treaty should be carried out; and to have seen to it that such provisions as the Treaty contained regarding the establishment of a league were of a sort too general to supply good targets for opponents in the Senate to shoot at. That question anyone can argue with himself.

One wonders whether Wilson realized, as the Conference took shape, how much he was being forced by hard realities to accept methods of procedure which contradicted some of his cherished principles; or what ammunition this would supply to his American critics. Most people will remember how the actual power became concentrated in fewer and fewer hands; how, even at the outset, it rested with the Council of Ten, made up of the heads of the delegations and the Foreign Ministers of the five great Allied and Associated Powers; and how, after Wilson's return from his brief trip to America, the power was wielded solely by the Big Four, i.e., by Wilson and the Premiers of the three great Allied democracies, except when something of particular interest to the Japanese came up; and shrank to a Big Three when the chief Italian delegates withdrew. Neither the Council of Ten nor the smaller group was ever authorized to take control.

This was hardly what Wilson, the self-appointed champion of the small peoples, the man who had accused the Allied Premiers of fearing that he would lead the small peoples against them, could have wished. But circumstances gave him no alternative. He was forced to realize that peace can no more be made by debating societies than can war; that the divorce of power from responsibility is impracticable; and that the discussion on issues about which public sentiment may become inflamed must be carried on in secrecy. The Council of Ten had to be replaced by the Council of Four, not only in the interest of greater speed, but because even ten leading statesmen seemed incapable of holding their tongues. With five hundred newspaper correspondents on the hunt for exciting news; with the peoples of Europe and America tense over the outcome, shell-shocked by war and victory, inevitably limited in their knowledge of the facts and still more limited in their ability to understand one another's points of view, there had to be strict secrecy. Statesmen could say biting things to each other, and part in anger. But after a night's sleep they could make allowances for each other's tempers and work in harmony again. But harmony might become impossible if their electorates, limited in knowledge and understanding, fired by nationalistic speeches or writings, insisted that their maximum demands should be fully satisfied. Hence settlements had to be made by a few men behind closed doors, if they were to be made in time, or even at all.

So Wilson had to see the smaller Allies, for whom he cared so much, reduced to the position of being merely asked to give consent—at public, "plenary" sessions of the Conference—to decisions made for them by the great Powers. His antagonists at Washington would not overlook the fact. In so far as the Treaty's prospects of adoption by this country were concerned, the most damaging circumstance was that the agreements reached in Paris were anything but "openly arrived at." Of course the President, in framing his Point about the new diplomacy, had been striking at the secret alliances of prewar days, and possibly at the secret treaties made while war was in progress. With all his faith in the peoples, he must even then have realized that treaties cannot be negotiated in the public view.

But most at least of the hundred and fifty American newspaper correspondents who had dashed to Paris, to "cover" one of the greatest stories in all history, had taken the phrasing of his Point quite literally. Finding that everything was being done behind closed doors, they and some of their editors were naturally outraged.

Wilson, sympathizing, did his best for them. He suggested that all the correspondents in Paris should try to find some method by which greater publicity would be feasible, but nothing came of it. There were communiqués, of course; and the meetings of the plenary sessions, being open to everyone, could be reported in detail. Delegates could, if they consented, be interviewed. But our correspondents were anything but satisfied, especially when they found that the President was less accessible than the Allied Premiers. He was much more burdened and more absorbed. Mr. Ray Stannard Baker did an admirable job in acting as his mouthpiece. But personal contact would have been much more effective in giving Wilson a "good press."

The negotiations which preceded the President's dash to America and back, negotiations which proceeded till the middle of February, when he sailed, gave him his two greatest successes at the Conference. At its second plenary session, on January 25, the Conference passed resolutions providing that a league of nations should be created as "an integral part" of the Peace Treaty, and that a commission should be appointed to draft a constitution (the Covenant) for it. This was Wilson's first great victory, won after many discussions, and owing much to British support. In the Commission, which held its first meeting in House's quarters at the Crillon, on February 3, he soon found that he was to have anything but smooth sailing. The British backed him consistently. While Lloyd George was skeptical about the League, a draft of the Covenant, deriving from both American and British plans, had been put into shape for presentation by the common labor of British and American experts. What was more, the British representatives on the Commission, Lord Robert Cecil and General Smuts, were no less pro-League enthusiasts than the President himself. Lord Robert had drawn up, for the President's revision, the resolutions of January 25.

With the French delegation it was different. Clemenceau, who had been worked on by House, was ready to agree that there should be *a* league; but he thought of it, naturally enough perhaps, as a means by which the Germans could be held down and France be made secure in the position she had claimed for centuries, as the first nation of the continent. The French representatives on the Commission, Léon Bourgeois and Larnaude, were ready to fight to the finish for the sort of league that the Tiger had in mind. Fortunately, the delegates of Italy, Japan, and the nine smaller countries represented on the Commission were in general sympathetic with the Anglo-American concept.

So things looked promising when Wilson took the chair at the Commission's first meeting. He asked at once that the American-British plan be accepted as the basis on which discussion should proceed. The French almost immediately opened fire. As Mr. Birdsall has pointed out, they were acting quite naturally. It was not merely that they wanted to hold the Germans down. To them, freedom was something that had been won by armies, conscript armies, and something that would have to be maintained by armies in the future. So the League would have to have armed forces at its command. And what country could unify and command these forces so well as France? Clemenceau even hoped that an international general staff, primarily French; of course, would be given some say in the raising and training of the League's troops, whether in Britain, America, or any other country.

To the British and American delegates this suggestion was fantastic. Their countries had never needed or liked conscription; and their peoples would never hear of any scheme for placing part of their armed forces under international control. In this country, the Constitution seemed to stand in the way. There were storms at the Commission's meetings. The French delegates were truculent, and returned repeatedly to the charge. It seems surprising that the Americans and British were able, in ten meetings, to secure the Commission's adoption of a league which would call for military measures only when the last hope of peaceable arrangement had vanished; and, even then, would not ask its members to bring their armed forces into play except by their individual choice. There would be a moral obligation, nothing else. Wilson, realizing that obligations under all international agreements are fundamentally moral ones, and that moral obligations are of compelling force with honorable men, was satisfied. Americans were sure to act honorably. And he was soon to tell a Boston audience of his belief that "the peoples" of the world were "in the saddle," and would see that their governments behaved properly in future.

His other great success in those first weeks at Paris, the Conference's wholesale acceptance of the system of mandates, was won in a series of contests which brought out the difficulties he was constantly to meet in reconciling abstract principles with national sentiments and interests, to say nothing of the obligations of treaties. No better plan for disposing of the colonies and dependencies which the Germans and Turks were to relinquish appears to have been suggested then or since. The mandate idea was not a Wilson monopoly (though it seems to have come to him independently); nor was he obliged to battle much with "looters" and "spoilers."

Before the opening of the Conference, it had been decided, with the President's full concurrence, that Germany should not recover her colonies. For this decision some of the Kaiser's former subjects were in considerable part responsible. German Socialists, in their anxiety to discredit the imperial government, had exaggerated the mistreatment of natives by German colonial officials; and Herr Zimmermann had put on paper plans for raising a million colored troops for Germany's army, and for the establishment of submarine bases in her African ports. Wilson's loathing of the mistreatment or conscription of colored peoples was probably the decisive factor in his decision that Germany should relinquish her overseas empire. Neither he nor other members of the Peace Conference could have been expected to consider how the Germans would be affected psychologically in being told that they were to lose their colonies because they were unfit to govern them.

As for the Near East, where the "Sick Man of Europe" was breaking up at last, two subjugated peoples of his misgoverned Asiatic lands, the Arabs of the Hejaz and the Armenians, would apparently be able to stand alone. The others, while certainly coveted by Allied imperialists, really needed some tutelage if they were to have order, and to make progress, as most of us understand the word. And far more, of course, was this true of the peoples inhabiting the islands in the Pacific which Germany had held. The new system would presumably give all the mandated lands and peoples protection against exploitation, conscription, and such abuses as the arms and liquor traffic, under the League's presumably watchful eye. Annexation would have given them none. Wilson's first idea was to have the mandated territories and islands administered directly by the League; his second, to have small European countries act as mandatories. But when, for reasons obvious enough, he saw that neither of these two plans was practical, he had to consent to guardianship by the great Powers and the British Dominions, which, by previous arrangement, had been expecting to annex most of them. Wilson would have no annexations at all:

> The world would say that the Great Powers first portioned out the helpless parts of the world, and then formed a League of Nations. . . . If the process of annexation went on the League of Nations would be discredited from the beginning.

That was the great principle; and he stuck to it. Tussling simultaneously with Bourgeois and Larnaude about the League, he had far from an easy time. French, Japanese, Italian, and Dominion delegates were all annoyed. By the last week in January, when the dispute about mandates was especially vigorous, the French newspapers were becoming vitriolic in their comments. Moreover, the Italians, the Japanese, and the Dominions could base their demands for annexation on treaties or solemn promises.

The case of the Dominions perhaps best illustrates the difficulties with which the President was faced. Nowadays one feels inclined to commend the foresight of the Australians and New Zealanders in wanting to annex Germany's insular possessions south of the equator, as a protection against Japanese attack. Nobody could think of them as "imperialists." Nor is it difficult to see why German South West Africa (of which the riches were not then fully known) was claimed, for the same reason, by the South Africans. All three Dominions had received definite promises. Lloyd George could not go back on them. He could not do anything but bring in the three Premiers to present their case. It was no more his fault that Mr. Hughes of Australia was cantankerous and unreasonable, than that time was wasted when Mr. Hughes's hearing apparatus went out of order, and proceedings had to stop until it was fixed again. What the British Premier could do, and did do, was to work for a sensible settlement. Debates and consultations followed fast: in the Council of Ten, in the Commission on the League, and in House's office at the Crillon. Since the Commission on the Covenant was drafting an article relating to mandates, the discussions in the Council of Ten and in the Commission (an interlocking directorate in so far as America was concerned) were intertwined.

In the Council a stormy scene or two occurred; and Wilson showed temper. House felt at times that he was too unyielding, and would have done better to congratulate his opponents on "their willingness to meet us more than halfway." There was even some fear that the Peace Conference would split on its first decisive test. But General Smuts greatly smoothed the way in offering a plan by which the disposable territories and islands would be placed under mandates providing control in three different degrees, according to the extent of their fitness to manage their own affairs. They were promised eventual independence, if and when they showed themselves capable of making use of it. There was a last flurry, when the French insisted upon the right to raise colored troops, even in mandated colonies. Here the President gave ground, on the understanding that such troops should be merely volunteers, and employed only for defense. Wilson could not always have his way, especially against a Premier who in the opinion of some of his people, was showing himself too pliant.

How close the contest had been was shown when General Smuts, presenting the final draft of the article of the Covenant on mandates, made a plea for its acceptance as it stood. Colonel Bonsal has given a vivid account of the session—of tense delegates having before them on the table "amendments which they thought were vital and which they intended to propose." And he tells of the speech, compelling in its modesty and sincerity, by which Smuts carried them away. He was ashamed of his draft, he said. It was not coherent, not even grammatical; but it was the best that the subcommittee which he headed was able to agree upon after a month's hard work. At least he could claim that it was designed to provide "ultimate self-government of all the peoples," and guardianship meanwhile. He would beg them not to alter it. The subcommittee had "weighed every sentence, every word." If they tried to introduce improvements, as he himself would like to do, he believed that it would "fall to the ground, not to be raised again" in their day. It was very faulty, yes; but it was an "opening wedge" by which they might "open wide a door to better things" after the world had enjoyed a breathing spell and men had become less "war crazed." In much these same terms Wilson was later to plead in this country for the infinitely more important adoption of the Covenant. He was to fail. Smuts, at Paris, did not. One of the reasons was that behind and with him was the President. Wilson had had to make some concessions as to details, but he had scored a real triumph.

By February 15 Wilson had reached what was perhaps the peak of his career. On that day he appeared before a plenary session of the Conference, to lay before them the draft of the Covenant which the Commission had produced. Considering all the difficulties, in surmounting French opposition in particular, the work had been done with surprising speed. When one thinks of the time consumed in the framing of most national constitutions, and remembers that the men who framed them had patterns before them, and were substantially of the same mind, the work of the Commission (which was first of all Wilson's) is impressive in the highest degree. Though Wilson's speech of presentation was a model in all respects, the proceedings in the plenary session were not altogether happy. Some of the smaller peoples, the Belgians in particular, had for some time been restive under the weight of the great Powers. Their delegates were primed to raise objections and offer amendments to the Covenant. Clemenceau, presiding, showed that the "steam roller," if unknown by that name in Europe, could work there very effectively. Its use, one would probably conclude, was unavoidable.

So the draft of the Covenant was accepted; and the President was able to leave for America in a confident and happy mood. The Allied statesmen had not proved nearly so difficult as he had feared. The peoples of Europe had seemed to look to him with all the confidence and hope he could have wished, despite the bad taste which some of the French papers had lately shown. The Conference had approved a covenant such as he wanted, and agreed to write it into the Treaty. He had had his way, too, about the question of mandates. Now he could look forward to a pleasant and comparatively restful month. He and Mrs. Wilson were to sail immediately for Boston. There he would make a speech, presenting the Covenant to his own people for their approval and support. After that he would have about a week in Washington. He would explain the Covenant to senators and congressmen, deal with bills passed by the lame-duck Congress before the session ended on March 4, and get reports from Democratic leaders about conditions of all kinds. There would just be time to plead the cause of the Covenant to the people in another speech before he and Mrs. Wilson boarded the *George Washington* for another restful trip.

Wilson was entirely set upon returning to Paris. The preliminary treaty was not nearly in shape for signature. They would be working on it while he was away. The military and naval terms would be drawn up. Information and suggestions on other terms would be waiting for him, too. Though Mr. Lansing would be titular head of the Commission in his absence, Colonel House would be his real representative. And of course they would be in almost constant touch by cable and wireless.

Wilson's elation must have added to his enjoyment of the westbound trip. The weather was satisfactory; and the *George Washington* made good time. The Under-Secretary of the Navy, Mr. Franklin D. Roosevelt, and Mrs. Roosevelt were on board, as was Mr. Francis, our Ambassador to Russia. Below were two thousand soldiers, in fine spirits at returning home and very appreciative of the warm friendliness their Commander in Chief showed them. The quiet days at sea were something of a lifesaver to the President; but he had a good deal on his mind. The short stay that he planned to make in Boston probably did not occupy him much. Formality was to be avoided as much as possible; and as for the speech he was planning, his mind was so full of the League that little if any preparation was needed.

But he must have realized that he would run into opposition at Washington. He had made some effort to forestall it by inviting the members of the committees of both Houses which dealt with foreign affairs to dine with him informally and talk over the League at ease. Colonel House had suggested the dinner. Wilson had thought that an address to Congress would be enough; but before he sailed the Colonel, better sensing the situation, had persuaded him to see what conviviality and freedom of discussion would do in softening opposition to the Covenant. Unfortunately, both he and his opponents in Washington were stiffening during the time of his voyage.

Wilson had made a reasonable enough request that senators should not publicly discuss the Covenant until he had had an opportunity of explaining it to them. Instead of complying, the senators most hostile to the League treated his request as an incentive to attack it bitterly. If Wilson could talk of it in Boston before they met, so could they in Washington—even though he could speak with authority as to its meaning, and they could not. Senators Johnson, Knox, and Borah demanded that the Treaty be concluded before the League was taken up; and Borah joined with Senator Poindexter in objecting to our membership in any league at all. The Covenant was raked fore and aft. Poindexter called it a breeder of wars, "a colossal burden of entangling alliances"; while the Democratic Senator Reed, not to be outdone in exaggeration by any Republican, discovered that it involved "complete surrender of America's vital right to defend herself" to a tribunal (the League Council, naturally) which "could be composed eight to one of the enemies of America."

Outside Congress, too, the President and the Covenant had been coming under fire. During a Lincoln Day banquet at the Waldorf, James M. Beck, whose ability was so often masked by spleen, had called Wilson's principles "a crazy patchwork of contradictions," and his foreign policy "a black stain of dishonor" upon the nation. Within the next few days Wilson had been attacked by both the friends and the enemies of Bolshevist Russia, alike excited over the testimony being given in Senate hearings by returned American consuls, by Mme. Breshkovskaya, and by Miss Louise Bryant (legally Mrs. John Reed). The enemies accused Wilson of showing sympathy with persecutors of Christianity, cold-blooded murderers, and advocates of free love; while Miss Bryant (who had failed to see any terrorism during her sojourn among the Bolsheviks) admitted that she had recently helped to burn the President in effigy. Senator Hiram Johnson appeared to sympathize with her feeling if not with her motives, when he talked about the "murder" of American "boys" by a Government which had sent them to Russia. Orators are sometimes so superior to mere definitions and dictionaries. Wilson apparently knew more or less about these attacks before he stepped on land, either from wireless messages or from newspapers delivered by tender. As the *George Washington* was nearing port there occurred a mishap, slight in itself, but amusingly suggestive, as one now thinks of it. Proceeding through a thick fog, the captain lost his reckoning. The President's ship was in a fair way to run aground. But Mr. Roosevelt, who as a yachtsman knew the waters well, located the ship's position and put her safely on her way again.

On February 24 the President and Mrs. Wilson, greeted by sirens and circling airplanes, were driving through crowded streets, to lunch quietly at the Copley Plaza with Mrs. Sayre, before Wilson left to make his speech at the Mechanics' Hall. The crowds were dense, since Boston was having a public holiday in the President's honor; but reporters noted that the applause was somewhat perfunctory. It might have been expected that even Boston would feel complimented in being chosen to receive and hear the country's President and triumphant chief delegate to the Peace Conference. But as Wilson, still audacious, must have realized when he made the choice, Boston was not only the hub of Senator Lodge, but perhaps the hub, in the Eastern States at least, of the kind of Americans of Irish origin whom he had more than once condemned.

Americans of Irish origin, whether hyphenate or otherwise, were incensed beyond measure just at this time by reports of what was happening in the old land. During the last two days of the *George Washington's* voyage, representatives of nearly all the important Irish organizations in America, to the number of over five thousand, had met in Philadelphia. The principal reason for the meeting was to see what could be done about having the cause of Ireland brought into the Peace Conference. Considering that Wilson had been visiting and hobnobbing with the King and the Prime Minister of Great Britain, much enthusiasm was hardly to be expected from Boston crowds in general. But there was a good prospect of his meeting with more friendliness from the people admitted by ticket to the Mechanics' Hall.

Seven thousand people taxed the capacity of the auditorium, as the President and Mrs. Wilson arrived, under the escort of the Governor and the Mayor. There were addresses of welcome, during which Mr. Coolidge, as reported, promised that Massachusetts would continue to support the President. There was singing, in which the audience failed rather dismally on "The Battle Hymn of the Republic," but recovered when "Onward, Christian Soldiers" had its turn. Then an alert and critical audience settled itself to listen. It was not especially impressed by the idealism and the generalities of the opening. And it found the President guilty of exaggeration, thanks to his exalted mood. Not even the idolized General Edwards, sitting there in uniform, would have been likely to tell Boston that American soldiers "were not like any of the other soldiers. They had vision . . . they were fighting in a dream." Nor did Wilson's listeners seem greatly stirred when he pictured the dawn of hope in Europe, the "new magic" that lay in the ideal of "settled peace"; or when he pictured the "unthinkable" results, the "bitterness of despair" that would ensue if the new hopes were dashed. Some eyebrows were raised when the audience was told that the world's peoples "were going to see to it that if their present governments do not do their will, some other governments shall." Was the President referring to this country?

Toward the end of the speech came a passage suggesting that Wilson was informed about the behavior of some of the senators. If America, he said, were to disappoint the confidence reposed in her, she would be abandoned to "those narrow, selfish, provincial purposes which [seemed] so dear to some minds." Then, as though anger had overcome him so suddenly as to make him indifferent to the sequence, the President lashed out:

I should welcome no sweeter challenge than that. I have fighting blood in me and it is sometimes a delight to let it have scope, but if it is challenged on this occasion it will be an indulgence.

This casting down of the gauntlet was greeted with hearty cheers by friends of the League in the Mechanics' Hall; but one wonders about the feelings of Colonel House and of Senator Hitchcock, the President's mainstay in the Senate, when they read of it. Wilson was not only carrying a chip on his shoulder: he was almost imploring anti-League and anti-Wilson senators to knock it off. Nor was he helping the prospects of the League by making its adoption so much a personal issue. A number of people at the Capitol were very content to have him do so. Democratic control of the Senate and its Foreign Relations Committee would end with the closing of the session on March 4. Of course the new Congress would not normally come together until December; but there were ways of seeing that it should convene much earlier.

Wilson's few days in Washington were among the busiest and disappointing of his life. He showed that his interest in domestic matters, especially the relations between capital and labor, was still alive. A hurried invitation was sent out to the governors of all States and the mayors of a hundred large cities to confer on the "vital questions affecting business and labor" which would be involved in the complete resumption of private enterprise. Wilson even found time to address the conference when it opened on March 3. But of course the question of the League was uppermost in his mind; and here he met with nothing but discouragement. The dinner given for the committees was so flat a failure that he later reproached House for having suggested it. Senator Borah had written that he could not be present, since the circumstances would prevent him from giving full publicity to whatever might transpire; and had sent his letter to the press. Senator Fall, afflicted with the same scrupulosity, had followed the same course. The senators and congressmen who did attend were greeted cordially; and the Covenant was discussed for hours in what seemed a good-humored atmosphere. But Senator Brandegee declared that he felt as though he had been dining with Alice in Wonderland; while others of the opposition group told reporters that the President showed astonishing ignorance of the provisions of the Covenant! It was reported around the Capitol that the President had not made so much as one convert.

And much worse things than that transpired. Democratic leaders, interviewed at the White House and the Capitol, informed the President that the Republicans had no intention of allowing him to carry on for long without Congress. A Senate filibuster, that abomination he had denounced two years before, would force him to call a special session in the near future. It would block the passage of certain appropriations without which Government could not go on. It was reported that Wilson, on hearing the news, "set his jaw," and announced that there would be no extra session in his absence. But he was soon to find that unless the Peace Conference could speed up its work, or unless he was willing to leave it before it closed, there would have to be a special session in his absence. For the filibuster went through as planned.

On the day the session closed and he was preparing to leave Washington for New York and Paris, thirty-seven of the senators who would sit in the new Congress bade him farewell by telling him what he might expect. A "round robin," which they signed, declared that the Covenant of the League "in the form now proposed to the Peace Conference should not be accepted by the United States." Since there were enough signers to block ratification of any treaty he might bring home, he would either have to secure changes in the Covenant at the bidding of Republican leaders, or get no covenant at all. Today, most people think that his only wise course would have been to retire from the Peace Commission, appoint another Commissioner (Mr. Taft, who would have been one of the best possible choices in the first place, might still have consented to accept a place), and devote much thought and energy to winning the support of the people.

Wilson does not appear even to have considered such a course. The people, as he correctly believed, were on his side. He was confident that they would give him victory later on. Since there was as yet no Treaty, the Covenant had still to be guarded at Paris, the more so as he had been advised to ask for amendments that would mollify some of the senators. He protested that the suggested amendments were unnecessary if nothing worse; and that if we should insist upon alterations, there would be nothing to prevent other governments from doing the same, and wrecking the structure. But he did not make up his mind either to ask for the amendments or to refuse.

In his indignation at the abuse of the Covenant, the failure of the dinner, the filibuster, the round robin, and the pressure put on him to have the Covenant altered, Wilson could not contain himself. He let go in a farewell message to the people, delivered at the Metropolitan Opera House, immediately before the *George Washington* was to sail. In one respect the occasion was an especially happy one. Mr. Taft spoke just before the President, explaining the main features of the Covenant, and pointing out how essential it would be to any lasting settlement. He did it in such admirable fashion that Wilson was able to confine himself to general pleas and arguments. In the main, he talked persuasively and even touchingly. He told of "a little limping group of wounded Italian soldiers," who had handed him a petition in favor of the League. "Their wounded limbs, their impaired vitality, were the only argument they brought with them." Then he spoke of the A.E.F., picking up from the band the words of America's favorite war song. He would not come back till it was over, over there, because he had "felt the crusading spirit of these youngsters who went over there not to glorify America but to serve their fellow men." America could not refuse to help the world, for if she did,

From being what I will venture to call the most famous and the most powerful nation in the world, we would of a sudden have become the most contemptible.

He had no fears of that:

I am going to tell the people on the other side of the water . . . that an overwhelming majority of the American people is in favor of the League of Nations.

Once or twice he laid the lash to the League's foes:

I cannot imagine how these gentlemen can live . . . and not be in contact with the events of their times, and I particularly cannot imagine how they can be Americans and set up a doctrine of careful selfishness thought out to the last detail. I have heard no counsel of generosity in their criticism. . . . I have heard nothing except, "Will it not be dangerous for us to help the world?"

But it was another passage which most stirred certain depths at Washington:

When that treaty comes back gentlemen on this side will find the Covenant not only in it, but so many threads of the treaty tied to the covenant [sic] that you cannot dissect the covenant from the treaty without destroying the whole vital structure.

In a comprehensive view of the peace settlement this was a statement of plain fact. Possibly Wilson did not intend it as a threat. Very probably he did. But one cannot assume that at this or any other point in his speech he gave way to mere pique or petulance. Many of the motives and many of the methods prevalent at the Capitol must have seemed immeasurably petty to a man who was risking everything he had, in order that his country might attain the eminence among nations that is won only by service.

Unfortunately, righteous anger, if Wilson's was righteous, may incur the same penalties as malevolence. "Gentlemen" at Washington reminded themselves that May and the special session were not far off. Wilson's western front was "flaming," as the papers say. He had a last reminder of this just as he was about to board the *George Washington*. He was asked to give an interview to a delegation of American friends of Ireland, headed by Judge Cohalan, one of the most active and abusive of all the hyphenates. He would receive the delegation, he said, but only without the Judge. Well, the Judge, who knew a good deal about politics, may also have thought hopefully about May days in Washington. Twisting the lion's tail, especially in Ireland's interest, was so popular that even senators not personally given to the sport found that refusal to join in was politically most unwise. And such tail-twisting could be useful, if not in helping Ireland, at least in making things difficult for Wilson, both at the Conference and later.

CHAPTER XVI

Victory on the Eastern Front

—————————◆—————————

Wilson's second eastbound trip cannot have been nearly so pleasant as the first. It was not only that his short visit in America had left a bitter taste. He knew that he was sailing into a very sea of trouble at Paris. He had always said that thirteen was his lucky number: he might have reflected, during those days at sea, that four seemed now to be his unlucky one. He had been told before he sailed, by people as friendly to the League as Mr. Taft and President Lowell, that he would have to secure at least four amendments to the Covenant if it was to stand any chance of adoption by the Senate. And he had to consider that the representatives of four great governments were going to make demands on him that he could not in conscience satisfy.

Since the early part of January the French had been asking that the Rhineland should be cut off from Germany, and made into one or more little republics which France would dominate, in fact if not according to any protocol. Disputes concerning the disposition of the Saar Valley were certain to be especially troublesome. Still greater difficulties were to be expected regarding the boundaries of Poland. While an early French suggestion that they should include the whole of East Prussia had now been dropped, Clemenceau and his delegation were insistent that the Poles should have Danzig. American and British experts were backing them, while Lloyd George was opposing them. Wilson's own mind was not made up.

As for Italy, her claims had not as yet been presented to the Conference; but the President knew that his position would be difficult when they were. He had already departed from his principle of frontiers following "clearly recognizable lines of nationality" by conceding to the Italians the Brenner Pass frontier. How would the Italian Government act when he returned to it, as he must do, on behalf of the half million Yugoslavs given over to them by the Treaty of London? The Japanese had also been very quiet so far, though they had persistently urged the insertion in the Covenant of a declaration establishing racial, or at least national, equality. Perhaps their insistence had been due mainly to pride, already wounded by such things as California's Alien Land Law; but they may have calculated that their demand would have a trading value, too. For it would not be long before the Conference would have to pass on their claim, under treaty, to all of Germany's former powers and possessions in the Shantung Peninsula.

As for Britain, until now the most co-operative of the great Allies, her ideas regarding reparations were clearly in conflict with the American understanding of the reservation laid down in the pre-armistice negotiations and accepted by the Germans. In Wilson's absence the French had conceded the British claim that pensions and separation allowances should be included in Germany's bill, as damage done to civilians by aggressive enemy action. American experts had complained by cable to the President; and had been directed to stand firm. And Wilson had received other disturbing news. House had cabled at least three times about French designs on the Rhineland, and had received two warnings from the President that no concessions in this matter could be made. Wilson's second cable showed that he was even a little troubled about his *alter ego's* own attitude.

Worry about all these things may have accounted for the fact that Wilson apparently landed at Brest in an irritated frame of mind. A surprise was awaiting him. Colonel House came aboard, carrying a set of maps, and retired with the President for a long private conference. Mrs. Wilson's much-quoted account of her husband's reaction to the interview may be explained in either of two ways. It is quite possible that time, devotion to her dead and defeated husband, and possibly her dislike of House, had blurred her memory as to just what took place. But it is at least as likely that Wilson, indulging in a fit of temper, was very unjust to his old friend. As Mrs. Wilson remembered it, the President "seemed to have aged ten years" when House took leave of him. When Mrs. Wilson asked what had happened, he declared that the Colonel had "given away everything"; had "compromised on every side," so that he would have to "start all over again."

The Colonel had done nothing of the sort. He had made things more difficult in one respect. He, like Mr. Balfour, had allowed Tardieu to persuade him that the French might be permitted to carry out their plans concerning the Rhineland for a limited time: perhaps five years, or until the League was properly functioning, even should this mean a longer period. But he had not committed the President. What is more, the Tardieu suggestion had been stillborn, thanks to the opposition of Lloyd George.

The episode has attracted attention as possibly marking the beginning of Wilson's estrangement from the most useful of his advisers at Paris. But the beginning is hard to find. "Ike" Hoover believed that people inimical to House had commenced to work on Wilson with some success during his first crossing on the *George Washington*. But the incident at Brest seems to supply the first trustworthy evidence that House's constant efforts to preserve harmony with the Allies, by conceding more to them than Wilson could approve, was undermining the position of confidence he had so long enjoyed, and in many ways so well deserved.

World history, even to the last decade, has been affected by developments at Paris during the two days following the President's return. The French were vigorously pushing their demands concerning the Rhineland. What was more, they were anxious to shelve the idea of a preliminary treaty, and conclude a final one, before too many of the troops of their Allies had been withdrawn. There seemed to be some question as to how such a change in procedure would affect the League. There were even rumors in Paris that the League might not be an integral part of the Treaty after all.

Wilson attacked the question of the Rhineland first. Lloyd George had already suggested to Clemenceau that if France would content herself with a mere demilitarization and temporary occupation of the Rhineland and Rhine Valley, Britain would agree by treaty to come to her assistance if the Germans should violate the terms before the League was functioning effectively. Wilson had hardly reached Paris before he made the same offer. Lansing, Bliss, and White were horrified. They knew that the Senate would never approve a treaty of this kind; and they could argue that the conclusion of such treaties would violate the principles on which the League was based, and suggest that the signatory governments had little confidence in it. But there was nothing they could do. Wilson was carried along by the belief that the people would force the senators to endorse whatever agreements he might sign. Future events were to be shaped much more by another decision which he apparently came to in these days. Issuing a sharp statement that the relation of the Covenant to the Treaty would stand unchanged, he decided to fall in with the French idea of concluding a final peace treaty then and there. Perhaps he merely felt that the conclusion of two treaties would keep him too long away from Washington. He had told the audience at the Metropolitan that he would not come back till it was over, over there. Perhaps, learning from his chief legal adviser that the Senate would have to approve the preliminary as well as the final treaty, he decided that it would be hard enough to get even one treaty ratified.

But the result of his decision, as Mr. Bailey has emphasized, was that the Peace Conference never really met at all. German delegates were to have been summoned to take part.in negotiating the final treaty. Now, they would not be called until the terms had been settled. And Hitler would one day be able to rave about the *Diktat* of Versailles. The decision had other unfortunate results. Everything would have to be done as speedily as possible. Articles drawn up by commissions and committees, with the idea that they would be modified at leisure, would be written into the treaty as they were. Some of them would be conflicting in effect. Above all, the reparation terms would take no account of the economic position in which Germany had been placed.

If Wilson foresaw any of these results, he was not troubled. Everything could be corrected through the League. He did not, in fact, have much time to think about results, for more immediate problems descended on him with a rush. By the time he had been back in Paris for a week, the Commission on the League of Nations had reconvened, and the Council of Ten, almost immediately to be converted into the Big Four, was discussing the Rhineland, the Saar, Poland, reparations, and Italy's frontiers. Consequently, within this week, disagreements which threatened to disrupt the Conference were beginning to appear. A crisis was starting to develop which would reach its height before the month was out and last well over into April. Then there would be a lull; but this would be merely a hush before another storm. It was all to be very wearing on Wilson, determined to uphold his principles in every issue, and working so much alone. The peak of the first crisis was to find him bedridden.

His difficulties, daunting enough in any case, were magnified by the necessity of securing amendments to the Covenant which might satisfy the senators. For he had finally been persuaded that this was a matter of necessity. He would have to get an amendment specifically excluding the working of the Monroe Doctrine, as we interpreted it, from the sphere of action of the League; another doing the same with regard to domestic issues, such as tariffs and immigration laws; a third, permitting us to quit the League if we should so desire; and still another, giving us full freedom to refuse acceptance of mandates. How the necessity of getting these amendments inserted was to affect the negotiations on other matters was immediately apparent when the President reconvened the Commission on March 22, and called it together again on March 24 and 26.

The first session had hardly opened before Bourgeois and Larnaude began again to demand changes that would bring the League into line with French wishes. The French delegates talked still more loudly at the second meeting when Wilson produced a draft of the amendments he was asking for. They made no trouble about those relating to domestic issues and the refusal of mandates; but they protested that the maintenance of the Monroe Doctrine would divert American interests and activities from European questions, and that permission given to League members to withdraw at will would dangerously weaken the whole structure. By both amendments, they insisted, France was being deprived of some measure of security. There was truth in these arguments; but Wilson was enraged on hearing later that Bourgeois had admitted that he cared nothing about the Monroe Doctrine, and regarded his protests merely as something to trade with. Perhaps the Japanese had the same motive in recommencing their demand for a racial-equality clause, though public sentiment in their country could sometimes take on an especially ugly form.

Even Lloyd George (apparently to the distress of his delegation) decided that he, too, could make use of the position in which the Senate had placed the President. He was apparently, and not unnaturally, upset by Wilson's pre-armistice threats of outbuilding the British Navy, and by the "second-to-none" policy for the expansion of our fleet, to which the President had publicly committed himself. Not desiring, for obvious and quite worthy reasons, to see an Anglo-German naval race succeeded by an Anglo-American one, he raised objections to the Monroe Doctrine amendment, at the same time asking that our plans for naval construction should be halted or even reduced. Of course Wilson would not hear of that. But, feeling the need of a united front against French demands for greater security along the Rhine, he did promise a conference on the limitation of naval armaments. That seems to have been a good idea in every way; but agreement was not reached until just before the fourth meeting of the Commission, on April 10. After the third meeting the President had decided to let the amendments rest awhile. Things were growing too warm for comfort in the discussions of the Big Four about other matters.

French demands were in the forefront; and the French press was now attacking the President with venom. Clemenceau had had to give up the idea of Rhineland republics; but, acting with much pressure from behind, he was demanding occupation for a period of thirty years, a system of inspection by Allied officers that would have involved the creation of something like an international general staff, the continuation of the treaties of guarantee until France decided she no longer needed them. Also the Saar Valley. Here again the President was plagued by his disagreement with the senators. Clemenceau, fearing that he would be subjected to still more popular pressure, had seen to it that accounts of such developments at Washington as the round robin were censored out of the French press. But he used his knowledge of the probability that the Senate would reject the guarantee treaty, as a way of bringing pressure on Wilson.

On March 29 came the famous scene in which Clemenceau accused the President of being pro-German, and flung himself out of the room. It was not to be until the middle of April that the compromise on occupation and demilitarization along the Rhine was reached. Then the press attacks on the President ceased overnight, as though someone had turned off a hot-water spigot. A little earlier the question of the Saar was settled; and a little later it was agreed that Danzig should have autonomy.

All this time the struggle over reparations was going on. On April 1 Wilson delivered himself of his famous and very un-Wilsonian ejaculation: "Logic! Logic! I don't give a damn for logic!" His legal experts had been insisting that he should not consent to the inclusion of pensions and separation allowances in Germany's bill. The concession he was making was, by general agreement, the most disastrous of all his decisions at Paris, both as to his sacrifice of principle and to the consequences which ensued. But at the time he made it he had no reason to believe it would have any other tangible result than to give Britain a larger, and France a smaller, percentage of what was collected from Germany. British and American experts seemed to agree that a reparations commission should arrive at a fixed sum to be demanded from the Germans, basing its calculations, not on Allied demands, but on German's capacity to pay. American influence in the commission would presumably be powerful. And American experts very properly informed the President that a sum fixed in this manner would be moderate, especially as compared with the astronomical French demands and the only less fantastic ones brought forward by certain of the British experts. Lloyd George seemed to change financial advisers according to his needs.

Finally, Wilson was in full expectation that the period of German payments would be limited to thirty years. Unhappily, after the President had agreed to the inclusion of pensions and separation allowances, he and the British came to a deadlock with the French. France demanded the full costs of the war and would hear of no time limit. Apparently her main idea was to hold the Germans down as long as possible. It was agreed that the occupation of the Rhine country could be continued if Germany failed to satisfy her creditors, and that even reoccupation might take place. If Lloyd George had stood firmly behind the President, Wilson might have been able to hold out for the sort of reparations settlement he had expected on April 1. But the British Premier was being attacked in the House of Commons for failing to keep his election promises.

Our delegation gave in. It was not Wilson who accepted the French demand for a reparations commission shorn of power to fix Germany's bill in terms of her capacity to pay. At the time he was sick in bed; and Colonel House accepted on his behalf. Wilson allowed the settlement to stand; but he seems to have chalked up another score against the Colonel. Unfortunately, he also chalked up a score against himself by not overriding House's decision when he was well again. Unfortunately, again, he endorsed the ambiguous and superfluous "war guilt" clause. That was to prove as good a talking point as the *Diktat* itself for a hysterical Führer.

The President's illness, which confined him to bed for some days after April 3, is a matter of considerable interest. For one thing, he showed his usual indomitable will by carrying on some business in spite of it. Then there seems to be some uncertainty as to its real nature.

It was supposed to be influenza; but there were people close to the President who believed, and still believe, that it was really a slight stroke. But the important thing is the marked change which a good many people saw in Wilson from about this time on. It was not only that his face twitched; not only that he looked "like a corpse." He seemed to some people more irritable, more rigid, but at the same time lacking in some of his old self-confidence. Perhaps such changes did occur; but in some great essentials the Wilson of earlier years lived on. Courage and determination always, audacity in crises—these resources he could muster still. And the sources he drew on for them remained as they had been: faith in God and the people. Faith in the people, in all peoples, was very much in evidence in the next crisis he was to face—the crisis arising out of Italy's demands.

The issue raised by the Italian claims had been simmering since before the armistice. Italian ministers would gladly have discussed it when Wilson was in Rome. Before and during his trip to America it had commenced to boil. Some of the heat came from Fiume, where Italians were somewhat more numerous than Yugoslavs in the town proper, but less numerous if the suburbs were counted in. A section of the Italians there were the most ardent kind of nationalists. Austrian rule, and the fact that they lived in a sea of Slavs, had made them especially eager to bring their city under the Italian flag. That it was the only decent port Yugoslavia could have; that the Treaty of London had left it to the Yugoslavs, made no difference to them. Crossing to what they regarded as their fatherland, a group of them found no difficulty in creating hot sentiment on their behalf. For Italians were unwilling that any other State, even one so new and weak as Yugoslavia, should have a decent port on "their" Adriatic Sea.

Orlando and Sonnino were soon under pressure to get Fiume, as well as the Adriatic provinces and islands promised in the London Treaty, with their half million Yugoslavs. They went to work on some of the American experts, and especially on Dr. Mezes, House's brother-in-law, and titular head at Paris of the experts of The Inquiry. Not forgetful of hospitality, they succeeded so well that two days after Wilson's return from Washington Dr. Mezes recommended to House that the Italian delegates should be given practically all they asked. The four American experts who were really entitled to advise the President on the question, and who worked as much as possible in the spirit of the Fourteen Points, reminded him that they had all along advised against letting either Fiume or Dalmatia go to Italy.

During a lull of some weeks, when other questions were in the forefront at the Conference, Dr. Mezes received considerable encouragement. His brother-in-law, Colonel House, anxious that the Conference should end speedily and harmoniously, and the League get under way, showed sympathy with his point of view. So did a group of distinguished American experts and advisers in other fields. It seemed to them that the progress of the Conference should not be impeded by what was a minor issue after all. Some of them appear to have argued that it would be better to place many Yugoslavs under Italian rule, than to have a small number of Italians governed by many Yugoslavs. The group came to be referred to as "upstairs," thanks to the location of House's rooms at the Crillon.

The question came to a head about the middle of April. The qualified experts had again appealed to the President against "upstairs" activity ten days before. Wilson, who liked Orlando, and was grateful for his support in the framing of the Covenant, tried, with the qualified experts' aid, to find some solution (making Fiume an independent port, perhaps) which would satisfy both the Italians and his own principles. But no way could be found. On April 14 he was forced to tell Orlando (in the interview which he compared, for the pain it gave him, to the one he had had with a sick and despairing mother when he was President of Princeton) that he could not go against the position of the qualified experts. If he ever thought seriously of wavering, he must have been stiffened by a fresh appeal which the qualified experts (re-enforced by our chief territorial specialist and chief adviser on economic matters) addressed to him when the "upstairs" group went to work on the other American Commissioners. Reminding him of his speech to them on the *George Washington,* they pointed out what conclusions could be drawn, if Fiume were taken from the Yugoslavs:

It would be charged that we had betrayed the rights of small nations. . . . Of all the world's statesmen the President alone repudiated a war for spoils and proclaimed the just principles of an enduring peace. . . .

Then, going on to deal with arguments that the refusal of concessions would bring Orlando's fall, and perhaps Italy's refusal of League membership:

Better a League of Nations based on justice than a League of Nations based on Italian participation bought at a price. The Italian Government may fall, but the Italian people cannot long withstand the opinion of the world. . . .

"Upstairs" could make no progress against an appeal like that.

The controversy over Fiume was still unsettled when the Peace Conference came to an end; but in several ways its results, both then and much later, were deplorable. Wilson, it will be remembered, tried to break the deadlock by the characteristic device of appealing, over the heads of their delegates, to the people of Italy—people who had seemed almost to idolize him less than four months before. His appeal was not only well reasoned, but moving:

America is Italy's friend . . . linked in blood as in affection. . . . America was privileged to initiate the peace . . . the compulsion is upon her to square every decision she takes a part in with those principles. . . . She trusts Italy. . . . Only upon these principles, she hopes and believes, will the people of Italy ask her to make peace.

The Italians, whose press presented them with Orlando's misleading reply to the appeal before they saw the appeal itself, were very much moved indeed, but not in the anticipated way. It seemed to nearly all of them that this man, who still called himself their friend, was a hypocrite bent on robbing them. The cry for Fiume became louder still. Not only Italians in Italy, but the vast numbers of people in America of Italian birth or origin, felt outraged. The "fortuitous concourse of atoms" antagonistic to Wilson and to the League was powerfully re-enforced.

There was some justification for this feeling, too. Wilson, perhaps remembering how he had been prevented from addressing the Romans, or annoyed at the efforts made in Paris to persuade him to shift his ground, was more unyielding than he had been to the French about the Rhine country and Poland's boundaries. Moreover, the appeal, which would have been unexceptionable as a published diplomatic note, gave Orlando and Sonnino good excuse for going home to embrace their angry countrymen. And in their absence the Big Three punished Italy for their withdrawal by making a final distribution of mandates in which Italy was ignored. Italy, like Germany, was wounded in her self-esteem.

Unfortunate, again, was the effect of the whole episode on Wilson's

relations with Colonel House. Though too much associated at the outset with "upstairs," the Colonel served Wilson faithfully through most
of the struggle, using every effort to find some compromise. At the
end he advised that Fiume should go to Yugoslavia. But Wilson and
the other three Commissioners apparently believed that he had tried
to present the opinion of "upstairs" as that of the qualified experts.
Documentary evidence neither fully establishes nor refutes the charge.
But from that time on the withdrawal of the President's confidence
from the Colonel was unmistakable. It is arguable, perhaps, that the
loss was more House's than Wilson's. It seems probable that House
would have remained abroad until the early autumn in any case. But
the President had never needed the Colonel as he was to need him in
the six months following the Peace Conference.

And there was yet one more unfortunate result of the dispute about
Fiume. On the day Orlando and Sonnino left Paris for Rome, the
Japanese, assuredly not by mere coincidence, asked that the remaining
Big Three should state what they were prepared to do about the disposal of the Shantung Peninsula. It is also significant that the Covenant
of the League, amended to meet some of the objections of the senators,
was to come up for adoption in a plenary session of the Conference on
the day following. The Japanese, who had never dropped their demand
for a clause concerning racial equality, could be expected to make
trouble if they had not received satisfaction about Shantung.

No part of the Peace Treaty, not even the Covenant itself, was to
be more grossly misrepresented to Wilson's people than was the Shantung article. Mr. Bailey has called particular attention to a passage in
one of the speeches of Senator Hiram Johnson:

To the Japanese Empire, with only 60,000,000 of people, we turned over
shamefully and cruelly 40,000,000 of Chinese. To the autocracy of the
Orient we delivered 40,000,000 Republicans of China. We made the Orient
"safe for democracy" by dismembering its only democracy and handing
the parts to the strongest autocracy on earth.

Mr. Bailey adds—and what informed person could disagree with him?
—that "it would be difficult to compress more errors into fewer words."
But it was not only senators who, for whatever reasons, misrepresented
the Shantung article. The substance of what they said was caught up
and repeated by the less respectable elements of our press, by political
orators, and even by people of the best intentions who knew little or

nothing of a vastly complex problem, and whose native sympathy with an underdog blinded them to such facts as were accessible. The irony of it is that, while Wilson agreed with reluctance to the settlement that was reached, it is now recognized by some authorities, at least, as one of the most defensible arrived at during the Peace Conference.

Certain basic facts are clear enough. Japan's treaty with Britain transferred to her all rights that Germany had possessed in the Peninsula. Since Britain, France, and Russia had taken similar rights in China unto themselves, and since the nature of Japanese "co-prosperity" was then little understood, the transfer, even had it been complete, would not have seemed nearly so vicious as it might strike one now. It is true that Lansing, Bliss, and White opposed it vigorously; but they did so when Wilson, in his reluctance, asked their opinion, and before he had explained the reasons why he might feel obliged to consent to it. Nor were they able to explain how he or the French and British were to deal with certain hard realities. The hardest reality was this: the Japanese were in the Peninsula; and no Power on earth was ready to make war in order to force them out. To refuse to bargain with them was to leave their control of the Peninsula (legally greater under treaties they had extorted from China than under their treaties with France and Britain) unchecked in any way.

But the Japanese were rather surprisingly willing to make terms. If the Peninsula was handed over to them by the Conference, they would give a written undertaking to restore sovereignty to China, and keep virtually nothing but economic rights. To accept their offer was to place faith in them. But since no one could eject them, and since their principal delegates at the Conference were regarded as men too honest to make an important promise without knowing that it would be carried out, to meet their terms was apparently the most sensible thing that the Big Three could do. And what was to become of the whole peace settlement and the Covenant should Japan and Italy refuse to sign; or should Japan link up with Germany and Russia, the two great Powers outside the League? The bargain was made; and Japan honestly lived up to it. But how could the people know what was the truth?

There are, of course, many other of Wilson's experiences and activities at the Conference which could be reviewed with profit here if space allowed. Certain of them suggest that his nerves were badly frayed. He was beyond measure enraged by the arrogance and discourtesy which humiliation caused Brockdorff-Rantzau to display when the German Commissioners arrived to receive the terms of the Treaty. He was bitterly contemptuous of Lloyd George's suggestion, made early in June, that several provisions of the Treaty should be moderated in Germany's favor. It made him "very tired," he said, to see men who had insisted on making the terms such as they were, now asking for their alteration out of mere funk lest Germany should refuse to sign. In a more normal frame of mind he would almost certainly have swallowed his natural irritation, and agreed with some of his advisers that he should get all possible improvements in the Treaty.

Other incidents of his last weeks in Paris—and especially his deplorable decision to throw aside the advice of his Near East experts and concur with Lloyd George in supporting the Greek seizure of Smyrna —suggest that his judgment was by no means what it had been. But, as things turned out, these episodes did little to affect the fate of the Treaty and the Covenant. Two others, of which one, especially, was in itself of the slightest possible importance, did. This last was the resignation from his very minor post at the Conference of Mr. William Bullitt.

Quite early in the Conference the question of trying to get things straightened out in Russia had come up; and some efforts in this direction had been made. When it had proved impossible to bring together representatives of the conflicting elements on the island of Prinkipos, Mr. Bullitt had been sent to Moscow by our Peace Commissioners, and with the unofficial blessing of Lloyd George, to ask for a statement of the terms on which the Bolshevik leaders would come to an agreement with the Allied and Associated Powers.

Mr. Bullitt, at that time well under thirty, and regarded by many as a very able and attractive young "parlor radical," had been performing the modest function of gathering documents and information, and conveying them to our Commissioners. But his undoubted ability and genuine interest in Russia seemed to fit him for the mission. On a lightning trip to Moscow he secured a statement of what seemed reasonable terms. He reported orally to Colonel House and the British Premier, and in writing to Wilson. He was naturally disappointed by what ensued. Preoccupation with matters which seemed to them more urgent, combined no doubt with dislike of Bolshevik theories and methods, caused the President and the British Premier to let the whole matter lapse.

Mr. Bullitt was indignant; and his indignation did not lapse. With little real knowledge of the problems that were being faced or the difficulties encountered in facing them, he grew more and more critical of the kind of peace treaty that was being worked out. He was so overcome by his feelings that, in resigning his post on May 17, he sent to the President of the United States a letter which was decidedly unusual. He began by reminding Wilson, in terms not unlike those used by the qualified experts on the Italian claims, of his promises and principles. He accused "the Government" (which could only mean the President) of delivering suffering peoples to "new oppressions" and creating new "international conflicts." Just where and how such offenses had been committed he did not specify. But he admonished the President of the United States that it was his duty to withhold his signature from the Treaty. The passage which followed seems the most curious of all, keeping in mind the position and beliefs of the recipient:

> . . . if you had made your fight in the open, instead of behind closed doors, you . . . might have established the "new international order based upon broad and universal principles of right and justice" of which you used to speak. I am sorry that . . . you had so little faith in the millions of men, like myself, in every nation who had faith in you.

This to Wilson! The episode is worth attention, not for its unusual character, but because Mr. Bullitt was later to give much aid and comfort to the enemies of the Treaty and the President.

The other incident of Wilson's stay at Paris which claims attention for the influence it was to have on his fortunes and his plans was the arrival of a delegation representing the friends of Ireland in America. They were much excited; for in Ireland something like real war had now begun. A declaration of independence had been issued; and Irish volunteers had been informed that, as "the army of a lawfully constituted government," they were entitled, both morally and legally, "to slay the officials and agents of the foreign invader" when acting in line of duty. Of necessity, they fought largely without uniforms or distinctive badges, exposing themselves to summary execution in case of capture, and creating the impression in British minds that they were no better than murderous outlaws. The British violated conventions, too, by destroying property beyond the dictates of military necessity and carting around hostages in lorries.

In this country feeling grew exceedingly bitter. The great Congress of Irish societies held at Philadelphia in February had decided to send a delegation of three men to the Peace Conference. Later on the Senate, convening in special session, voted an expression of "its sympathy with the aspirations of the Irish people," and its desire that our Peace Commissioners should "endeavor to secure for Edward [sic] De Valera, Arthur Griffith, and Count George Noble Plunkett, a hearing before said peace conference." At least some of the senators who voted this directive to the Peace Commissioners must have known that our delegates could not infringe the rule (as dear to us as to any people on the earth) that no country may interfere officially in what another regards as a domestic issue. The senators had insisted on having the principle underlined by an amendment to the Covenant. But the senators also knew that, since the President had declared the right of small nations to have governments of their own choice to be one of our war aims, it would be easy to indict him before the people (uninstructed in diplomatic conventions of all sorts) as having violated his principles and tricked the nation, if he could not succeed in doing something for Ireland. Considering that British public opinion was also much inflamed by reports of Irish cruelties, the senators who had voted the directive had deeply embarrassed the President.

The Irish delegates reached Paris in March, long before the Senate had convened, and at a time when Wilson was leaning heavily on British support against French demands for Germany's dismemberment. Moreover, he was just beginning to meet objections to an amendment of the Covenant concerning the Monroe Doctrine on which the senators placed much weight. As Colonel Bonsal puts it:

The delegates were being asked in the Monroe Doctrine reservation to exclude all American questions from their field of operations. With what grace, then, could he barge in with Ireland?

Wilson, who had no time or energy to spare for side issues; and had always disliked pressure groups, was very angry. "My first impulse," he said, "was to tell the Irish to go to hell, but, feeling that this would not be the act of a statesman, I denied myself this personal satisfaction." But he was only blowing off steam. For he took the most practical means at his disposal of helping Ireland, by pointing out to Lloyd George that the more extreme Irish-Americans were sure to start a campaign against the peace settlement unless some satisfaction was given them.

The denouement presented some of that curious blend of tragedy and humor which has run through a good deal of Ireland's recent history. The President received the delegation, headed by Frank P. Walsh, former co-chairman, with President Taft, of the War Labor Board. The interview was apparently satisfactory. There seemed even to be some prospect that Lloyd George, hoping to placate the most bitter enemies of his country in America, would facilitate the appearance of De Valera, Griffith, and Plunkett at Paris. He invited Mr. Walsh and his fellow delegates to call on him; and placed a destroyer or torpedo boat (accounts vary) at their disposal for a visit to Ireland. It was even arranged that they should pass through Dublin in some state, with a guard of honor from the Castle.

Suddenly the whole picture changed. Lloyd George's desire to accommodate vanished; and the President announced that any further efforts of his to meet the wishes of the Irish-American commissioners and their backers in the Senate would be fruitless. All accounts agree on this; and most of them on the behavior of the Irish-American representatives in Dublin; but only Colonel Bonsal's contemporary diary goes into the matter in detail. The commissioners were seasick on the crossing; and this was the explanation given by one of them regarding what followed:

". . . we were feeling pretty peaked when we landed . . . and as is, I suppose, natural, with such a warm-hearted people, perfect strangers came up to us and . . . offered us nips and indeed they forced them upon us . . . Irish whiskey . . . must be dangerous until you get used to it. . . ."

Colonel Bonsal asked what happened next.

"Of course I don't know," came the answer, "but I'll tell you what they say happened. We were driving down Sackville Street in a jaunting car and all Dublin was cheering us. They say I took the driver's seat and announced that we Irish Yankees had come to proclaim Ireland a nation, and the police inspector . . . said that I called upon all within sound of my voice to join the boys from America and throw George the Fifth into the Shannon!"

Very humorous all of this, and, as Lloyd George said, "how natural." But what was the impression in America on people who knew nothing of the "nips"? The British Government had objected to free speech on the part of Irish-American representatives, and President Wilson had shown no sympathy for Ireland. And there was a flare-up in the House of Commons when the three Americans issued a statement on the "atrocities" committed by the British in Ireland, based, so they claimed, on "unimpeachable authority." One of the things that makes Dublin so charming is that you can always learn the most surprising things on "unimpeachable authority."

The Irish-American commissioners kept up their pressure to the end of the Peace Conference, and beyond. On June 11, just after the Senate resolutions had been passed, Mr. Walsh and former Governor Dunne of Illinois had a rather stormy interview with the President, in which Mr. Walsh confessed his inability to "disentangle . . . official and unofficial business," and complained that nothing had been done. The President pointed out that no small nation had been admitted to plead its cause, and that none could be, except by unanimous consent. And he reminded Mr. Walsh that he "was well on the way to getting Mr. De Valera and his associates over" when the Irish-American commissioners "kicked over the apple cart" by their speeches in Ireland.

The Irish-American commissioners next asked for information as to what would be done about the Senate resolution by the Peace Commissioners as a whole; and demanded the creation of an impartial committee, to report upon existing conditions in Ireland. On June 20 they announced that the American Federation of Labor had voted unanimously that the Irish Republic should be recognized. When Mr. Joseph Grew, in his official capacity as Secretary General to the American Peace Commission, informed them that only Clemenceau, in his capacity as President, could in any case present the Irish question to the Peace Conference, they attempted to "put the heat on" the Tiger, by reminding him that matters of "material interest" to France were even then occupying the attention of the Senate; and that there were 20,000,000 persons of Irish blood in the United States. The Tiger's answer does not seem to be accessible; but Mr. Walsh's letters suggest that indignation had by this time quite run away with him. The Senate Foreign Relations Committee was to give him his chance to speak his mind about the Treaty and the League.

How much did Wilson accomplish at Paris? Adding up his successes, instead of pointing out his failures, one reaches an impressive total. Moreover, most men who knew the Conference from the inside, or have reviewed it as scholars, agree that the total could scarcely have been greater. General Smuts set down his estimate in 1921:

He arrived at the Paris Peace Conference . . . [and] . . . plunged into that inferno of human passions . . . like a second Heracles [determined] to bring back the fair Alcestis of the world's desire. There were six months of agonized waiting. . . . And then he emerged with the Peace Treaty. It was not a Wilson peace. . . . It was not Alcestis, it was a haggard, unlovely woman with features distorted with hatred, greed, and selfishness, and the little child that the woman carried was scarcely noticed. Yet it was for the saving of the child that Wilson had labored until he was a physical wreck. . . . Others had seen with him the great vision, others had perhaps given more thought to the elaboration of the plan. But his was the power and the will that carried it through . . . the Covenant is one of the great creative documents of human history.

The Treaty as a whole was bad, but,

It was not Wilson who failed. . . . It was not the statesmen that failed, so much as the spirit of the peoples behind them . . . not the greatest man . . . in the history of the race would have saved that situation.

But Wilson, in securing the adoption of the Covenant, had won "undying honor" that would "grow with the growing centuries."

CHAPTER XVII

President, Senate, and People

———————◆———————

W HEN JOHN SHARP WILLIAMS, bidding farewell to the Senate in 1923, declared that he would rather be a dog baying at the moon than continue sitting in that illustrious body, he was obviously enjoying himself, and getting something out of his system. No one knew better than he how much ability in the aggregate there was among his late associates, or how well they could dispose of matters before them, when they chose. But neither did anyone know better the exaggerations, distortions, and sheer absurdities of which some senators were capable when they were out to strike down a man, a party, or a cause. Williams, as a strong supporter of the President, had good cause to remember the Senate debates on the Treaty and Covenant, which recommenced almost as soon as the Sixty-sixth Congress convened in special session, on May 19.

It would be difficult to believe that some of the speeches were ever made, if one had not the cold testimony of the *Congressional Record*. And it is hard to see on what they were based, apart from hearsay, imagination, and animus. Senator Hiram Johnson, even then presumably long past his salad days, offered some of the most extraordinary performances. He shouted that, by entering the League, we should be inextricably bound in "the sordid, cunning, secret, and crafty designs of European and Asiatic governments"; that the country's "blood and its bone" would apparently be for all time "commandeered." He warned of "a tremendous propaganda, financed with hundreds of thousands of dollars," to force "an English document" upon the American people. He produced more fiction, by asserting that Britain could have as many votes in the League as she saw fit to demand; and almost outdid himself in declaring that the Monroe Doctrine reservation "could not have been written with any other purpose than the destruction of the Monroe Doctrine." With an eye on his California constituents, and quite ignoring both the specific exclusion of all domestic questions from the jurisdiction of the League, and the Peace Conference's refusal to give the Japanese the racial-equality clause which they had asked for so persistently, he declared that, under the League, California's alien land law could not have been passed without the consent of other Powers. Another dazzling flight of pure fancy, which also might have its value when the people next went to the polls, allowed him to picture American soldiers fighting the Irish people, to keep them under Britain's yoke. And he scaled the heights of humor when he, a very isolationist of isolationists, accused Wilson of treachery to American altruism!

Mr. Johnson had once and again called "history" to his aid; but in this, he was far outclassed by Senator Sherman of Illinois. Wilson's administration, guilty of "the infamous, criminal insanity of the attempt to barter [Americans] and their posterity to the Old World," was "a hybrid between a French Revolution and an oriental despotism." Apparently, it brought to the Senator's mind a horrible nightmare, in which postured such formerly unacquainted figures as Caligula, Jack Cade, Abdul Hamid, and Karl Marx. "History would forget the reign of Caligula in the excesses and follies of the American Government operated under the League of Nations." At Washington, the ghost of Marx, as represented by some of Wilson's appointees, was even now squeaking and gibbering across the way from "the menacing shade of the Commander in Chief." If Senator Sherman's assemblage of historic figures was a bit bewildering, he showed more dramatic talent than regard for senatorial dignity, in offering his respects to a former President of the United States, the pro-League Mr. Taft: "If he were to put on a kimono and shave off his mustache . . . he would be the prize dowager of the whole beauteous sisterhood."

Progressives and Republicans had no monopoly of the Senate's leading acrobats and humorists. One of the highest prizes certainly went to a Democrat, Missouri's isolationist Senator Reed. For he could make even mathematics humorous. He calculated that the membership of the League would comprise fifteen white nations and seventeen "black, brown, yellow, and red" ones—including, incidentally, Cuba! That, he pointed out, was bad enough; but let the Senate consider that the white populations represented would be outnumbered by the differently pigmented on a scale of nine to one. Again there was tender solicitude for constituents. "Oh, you men of the South . . . Liberia . . . is given a vote equal to the vote of the United States." And this despite the unfortunate addiction to cannibalism of many of Liberia's citizens. Yes, and who could say that Liberia might not obtain a seat in the League Council? Why stop at Liberia? There were the Haitians, who sacrificed children to their idols; there were the people of Panama, where two thirds of all births were illegitimate. The vote of one dusky Panamanian was to be equal to that of two hundred and twenty white Americans! O infamy! O infamy!

No doubt most of Wilson's opponents in the Senate left the chamber, or bit their lips, or hung their heads, while such displays went on. And perhaps it did not matter that undergraduates, picking the juicy passages, shouted with glee over debates in the higher legislative chamber of a government they were taught to respect. But the effects of some of this verbiage were desperately serious. Whether we should or should not have entered the League, there was too much truth in Wilson's bitter cry: "They have poisoned the wells of public sentiment." The Covenant was unquestionably open to much criticism on some points; but American public sentiment, in so far as it really rejected the provisions of the Covenant, did so mainly for non-existent reasons. Distortions, perversions, and misstatements were soon spreading out and out—carried, not only by the lower type of anti-League and anti-Wilson newspapers, but sometimes, innocently enough, by papers not endorsing them, but alert for "snappy" headlines and readable copy. They were also carried (here again quite frequently in perfect innocence) by partisan speakers of all degrees into gatherings of all kinds. Some of the Senate exhibitionists would soon be encouraging great gatherings to hiss and boo and scream "Impeach him!" whenever they made mention of the President. Honest opponents of the League who stuck to facts were, by comparison, too dull to have the same appeal.

There were Democrats who, for one reason or another, attempted to stem this tide, but their advocacy of the League seemed weak and ineffective as against the passion of its foes. The old supporters of the League to Enforce Peace were much in the same case. Moreover, the Republicans who had given them distinguished leadership, while as anti-isolationist as ever in principle, grew increasingly critical of the

Covenant, despite the changes in it made at their request, and at some cost to Wilson's principles.

So the League's enemies "poisoned the wells of public sentiment." For how were the people, of whom only a very few had ever read the Covenant, to know what was false and what was true? Some of the men who misled them were great men, in the popular eye at least. Was not Senator Johnson being considered as a possible President? How could the people know that there was nothing "sordid, cunning, secret, and crafty" about the League; that not a word in it authorized any other country, or all countries, to "commandeer" a single dough-boy or a coast-guard boat? How could they know that the Covenant was not "an English document"; that it guarded the Monroe Doctrine; that it could not prevent the Californians from passing all the alien land laws that they might desire? How could they decide that, instead of perpetuating British rule in Ireland, the League would give us our first opportunity of bringing the matter into diplomatic discussion, without infringement of international amenities? As for "Britain's six votes to our one," would Wilson, of all people, ever have given his consent to that? Anti-League orators and editors never mentioned such factors as the difference between the Council and the Assembly, the necessity for unanimous decisions, the doubt as to whether British influence with the Dominions was more powerful than our own with certain of our neighbors. There being in those days no Gallup polls, one has little to go on, in estimating public sentiment. But it seems a fairly safe assumption that popular endorsement of the League, un-mistakable in the spring, was weakening before Wilson got home again from Paris.

People who distorted or utterly falsified the meaning of the Cove-nant could find receptive audiences in any State of the Union. Thanks largely to the President, we had been in the war so short a time; had, comparatively speaking, got off so easily; and had held ourselves so much apart that isolationism was still almost as natural and traditional with most of us as the spirit of free enterprise.

Anti-British feeling lay close to the surface, too; and the anti-Wilson and anti-League forces were shrewd enough to appeal to it, and strengthen it, in their attacks upon the Covenant. It was easy to pass over the British people's centuries of struggle for self-government, and the fact that their success had supplied the first roots of our freedom, as well as offering inspiration and a model to countless liberals in

Europe. There were voters who had never known these things, voters who had forgotten them. On the other hand, it was easy to stress the blot which Britain's treatment of Ireland had left on her record; and to adopt the sophomoric position that "imperialism" always and everywhere (except in the Philippines, the Caribbean, and Panama) had been an evil thing. From that, it was not too difficult a step to persuade some of the people that "imperialism" was all that the British had been fighting for; that we had been her cat's paws in enlarging it; and that we should bind ourselves to go on playing the same humiliating part by entering the League.

Against the native and familiar elements of isolationism and dislike of the British, inflamed by ignorance or malice, Wilson was preaching altruism to the people. That, too, was native and enduring; but the people never before had had much occasion or incentive to practice it, except in providing generous relief where there was physical distress. The war had given it a more idealistic complexion, so long as there was a sentiment of brotherhood in arms. But the new complexion was disappearing rapidly. Most of the people were less immediately concerned about isolation or altruism than about wages, dividends, and the price of food.

Wilson, absorbed and wearied by his quest for American leadership in a new world order, soon found himself trying to reduce the cost of living, and making new enemies to his administration and his policies at every step. The packers were all for reducing the price of beef on the hoof, but not on the counter. They were incensed by an investigation that the Federal Trade Commission had just wound up, and by the President's action in throwing on the market masses of cold-storage products, which had been held back for the troops. The farmers would hear of no reduction in the price of grain; the planters wanted a higher price for their cotton. The middlemen and stock manipulators were annoyed when Wilson asked Congress for power to cut their profits: the "profiteers," when he sought authority to punish them. Labor had been uneasy all through the year, and had staged some serious strikes. The activities of the I.W.W., and of some agitators who did not stop at criminal acts, had produced an atmosphere in which settlements were sometimes difficult. In the summer of 1919 the price of altruism in America was dropping rapidly. So was the popularity of the President and his policies.

If all the elements and forces in the country which earnestly believed in justice, self-determination, and international organization for enduring peace had held together, the prospects that public sentiment would remain behind the League would have been more promising. But bitter condemnation of the Treaty by the left-wing liberals broke the ranks, to the great advantage of some of the country's most conservative and nationalistic elements. No one could blame the "radicals" for criticizing the Treaty, as J. M. Keynes, George Lansbury, and many others were doing in England; and as Wilson was ready to do at any time. But their demand for its rejection was quite another thing. They might have been well advised to ponder the most popular of Bairnsfather's "Ole Bill" cartoons, in which one Tommy in a shell hole is admonishing a complaining mate: "Well, if you know a better 'ole, then go to it." They were not only emptying out the baby with the bath, but helping to prepare the return of the kind of government at Washington which they least liked. Their numbers and the circulation of their organs were both small; but who can say to what extent the opinions of a group of intellectuals (history offers many a case in point) may be diffused?

Take the articles from the *New Republic* of May 1919, which were read into the *Senate Documents*. They were well written. They were well reasoned, if one started from certain premises. One of these was that Lloyd George, Clemenceau, and Orlando were part of "an old order that accepted war and conquest as natural, necessary, and, on the whole, salutary phenomena!" Clausewitz, Nietzsche, Treitschke, and Spengler would hardly have laid claim to such wide influence. Another premise was that the only hope for "a tolerable international order" lay in "the rise of a party dominated by the workers." From such a standpoint it was not difficult to condemn the whole peace settlement for its failure to "moralize nationalism by releasing it from class bondage and exclusive ambitions." How this objective could have been attained at Paris the *New Republic's* editor did not say. It was enough to point out the sheer wickedness of the Treaty:

> The European politicians who with American complicity have hatched this inhuman monster have acted either cynically, hypocritically, or vindictively, and their handiwork will breed cynicism, hypocrisy, and vindictiveness in the minds of future generations.

The senators may have been a little startled by some of the premises of the *New Republic's* editor, and by some of the angles of his attack; but Wilson's opponents must have found his conclusions highly satisfactory. They must have been pleased to read that Americans who should "connive at" the Treaty would "be delivering themselves into the hands of their enemies, the reactionaries and revolutionists." They must have been gratified to see the Covenant condemned for its "compulsory features" and "guarantees involving force," especially at a time when some English "radicals" were anathematizing the President for failing to produce a league with "teeth in it." Better still was it to read that these compulsory features and guarantees should be removed, "on the plain unimpeachable ground of American safety." That was the stuff!

And there was more of it. The acceptance of the Treaty itself would be "a violation of faith"; its rejection (here some of the senators may have blinked a little, even in their satisfaction) would "clearly and emphatically testify to a formative connection between religion and morals and economics and politics."

The aid and comfort given to each other by our extreme left and extreme right wings in opposing the Treaty and the Covenant brings to mind Mr. Churchill's pre-war remark that the reds and blacks of Europe were like the North and South poles. You traveled in opposite directions to get to them; but when you arrived, you met the same cold winds, fatal to all such growth as goes on in temperate zones.

Of course the *New Republic* did not stand alone even in the *Senate Documents*. The *Nation* came in to do its part in preparing for the defeat of Wilson's policies, domestic and foreign, and the right wing's triumphant return to power at the White House and the Capitol. Its columns showed it possessed of information that must have been very difficult to come by. It was able to inform the people that "the Government probably was more ignorant of politics and affairs abroad than many a private individual or organization"; that "a great deal of authentic information from abroad was not permitted to enter the doors of the State Department at all"; and that "the small residue of true report which found lodgment there was . . . self-discredited and rarely considered." Settled in another comfortable armchair, the *Nation* could not forgive the President for his failure to "insist" upon the abrogation of the secret treaties.

Periodicals now almost forgotten took up the cry. In *Reconstruction,* Amos Pinchot denounced the League as an organization which undertook to "control all nations within [sic] and without by a system of drastic punishments including national starvation," and as "essentially a balance of power." Voices were raised on the other side, of course. In the *Century,* Herbert Adams Gibbons took a very different point of view:

> We went to Paris burning with zeal to reform the world. . . . Idealism? There was none, we said, except among ourselves . . . but when we were asked to assume responsibilities in the Near East, to mount guard on the Rhine, to see through the job that we had begun, to pay our share, and to put the Monroe Doctrine and the Panama Canal and immigration on the table we turned sorrowfully away from our vision of a durable world peace and went to live in a glass house like the other fellows.

But it was not from the now lamented *Century,* or other magazines of its type, that Wilson might most confidently have expected support. He was wounded in the house of his friends.

With Wilson, the Treaty and the Covenant coming under such cross fire, Senator Lodge found that things were shaping up nicely. Presumably, Wilson could be forced to make his choice between two very disagreeable alternatives. He could be required to accept, at the bidding of the Republicans, and for the greater glory of the Republicans, "reservations" to his precious Covenant which would amount to actual and important changes. This being so, he would have to go, hat in hand, to the governments of the signatory Powers, perhaps even to the new German government at Weimar, to beg for their consent. Should he refuse, ratification of the whole Treaty could be blocked. Provided all, or almost all, the Republican senators could be held in line, there would be sufficient votes. For assistance was to be expected from at least three Democratic senators: Reed of Missouri, Walsh of Massachusetts, and Shields of Tennessee.

The matter would require some careful handling. If Senator Lodge's announced purpose was to be carried out; if the Covenant was to be drastically altered, or repudiated altogether, in case the President and the Democrats proved obstinate, there were two groups with widely differing views that would both, for the present, somehow have to be satisfied until the task was done. There was "the battalion of death," so styled by one of its members: eight senators pledged to work for the elimination of the Covenant from the Treaty. They were sometimes to be seen lunching together; and a glance at their lunch table was enough to show how indispensable Senator Lodge found them.

Messrs. Knox, Moses, Fall, Poindexter, and Brandegee were pillars of the party. Messrs. Hiram Johnson, Borah, and Reed were specialists of the first order in misrepresenting the Covenant and other features of the peace settlement to the people. They were effective in the Senate, but still more so in public meetings where passion would drive out all reason. Consequently their speeches had good news value for the press. Some straight Republican members of the battalion were only a degree less talented in this respect. So the battalion, constituting Senator Lodge's shock troops, and claiming to possess the sympathy and support of at least eight other senators, had to be treated with the indulgence which the janissaries had once received from Turkish sultans.

Equally indispensable, in view of their voting power, was a group of Republicans far from ready to follow the janissaries in objectives or in tactics. Moderate and clear-sighted senators of both parties doubtless saw, as leading Allied statesmen did, that the importance of "reservations" was easy to exaggerate. Even within the League, national sentiments and interests would be at work. No nation was likely to live up to Article X in particular, when put to a serious test. What really mattered was not the letter of the text, nor even the specific obligations the Covenant imposed, but the co-operation of all great peace-loving peoples to place restraint upon governments indifferent to law and to morality. Most of the Republican senators were in favor of the League. They would vote for "mild" reservations—in some degree from conviction, and also to keep the party line. But they were likely to balk at drastic ones, endangering the peace settlement through possible objections raised by other signatory States, and through a serious contest between the Senate and the President.

Public sentiment, if commencing to move against Wilson, had not moved much. So the "mild reservationist" Republicans in the Senate, estimated toward the close of the summer to number from twenty to twenty-five, and headed by one member of the Foreign Relations Committee, Senator McCumber, might easily come to terms with the forty Democratic senators of like mind. Such an arrangement would give Wilson and his party a substantial, if incomplete, victory to place to their credit.

Ratification under harmless and perhaps wise reservations would almost certainly have gone through, if everyone had thought of country before party and personal animosities, and had made concessions of some sort. Impossible as it is to know the motives of any man, there is almost conclusive evidence that Senator Lodge was moved throughout by partisanship and personal animosity. Wilson seemed to put his party's interests into the background; and there is no reason to suppose that his dislike of Lodge in any way changed his course. Few will deny that he was too unyielding; but his great test did not come until late in the autumn, when he was a broken man, shut off from normal sources of information and advice, and too sick to estimate possibilities and consequences.

Thus even in the summer of 1919, when issue was first really joined in the great Wilson-Lodge struggle, the advantages lay heavily with the Senator. When the President, just arrived from Brest, submitted the Treaty officially to the Senate, on July 10, he looked rested and fit; and said that he felt so. Men who had been shocked by his appearance during the last months of the Conference may have shared his illusion that such recuperation as the sea voyage had brought to him would last. But as the cares of handling domestic questions, anxiety for the Treaty's fate, and the heat of a Washington summer closed in on him, the illusion was soon dispelled. "I am at the end of my tether," he once confessed. And even had he been well; even had he been less absorbed in all the domestic questions which the country's readjustment to peace conditions and his long absence in Paris had brought crowding in on him, he could not have done much about the Treaty during the summer weeks, save to watch the moves of his antagonists.

Senator Lodge, perhaps as cool, shrewd, and experienced a politician as Washington has seen, apparently realized what hindsight makes it easy for us to see—that time was on his side. It was not only that he had to step softly, in keeping the "battalion of death" or the "mild reservationist" Republicans from breaking ranks. The people, welcoming returned and often disgruntled soldier relatives, uneasy about taxation, the cost of living, labor disputes, prohibition, and other troubles at their doors, were losing interest in Europe week by week. If disputes about the Treaty were protracted long enough, many were likely to grow tired of the subject. At the same time, many others might be persuaded by orators or editors that common prudence forbade our entry into the League.

To have hearings before the Foreign Relations Committee should also help. As Mr. Taft once charged, the Committee had apparently been "packed" with the ablest enemies of the League. Six members of the battalion of death, besides the equally hostile Senator Brandegee and the pliant Senator Harding, would assure Senator Lodge, its chairman, of a majority of its seventeen members. It could subpoena hostile witnesses, and question all witnesses in such a way as to bring the President and his peace settlement into ill repute with the people. For even pro-League newspapers of the highest type could not avoid reporting the more noteworthy parts of the hearings. The fact that a change in public sentiment was likely to affect the attitude of some senators may well have seemed to the hostile majority of the Committee another reason for delay. Given time, the Republican mild reservationist group might come thoroughly into line. Despite the fact that conditions in both Europe and America made the earliest possible ratification (or even rejection, if rejection it must be) of the Treaty desirable, despite the protests of the President, of its own Democratic minority, and of pro-League papers, such as the *New York Times,* the Committee on Foreign Relations did not report the Treaty to the Senate for two months. Perhaps the chairman had still another reason for delay. The President, being tired and strained, was apt to show himself imperious.

As the weeks passed, Wilson did play into the hands of his antagonists; but he was far from being as unreasonable and imperious as he has sometimes been pictured. He would have been something more than human if he had been able to preserve a complete poise. The pressure on him was tremendous, both as to foreign and domestic issues. Cablegrams kept coming in from Paris, where the Peace Commissioners of the great Powers were still meeting, now dealing mostly with what had been Austro-Hungarian affairs. Colonel House, acting for him in London, primarily if not entirely on League business, also sent frequent messages.

At home, besides all the problems of readjustment that had to be dealt with, a threatening situation in the relations of capital and labor claimed his attention constantly. Ever since a strike of the marine workers in New York in January, such questions had been coming up. At the beginning of August came the revolutionary "Plumb plan": the suggestion of the railroad brotherhoods, through their counsel, Mr. Plumb, that the Government should take over the roads and place their operation in the hands of their employees. Wilson had probably given some impetus to this movement in his cabled message to Congress on the opening of the special session. As he saw it, the question of labor was not that of making it effective in industry and commerce, but of seeing that wage earners secured "progressive improvement" in working and living conditions. This should involve "the genuine democratization of industry, based upon a full recognition of the right of those who work, in whatever rank, to participate in some organic way in every decision which directly affects their welfare, or the part they play in industry."

All in all, conditions were working up to the Boston police strike in September and the great strikes of the steel workers and miners two months later. The President had constantly to think of industrial relations, and of the many bills for dealing with them which were being brought into Congress. To add to his concern about affairs at home came reports from various members of his Cabinet, showing that the delay of the Foreign Relations Committee in dealing with the Treaty was holding up reconstruction, trade, demobilization, even budgeting. Both Cabinet members and other advisers were pointing out that delay was robbing the people of much of their interest in the League. He showed no more impatience than the editor of the *New York Times,* who wrote of "the disgrace and humiliation of the Senate's perverse behavior."

Again, it must have seemed to the President that the struggle over the League had been dragged down to a deplorably low plane. As early as March the New York *Sun* had declared that "the Wilson scheme for a League of Nations" had been a partisan issue ever since the President had spoken in Boston; and had reminded its readers that "the nineteen-twenty national campaign [was] already on." Anti-League organizations were springing up. There were at least two of them in New York. Speaking for "The League for the Preservation of American Independence," George Wharton Pepper disclosed that the struggle in progress was "between the President on one side and Americanism on the other!" Still more extraordinary were statements issued by "American Women Opposed to the League of Nations." Referring feelingly to the death of American soldiers "in the waterless deserts of Africa, in the feverish jungles of Asia, in the icy fields of Russia," the ladies asked whether these men were to die "for England and Japan and the International Money Power."

The Council of the League could Order America to send soldiers—
YOUR BOYS, YOUR MEN—TO SHOOT DOWN THE PEOPLE OF
IRELAND, INDIA, KOREA, EGYPT, AND SOUTH AFRICA, AND
TO BE SHOT DOWN IN THOSE DISTANT LANDS.

There was a humorous side to such evidences of the work anti-League
propaganda was doing. C. S. Hamlin of the Federal Reserve Board,
attending a grange meeting in a small Massachusetts town, was asked
whether it was true that "under the League of Nations the Pope of
Rome would be the universal sovereign of the world." Opposition
seemed to be multiplying everywhere. Reports came in of a deal between the Hearst press and Senator Hiram Johnson. The *Chicago
Tribune* had lined up with the extreme isolationists some time before,
though its tone was later to become more moderate. Such things were
to be expected. But it was discouraging that Mr. Taft not only came
out in favor of an extensive set of reservations, apparently for the
appeasement of the violent isolationists, but implied that Wilson was
trying to monopolize all credit to be drawn from the peace settlement,
and was doing it for political reasons.

Even the President's own party was giving trouble. With the exception of three or four men, it was supporting him in the Senate; but
disturbing reports came in from the outside. Hardly more than a week
after his arrival from Paris, a State Democratic convention in Missouri
decided that the party in the State and in the nation was facing disaster under its national leadership. Mr. Frank Walsh and other
friends of Ireland were accusing defenders of the Treaty in the White
House and the Capitol of trying to make political capital out of the
peace. This Democratic group declared that the Covenant constituted
a betrayal of all of Wilson's principles. Its ratification would drive 95
per cent of all Democrats of Irish origin out of the party. This, of
course, was an undoubted exaggeration. While Tumulty believed, on
the basis of various reports, that the great influence of Cardinal
O'Connell and Cardinal Hayes was being thrown against the League,
Cardinal Gibbons was clearly on the other side. In a published interview he had expressed his hope that the President and the Senate
would be able to agree, and his belief that "an early adoption of the
League of Nations [would] infuse intense joy throughout the United
States."

But, all in all, the party was not giving Wilson the support he needed
so badly. Even Mr. Lansing made things difficult for him when, ap-

pearing at the Senate hearings, he gave it as his opinion that Japan would have signed the Treaty without the Shantung article. Obviously, the President had reasons for proceeding as carefully as Senator Lodge. Warned by senators of both parties that the Treaty could never be ratified without reservations on the Covenant and on the Shantung article, and that Democratic senators were showing an increasing tendency to join the mild reservationist Republicans, he had to give some ground. At first he had announced, through Senator Hitchcock, that the discussion of any reservations by Democrats was "premature." But he never quite closed the door; and on September 3, the day on which he left Washington to make the speaking tour which ended in his collapse, Senator Swanson restated to the people the position he had taken before the Senate Foreign Relations Committee and would cling to until the end. He would accept reservations, so long as they merely stated America's interpretation of the Covenant without altering its meaning, and so long as they merely accompanied the act of ratification without being a part of it.

He felt that his position was reasonable and secure. Many influential friends of the League were at least content with it. The *New York Times* believed that America would have such power and prestige within the League that she could secure changes when she needed them. George W. Wickersham, good Republican and faithful member of the League to Enforce Peace, felt that ratification should come at once, and amendment later on. President Eliot gave a letter to the press, insisting that immediate ratification was the important thing, whether reservations were attached or not. Mr. Herbert Hoover, speaking to an engineering society, took the same point of view.

But the decision lay with the mild reservationist Republicans. What they would do, no one could say. In general, they seemed to be with the President. Like him, they were apparently against any changes in the Treaty which would require fresh negotiations with any of the Allies or with the government at Weimar. But they could not always agree among themselves, and might give way to party pressure. The President tried persuasion. For a month after his return he constantly invited senators of both parties to consult with him at the White House. He was told again and again that these conferences were producing excellent results. But Senator Lodge was also at work. On August 12, after three months of comparative silence, he attacked the Treaty in a two-hour speech on the floor of the Senate. He cleverly borrowed Wilson's *leitmotiv* of service. America, he said, must have freedom to pursue her task of serving all the world. He managed to make this plea a basis for demanding reservations which virtually eliminated Article X, and made other important changes in the Covenant. What was more, he demanded that our ratification of the Treaty should not go into force until these reservations were accepted by four (that is to say all) of the other great Allied and Associated Powers.

The galleries were in raptures. No doubt they were well stocked with anti-League people; but the press reported that marines, returned from France, joined in with the applause. According to the *New York Times,* the cheering was "much like the roar that breaks loose at a ball park when the home team wins the game in the ninth inning." Senator Williams replied, scoring Lodge for pandering to hyphenates. There was a storm of hisses then. This may have produced some thought in certain mild reservationists. So also, perhaps, did public reaction to the hearings before the Foreign Relations Committee which were in progress through August.

Perhaps it would be proper to assume that the Committee's object was to get light on the Treaty, and especially on the Covenant. Forgetting propriety, and running through the stout volume in which the report of the hearings is officially set out, one gets the feeling that he is reviewing proceedings rather like those with which the Spanish Inquisition has generally been credited. Wilson, of course, is the contumacious heretic. Senator Lodge has Torquemada's role. But the hearings were no joking matter. For all Wilson's seeming composure when the inquisitors were examining him, the experience must have imposed a heavy additional strain, at a time when he was least able to bear it. That he was more than fatigued is evident. The one feature of the President's testimony which has seemed almost impossible to reconcile with his character was very probably an indication that his collapse was close at hand.

On at least one point Senator Lodge and the members of the battalion were really seeking light. They showed great pertinacity in trying to discover just how the Treaty and Covenant had been made. Success would answer a triple purpose. It would show what personal blame could be made to rest upon the President; and it would support the strict constructionist but outmoded claim that the Senate was entitled, not only to reject or ratify treaties, but to have a part in making them. Moreover, this attempt gave the battalion of death an excuse for insisting that the Committee was entitled to see all documents throwing light on the proceedings of the Peace Conference, even to reports of discussions of the most confidential kind. Wilson and Lansing correctly held that their publication would be contrary to public policy. The revelation of sharp contests and sharp words, which statesmen-delegates had composed or overlooked after a sound night's sleep, was too apt to stir up mutual irritation between peoples, especially when demagogues were ready to make use of them.

A still stronger argument was that records of confidential proceedings could not honorably be made public by one of the governments without permission from the rest. Our own delegation had refused Clemenceau permission to place the minutes of the Commission on the Covenant before the Chamber of Deputies, almost certainly in fear of the recriminations which our opposition to the creation of an international army would have stirred up. Senator Knox, as a former Secretary of State, must have appreciated these considerations even better than Senator Lodge; but he seemed as ready as any of the battalion to let the people gain a false impression by Committee sneers concerning "open diplomacy." Witnesses were frequently questioned as to their ability or willingness to submit such documents to the Committee as the President and Mr. Lansing found it necessary to refuse. There was a long array of witnesses. The causes of countries or districts from the Aaland Islands and Albania down through the alphabet to Ukrainia were presented by aggrieved representatives, and solemnly considered by senators without benefit of experts.

One of the representatives (pleading Italy's claims to Fiume) was Congressman Fiorello LaGuardia; but the protagonists of Ireland furnished by all odds the most voluminous and picturesquely presented evidence. Mr. Norman Davis and Mr. Baruch were examined on the financial and economic clauses of the Treaty; Mr. David Hunter Miller on the League; and the President and Secretary of State on many things.

What makes one feel that the hearings were inquisitorial is not merely the fact that the President's cross-examination was apparently aimed at making him incriminate himself. Still more conclusive is the attitude of the majority of the Committee toward other witnesses. Mr. Miller, whose part in the drafting of the Covenant would have made him one of the most acceptable of all witnesses before a committee primarily bent on seeking light, was treated with bare civility. According to Senator Lodge's own statement, the hearings could have been, but were not, reopened for the examination of Colonel House, whose intimate knowledge of all that had happened at Paris rivaled the President's. He would, presumably, have been a star witness for the defense. But the Irish-Americans, who had lacked opportunity to get inside information at Paris about anything save their own hopeless and partly self-frustrated quest, were given the most cordial consideration, and urged to testify about things of which they knew little or nothing. Nor would mere respect for the votes of American friends of Ireland account for this. Mr. Bullitt, whose part in the actual Conference had been little more than that of a clerk, received flattering attention and warm thanks. Because it was the attitude of the Committee toward the Treaty, and the sort of testimony it sought, which counted most in affecting public sentiment toward Wilson and the League; because, again, most of the evidence presented was too detailed even for the briefest review here, it may be permissible to concentrate on the appearance of the President, the friends of Ireland, and Mr. Bullitt.

The President's appearance before the Committee, on August 19, was not technically a part of the hearings, and took place at the White House. It received extraordinary publicity. It was referred to as unprecedented in the annals of Congress. A whole staff of reporters was present, some transcribing while others took notes, so that their papers should have verbatim accounts without delay. At ten o'clock in the morning a very tired President sat down in the East Room, with Messrs. Lodge and Knox within arm's length, and Messrs. Borah and Brandegee across from him. Able Democrats of the Committee did their best to defend the President; but all the advantages lay with the prosecution, in strategic position as well as in numbers. They had been able to decide beforehand what questions should be asked and who should ask them. Mr. Fall even had a written list of twenty, which the President would be permitted to answer at leisure—and the newspapers to print at once. Some of them were tricky and technical, some wide of the main issues, and some apparently designed (as, e.g., one treating the whole mandates system as a sham) to disgust the newspaper-reading public with the peace settlement.

Generally speaking, the President's performance was admirable. At all times, and under much provocation, he was extremely courteous, and seemed composed. After an inquisition of three and a half hours he invited all the senators to lunch with him. To all outward appearance, the lunch proved a great success. It was, so the reporters heard, quite "jovial," the host entertaining his guests with plenty of stories, and the guests all "in good humor when they emerged." One of them confided to a reporter that the lunch would have cost him five dollars at a good hotel, even though no alcoholic drinks were served.

The inquisition itself had been very far from jovial. At its opening the President had read a statement which he had "taken the liberty" of drawing up. With admirable directness he had gone straight to Article X, pointing out that the Council of the League could do no more than advise action; that it could not do even this without the vote of the United States; and that, even should action be advised with our representative's consent, the only obligation resting upon us would be a moral one. He admitted that moral obligations were in fact the most binding ones, but emphasized that only in cases where States were guilty of "external aggression" could any arise. He had no objection to a reservation declaring the right of our Government to decide whether such obligation existed in any given case, provided the reservation merely *accompanied* the resolution of ratification, leaving unaltered the text of the Treaty. He could not accept reservations or amendments calling for re-negotiation with the many signatory governments. He would feel "the greatest reluctance" in asking the Germans to re-negotiate; and as for all the Allied governments, the difficulty of getting them to agree at Paris upon a single text had convinced him that, once America began to alter the Treaty, other States would follow her example until its whole meaning was obscured.

Democratic members of the Committee supported him by pointing out that all treaty obligations were ultimately moral ones, and that it would be impossible so to frame any international agreement that differences of interpretation would not arise. Senator McCumber was impressed. But Senator Lodge and the members of the battalion were not. Some of them adopted a surprising line of argument. If every member of the League, they argued, established the right to decide upon its own moral obligation in every case, the whole article would have so little compelling force as to be nothing, in the words of Senator Brandegee, but "a rope of sand." This, of course, was only too true; but the main point made by these men in addressing public audiences was that "the rope of sand" would drag us constantly into war.

We, but we alone, it seemed, would always treat moral obligations as compelling ones.

Indictments, implied when not direct, were leveled thick and fast. The battalion, in order to discredit the President and the peace settlement, made the usual demand for documents which could not be produced. Of course the Shantung article of the Treaty was given full attention, and Mr. Lansing's opinion quoted, in order to refute the President's. When it came to the votes in the Assembly given to the British Dominions, the battalion was able to call attention to what seemed to be confusion in Mr. Miller's views. They were obviously much less interested in obtaining light than in discrediting the President's statements. Senator Lodge, who let members of the battalion do practically all of the talking, declined the President's offer to be questioned further after lunch. But he informed the reporters that he was "disappointed in the information gained."

Thanks to the fact that the senators asked Wilson for little "information"—and that little mostly on matters already covered by others—it did not, in fact, get much. But it got some misinformation that was infinitely damaging. Questioned at different times, and with great thoroughness, by Senators Johnson and Borah, Wilson asserted emphatically that he had not been informed, officially or unofficially, prior to his arrival in Paris, about any of the secret treaties between the Allies. It was an astounding statement, contradicting a mass of evidence, some of which the members of the Committee must have had. The terms of some of the treaties had even been published in our papers a year before the President first left for Paris. The Fourteen Points had been framed in part to provide a revision "in a liberal sense of the war aims which had been crystallized in the secret treaties." The Lippmann-Cobb commentary on the Fourteen Points had referred to the Treaty of London.

In the words of one who especially studied the President's statement, there are just two possibilities: "that the President lied" or that, "not remembering the time and circumstances of his learning of the treaties, he felt that he was telling the truth." "Until, and unless," this study continues, "evidence [that he was lying] is brought forward . . . the latter alternative is the only one tenable." One must subscribe to that. Even if one could grant the possibility of Wilson's having so belied his character, his falsehood would not have made good sense. He could not have expected it to stand; to have been hoodwinked would not have been to his credit; and, more than all, he could not have failed to realize that he would not be furthering the Treaty's chances of ratification by picturing America's principal prospective partners in the League as indifferent to common honesty. Almost beyond question, his condition of health supplies the key to the riddle. Complete lapse of memory on some one point is said to be entirely possible in a person close to a paralytic stroke, especially when under severe strain. But his lapse did grave harm.

No sooner was the hearing over than Senators Borah, Knox, and Johnson issued a statement declaring that America would be asked, under the Treaty, to guarantee indefinitely the terms of secret treaties concealed from her Government until the opening of the Peace Conference; and would be under a moral obligation of compelling force to take part "in the disturbances, the conflicts, settlements, and the wars of Europe and Asia." Moreover, "Europe would be under the same impelling force to take part in the settlement of American affairs." This statement raises more questions than Wilson's apparent lapse of memory. Is it possible that these senators, who had ample evidence concerning his misstatement, believed it? How had the "rope of sand" become a mighty force again? Just why and how did the statement reach the press together with the report of the hearing? Perhaps the day will come when these questions will yield to study, too.

That friends of Ireland were anxious to appear before the Committee was natural. It was natural that they were guided by their feelings, and that affection for the land of their origin should be strong in them. But the Committee could hardly have expected their appearance to produce anything but what it did: misrepresentation of the meaning of the Covenant; loud cheers from the spectators; snappy headlines and copy for the press; and added evidence of the battalion's bias. Mr. Frank Walsh, speaking as head of the delegation sent to Paris, made no claim to the possession of information concerning the Peace Conference, save what he had gathered from talks with the American Commissioners, from plenary sessions reported in detail by the press, and from hanging around the Crillon until he "wore out several pairs of shoes." His admission that he had not had time to read a speech in which Senator Walsh of Montana had argued that the League offered the best promise Ireland could have for her future, suggested that he was not giving the subject much study.

His fellow witnesses had no more, if as much, to offer when it came down to facts. Yet the majority of the Committee heard them eagerly. Senator Johnson begged them to take all the time they wished. He was ready to spend the rest of his days in listening. Senator Borah decided that it was better for the Senate to adjourn for lack of a quorum, than that an interruption of this hearing should occur. Apparently these witnesses were producing what most of the Committee wanted.

Judge Cohalan, no doubt remembering a night in March, led off. Lloyd George was nothing but a fig leaf to cover the rule of Britain by the Cecil dynasty, now headed by Mr. Balfour and Lord Robert, "father of the proposed League of Nations." This was not only a menace to America, but a grievous thing for the oppressed Canadians. "Why should not our great neighbor on the north, which Cecil undoubtedly hopes to use someday as a weapon to smite us . . . have an opportunity of taking its place among the republics of the earth?" If America were to enter the superstate referred to as the League, the Cecils "would put us in the position of again being a vassal state of England." There was much more of this. Mr. Walsh, who must have found the Judge's oration somewhat embarrassing, was satisfied merely to maintain that the President's best friends must save him from "the wreck of the great mistake" he was making about the League. But members of the Committee pressed him for information about the doings of the Peace Conference. Senator Johnson, on hearing of his sacrificial offering in footwear, was anxious that the record should show him as speaking from "personal knowledge."

Mr. Walsh, essentially an honest man, allowed his feelings to get beyond control. The Administration had made us a cat's paw for British imperialists, and was still concealing from the Senate "secret agreements" which would add to the ill-got spoils of the Allies. Spurred on, perhaps, by the applause he drew, he went on to protest that League membership would surrender Americans "to the conception of monarchy as opposed to the republican form of government!" There was not a great deal that the other witnesses could add; but Mr. Bourke Cockran apparently drew even more applause. He did not "intend the slightest reflection on the President of the United States" [there was laughter at this point]; but the President "by placing his person . . . in the power of a foreign Government" had allowed himself to be coerced. The Committee listened patiently to more speeches in this vein, but apparently never thought of summoning any of the Americans of Irish origin, as well acquainted with the doings of the Peace Conference and Ireland's grievances, who would have brought some common sense to the hearing. But, after all, who were the members of the battalion to be critical? Without the passions of centuries to deprive them of moderation and respect for facts, some of them could rival Judge Cohalan at his best. The poisoning of the wells of public sentiment went on.

The hearings came to an end, on September 12, with the appearance of Mr. Bullitt. It was perhaps a fitting climax. Mr. Bullitt's evidence was not only the most damaging to the chances of the Treaty and the Covenant which the Committee heard, but the most wounding to Wilson, and the most pleasing to his antagonists. Moreover, his conduct was so unusual as even yet to be a matter for wonderment. It has been alleged, and may be true, that Mr. Bullitt was not a party to the issue of the subpoena which summoned him. But an article which he had published in the *Nation* must have whetted the battalion's appetite. It has been said, and may be true, that before appearing he felt some qualms about giving the testimony he had in mind. If so, he must valiantly have conquered them. For he appeared before the Committee carrying a set of carefully arranged documents, some of which most men would not have felt entitled to produce at all. He first displayed some papers on his mission to Moscow, adding, for good measure, accounts of conversations with people who included Lloyd George and Lloyd George's secretary Philip Kerr, later (as Lord Lothian) British Ambassador to the United States. These accounts represented the British Premier as a politician of the lowest type.

Mr. Bullitt next helped to satisfy the burning curiosity of the senators as to the origin of certain articles and phrases of the Covenant by producing a set of drafts, of which one had been personally typed by Wilson, and presented to Mr. Bullitt as a souvenir by Colonel House, before the Peace Conference opened. It does not seem that these drafts were especially confidential; but most junior functionaries would not have felt entitled to give out documents which had come to them in line of duty without the permission of their authors, his former chiefs. All testimony offered was of course accessible to the press, as well as to the government printer. In producing more or less confidential papers relating to his Russian trip, Mr. Bullitt did ask to be excused from making public certain telegrams which would have revealed one of the State Department's secret codes. But with apparent reluctance he produced a personal note, marked "private and confidential," which he had received from Mr. Kerr. When he came to the peace settlement, he was apologetic about his inability to supply minutes of discussions of which the publication had been refused by the President and Secretary of State. Yet he volunteered to tell what he knew about one phase. His remarkable letter of resignation to the President and a companion piece dispatched to Colonel House were added to the pile for the printer. When testifying, in response to questions, that Mr. Lansing, General Bliss, and Mr. White had "objected very vigorously" to numerous provisions of the Treaty, he more than once referred to records he had kept of conversations he had had with them. Having demurred to the production of these records, and having been told by Senators Lodge and Knox that he would not be asked for them, he volunteered to produce the record of a conversation he had had with Mr. Lansing. While occurring after Mr. Bullitt's resignation, this, so Mr. Lansing had supposed, had been entirely personal and confidential:

Mr. Lansing then . . . said: "I consider that the League of Nations at present is entirely useless. . . . The League of Nations can do nothing to alter any of the unjust clauses of the Treaty except by unanimous consent . . . and the great Powers will never give their consent. . . . I believe that if the Senate could only understand what this Treaty means, and if the American people could really understand it would unquestionably be defeated." . . . He thought . . . that Mr. Knox might instruct America in the real meaning of it.

There were immediate reactions to this testimony. On September 16 the *New York Times* printed an authorized statement from Mr. Kerr, describing the account, as received in Paris, of Mr. Bullitt's conversations with Lloyd George and himself as "a tissue of lies." On the preceding day the *Times* had suggested that Mr. Bullitt apparently did not feel bound by obligations of confidence which "gentlemen of non-Bolshevist notions of honor would have sacredly respected." Mr. Lansing, wiring the President a very different account of his confidential talk with Mr. Bullitt, and promising all possible help in securing the ratification of the Treaty, characterized Mr. Bullitt's conduct as "despicable and outrageous." The reactions of the majority of the Committee had been quite different. "We are very much obliged to you indeed, Mr. Bullitt," said Senator Lodge, when the witness had finished. It is not on record that such people as Messrs. Lansing, Miller, Baruch, and Davis received any thanks at all.

CHAPTER XVIII

Debacle on the Western Front

———————•◆•———————

Mᴏʀᴇ ᴛʜᴀɴ ᴀ ᴡᴇᴇᴋ before the hearings closed, the President had gone out to meet the people of the Middle West, Far West, and South, hoping to purify the "wells of public sentiment." Such a trip had been in his mind all through the year; and by September its necessity was obvious. How the wind was blowing was indicated by a poll of the Senate on an amendment for the restoration (on paper) of all rights in the Shantung Peninsula to China. Although its adoption would have constituted a serious alteration of the Treaty's terms, forty-four senators favored it, and twelve declined to commit themselves. And the Republican mild reservationists were reported to be far from the President's position in other ways. While still supposedly objecting to reservations or amendments requiring fresh negotiations with other Powers, they were said to feel that they could support the Lodge program, in the belief that it would be swallowed without negotiation by the other signatory governments. Perhaps in general their belief was justified; but what about the Shantung article? And the President did not agree with them.

It was apparently as clear to some of Wilson's friends and sympathizers as to himself that he would need the fullest support he could persuade the people to give him. Some of them sent suggestions as to the kind of speeches he should make. From Mr. D. H. Miller he obtained (but this was probably by request) a set of comments on Article X, and on all the arguments which its opponents had brought up. Senators McCumber and Phelan, both anxious to be helpful, sent advice that was curiously similar in some ways. Mr. McCumber wrote that the most serious popular opposition to the Treaty was coming from "Sinn Fein followers in the United States . . . misled by false assertions and instructions." Hence the President should explain away the beliefs that Britain's power in the League would be six times that of ours, and that our membership would compel us to help the British in holding down Ireland, Egypt, and India. He would have to deal carefully with the Shantung article, too, since next in seriousness was the opposition of people "to whom the mention of Japan [was] as a red rag to a bull." Senator Phelan wrote that the "Irish" were "in a fair way to leave the Democratic party," and begged that Wilson would do his best to argue them out of their grievances and their fears. Other people advised the President to say little about ideals and principles, and get down to actual cases.

Thus armed, but with no time to prepare the many speeches he was to make, he gathered up what vitality remained to him, and set out hopefully on September 3. To reporters at the station he seemed well and even jovial. Dressed in a blue coat, white trousers, and white shoes, he did not seem like the aging and desperately strained man about whom those closest to him were worrying. As the train pulled out for Columbus, Ohio, it carried quite a numerous party. There were twenty picked reporters and three moving-picture men, besides the secretaries, messengers, and secret-service guards. And of course Mrs. Wilson, Admiral Grayson, and Mr. Tumulty went along, all bent on taking care of the principal passenger.

Nothing that Wilson ever said or did was greater evidence of his courage and his determination to see the Covenant ratified than was this tour. In the campaigns of both 1912 and 1916 he had shown his dislike of speaking trips; but now he had been eager to go, despite all the warnings his doctor could give him. His itinerary called for visits to twenty states and even more cities. He planned, after its conclusion, to take a turn through New England, and especially to meet the two Massachusetts senators on their home ground. Practically all of his nights would be spent on a moving train; and he knew what sort of things would fill his days. To avoid giving offense, he would have to attend receptions, dinners, and lunches; to shake hands with lines of people; to grant interviews to local party chiefs.

What he did do would have seemed prodigious, even had he been in the best of health. Up to its abrupt ending, on September 26, the trip gave him just twenty-two days for speaking; and, since he would not speak on Sundays, even for the League, he had in reality just nineteen. Yet he covered fifteen states, delivered some thirty important speeches, to say nothing of minor ones, and managed to attend to affairs as well. Day by day there reached him messages about Fiume (one hundred and twenty pages on one day); about Greece and Russia and Hungary and Mexico, and other countries, too. He may have passed over some of them, but his papers show that the most urgent matters were dealt with. Then reports on political conditions were constantly coming in from Washington: estimates of the impression he was making; advice to keep his speeches on a practical level; suggestions as to the matters regarding which the people were still confused.

Some reports of trends in the Senate and the country were encouraging. The League to Enforce Peace was working for ratification vigorously. Mr. Lansing was doing the same, though the effects he got were diminished by his refusal to comment on the Bullitt interview. A movement in favor of the Treaty was beginning to gain headway among Americans of Irish origin. Of course there were also unpleasant reports. For example, much publicity was given to an address delivered by Chancellor Day of Syracuse University at the opening chapel service of the fall term. The Chancellor was reported as having compared Wilson to Emma Goldman; accused him of an "unthinking, blind egomania of socialism"; and demanded that he should take the first train back to Washington. But the news that really stirred Wilson was that of Mr. Bullitt's testimony. A long telegram from Mr. Lansing, explaining that he had told Mr. Bullitt that he recognized the faults of the Treaty to have been probably unavoidable; that it should certainly be ratified; and that it was only in speaking of American membership on League commissions that he had expressed doubt as to whether the Senate and the people would ratify the peace settlement, did not much placate the President. The whole incident, he told Tumulty, confirmed suspicions of the Secretary he had long felt. He would have demanded Mr. Lansing's resignation on the spot, if the news had come to him in Washington.

The effects of the Lansing-Bullitt episode probably gave Mrs. Wilson grounds for feeling even more worried than she had been during the first half of the trip. The President had been suffering from headaches almost from the start, and these steadily became worse. She used to find him sitting in one chair with his head resting on the back of another, while he dictated to his secretaries on official business.

Some of the newspapermen began to realize that the President was far from well. Knowledge of his splitting headaches could not be concealed from them. But, seeing him at such close quarters, they seem to have felt more admiration and affection for him than pressmen had ever done before. One of them, reporting how well Wilson had held a San Francisco audience, made uncomfortable and uneasy by the packing of the auditorium with twice as many people as it could properly accommodate, remarked on his "extraordinary" powers of endurance and self-control. Before the speech he had had a blinding headache for two days. But it was not only that the reporters admired him. Charles Grasty wrote that he had never known a President "so entirely free from presidential consciousness" and from "any petty vanity." Wilson had succeeded in "domesticating" the train, and had become a sort of paterfamilias to everyone on board. Grasty wrote, too, that he was getting "cumulative effect from his missionary work." That, no doubt, was one of the things that helped Wilson to hold out. His audiences grew larger and more cordial. But he had something else to spur him on. Senator Hiram Johnson was trailing him, repeating *ad nauseam* the sort of things he had been saying in the Senate. In Minneapolis and St. Paul he succeeded in working his audiences to a pitch where they shouted "shame" when the names of their senators, Kellogg and Nelson, were mentioned. Both of them were rated as mild reservationists. Senator Borah and other members of the battalion were also on Wilson's trail.

So, ignoring all warnings, the President kept on. He could not help striking an idealistic note from time to time, but he did not forget the advice he had received. All the arguments which had been used against the Covenant were dissected one by one. On September 25 he delivered at Pueblo one of the longest and most important of his speeches. In one respect he neglected the advice he had received. Pointing out that much of the criticism of the League was coming from the hyphenates, he defined a hyphenate as a man who carried "a dagger that he [was] ready to plunge into the vitals of this Republic" whenever he should see fit. But his defense of the Covenant was as definite, as clear, and convincing as ever he could have made it when at his best; and his appeal for its support, without being sentimental, was touching. He talked of his "clients in this case . . . the children . . . the next generation." He told of pledges made to the men whose graves he had seen in the cemetery at Suresnes, and of his determination to see that these pledges were carried out. He appealed to his listeners' pride. Could Americans wish to be exempted from responsibilities which other members of the League would bear?

And then, as in the old days, he brightened up the occasion with a joke. He told of two hot-tempered and rough-tongued men, who were persuaded to promise that they would stop swearing at each other inside the town. But by the time they got outside town they did not want to swear at all. The passions of nations, he pointed out, were very much like those of individuals. Then he wound up with his never-deserted theme. Through America the world was to be led into such "pastures of quietness and peace" as it had never dreamed of before. That was the last great speech he ever made. His first collapse came that night; and, realizing the sheer impossibility of going on, he had to let Mrs. Wilson and Dr. Grayson take him home. No one realized just at first how serious his condition was. At Washington he was able to walk from the train to his car. In the days that followed he felt well enough to enjoy a drive and a movie, and to read the Bible to his wife. But on the night of October 3 they found him unconscious. He was paralyzed on his left side.

"Oh! if he had been frank about his illness," wrote Franklin Lane about the President later, "the people would have forgotten everything, his going to Paris, his refusal to deal with the mild reservationists—everything would have been swept away in a great wave of sympathy. But he could not be frank; he who talked so high of faith in the people distrusted them; and they will not be mastered by mystery." Lane must have written this in one of those moments of haste and impatience which were by no means foreign to him; but there were doubtless many people who, entirely misunderstanding Wilson, subscribed to the judgment at leisure. It may well be felt that there was too much "mystery" about the White House in the months following the President's collapse; unnecessary mystery, it seems; mystery that was harmful to the country, to Wilson, and to the cause he had most at heart. But, if so, was he to blame? On medical orders he was at first kept *incommunicado* except to Mrs. Wilson, Admiral Grayson, and "an occasional tight-lipped doctor." Members and connections, such as Dr. Axson and Mr. McAdoo, who were allowed to speak to him, must have had their orders. What did he know about his own condition, about its causes, about the reports concerning it that were given out, about the rumors that were current?

Of course Mrs. Wilson and Dr. Grayson knew the truth. In the first terrifying days Dr. Dercum, summoned from Philadelphia, gave Mrs. Wilson a biography of Pasteur, to comfort her with the knowledge that a man could do some of the finest work of his career after having had a stroke. Tumulty, Secretary Houston, and probably a few others knew; but no announcement of the truth was made. For months Admiral Grayson would say no more than that the President was suffering from that ill-defined malady referred to as a "nervous breakdown," along with "indigestion and a depleted system." Dr. Grayson may have been acting on his own judgment, or on that of others. In either case, it must be assumed that fear of the effects some accidental discovery of the truth would have upon the patient was the impelling motive. It is quite possible that Dr. Grayson continued to issue such reports on the President's own orders. Wilson would have gone far to keep his leadership, so long as any hope remained that his peace plans could be carried through.

But it seems more probable that he himself was deceived. He was unconscious for the first few days, and probably not himself mentally for at least a month. Is it likely that Dr. Grayson and Mrs. Wilson, concerned above all things to keep his morale high, felt justified in letting him know what had occurred? And like any other sick man, he must have relied upon his wife and his doctor—in this case an exceptionally devoted wife and a doctor who had been an intimate friend for years. In all likelihood they coaxed him along from week to week, holding out hope that if he would be patient for just a little longer, and do as he was told, he could expect to be all right again. With so much work still ahead of him, he must have been more than ready to believe that his inability to use his left arm and leg and the impairment of his vision and his speech were temporary conditions that would yield to treatment before long. It is easier to say that the mystery was unfortunate than to fix the blame. It seems impossible to place it, as Lane did, upon Wilson.

People who did not realize that it was as important to keep the President cheered up as to keep him away from official cares and from arguing about business, may have been puzzled at learning that he was allowed to see some visitors. During the first six weeks or so he was inaccessible to any members of his Cabinet or of Congress except Senator Hitchcock, and was seldom seen even by Tumulty. Yet he was able to enjoy a visit from the King and Queen of the Belgians, and find great pleasure in examining a regal gift of china they had brought. Newspapermen, alert for "human-interest" details, innocently but delightedly misreported the Queen as saying that she had found him wearing a "torn" sweater. One result was to bring protests and gifts of darning wool from indignant ladies to the mistress of the White House; but another may well have been to make Cabinet members and friendly senators wonder why the same access was denied to them. They may have wondered again, a fortnight later, on hearing that Wilson had entertained an embarrassed young Prince of Wales.

Another puzzling thing was that, while bill after bill became law without the President's signature, several presidential pronouncements, including a veto of the Volstead Act, came out of the White House. But they did not necessarily come from Wilson; and rumors about his sanity were current in Washington for months. One reason for shutting out visitors may possibly have been that Wilson's illness, combined with his anxiety about the League, had rendered him morose. One gets some insight as to his state of mind from the famous Hitchcock-Fall visit to his bedside. The visit is still more noteworthy in calling attention to a gap in our Constitution which caused much trouble in 1919, and may still do so at any time. As soon as it was realized that the President's condition, from whatever cause, was serious, and that the time of his recovery could not apparently be fixed, the question of carrying on the administration came up. The Constitution provides that the President's duties devolve upon the Vice-President in case of his disability. But it does not say who shall decide that the President is incapable of performing his duties.

Whether or not Wilson was able to consider the matter, and make his wishes known, the decisions reached did not impress the public favorably. On the advice of the President's physicians, Mrs. Wilson consented to deal with all communications, oral or written, which came to the White House. She decided (with Dr. Grayson's advice, when she felt it was needed) which of them should be brought to the attention of the President. She might, and sometimes did, send important papers to Secretary Houston or one or two other persons in whom she had especial confidence, to be acted on in Wilson's name. Replies to communications, when there were replies, were issued through or by Mrs. Wilson, too. When knowledge of this arrangement got about, and doubts about the President's mental condition were not dispelled, people complained that the most important functions of the Government were being discharged by amateurs. Who, it was asked, was in actuality the President? And then there was the question of the Cabinet. During the President's previous absences the members of the Cabinet had come together at the usual intervals; but that had been with his consent. Now Mr. Lansing, as ranking member, apparently took consent for granted; and summoned a meeting during the first days. He was soon told by Dr. Grayson that the President had been informed, had shown irritation, and had inquired by what authority the summons had been sent out. Mr. Lansing, in some perplexity, called attention to the constitutional provision that, when a President was disabled, the Vice-President should take over his duties. This did not help at all. Mr. Marshall, a modest man, declared that it would be a tragedy both for him and for the country if he had to act as President; while Mr. Tumulty and Dr. Grayson made it clear that they would fight any attempt to establish the President's disability. The Cabinet met for discussion, since the country's business would not wait; but except when an occasional message arrived from the White House, it had no leadership. Neither had the party; and neither, in some essential matters, had the nation.

All this provided a background for the Hitchcock-Fall visit. During the first two months of Wilson's illness Senator Fall more than once informed the Foreign Relations Committee of his belief that Mrs. Wilson was functioning as President, and that an investigation should be made. At the beginning of December he told the Committee that he was in a position to state that the President would not object to having the situation looked into, and that he was ready to undertake the task by a visit to the sickroom, if the Committee would depute him to make it. Another member, realizing that no one of them had shown greater animus toward the President and his ideals than Mr. Fall, suggested that Senator Hitchcock should also go. Senator Lodge arranged by telephone for a visit that afternoon. There was an element of comedy about the affair. According to Senator Hitchcock, the visitors found the President well braced up for the interview. His left hand was concealed by the bedclothes, and with his right he gave Senator Fall so strong a handshake as to startle him. They talked of

Mexico; and after the interview Senator Fall admitted to the press that he had found the President's mind "vigorous and active."

But the interview had its unpleasant side. Mrs. Wilson wrote later that, having avoided shaking hands with Mr. Fall, she had stayed in the room and written down everything that was said, telling the visitors of her determination that there should be "no misunderstandings or misstatements made." And Wilson's resentment was so bitter and lasting as to suggest that he was soured. More than a year later he told Secretary Houston about the visit, complaining of having been intruded upon by a "smelling committee." Perhaps he did not speak as intemperately as Mr. Houston quoted him from memory:

> After the Committee had . . . discovered that I was very much all here, the Committee turned to leave. Senator Fall paused a moment and said: "Mr. President, I want you to know that I am praying for you." . . . If I could have got out of bed I would have hit the man. . . . He must have known that God would take the opposite view from him on any subject.

But there is other evidence regarding Wilson's frame of mind. In September 1920 Secretary Lane, a discriminating admirer, lamented that the President had grown sullen. "The little Wilson (as distinguished from the Great Wilson)," he wrote, "is now having his day." Lane's personal experience illustrates the difficulties which the President's seclusion created for others. Though he longed to stay in public life, and had refused handsome offers rather than desert the President, the Secretary decided in November 1919 that it was necessary for him to resign at once. The expenses of living in Washington had run him into debt, and he foresaw (only too correctly as it proved) the return of a dangerous illness, which would prevent him from making provision for his family. His loyalty forbade him to go without talking to the President; but, access being denied him, he was forced to resign by letter after three months' waiting.

Some of the messages and letters on domestic questions which did come from the White House at this time were unfortunate. The most significant had to do with the relations between capital and labor; and of these the first was issued about a week after the President's collapse. Since the question of industrial relations had for years appeared to interest him more than anything except the League, this was quite in character. So was the tone of his communications to a labor conference, and to a national industrial conference which he had called, in order that methods of conciliation should be thoroughly explored, and agreed upon if possible. The industrial conference was a flat failure. President Eliot, whose interest in industrial relations rivaled the President's, and who had eagerly accepted an invitation to be a member of the conference, wrote of it as "most mortifying . . . because of lack of knowledge, intelligence, and public spirit." The labor group, which had brought in a program to which neither the representatives of the employers nor those of the public were willing to agree, deserted early; and was immediately followed by the representatives of the public, with the exception of Mr. Eliot.

Perhaps this accounted for some of the sternness shown by the President or whoever was acting for him, when the United Mine Workers denounced a wage agreement made under sanction of the Fuel Administration for the duration of the war, and voted a strike in all bituminous mines, unless large concessions were made as to wages and hours. A sharp message went to the miners from the White House, stressing the grave effects a strike would have; pointing out that other classes of workers had postponed action until the Government's efforts to reduce the cost of living had been tried out; "solemnly" requesting that the strike be called off; and warning the miners that protection would be given to national interests. Of course this again was, in substance, to have been looked for. So also were further communications, leading to the establishment of a commission to place the relations of owners and miners on a more satisfactory basis. But there was an aftermath showing what harm the abnormal situation at the White House might do in any issue. The Fuel Administrator, Harry Augustus Garfield, President of Williams, one of Wilson's close friends since they had served together on the Princeton faculty, believed that a report he had sent the President had been altered in transit. In consequence he resigned. But the matter was not closed. Mr. Garfield was convinced that the letter accepting his resignation was too curt to have been written by the President's orders. He was not the kind of man to make such assertions recklessly. But through whatever means, and with whatever mistakes, the executive went on functioning.

In December came the annual message to Congress. Some parts of it were calculated to stir the President's critics. Left-wing liberals may have "viewed with alarm" a request that Congress should "arm the

Federal Government with power to deal in its criminal courts with those persons who by violent methods would abrogate [America's] time-tested institutions." High tariff men no doubt disliked the reminder that "if we want to sell, we must be prepared to buy." But most of the message, calling for such things as a better budget system, audit by permanent officials, the adjustment of industrial relations, and aid to veterans in returning to civil life, was sensible to the point of flatness. This was just as well, considering that the administration's friends and foes alike were again involved in a maze of debates about the Treaty and the League.

In this struggle it was not only the devious course of Senator Lodge which would have "broken the back of the most supple rattlesnake"; it also was the complexity of the moves of all the parties to the dispute. One says "all" parties, because there still were differences of opinion in both Republican and Democratic ranks. Not many men in the Senate stood either for complete acceptance or complete rejection of the Treaty and the Covenant. Of certainties in the situation there were only the same old two: that more than two thirds of the senators were ready to ratify the Treaty and Covenant if alterations of some kind were made; and that nothing like two thirds would vote for ratification without reservations of some kind. Even the sick and secluded President knew that. So senators went on splitting hairs in the manner of early Greek theologians, trying desperately to find a basis for compromise in new versions of the reservations the Committee had reported out. Those relating to Article X alone would make a small booklet.

But the question was not to be settled by all the verbal ingenuity that all the senators could show. As October and the first week of November passed, the position became relatively stabilized. The amendments offered by the Committee were thrown out, and a set of reservations, fourteen in number (in ridicule of the Fourteen Points, it was said) were fixed upon as the Lodge program. And the mild reservationist Republicans were supporting them. In vain Mr. Taft had gone to Washington to plead with this group, which held the balance of power. Senator Kellogg, accused of lacking "guts" to stand up for what was right, merely cursed the President; wished the Treaty in hell; and insisted that the mild reservationists could not help themselves. Mr. Taft was also informed that the trusted Mr. Root "had been acting like a Machiavelli" throughout the whole affair. So much for party politics! The battalion of death was beginning to be confident that ratification on any terms would be impossible. Just what Senator Lodge hoped for, apart from humiliating Wilson and his party, and discrediting them with the people, as willing to endanger the nation's interests, it is impossible to say. The secret wishes of a man like the Senator are not recorded for posterity. But before the decisive vote was taken a correspondent of the *Times* of London reported him as considering the Treaty dead.

November 7 was an important day. The Lodge group presented a reservation to the preamble of the Covenant, thus lying outside the regular fourteen. It directly assailed the President's position, by providing that all reservations subsequently adopted should be "a part . . . of the resolution of ratification." As such, the reservations would have to be accepted by three of the governments of Britain, France, Italy, and Japan, before ratification could be regarded as having taken place. That meant, of course, the re-negotiation to which the President had steadily been opposed. Moreover, the vote would give the first decisive trial of strength, showing whether the mild reservationist Republicans would stand behind the Lodge program. It was adopted by forty-eight to forty. If Senators Gore, Reed, and Walsh of Massachusetts had not supported Senator Lodge, the majority would have been only two.

Within the next ten days all but one of the fourteen reservations were passed. Most of them merely underlined existing provisions of the Covenant; some were possibly wise safeguards against future contingencies. Regarding the Shantung settlement, it was provided merely that our assent should be withheld, not that some unspecified forces should eject the Japanese in some unspecified fashion, as the Committee report had seemingly called for. But most notable was the phrasing of the reservation to be adopted on Article X, as framed by the senior Senator from Massachusetts, who had once contended so vigorously that force should be put behind provisions for preserving peace:

The United States assumes no obligation [i.e., either legal or moral] to preserve the territorial integrity or political independence of any other country or to interfere in controversies between nations . . . or to employ the military or naval forces of the United States under any article of the Treaty for any purpose unless in any particular case the Congress . . . shall by act or joint resolution so provide.

That had been our position without any League. Wilson's proud boast that Americans would not wish to escape from obligations accepted by other Powers found no acceptance there.

The President's position was unchanged. He would accept "reservations" explaining our interpretation of certain articles of the Covenant, but not textual changes which would call for negotiations with other governments. And, above all, there should be no reservation, explanatory or otherwise, by which America disclaimed all obligations, moral as well as legal, under Article X. It is easy to say that he was stubborn and unrealistic during all the struggle that ensued. The judgment is a common, perhaps even a general, one. But he was not showing blind, unreasoning obstinacy. That was not in his nature. He had been obstinate in Paris during the preceding spring, but had always made concessions necessary to avoid the wrecking of his plans. Sick and secluded as he now was, greater obstinacy on his part would have been understandable. But this excuse need not be pressed. It seemed to him that the nation's good faith and honor and championship of peoples less secure and fortunate were involved.

Perhaps he was realist enough to see that Article X had small chance of being lived up to by governments which accepted the Covenant; but if he agreed to sheer repudiation such as this, he would be justifying, if not inviting, demands for re-negotiations of far-reaching character, especially on the part of France. He knew by this time that the Senate would never ratify any treaty promising our armed assistance to the French, in case danger threatened from her embittered and too populous neighbor. How was France to satisfy her longing for security by membership in a League, newborn and congenitally weakened by the elimination of this article? What would she get as payment for her concessions at the Peace Conference? Even in 1919 it was clear enough that she would revert to armaments and alliances.

After all, what actual danger to America, what infringement of the Constitution, could the ratification of Article X involve? No delegate to the League Council could ever commit the nation to armed hostilities unless, to use Senator Lodge's words, "in any particular case the Congress . . . [should] by act or joint resolution so provide." A moral obligation would rest upon Congress; but how was peace to be preserved, if we, of all the world's great peoples, so safe and populous and rich and peace-loving, acknowledged no moral obligation to help in preserving it? He had meant what he said, when he told the audience at the Metropolitan, on March 4, that, should we refuse to play our part, this "most famous" and "most powerful" nation "would of a sudden have become the most contemptible." Perhaps he should have remembered an earlier statement he had made: that the League's success would depend less on definite commitments than on the spirit in which all nations entered into it. But was such political philosophy to be expected from a great idealist, shattered in health and nerves; exasperated by incessant and preposterous misrepresentations and misstatements about the Covenant; cut off from anything like a normal supply of information or counsel; and exaggerating, perhaps, the force of his will power, because it constituted so much of what was left of him?

Senator Lodge was more obstinate in his insistence on definite provisions, without having any of the excuses which existed in Wilson's case. Moreover, Wilson was sure that the people would give him victory in the end; Lodge, not greatly respecting the people's judgment, was glad to let the Senate exhibitionists mislead them, while he pursued his strategy at the Capitol. Wilson was not realistic. He did not accept the facts, because he would not believe them to be facts. His faith that the people would understand and follow him seems to have been deepened, if anything, by his illness. A year later, when his touch with the outside world had been restored for months, it was impossible to make him even doubt that the people would elect another Democratic President and Congress, in order that America should join the League. The contrast between this flight from realism and his shrewd appraisal of his chances in 1916, when the party's prospects were brighter far, is worth considering.

"The Fates" seemed to conspire against him and his great project in the fall of 1919. For, in partnership with Senator Lodge, they excluded from the Senate hearings a supporter of the peace settlement unrivaled in the combination of inside information, coolness, shrewdness, and tactfulness. By a curious coincidence, Colonel House, who had remained in Europe until the end of September, transacting League business, was struck down by illness at almost exactly the same time as the President. Unable to leave his bed, still less to present himself before a hostile Senate Committee, for some time after he arrived in this country, he saw the dangers that threatened the Treaty, and was more than anxious to give what aid he could. In his helplessness he turned to his old friend and interpreter, Colonel Bonsal, who knew

Senator Lodge, and in a personal sense liked him. Colonel Bonsal went twice to see the Senator. Would the Foreign Relations Committee hear Colonel House as soon as he was able to appear? Senator Lodge thought it so improbable as hardly to be worth considering. The Committee had closed its hearings, and had secured what information it needed.

But something came of Colonel House's efforts all the same. Senator Lodge proved less unyielding than on the Senate floor. Sitting down with Colonel Bonsal, he took up a copy of the Covenant, wrote in the minimum alterations he would accept, and added his signature. Colonel Bonsal, sure that the Senator's concessions were substantial, hastened to telephone the news to the bedridden Colonel House, who was overjoyed. Then, rushing to a post office, Colonel Bonsal confirmed his telephone report by sending the precious document. Colonel House, of course, relayed the document to the President. Since then it has not been heard of.

Speculation as to what happened is fruitless; but a page in Mrs. Wilson's *Memoir,* dealing with events which took place two weeks later, lends color to more than one surmise. Mrs. Wilson writes that Senator Hitchcock called on the morning of November 19, assured her that the Treaty could not be ratified unless the Lodge amendments and reservations were accepted by the President, and persuaded her to plead with him. Returning to the waiting Senator, Mrs. Wilson told him that the President considered it "better a thousand times to go down fighting than to dip your colors to dishonorable compromise." She added that she would never again ask the President "to do what would be manifestly dishonorable." If so friendly and so influential a supporter of Wilson and his policies was so reproved, what chance could there have been that a message from Senator Lodge, transmitted by Colonel House, would be considered favorably? It may be that the President in his regrettable but understandable moroseness regarded it as unworthy of notice. It may also be that Mrs. Wilson, who not only shared her husband's feelings toward Senator Lodge, but disliked and distrusted Colonel House, decided that she would needlessly disturb the President by giving him the message. Colonel Bonsal raises another question: how did this episode affect the Senator? Almost any man will harden his heart under what seems a snub; and meekness was not among the Senator's virtues.

Even the most touching appeals were helpless to break the deadlock between the Senate and the White House. The danger to the Treaty was realized even in Europe; and a plea to the American people came from the ruined University of Louvain, a spot where so much American sympathy and indignation and desire to help in restoration had centered. Belgium herself, it said, after all her trials, was disappointed in the settlement. But the acceptance of the settlement offered the best hope of peace; and its proper enforcement depended on the participation of the United States. How little the professors at Louvain knew of politics in America!

On November 19 the expected happened. Senator Lodge offered a resolution that the Treaty, as modified by the fourteen reservations, should be ratified. The Democratic senators, forewarned by Senator Hitchcock, listened to an admonition from the White House which had the force of a command:

. . . in my opinion the resolution . . . does not provide for ratification, but rather for nullification of the Treaty. . . . I trust that all true friends of the Treaty will refuse to support the Lodge resolutions.

The President had his way. The resolution, needing a two-thirds vote for passage, did not come near to securing even a majority. After a long wrangle Senator Hitchcock, hopeless but faithful, was allowed to offer a substitute resolution, calling for ratification of the Treaty as it stood. After this was defeated, there came what was in some respects the most remarkable development of the day. Senator Knox proposed a concurrent resolution of the Houses to the effect that "the state of war between Germany and the United States [was] . . . hereby declared at an end." And Senator Lodge, who had once declared a separate peace unthinkable, supported it. Instead of passing it, the Senate adjourned.

CHAPTER XIX

Journey's End

————————◆◆————————

I T SEEMED TO MRS. WILSON that the most immediate and obvious effect upon the President of the Senate's votes of November 19 was to increase his determination to get well, in order to carry on the fight. But improvement came slowly. Before Christmas he was able to sit up for a part of every day; but the members of the Cabinet found it almost impossible to communicate with him except through his doctor. He seemed "too done up to stand any strain or worry." Thanks to his weakness, his seclusion, and the fact that no official statement as to the nature of his illness was even yet issued, official Washington was still puzzled. Rumors regarding his very sanity were still current. So were doubts as to who was exercising the powers of the chief executive. Early in January, when the Attorney General, the Under-Secretary of State, and the Secretary of Agriculture were asked to revise the draft of a message from Wilson, to be read at the coming Jackson Day banquet, Mr. Houston, noting certain curious and provocative misstatements it contained, "doubted if the President had had anything to do with [its] preparation." Houston's assumption was a daring one; but he was then as ever a faithful and admiring follower of Wilson's, and apparently in possession of Mrs. Wilson's confidence. It was no wonder, then, that the rumor factory kept at work; but there was a side to its activities which can be remembered only with disgust. There were people, apparently decent in other ways, who did not hesitate to show satisfaction regarding the President's illness; to say it served him right; even to connect it with attacks upon his private character, which men long and intimately associated with him knew to be monstrous. Such improvement in Wilson's physical condition as could be noted, was not matched by any improvement in the prospects of the League.

Most of the President's friends and well-wishers were ready now to beg him to co-operate in getting the Treaty ratified, no matter what reservations the senators might demand. The vote of November 19 had scarcely been taken when Colonel House, undeterred by the snub he had received in connection with the Lodge-Bonsal episode, sent two letters within four days, advising a line of policy that might have saved both the Treaty and Wilson's principles; might even have forced Senator Lodge to yield some ground. The President, Colonel House pointed out, had only to declare that being unable to accept the Lodge reservations, he was throwing all responsibility on the senators. He would thus reaffirm his loyalty to the Allies, and make ratification, under some set of reservations, certain. His sacrifice would be regarded as "the act of a great man." It was not improbable that his personal withdrawal from the struggle would moderate its bitterness, so making it possible for mild reservationists of both parties to win concessions from Senator Lodge. The rejection of the Treaty was the thing to be avoided at all costs. House obviously put his heart as well as his brain into those letters; but whether the President ever heard of them or not they were utterly ignored.

Appeals and arguments to much the same effect came from other influential quarters. Some of them probably did more to stiffen the President than to soften him. Mr. Bryan, speaking at the Jackson Day dinner, attacked his stand, and maintained that the Democratic minority in the Senate was not justified in using the two-thirds rule to block the Republican majority. More irritating still was a step taken by Sir Edward (now Viscount) Grey. Lord Grey had spent the autumn in this country, on a "good-will" mission, and in the hope of discussing the Turkish peace treaty with the President. Prior to his illness, Wilson had greatly looked forward to meeting him; but, for reasons still somewhat obscure, did not give him an interview. The distinguished visitor talked with men of various views, including Senator Lodge. Anxious to have us in the League on almost any terms, and perhaps misreading the situation at Washington as presented by a shrewd senator who had earned Britain's gratitude in the days of our neutrality, he acted with doubtful propriety. At the end of January he published a letter in *The Times* showing sympathy with the Lodge position, and giving it as his opinion that Britain would accept the Lodge reservations, if need be. Judging by some of the reactions he produced, he was pouring oil, not on the waters, but on the flames. The President declared him guilty of the "grossest possible breach of courtesy."

But other appeals were sent to the White House by organizations and individuals whose motives and methods were beyond question. One bore the signatures of Cardinal Gibbons, Ray Stannard Baker, Isaiah Bowman, Stephen Duggan, Edward Filene, Norman Hapgood, Hamilton Holt, David Hunter Miller, Ellery Sedgwick, and Ida Tarbell. These appeals bore little fruit. An unofficial statement issued from the executive offices in December suggested that the President might take the course advised by Colonel House. But the letter read in Wilson's name at the Jackson Day banquet in the capital (purged of the misstatements it had at first contained) showed him still full of fight. The American Government must either refrain from making changes that would "alter the meaning" of the Treaty, or refuse to ratify it at all. He could not "accept the action of the Senate . . . as the decision of the nation"; and, if national sentiment was in doubt, "a great and solemn referendum" would be provided by the elections of the coming autumn. He was making the ratification of the Treaty more than ever a partisan issue; but it was so natural for him to turn confidently to the people that this probably did not even occur to him.

But in the dreary postlude to the voting of November 19 which went on from December to March, it was Mr. Lodge who had the principal and certainly a much less creditable role. During January the coilings and uncoilings of the supple Senator were something to marvel at. He still had to be careful. All kinds of voters were demanding that the Treaty should be ratified; and most of them were in clear agreement with the President that no fresh negotiations with other governments should be called for. A poll of 17,000 Protestant, Catholic, and Jewish clergy gave all but 800 votes for the Treaty; and another, held at hundreds of universities and colleges, showed nearly two thirds of 150,000 voters demanding ratification with mild reservations or none at all. Only one fifth supported Senator Lodge's stand. From chambers of commerce, from the American Federation of Labor, from railroad brotherhoods, from women voters, from granges, the same demands came in.

Senator Lodge, not much interested in public opinion, but very much interested in votes, took heed. In the last days of January the battalion of death discovered that he was conferring with eight mild reservationists, of whom four were Democrats. He was even reported to have said that progress was being made. Perhaps he was merely making a gesture: or perhaps he thought that some slight concessions would have political value, now that the President and the Democrats had been thoroughly rebuked and curbed. But the members of the battalion of death were taking no chances. Senator Lodge was peremptorily taken out of a conference with the eight reservationists, and brought before the battalion, rather as Balkan premiers were summoned to Berchtesgaden a short while ago. He did not long maintain his frosty dignity under the lash of Senator Borah's tongue. Any appearance of compromise, he was told, amounted either to betrayal or to hypocrisy. The conferences must stop at once. They did. Senator Lodge apparently decided that the battalion and their friends might disrupt the party; whereas the mild reservationists could be counted upon to stay in line. He announced that he could not accept the slightest deviation from his "reservation" on Article X.

In vain Mr. Taft suggested that, when the League Council (with our representative's concurrence) advised action in any case, Congress should decide what moral obligation, if any, then rested upon our Government. In vain Democratic senators announced their willingness to concur with Mr. Taft. In vain Wilson endorsed a set of interpretative reservations submitted by Senator Hitchcock, declaring that the United States assumed no obligation under Article X to employ its armed forces or an economic boycott, except as Congress should in any given case decide. Not only did bickering and hairsplitting go on, but senators enjoyed themselves by adding new reservations or amendments to the old. One, completely irrelevant but actually passed, reaffirmed American sympathy with the aspirations of Ireland. It must have been a relief to all sensible and honest senators when, on March 19, the Treaty accompanied by the Republican reservations was again voted down, and the sorry business brought practically to an end. A joint resolution declaring the state of war with Germany as at an end passed both Houses; but the President's veto was sustained.

Wilson received the news more quietly than some of those about him had dared to hope, but it cut him to the quick. "They have shamed us in the eyes of the world," he said. In his veto message he declared himself unable to "become party to an action which would place ineffaceable stain upon the gallantry and honor of the United States." For a moment he seemed even to doubt whether the people would follow him. But this mood quickly passed. He was soon looking to the "solemn referendum" of the autumn with perfect confidence.

Meanwhile, as winter gave place to spring, he regained some liberty of movement and some of his old grasp on affairs; but not, it seems, his old self-control and soundness of judgment. He was promoted to a wheel chair; and while the Senate argued the Treaty, he often sat outside the window of Tumulty's office, haggard but hopeful, and very anxious for the news. Sometimes he tried to work at official papers in his chair, at others listened while Mrs. Wilson read aloud. Soon he was able to go for short motor rides, and to enjoy the moving pictures, which producers sent in abundance to the White House. But he was crippled in more ways than one. He was still a hot, impatient perfectionist and patriot; but the "practical" President of pre-war years, even the negotiator at Paris, who had realized that politics must always observe the limits of the possible, and take all permissible account of public sentiment, was hardly to be found in him.

Take his dismissal of Mr. Lansing from the secretaryship of State. It would be difficult to contend that he did not do the proper thing; but he did it in anything but a proper way. Since, more than most presidents, he had chosen to be his own Secretary of State, the titular holder of the office had to be a man of his own views. Lansing's unconcealed lack of sympathy with his ideas for a new world order, shown at Paris, before the Foreign Relations Committee, and by Mr. Bullitt's breach of confidence, made his replacement entirely understandable. But the only reason for his replacement by Bainbridge Colby which reached the public was that he had gone beyond his powers in summoning the Cabinet after the President's collapse. That, the President explained to Mrs. Wilson, was an official transgression, whereas the others were "personal." But the dismissal, especially as made use of by the President's antagonists, seemed to many people a heavy punishment for a slight offense, administered by a man so small as to be jealous of his power. Moreover, the President had written Lansing with a harshness understandable only in view of the handicaps and disappointments that he was suffering.

Such harshness showed again, when the Italian-Yugoslav dispute about Fiume, smoking since the Paris Conference, erupted during the winter months. In brief, Great Britain and France, departing from a tripartite agreement concluded with our State Department in December 1919, brought pressure upon Yugoslavia to submit either to a new solution of Adriatic questions more acceptable to Italy, or to the literal execution of the Treaty of London. Though the Franco-British *démarche* gave good ground for protest, it could have been handled tactfully. The President's cables almost burned up the wires. He could not possibly be a party to proceedings inconsistent with Article X; to an arrangement "unfair in principle and . . . unworkable in practice," rewarding the aggressor "at the expense of the small and weak," and constituting "a positive denial of the principles for which America entered the war." Wilson even threatened to take the lead in making a separate peace with Germany. This at the moment when he was straining every exhausted nerve to prevent senators from torpedoing the peace settlement! Was the man who made this threat the negotiator of the year before, the negotiator who knew when circumstances were too much for him?

Certainly his appearance and bearing suggested a grievous change. Witness Mr. Houston's account of a Cabinet meeting held at mid-April, the first meeting at which the President had presided since his collapse:

It was enough to make one weep to look at him. One of his arms was useless. In repose, his face looked very much as usual, but, when he tried to speak . . . his jaw tended to drop on one side, or seemed to do so. His voice was very weak and strained. . . . He put up a brave front and spent several minutes cracking jokes. Then there was a brief silence. . . . Someone brought up the railroad situation for discussion. The President seemed at first to have some difficulty in fixing his mind on what we were discussing. Dr. Grayson looked in the door several times as if to warn us not to prolong the discussion. . . . Finally, Mrs. Wilson came in, looking rather disturbed, and suggested we had better go.

A fortnight later, when the Cabinet met again, "the President seemed much better and took a much more lively part in the discussions"; but even then, and apparently to the end of the administration, a new formalism attended the relatively few Cabinet meetings that were called. Members, when entering, were announced, since the President could not distinguish their faces. From more than one direction darkness seemed to be closing in on him. Apart from the indefatigable efforts of his family, Dr. Grayson, and a few intimates to make him happier, cheer came to him only occasionally. He had the pleasure of summoning the first meetings of the Council and Assembly of the League, and of being the recipient of a Nobel peace prize.

Disabled and disappointed as he was, Wilson ran true to form in living up to his sense of duty. Mr. Tumulty wrote that up to his last day in the executive offices he acted as he would have done if he had expected to be President for life. And in 1920 he no longer had the inspiration of being able to plan an economic and social structure in line with his ideas of American democracy, in full confidence that his plans could be carried out. His party and national leadership could not be recovered in anything like full measure unless an immense improvement in his health took place. Conditions in the country did not call immediately for reforms, but for readjustment to peace times. Nearly all the matters that had weighed on him after his return from Paris—strikes, taxation, prices, living costs—still crowded to the front. Some constructive legislation did come through. In June the Federal Power Commission was brought to birth, and the bill to establish a budget system reached the President's desk for signature; in August the woman suffrage amendment was ratified at last, thanks partially to the President's urging. But pressure from economic groups was still brought to bear. For example, the cotton growers were asking the Government to supply the Germans with money for purchasing cotton, accepting payment in German bonds, but were outraged by the suggestion that they might accept payment in German bonds themselves.

With the public discontented and confused, with his term of office running out, with an election coming on, and with his vitality at low ebb, Wilson might very excusably have avoided political conflicts, or tried to placate discontented groups in the nation. Instead, he sharply rebuked Congress, when he regarded it as acting unwisely, and did what he could to correct what seemed to him its mistakes. In a telegram to railroad union officials who complained of the cost of living, he accused Congress of delaying relief month after month, and of having for its "dominating motive . . . political expediency rather than . . . the public welfare." Supported by the Federal Reserve Board and by the Treasury, he struck at those who seemed to him mere self-seekers. He would not hear of the soldiers' bonus; he vetoed a joint resolution extending the life of the War Finance Corporation; and his last official act, on March 3, 1921, was to kill an emergency tariff act, designed as a first step in bringing high protection back again. Reluctantly, and again with Treasury support, he had felt compelled to veto even the bill establishing the budget system, as involving encroachment upon the powers of the executive. No one could accuse him of playing politics to further that victory in the November elections on which he had set his heart.

Long before the national conventions were held, and the party campaigns got under way, Wilson's position had been fixed. It had, in fact, been fixed with the writing of his Jackson Day letter. In so far as the Democratic party would allow, the election was to be a referendum on the League. As early as May 9 he telegraphed the Democrats of Oregon that it was "imperative that the party should proclaim itself the uncompromising champion of the nation's honor and . . . therefore indorse and support the Versailles Treaty and condemn the Lodge reservations." If one is inclined to regard this as mere partisanship or stubbornness, it is well to remember that some distinguished Americans against whom these charges could not lie were no less emphatic than he. President Eliot, reminding the readers of the *Atlantic Monthly* of Wilson's promise in his Flag Day address of 1917, that "a new glory [should] shine in the face of our people," went on bitterly:

That glory did shine, until Republican Senators began, first, to interfere—without Constitutional right—in the negotiations which were going on in Paris, and so to diminish the influence and authority of the American delegate . . . and then to urge the whole American people to . . . adopt the selfish, timid and dishonourable course advocated by the opponents of the League. . . . The League of Nations . . . is in operation . . . but its beneficent action is crippled by the absence of the United States. . . . The Republican party has turned its back on its own principles of 1860 and 1918.

Later in the same article he protested against the epithets which "Republican official documents and the speeches of Republican orators" were applying to the President ("autocrat . . . hypocrite . . . insincere . . . meanly jealous"), and quoted a sentence printed in a Philadelphia newspaper in 1797:

If ever a nation has been debauched by a man the American nation has been debauched by Washington; if ever a nation has been deceived by a man, the American nation has been deceived by Washington.

But even in 1920 the influence of the *Atlantic Monthly* with the people in general was small as compared with that of the *Chicago Tribune;* and no Democratic voice seemed strong enough to prevail against the booming tones of Senator Johnson. The party was sadly deficient in speakers. It also seemed sadly deficient in morale.

Wilson took practically no part at all in the activities of the Democrats, beyond attempting to make the League the dominant issue. Mr. C. W. Stein recently reviewed what evidence there is for the assertion that he wanted a third term. Though there were many people who hoped he would seek nomination; though men in Wall Street placed bets on his getting it; though Mrs. Wilson may have wished for it, conclusive evidence of his own desire for it appears to be lacking. Perhaps if this had seemed the only possible chance of saving the League he would thus have sacrificed what little was left of him. It is not possible to say more.

As it was, no one, not even Homer Cummings or Bainbridge Colby or Carter Glass, could persuade him to interfere with the elaboration of the party platform except in seeing that it gave full endorsement to the League, still less to express the slightest preference, before or during the San Francisco convention, for any Democratic candidate. He based his stand on principle; but the fact that his son-in-law and old friend, Mr. McAdoo, was much favored for the nomination, practically precluded him from giving any word or sign. Real admiration and affection for his son-in-law, to say nothing of family ties, forbade opposition; and they, not less than good taste, forbade endorsement, too. As President Eliot freely admitted in his *Atlantic Monthly* article, some Democrats as well as many Republicans had "somehow acquired an utter distrust of the character and conduct of President Wilson," regarding him as "shifty," as "cold," as "inconstant." Did Mr. Eliot forget how well the public had been instructed to find a number of unpleasant qualities in the person of the chief executive? Mr. Lane remarked how unfair it seemed that the candidate of 1920 would be handicapped by Wilson's unpopularity.

It was hard to believe that this was the same man whom vast crowds in America and Europe had cheered' so frantically so short a time before, especially if one called to mind how recklessly he had sacrificed everything in doing what seemed to him his duty as the people's interpreter. In more than one respect he was well advised to keep aloof from convention politics. Yet the convention paid him a striking tribute. As the proceedings opened, a great flag was drawn up, to show his portrait. A stampede began, with delegates parading and cheering him, until this offer of homage looked like an effort to draft him for a third term. There was a bitter fight in the Resolutions Committee over the endorsement of Wilson's stand on the Treaty; but Carter Glass, insisting that the President could not have broken faith with the Allied governments, at last carried the day. When the results were known, he seemed well content that the nominations had gone to his friend and admirer, Governor Cox, and to Franklin D. Roosevelt. Mr. Cox seemed a trifle hesitant about connecting himself too closely with an unpopular President and a doubtful cause, until attacks upon Republican "corruption" appeared unpromising. But a visit to the White House apparently altered his attitude, and even made him something of a crusader for the League.

As the election drew near, the President stood serene in his confidence that the "moral sense" of the electorate would carry the Democratic candidate and cause to victory. He was soon forced to realize that he could do no real speechmaking; but he gave what help was possible. On October 3 he issued an appeal to the people, admonishing them that the country's honor was at stake, and expressing his amazement at "the gross ignorance and impudent audacity" shown by the opponents of the Treaty, in inventing a type of Americanism grossly selfish, indifferent to the ideals for which America had fought, and lacking foundation "in any of the authentic traditions of the Government." About a week before the election, he followed up this appeal by addressing, from his invalid chair, a small group of pro-League Republicans. It was the first formal address he had made since his collapse; and it was a tame effort as compared with the great orations of other days. No opponent of the League, he pointed out, had proposed "any other adequate means of bringing about settled peace."

There was infinite pathos in the Wilson of those days. No longer capable of sizing up public sentiment, no longer able to grasp and deal with the realities of politics, he did not know that the "solemn referendum" of November would not be on the League so much as on the President, his method of governing, and the policies by which he had angered so many of the people, in trying to make the country a better place for all of them. He had forgotten that a slump in idealism is apt to come as a natural reaction from the sacrifices people make, the ideals from which they draw consolation and confidence, while a war is in progress. Perhaps he would have been able to check the reaction of 1919 by constant and strong appeals, if he had started soon enough. But he had been away in Paris when it had first set in, leaving a free field to men who were eager, for different reasons, to encourage it. His September speaking trip had offered too little and too late.

Nor does he seem to have realized that his opponents, almost certainly by calculation and with much aid from himself, had delayed decision on the Treaty and the League so long that the electorate was saying in effect: "A plague on both your houses. Let's drop the whole affair. Let's leave the European governments to squabble about Fiume or whatever may divide them, and go back to being just Americans, minding our own business, and letting other peoples mind theirs." He did not see that the nation, at least as generous as any other in world outlook, was so certain of its security, and so distrustful of all peoples overseas, as to feel that it would be giving much and getting little or nothing in return by entering the League. The people had willingly been lifted up to belief in international co-operation for peace, by patriotic and clear-sighted men, of whom the most eminent had in general been Republicans. But gradually they had been confused and disillusioned by flagrant misrepresentations and misstatements, from the mouths sometimes of honest men; by concerted and shrewd attempts to increase their distrust of "foreigners"; by a bedlam of arguments; and by the degradation of a great ideal to the level of a party struggle for power and spoils. Who was there to call up again their faith and generosity? Probably not even Wilson could have repaired the damage done, had he been restored miraculously to all his powers. And there were no Democratic believers who were both able and willing to become great pro-League evangelists. The people, his inspiration and the source of his strength, had gone away from him and his great project. There was no one to call them back.

The party he had brought back to power, and to which he had given distinction in principles and in legislative achievement not to have been conceived of in 1912, was weakened in many of its parts by sectionalism and self-seeking. The late Professor (and Ambassador)

Dodd, whose admiration for Wilson sometimes carried him too far, did not exaggerate concerning this:

> Its national organization was Wilsonian while the leading state organizations were opposed to him. In Georgia, Hoke Smith and Thomas Watson united their Negro- and Catholic-baiting organizations to defeat the President's programme. In Alabama there was no enthusiasm for the "new freedom." The New York Democracy was then as ever opposed to any Democratic leader who could carry the country. . . . In Massachusetts, Senator Walsh rivalled Lodge in chasing the Irish, Italian, and German vote. Thomas Taggart of Indiana and George Brennan of Illinois were only smaller Tammany politicians seeking to undo the only man who had given the Democratic party a real standing in the country. In Missouri, Senator Reed sought to be returned as a delegate to the Democratic convention, simply for the purpose of fighting Wilson.

Hence men of many groups and both parties who cherished grudges against the President had their day. New England businessmen abused him on account of the income tax; because he had men of "socialist" leanings in the administration; or as a Southerner spending public money for Southern projects, such as Muscle Shoals. Many of their employees would equally have none of him, being persuaded that he was anti-Irish, anti-German, or anti-Italian. They forgot that such charges held only to the degree that the President was first and foremost pro-American.

"America First," his own proud phrase, was even then twisted into the selfishly nationalistic slogan of a later time. In the Middle West he was berated as pro-British (and so he was, as compared with William Hale Thompson, though almost the reverse, when you considered his position and that of Senator Lodge during the years of American neutrality); as an "internationalist" ready to sell out his country; and as a man indifferent to the farmers' needs! Whether in New England or farther west, the Negro vote, vastly swelled in Northern cities by the war's industrial demands, was mobilized against this friend of colored Americans. He had not prevented segregation in Washington; though how he could have done so was not explained. Naturally, his party had to suffer for all his sins, real or alleged, and especially for his "autocracy." To this last charge there was, of course, substance, provided one disagreed with Wilson's conception of the presidency. But there was hardly enough to permit comparison with the bloodiest tyrants known to history. This was all part of the great political game, played on its lowest levels; and the teams were too unequal to leave the issue in real doubt.

Fantastic as it now may seem, there were Republicans who argued (some doubtless in all sincerity) that votes for their party would be votes for our entry into the League. That great Republican champion of the League principle, Mr. Taft, put the case plausibly in the *Yale Review*. Enough Republican senators to block ratification until Article X was nullified—men fixed in their opposition "by the bitterest kind of discussion"—would hold over through the election of 1920 in any case. Moreover, they could count on a couple of Democratic senators, and almost certainly on some re-elected Republicans. Hence a Democratic victory, claimed Mr. Taft, could bring only a continuation of the deadlock. But from a Republican victory one could expect America's participation in the League, with the "enormous advance" in the prospects of enduring peace offered by "limitation of armament, the provision for enforcing submission of all disputes between two nations to an impartial hearing by use of a universal boycott and voluntary force by any member of the League, and open diplomacy."

Mr. Taft admitted that the Republican platform had been made noncommittal on the subject, in order to prevent a bolt by a dozen isolationists; that Mr. Harding had promised, if elected, to sign the joint resolution for a separate peace with Germany; and that he had talked only in "vague and general" terms of an "association" of nations to replace the League. And he seemed to forget that the formation of such an association of nations to replace the League was obviously impracticable. So he found it "fairly clear" that a Republican victory would put us into the League, while a Democratic victory would keep us out. Looking back now, it seems "fairly clear" that Mr. Taft, as anti-Wilson and anti-Democratic as he had ever been pro-League, was working hard to persuade himself. And it seems more than fairly clear that he was not in the confidence of his party's effective leaders. But how were the people, hearing such arguments from many sources, to realize that the contentions of the one-time pro-League ex-President held no better than did a sieve?

When the Republican landslide came, Wilson, unprepared as he was, showed much of his old-time nerve. He was bitter about the methods which had been used to rob Americans of their idealism, and involve them in what seemed to him disgrace. He was sad about the "tragedy of disappointment" that he saw in store for them. But he did not seem especially depressed. He was cheered by a letter from his old friend, Senator Williams of Mississippi, promising to keep up the fight, and reminding him that the League was "on its feet, learning to walk, Senate coteries willy-nilly." Fortunately, Mrs. Wilson was able to enlist his interest in the new home she was busily planning. The first question to be decided was whether they should live in Baltimore, Washington, Richmond, Boston, or New York. With true Wilsonian system, a chart was drawn up, allowing to each city so many points for climate, for friends, for "opportunities," for freedom, for amusements, and for libraries. Boston, for example, received high points for libraries and for freedom, but very few for climate or for friends. Richmond, scoring high in friends and climate, was unsatisfactory in other ways. Washington being victor in the contest, ideas for building a house were happily discussed, and the President apparently shared Mrs. Wilson's interest in filing pictures of architectural details.

When building did not prove feasible, the problem of finding a house that would be adequate, well-situated, and within their somewhat restricted means, proved an engrossing one for weeks. Finally, Mrs. Wilson set her heart on securing the subsequently famous S Street house; and the President had the rare pleasure of presenting her with the deed as a surprise. Even then there were questions of alterations and decorations and furnishing, to take his mind away from vetoes, elections, and "Senate coteries." And he was commencing to detach himself from them in other ways. He was thinking once more of writing the *magnum opus* he had planned before his entrance into New Jersey politics. Only one page was ever written, a page of touching dedication to his wife. But it was pleasant to think about the book. Life with Mrs. Wilson in the S Street house promised calm and happy days, as the time for Mr. Harding's inauguration drew near.

There was nothing dramatic about Wilson's last day in office, except the tragedy that lay in his shattered body and shattered hopes, and the gallantry with which he bore up under it. For a man with nerves so badly shaken, the sharp transition from power to impotence, even the change of physical surroundings, involved considerable strain. Such little physical exertion as was required from a retiring President by the ceremonies at the Capitol was no small thing for him. Had he been making way for a successor with some at least of his ideals, hope might have buoyed him up. But what hope could he feel in handing over his office to a pliant member of Senator Lodge's group? Friends pointed out that he could avoid the ceremonial without discourtesy; but, correct and resolute to the last, he insisted on going through with it. He could get along, he said, with his "third leg," his old blackthorn.

So he rode side by side with Mr. Harding to the Capitol, appearing as an aged and battered contrast to the handsome, robust son of Ohio, who was receiving vast applause, without having said or done anything that one could especially call to mind. It was very much in contrast with a number of drives, of which the cheers for Mr. Harding must have reminded him. There was quite a contrast again when they reached the Capitol, and Mr. Harding, to the accompaniment of even greater cheers, mounted casually the long flight of steps, leaving the man who was still President to be taken to a lower entrance, where an elevator was available. The formalities in the President's room did not amount to much; but there was one incident which has proved irresistible to newspapermen and diarists and Hollywood. Senator Lodge, as in duty bound, came to announce that the two Houses of Congress, being ready to adjourn, awaited the President's pleasure. However well the Senator had succeeded in squaring his actions with his conscience, it must have been Wilson's conviction that this man, who faced him superciliously in cool triumph, had not only reversed his position on League and separate peace without an apparent qualm, but had been guilty of the far worse offense of helping to debauch the people, by inducing them to turn their backs on their tradition of generosity, and persuading them that the highest patriotism was expressed in terms of national selfishness. As a result, the other peoples of the world would have only a crippled League to depend upon. Whatever was in Wilson's mind, repulsion was so evident in his attitude that some of those who stood about him as he faced the Senator doubted whether his composure would be equal to the strain. But self-control enabled him to preserve an icy courtesy. It was all over then; and Mrs. Wilson could take him to their new home; and Dr. Grayson could order him to take the first real rest he had had for many years.

In fact, he soon found that there could not be much except rest for him in the years (only three, it was to prove) that lay ahead. He resigned himself reluctantly. Just before Mr. Harding's inauguration he had formed a law partnership with his last Secretary of State, Bainbridge Colby; and soon after the inauguration the offices of Wilson and Colby were opened in Washington and New York. They were not open long. Such knowledge of any but constitutional law, as Wilson had once had, must have been well-nigh obliterated by the intervening experiences of forty years; and the doctors would not hear of his going to his law office for more than an hour a day, nor of his going at all, until he was stronger. Mrs. Wilson tells us that numerous clients appeared, some offering rich fees, but that there was only one of them whose case, as Wilson saw it, could be handled with propriety by a former President and Secretary of State. Soon Mr. Colby had to go on alone.

So there was nothing for Wilson to do but to become a member of the leisure class; and there was nothing that Mrs. Wilson did not do to make the time pass pleasantly. There were family visitors and little celebrations of family anniversaries; there were drives and moving pictures and endless games of Canfield (with Wilson's scores recorded scrupulously over many months!). There were almost weekly visits to Keith's Theatre; and there were many magazines with pictures which he could go through, without straining his eyes. And always there were many books and magazines to be read aloud. Detective stories, for a time in high favor, gave way to Scott and Dickens; and Bagehot, the favorite of early days, was a familiar friend in these last ones. Sickroom etiquette took the place of the insistence upon correctness that had become second nature to Wilson. Friends found him, and sometimes lunched with him, in his own room. There, in a dressing gown, he took all his meals, as much at ease as his old enemy, neuritis, would allow.

The friends who came formed a distinguished company, and one which could remind him of nearly all the important phases of his career. There were men, like Cleveland Dodge and Bliss Perry, who could talk of the old times at Princeton; men, like Senators Glass and Swanson, with whom he could live over political battles in Washington; there were others, such as Bernard Baruch and Henry Morgenthau, to recall the days of neutrality and war and peacemaking. To bring back the great moments of the Peace Conference came Clemenceau, almost incredibly gay and agile for his years; Lloyd George, sympathetic but very ready to record his host's failings; and Americans who had been closely in his confidence, such as Ray Stannard Baker and Frank Cobb. Deplorably, the list of visitors received did not include Colonel House; although there is no doubt that the Colonel longed to see and comfort his old chief; and although his eldest daughter is quoted as having said that her father's affection for the Texan never died. Very few of the visitors have left on record accounts of their visits, but Professor Bliss Perry's is enough:

He sat at the right of the fireplace in his library, slumping a little in his chair, and holding a cane. His head, which he had always carried high, was bent, as if he had been bludgeoned. His voice was distinct, but low, slow, and without animation. His mind, however, seemed to me as clear as ever, though not so alert. We talked a little of the old days at Princeton, thirty years before, when we used to discuss Stevenson and Walter Bagehot. He spoke of the Peace Conference, saying that he thought that General Smuts had the best mind of any of the men whom he met in Paris. . . . He asked me about the political situation in Massachusetts, and spoke grimly of Henry Cabot Lodge. No Scotch-Irish Presbyterian ever found it easy to forgive his enemies! And then, with a sudden flash of that indomitable religious faith which lay deeper than anything else in his nature, he assured me that a revival of moral idealism was bound to come to our American people.

He lived and died in certainty that the people would sooner or later justify his pride and faith in them.

His family, friends, and physicians did their utmost to reconcile him to his invalidism; but he was never reconciled. Sometimes he could view the situation with grim humor, as when he remarked to Mrs. Wilson that he was "having the unique experience of attending [his] own obsequies." But he made every effort possible to preach his old ideals. It was very difficult; for neither brain nor hands nor voice nor eyes would serve him very well. Since he found it hard to write, the famous typewriter was brought out again. But typing with one hand was too tedious, especially since the clear-cut ideas that once had come so readily now had to be sought for, and laboriously joined. As for speaking, that was still more difficult, even when a prepared text was used. It involved much nervous tension beforehand, as well as effort at the time. Then there was the danger of an emotional reaction to signs of kindness and of sympathy in the audience. On at least one occasion he "choked up" when trying to address admirers from a window of his house, and had to wave them away.

Still, even in his last months he did manage to be heard. He wrote an article which the *Atlantic* was glad to print. It was a protest against the return to "normalcy," commenced under President Harding, and about to go forward under President Coolidge, whom Wilson described to Lloyd George as "no one in particular." He was especially grieved over the reversal of his tariff policy. The passage of an emergency tariff act soon after he left the White House had prepared the way for the Fordney-McCumber tariff (then the highest in our history) in September 1922. He had always linked high tariffs with privilege. The war, he wrote in the *Atlantic,* had "made the world safe for democracy"; but "democracy [had] not yet made the world safe against irrational revolution." The underlying trouble was that "a Christian conception of justice," the permeation of our civilization with the spirit of Christ's teachings, was lacking. Were there not capitalists who still used other men as "mere instruments of profit"? It was one of the briefest of his articles, and not especially original; but it cost him an infinity of pains. It was "primed and polished" late into the night, when he should have been sleeping.

He made long and painful preparations, too, for his first speech on the radio, delivered on the eve of his last Armistice Day. Perhaps if he had known that it was to be his valedictory, he might have spoken less bitterly:

> . . . the stimulating memories of that happy triumph are forever marred . . . by the shameful fact that when the victory was won . . . by . . . our own incomparable soldiers—we turned our backs upon our associates and . . . withdrew into a sullen and selfish isolation, which is deeply ignoble because manifestly cowardly and dishonorable . . .

He even complained that France and Italy had "made waste paper of the Treaty of Versailles." But his bitterness was not the bitterness of despair. He looked forward, he told his listeners, to a day when Americans should "inevitably be forced by the moral obligations of freedom and honor to . . . assume once more the role of courage, self-respect, and helpfulness which every true American must wish to regard as our natural part in the affairs of the world." Except in the unaccustomed use of the word "forced" in connection with the people, this last passage was as Wilsonian a valedictory as he could have delivered at his best.

The grim mood reflected in this Armistice address was not constant as Wilson's end drew near. There is more reason to believe that it reflected only the thoughts which the occasion conjured up. One day, while all his faculties were still with him, Wilson startled one of his daughters with the remark: "I think it was best after all that the United States did not join the League of Nations." Naturally, she asked why.

He answered, "Because our entrance into the League at the time I returned from Europe might have been only a personal victory. Now, when the American people join the League it will be because they are convinced that it is the right thing to do, and then will be the *only right* time for them to do it." Then with a little humorous smile—"Perhaps God knew better than I did after all."

God and the people to the end. On February 3, 1924, Woodrow Wilson died.

In more than one respect tragedy went with him to the grave. In the pre-armistice and peace negotiations he had done his best, even though not very successfully, to give the Germans a peace of justice, a peace based on his principles. Yet the highly respected *Deutsche Rundschau* led the German press in writing of his "poison fangs," and the obligation of the German people to "shout [their] curse after him into the grave." He had shown himself such a friend of all peoples, and of the underprivileged and oppressed of all peoples, as the world had rarely seen. Yet the chorus of respectful and admiring tributes which came from the British press was broken by the strident cry of London's left-wing *Daily Herald:* "It is not a tragedy that he is dead— it is a relief. The tragedy was that he failed so disastrously. . . ." In general, the French papers, like the British, spoke in terms of homage and gratitude. And among them the *Matin* offered a tribute which would have gone straight to the heart of the dead President:

The imperishable merit of Wilson is that of having brought into unison the ardent voice of the East and the indifferent voice of the West, and of having cast in one and the same mold 110,000,000 men of every race, every tendency, and every origin.

For more than twenty years we Americans have differed in our own estimates. Because many of us are concerned that such mistakes as Wilson made, or seemed to make, shall not be made again, it is natural for us to be critical. So it seems worth while remembering some sentences that lie embodied in the unsparing and perhaps too highly colored exposition of his temperamental faults which Lloyd George (who never knew him either intimately or in normal circumstances) has given us:

But no one can doubt that he was a supremely able man . . . that he honestly consecrated an upright character and a fine intellect to the service of mankind, no one will deny who is not afflicted with a party spirit so charged with rancour as to have become an insanity of the soul.

And John Sharp Williams, at the time of the Republican landslide of 1920, wrote a sentence worth remembering:

Woodrow Wilson, the first martyr to the cause, is the seed of the Church.

But some of us may prefer to eschew all argument, and endorse the words of Professor Bliss Perry:

. . . If his career ended with his burial, as in some stormy Elizabethan play, it would be fitting to call Woodrow Wilson's life a tragedy. Take up the body and let "the soldiers' music and the rites of war speak loudly for him." But in the case of the true visionary, those trumpets of the sad fifth act and the fall of the tragic curtain are impertinences. Upon idealists such as he the curtain does not fall: the play evolves into the eternal drama that makes up the life of humanity. The illogical, impertinent bullet that pierced Lincoln's brain has now become a portion of his glory. "I meet him at every turn," said Thoreau of John Brown after he was hanged. "He is more alive than ever he was." Those who hated Wilson in his lifetime and those who loved him can agree at least in this: that his ultimate fame will depend upon the triumph of the political ideals which he clothed with fitting words. We make our guesses even now, but fifty years hence we shall begin to know something of the verdict of mankind.

GETTING TO KNOW WILSON IN A WELL-EQUIPPED
LIBRARY

How would a person, interested but not bent on deep study, go about it? For any aspect of Wilson's life and work up to his first sailing for Paris, in December 1919, the trail would start from one or more of Ray Stannard Baker's eight-volume *Life and Letters.* For the President's experiences at Paris, Mr. Baker's three volumes on that special phase, *Woodrow Wilson and World Settlement,* checked against recent studies of the Peace Conference, would supply a good take-off. But to get one's own understanding of a man's principles, ideals, and plans; of his style, his oratory, and his statesmanship, one must make his personal acquaintanceship through some of his speeches and writings. The six volumes of *Public Papers,* edited by Mr. Baker and the late Professor Dodd, supply the need, and are very good reading. For the years 1912 to 1919, and in a different way, President Seymour's *Intimate Papers of Colonel House* are exceedingly useful, and better reading still.

The House *Papers* help to save one from the danger of viewing and judging Wilson in the light of these later years; and so do articles about him written by contemporaries less close to him than House. Such periodicals as the *Quarterly,* the *Atlantic,* the *New Republic* and the *Review of Reviews* (my selection is quite arbitrary) are sprinkled all through with them; and the *Readers' Guide* tells one where to find them in short order. They are rich in new facts and views. The cartoons in the *Review of Reviews* supply much besides humor. Profit and enjoyment are also to be had by running through editorials and news reports in great dailies, whether, like the *World,* they looked on Wilson's works and found them good; or, like the *Sun,* had little or nothing to commend.

Wandering over to the section of the library given to biography and autobiography and published diaries and letters, one may see our twenty-eighth President, or at least the people and circumstances surrounding him, through the eyes of other prominent public men. H. F. Pringle shows how he appeared to Presidents Taft and Theodore Roosevelt; J. B. Bishop (to say nothing of Owen Wister and W. R. Thayer) throws additional light upon the antipathy between the Rough Rider and the first Democrat to succeed him at the White House; while Colonel Roosevelt himself places his bitterness on record in his *Correspondence* with Henry Cabot Lodge. The best that anyone has ever said of Lodge was said twenty years ago by his friend, Bishop William Lawrence; and the latest appraisal of *The Gentleman From Massachusetts* was offered this year by Karl Schriftgiesser.

The names of other merciless critics, of people approving but sometimes critical, and of enthusiastic friends, will appear on the backs of many books in this section. Claude Bowers' *Beveridge,* C. O. Johnson's *Borah,* S. H. Acheson's *Joe Bailey,* and the first La Follette's *Autobiography* are representative of books showing types of opposition which Wilson had to meet. Bryan's sometimes enigmatical attitude comes out in Paxton Hibben's *Peerless Leader* and J. C. Long's *Great Commoner.* Josephus Daniels' *Wilson Era* makes Bryan a more devoted Wilson man than his biographers have found him. Henry James's life of the approving but critical Charles W. Eliot can be read for pure delight. So can the passages about Wilson in Bliss Perry's *And Gladly Teach,* to say nothing of Burton Hendrick's still enchanting *Life and Letters of Walter Hines Page.* For outright encomiums there are such books as G. C. Osborn's *John Sharp Williams.* Affectionate understanding by those closest to Wilson is diffused through such volumes as Mrs. (Edith Bolling) Wilson's *My Memoir,* Mrs. (Eleanor Randolph) McAdoo's *The Woodrow Wilsons,* Joseph Tumulty's *Wilson as I Knew Him,* and Mrs. E. G. Reid's *Woodrow Wilson.* Critics, friends, and devotees again appear in the authors of short accounts of Wilson's life and works (the librarian has probably a small shelf of them), with R. E. Annin displaying hostility so bitter as to be destructive of all objectivity, and W. E. Dodd showing, in his still very useful *Woodrow Wilson and His Work,* how far devotion can lead a good historian. Reading biographies sometimes leaves one a bit confused about chronology; so that Pennington and Bolling's *Chronology of Woodrow Wilson* may come in handily. The *American Year Book* for the years in which it was published is highly useful, too. F. L. Paxson's fine volumes carry part of the story; and Mark Sullivan's *Our Times* supplies a brightly variegated backdrop.

Books already mentioned (those of Tumulty and Daniels in particular), and also the best short general accounts, such as the ones by David Lawrence and William Allen White, give one an idea of Wilson's part in the great game of state and national politics. But there are other volumes to be added, such as James Kerney's *Political Education* and Champ Clark's *Quarter Century.* With a salt shaker at hand, one may even enjoy the treat of reading W. F. McCombs' *Making Woodrow Wilson President.* As Wilson enters the White House, one begins to see him in the perspective offered by other presidents. Here E. S. Corwin takes over with *The*

President, Lindsay Rogers with articles, and G. F. Milton with *The Use of the Presidential Power.* Harley Notter's *Origins* prepares one for Wilson's adventures in international affairs, and William Diamond's recent *Economic Thought* for his efforts to meet the people's economic and financial needs. One may go on from Diamond to such books as Smith and Beasley's *Carter Glass,* or Glass's own *Adventure*—even perhaps to such general books as Seager and Gulick's *Trust and Corporation Problems* and E. E. Schattschneider's *Politics, Pressures and the Tariff.* Members of Wilson's Cabinet supply much information on his views and activities as President through such books as D. F. Houston's *Eight Years,* Frederick Palmer's *Newton Baker,* and F. K. Lane's *Letters.*

If one is especially interested in seeing Wilson and the country drawn towards and into the world conflict, Ray Stannard Baker's *Life and Letters,* the *Public Papers,* and the House *Papers* may be supplemented by the works of Charles Seymour, Carlton Savage, Alice Morrissey, Edgar Turlington, and others. Richard Van Alstyne's recent *American Diplomacy in Action* provides, in brief space, a fresh and provocative review. For Wilson as a war leader, enough books have already been mentioned to give anyone a start. As for the armistice, H. R. Rudin's recent study provides not only a start but a finish.

Some readers may be most interested in Wilson's personal war, which opened with the pre-armistice negotiations, and seemed to end with Mr. Harding's arrival at the White House. In Wilson's view it was a war to make the American people the benefactor of all peoples, in seeing to it that the world should have not only just but lasting peace. This war of his was waged on two fronts: at Paris, then at Washington. What happened at Paris has offered in itself a battleground, during a quarter century, for diarists, commentators and historians. Fortunately, Paul Birdsall's *Versailles Twenty Years After,* Thomas Bailey's *Woodrow Wilson and the Lost Peace,* and three review articles in the *Journal of Modern History* (December 1929, September 1939, and March 1944) by R. C. Binkley, Paul Birdsall, and Bernadotte Schmitt, offer relief maps of the most complicated diplomatic negotiations so far known. For Wilson's part one may proceed (with due caution) from the three great stand-bys for his whole career to such personal accounts as Lloyd George's *Memoirs of the Peace Conference,* Robert Lansing's cold and critical narrative of the *Peace Negotiations,* and Colonel Bonsal's entertaining *Unfinished Business.* There are others of equal value. Indeed one may pick up information on Wilson's role from the most specialized and documented studies. René Albrecht-Carrié's *Italy at the Peace Conference* is a case in point.

Since Mr. Baker did not carry his account of Wilson's activities and experiences in the United States beyond the date of his first sailing for Paris; and since Colonel House never saw the President after Wilson left the Peace Conference, only one of the three great stand-bys, the set of *Public Papers,* is available for the greatest of Wilson's struggles at Washington, and for his last sad years. One gets little real idea of the conflict with the Senate from J. B. McMaster's *The United States in the World War,* G. A. Finch's *The Treaty of Peace with Germany in the United States,* and the *American Year Book* for 1919. Senator Lodge's apologia, *The Senate and the League of Nations,* does little more than show the weakness of his case. So some reading of the *Congressional Record* and the *Senate Documents,* advisable but optional for earlier phases, becomes a matter of necessity for 1919 and 1920. But this reading is at once so amusing and so shocking at many points that one soon becomes engrossed. Then the books by and about Wilson's relatives or close friends, and various prominent figures in politics must come out again. So must the *Readers' Guide,* and perhaps the index to the *New York Times.* But one must go if possible to the Library of Congress, asking Mrs. Wilson's permission to see the strange assortment of papers which came under her husband's eyes and her own from the summer of 1919 on. Miss Brand will direct one to other manuscript collections, too.

Index

205
16958 3